The Free Speech Century

The Free Speech Century

EDITED BY
LEE C. BOLLINGER
and
GEOFFREY R. STONE

OXFORD
UNIVERSITY PRESS

OXFORD
UNIVERSITY PRESS

Oxford University Press is a department of the University of Oxford. It furthers
the University's objective of excellence in research, scholarship, and education
by publishing worldwide. Oxford is a registered trade mark of Oxford University
Press in the UK and certain other countries.

Published in the United States of America by Oxford University Press
198 Madison Avenue, New York, NY 10016, United States of America.

Library of Congress Cataloging-in-Publication Data
Names: Bollinger, Lee C., 1946– editor. | Stone, Geoffrey R., editor.
Title: The free speech century / edited by Lee C. Bollinger, Geoffrey R. Stone.
Description: New York, NY : Oxford University Press, 2019.
Identifiers: LCCN 2018008341 | ISBN 978-0-19-084137-9 (hard cover) |
ISBN 978-0-19-084138-6 (pbk.) | ISBN 9780190841393 (updf) | ISBN 9780190841409 (epub)
Subjects: LCSH: Freedom of speech—United States. | United States. Constitution. 1st Amendment.
Classification: LCC KF4772.F737 2019 | DDC 342.7308/53—dc23
LC record available at https://lccn.loc.gov/2018008341

3 5 7 9 8 6 4

Paperback printed by Webcom, Inc., Canada
Hardback printed by Bridgeport National Bindery, Inc., United States of America

To Jean and Jane

And to the next generation:
Emma, Colin, Katelyn, Sawyer, and Cooper
Julie, Mollie, Maddie, Jackson, and Bee

CONTENTS

PART FOUR   NEW TECHNOLOGIES AND THE
FIRST AMENDMENT OF THE FUTURE

ACKNOWLEDGMENTS

We are, of course, deeply grateful to our authors, all of whom took time out of their very busy and eventful lives to contribute important and illuminating essays to this volume. It is, indeed, difficult to imagine a more distinguished or more thoughtful group of commentators to reflect on the issues that are the focus of this work. And we are delighted to report that every one of them was an absolute pleasure to work with.

Columbia University and the University of Chicago, our respective home institutions, share many similarities, but one that bears noting here is that they both offer the most conducive environments for conducting serious scholarship. It is to our very great benefit that we serve on their faculties, and this volume is a product of that special intellectual atmosphere.

We also grateful to Dave McBride and to the entire staff at Oxford University Press who worked with us so diligently and so energetically to bring this volume to publication. Needless to say, this would not have been possible without their assistance and their guidance.

On a personal level, we want to express our love and gratitude to our families and especially to Lee's spouse, Jean Magnano Bollinger, and Geof's partner, Jane Dailey. A perfect relationship brings a lot of shared ideas and substance along with the emotional balance necessary to bring words into being.

Because this work is largely a reflection on the contributions of many distinguished jurists over the past century, we wish to express our appreciation, not only as editors, authors, and First Amendment scholars, but also as citizens of this nation to those extraordinary individuals, including such remarkable and courageous jurists as Learned Hand, Oliver Wendell Holmes Jr., Louis Brandeis, Hugo Black, William Douglas, and William Brennan Jr., whose contributions to the strength and vibrancy of our American democracy must never be forgotten.

And, finally, we owe more than we can say to Carey Bollinger Danielson. From the very beginning of this project, Carey oversaw every detail of the editing, cite-checking, organizing, copyediting, and coordinating of this work. She has been tireless in her efforts, generous with her time, and an absolutely perfect colleague. Given our other commitments, we can honestly say that, without Carey, *The Free Speech Century* would never have seen the light of day. Thank you!

Lee C. Bollinger
Geoffrey R. Stone

LIST OF CONTRIBUTORS

Floyd Abrams, Senior Counsel, Cahill Gordon & Reindel LLP. Adjunct Professor, New York University School of Law

Emily Bell, Director of the Tow Center for Digital Journalism at Columbia Journalism School

Monika Bickert, Head of Policy Management, Facebook

Vincent A. Blasi, Corliss Lamont Professor of Civil Liberties, Columbia Law School

Lee C. Bollinger, President, Columbia University and Seth Low Professor of the University

Sarah H. Cleveland, Louis Henkin Professor of Human and Constitutional Rights, Columbia Law School; Member, United Nations Human Rights Committee

Heather K. Gerken, Dean and Sol & Lillian Goldman Professor of Law, Yale Law School

Tom Ginsburg, Leo Spitz Professor of International Law, University of Chicago Law School

Lawrence Lessig, Roy L. Furman Professor of Law and Leadership, Harvard Law School

Catharine A. MacKinnon, Elizabeth A. Long Professor of Law, University of Michigan, and the James Barr Ames Visiting Professor of Law, Harvard Law School (since 2009)

Robert C. Post, Sterling Professor of Law, Yale Law School

Albie Sachs, Former Justice of the Constitutional Court of South Africa

Frederick Schauer, David and Mary Harrison Distinguished Professor of Law, University of Virginia

Geoffrey R. Stone, Edward H. Levi Distinguished Service Professor of Law, University of Chicago Law School

David A. Strauss, Gerald Ratner Distinguished Service Professor of Law, University of Chicago Law School

Cass R. Sunstein, Robert Walmsley University Professor, Harvard University

Laura Weinrib, Professor of Law, University of Chicago Law School

Tim Wu, Isidor and Seville Sulzbacher Professor at Columbia Law School

INTRODUCTION

As suggested in our title, *The Free Speech Century*, this volume commemorates the hundredth anniversary of the Supreme Court's first decisions interpreting the First Amendment's guarantee that "Congress shall make no law . . . abridging the freedom of speech, or of the press." Over the past century, we have seen an extraordinary evolution in the ways in which the Court has given meaning to that guarantee. Through a series of false starts, shifting doctrines, and often controversial and surprising outcomes, the Justices have struggled to fulfill the promise of that guarantee. In so doing, they have exemplified Justice Oliver Wendell Holmes' insight in 1919 that "all life is an experiment"—including the constitutional guarantee of free speech.

To explore the past, present, and future of this First Amendment "experiment," we have convened a group of truly extraordinary scholars to examine the free speech century, and beyond. In Part One, "The Nature of First Amendment Jurisprudence," chapters by Vincent Blasi, Frederick Schauer, Laura Weinrib, and Heather Gerken address some of the fundamental interpretative challenges posed by the First Amendment and the processes by which the Justices of the Supreme Court have grappled with those challenges.

In Part Two, "Major Critiques and Controversial Areas of First Amendment Jurisprudence," Floyd Abrams, Lawrence Lessig, Robert Post, David Strauss, Catharine MacKinnon, and Cass Sunstein examine ongoing areas of uncertainty and controversy in contemporary doctrine, addressing such issues as campaign finance regulation, free speech on campus, national security and secrecy, sexual expression, and the continuing vitality of the clear and present danger standard.

In Part Three, "The International Implications of the First Amendment," Albie Sachs, Tom Ginsburg, and Sarah Cleveland investigate the impact of American free speech jurisprudence across the globe. To what extent has our conception of free speech been embraced by other nations? To what extent have other nations rejected our understanding of free expression? And what explains the choices that we and other countries have made in our respective approaches to these issues? These are fascinating and critical questions as we look to the future.

And speaking of the future, in Part Four, "New Technologies and the First Amendment of the Future," Emily Bell, Monika Bickert, and Tim Wu delve into the often vexing challenges that the advent of the internet and other forms of new technology pose to our current understandings of the First Amendment. Are the fundamental premises of Holmes' "experiment" still relevant? How should we address such issues as fake news, tribalism, polarization, globalization, and foreign interference? Is it realistically possible to maintain our own conception of free expression in a world in which the boundaries between nations are rapidly dissolving? As Tim Wu asks in the final chapter in this volume, "Is the First Amendment obsolete?"

We are proud of the remarkable collection of chapters we have gathered in this volume. They present a range of different and often conflicting perspectives on some of the most critical issues of the day. And, true to Justice Holmes' understanding of the First Amendment, they make clear that our commitment to free expression remains a challenging and often puzzling "experiment." We hope that, in this work, we have enriched understanding and provided readers with a rare opportunity to explore the views of some of our nation's most accomplished and most distinguished scholars.

The Free Speech Century

Dialogue

Bollinger: Let's begin with a word about why we have brought together this group of distinguished First Amendment experts to contribute chapters to this volume. There are three primary reasons to start with. The first is reflected in our title, *The Free Speech Century*. The year 2019 will mark the hundredth anniversary of the very first decisions of the US Supreme Court interpreting these simple, unadorned words of the First Amendment: "Congress shall make no law . . . abridging the freedom of speech, or of the press."

Those three cases—*Schenck, Frohwerk*, and *Debs*—all emerged out of the intense emotions surrounding the nation's involvement in World War I.[1] A tidal wave of patriotic fervor and intolerance spread across the country, crushing dissent. Even a leader of a political party and a candidate for president of the United States, Eugene Debs, was imprisoned merely for delivering a speech in which he praised the courage of individuals who refused to be drafted. The defendants in all three cases sought the protection of the First Amendment. Justice Oliver Wendell Holmes Jr. authored the opinions for a unanimous Court rejecting that argument in each case. It was an inauspicious start for the constitutional right of freedom of speech and press, as we have come to know it. But in *Schenck*, Holmes put forward a test that had more staying power than the outcomes in these particular cases. Speech, he wrote, can only be suppressed when the government can demonstrate a "clear and present danger" of harms the government has a right to prevent.

Within a matter of months, in another similar case (*Abrams*), Holmes changed his position on what might constitute a clear and present danger and, in some of the most compelling language ever written about freedom of speech, he launched a historic mission to define and give meaning to the right.[2] Through thousands of cases, reams of scholarly commentary, and intense and sometimes heated public debate, there emerged in America a jurisprudence of freedom of expression that is the most elaborate, the most doctrinally detailed, and the most speech protective of any nation on Earth, now or throughout history. And because of this unique history, it is worth stepping back after a century of experience to reflect on what we have witnessed.

The second reason for the book is related. Another of Justice Holmes' early observations was to suggest that we should think about free speech as an "experiment."[3] This was a way of building into our First Amendment jurisprudence a commitment to self-criticism, even skepticism, which is especially needed for an idea that so easily takes on the character and aura of a fundamental—even sacred and therefore unchallengeable—principle of the society. Approaching what we have created—whether it be with *New York Times v. Sullivan*,[4] which set constitutional limits on the law of defamation; or with the Pentagon Papers,[5] which struck the balance between the government's legitimate interests in secrecy and the public's right to know; or with *Citizens United*,[6] which addressed the possibilities of regulating money in politics—with a detached and critical eye is vitally important. We have sought to create and celebrate that spirit in this book.

The third reason for this volume is that, at this moment, the world may be changing in ways that unsettle and even upset some parts of the elaborate edifice of First Amendment jurisprudence we bring with us into this new century. The interests at stake in some areas of traditional doctrine may be undergoing significant changes that will call for new balances. The introduction of new technologies of communication always has profound effects on human thought and discussion, and this is most certainly true now with the internet. Meanwhile, the increasing interdependence of the modern world, shaped in large part by the internet itself, is bringing globalization to the doorstep of the First Amendment. All these changing and new circumstances by themselves constitute reason enough to take advantage of the hundredth anniversary and to ask how we should think about freedom of speech and press for the future.

Stone: It is interesting to imagine how challenging the task of giving meaning to the fourteen relevant words of the First Amendment might have seemed to the Justices in the spring of 1919: "Congress shall make no law abridging . . . the freedom of speech, or of the press." At first blush, the task might have seemed easy. As Justice Hugo Black declared some forty years later, "The phrase 'Congress shall make no law' is composed of plain words, easily understood. [The] language [is] absolute. [Of] course the decision to provide a constitutional safeguard for [free speech] involves a balancing of conflicting interests. [But] the Framers themselves did this balancing when they wrote the [Constitution]. Courts have neither the right nor the power [to] make a different [evaluation]."[7]

Anticipating this argument, Justice Holmes in *Schenck* offered his brilliant hypothetical of the "false cry of fire in a crowded theater" to demonstrate that the First Amendment obviously could not mean what it appears to say.[8] But that opened up an extraordinary can of worms, because if it doesn't mean what it appears to say, what does it mean? If the First Amendment does not protect the person who falsely yells "Fire!" in a crowded theater, what other speech does it not protect? And how is the Court to answer that question? Should it look to the original understanding of the Framers of the First Amendment? To the purposes of the First Amendment? To the philosophy of free expression? To logic and to the benefits of experience over time?

It seems doubtful that the Justices in the spring of 1919 were thinking very clearly about the extraordinary array of issues they and their successors would confront over time: Was the First Amendment limited only to "political" speech, as Robert Bork would later argue?[9] Did it not protect artistic expression, scientific inquiry, sexual expression, and commercial advertising? What about false statements of fact such as perjury, fraud, defamation, and political lies? What about threats? What about express advocacy of law violation? Two years earlier, in his famous opinion in the *Masses* case, then federal district court judge Learned Hand had suggested that such speech is not within the protection of the First Amendment.[10] What, one wonders, did Justice Holmes and his colleagues on the Supreme Court think about Hand's opinion in *Masses*?

And then there is another whole set of issues. If clear and present danger is the test adopted by the Court in *Schenck*, then is that also the test when the government says "no one may give a speech in a public park," or "no one may write graffiti on a public building," or "no one may hand out leaflets on a public street"? Does the test embraced in *Schenck* apply to those cases as well? If not, why not? And what about flag burning and spending money to elect candidates, and refusing to make a wedding cake for a gay couple? Are those cases like *Schenck*, or are they different?

And, of course, it's even more complicated than that, because although Justice Holmes used the language of clear and present danger in *Schenck*, he did not repeat the phrase in the two subsequent opinions he wrote for the Court only a week later—*Frohwerk* and *Debs*. Moreover, even though he used the phrase in *Schenck*, no one today would argue that he actually applied the test—as it later came to be understood—in *Schenck* itself.

In short, the evolution of First Amendment jurisprudence over the course of the past century has been a long, complex, and difficult journey. The Supreme Court has often moved in fits and starts, sometimes forward and sometimes backward, as times have changed, the perspectives of the individual Justices have changed, and technology has changed. How we got to where we are today is a fascinating and important story, because it lays the foundation for how we might move forward into the future. The chapters in this volume seek to shed important light on the nature and wisdom of that evolution.

Bollinger: Just as it is interesting to look back and see the array of free speech issues that followed the launch of First Amendment jurisprudence in 1919, and to imagine how hard it would have been then to foresee what unfolded, so it is important for us now not to look back and take for granted what has evolved and to be cautious about our own abilities to foresee with accuracy what lies ahead. Freedom of speech has become so much more than just a legal principle. It has become a part of the national identity, and in so many ways we have learned to define ourselves as a people through the process of creating the principle itself. To talk about free speech is ultimately to talk about the ends of life—about the mentality underlying censorship, about what we seek to achieve through human intellect and discussion, and about what speech can do that's evil and harmful and how we must learn to deal with that reality.

Holmes began to take us down this path with his powerful dissent in *Abrams*. First he offered this assessment of human nature and of the counterintuitive character of free speech:

> Persecution for the expression of opinions seems to me perfectly log-
> ical. If you have no doubt of your premises or your power and want a
> certain result with all your heart you naturally express your wishes in law
> and sweep away all opposition. To allow opposition by speech seems to
> indicate that you think the speech impotent, as when a man says that he
> has squared the circle, or that you do not care whole-heartedly for the
> result, or that you doubt either your power or your premises.[11]

From this observation about the elementary human instinct for belief, cer-
titude, and insistence that others not oppose you, Holmes famously urged this way of being in the world:

> But when men have realized that time has upset many fighting faiths, they
> may come to believe even more than they believe the very foundations
> or their own conduct that the ultimate good desired is better reached
> by free trade in ideas—that the best test of truth is the power of the
> thought to get itself accepted in the competition of the market, and that
> truth is the only ground upon which their wishes safely can be carried
> out. That at any rate is the theory of our Constitution. It is an experi-
> ment, as all life is an experiment.[12]

But together these fundamental insights mean we must learn to live with a profound tension: a long-term perspective on the greater ends of life that may subdue, but presumably never fully defeat, the basic human impulse to limit and control the disorderly world of ideas and expression. Free speech is not for the faint of intellect.

Stone: In working out the details of this "experiment," the Supreme Court gradually came to understand several critical insights about the practical realities of protecting the freedom of speech and of the press. These insights have played a central role in the way the Court, over time, gave content to the First Amendment.

First, the Court learned about the so-called chilling effect. That is, the Court learned that people are easily deterred from exercising their freedom of speech. This is so because the individual speaker usually gains very little personally from signing a petition, marching in a demonstration, handing out leaflets, or posting on a blog. Put simply, except in the most unusual circumstances, whether any particular individual speaks or not is unlikely to have any appreciable impact on the world. Thus, if the individual knows that he or she might go to jail for speaking out, he or she will often forego his or her right to speak. This makes perfect sense for each individual. But if many individuals make this same decision, then, in the words of Professor Alexander Meiklejohn, the net effect will often be to mutilate "the thinking process of the community."[13] Recognition of this "chilling effect," and of the consequent power of government to use intimidation to silence its critics and to dominate and manipulate public debate, was a critical insight in shaping our First Amendment jurisprudence.

Second, the Court learned about what we might call the "pretext effect." That is, the Court came to understand that government officials will often defend their restrictions of speech on grounds quite different from their real motivations for the suppression, which will often be to silence their critics and to suppress ideas they don't like. The pretext effect is not unique to the realm of free speech, but it is especially potent in this context, because public officials will often be sorely tempted to silence dissent to insulate themselves from criticism and preserve their own authority. Of course, the very idea of the pretext effect turns on what we mean by legitimate and illegitimate reasons for restricting speech. One thing the Court came to understand is that the First Amendment forbids government officials from suppressing particular ideas because they don't want citizens to accept those ideas in the political process. This principle, which was first clearly stated in the Supreme Court in Justice Holmes' dissenting opinion in *Abrams*, is central to contemporary First Amendment doctrine and rests at the very core of the pretext effect's strong suspicion of any government regulation of speech that is consistent with such an impermissible motive.

Third, the Court learned about what we might call the "crisis" effect. That is, the Court came to understand that in times of crisis, real or imagined, citizens and government officials tend to panic, to grow desperately intolerant, and to rush headlong to suppress speech they can demonize as dangerous, subversive, disloyal, or unpatriotic. Painful experience with this "crisis effect," especially during World War I and the Cold War, led the Court to embrace what

Professor Vincent Blasi has aptly termed a "pathological perspective" in crafting First Amendment doctrine.[14] That is, the Court has structured First Amendment doctrine to anticipate and to guard against the worst of times.

Over time, these three insights led the Court to articulate three of the central principles of contemporary First Amendment jurisprudence: (1) a strong presumption against the constitutionality of viewpoint-based restrictions, (2) a greater tolerance for content-neutral restrictions, and (3) an understanding that some forms of speech have only "low" First Amendment value and therefore are not entitled to the "full" protection of the First Amendment. Thus, the Court came to view quite differently a law forbidding criticism of a war, a law regulating leafleting, and a law restricting defamation or threats.

Bollinger: It is important for our readers that we highlight an underlying theme in the important First Amendment lessons you have just articulated—namely, that over time the Court has come to see the dominant purpose of the constitutional right of freedom of speech and press as necessary to fulfill the prior commitment to live in a democracy. When sovereignty resides in the citizenry, then there can be no place for the State to tell the people what they can and cannot say or hear. The process of self-government must be insulated from the intrusion of official censorship, and it is the proper role of the judicial branch to provide that insulation. The case that most clearly announced and fully articulated this basic theory of the First Amendment was the *New York Times v. Sullivan* decision in 1964, although there are echoes in some of the earliest opinions of Justices Brandeis and Holmes.

Now, to be sure, the actual scope of protection of speech afforded by the democracy rationale overlaps with the discovery-of-truth rationale, but it does seem to start from a somewhat narrower notion. It has the distinct merit of deriving the meaning of free speech from the broader constitutional document, which is all about establishing a democratic political structure. Since federal judges are appointed and then afforded lifetime tenure, there is a natural anxiety of institutional legitimacy insofar as they tell the other elected branches what they should or should not do under the Constitution. And, as you and I have noted, once you begin thinking about what the words "the freedom of speech, or of the press" actually mean, and you realize (1) it can't possibly mean all expression and (2) the Framers were vague at best about what it does or might mean, you really have to come up with a philosophy to guide you, and under the circumstances it is natural to gravitate to a practical end consistent with the larger constitutional text. Interestingly, the other most commonly expressed theory of free speech, especially in the arena of international law—namely, that it is meant to secure a basic "human right" essential to individual human dignity, without regard to any broader social or political benefits—has never gained much traction in the US jurisprudence.

There is a dilemma with the democracy rationale. Most censorship does not fit neatly into the model of the "government" prohibiting "citizens" from exchanging thoughts and ideas. It is usually the government with the full support of the majority of citizens deciding through the democratic process what speech should be disallowed and punished. This leads to another sobering realization: over the past century, in the two periods when the nation endured the most severe bouts of fear and intolerance (namely, World War I and the so-called Red Scare that followed, and the McCarthy era of the 1950s), the judiciary did not serve as the bulwark of protection against extreme censorship. Perhaps the developments in First Amendment doctrines over the course of the last half-century will change the outcome the next time the country faces war, fears of international conspiracies, or economic depressions.

For my part, I have long been fascinated by another way of understanding what has evolved in the thinking about freedom of speech, especially as it is revealed in cases involving speakers with extremist ideas or those who are obviously harmless or inconsequential but have been swept up in the fever of persecution. Every free speech case has two dimensions. One is the "speech," which leads us naturally to think about why we would want to protect this form of human activity and, in doing so, to ask what value we can expect to derive from expression. The other is the act of censorship itself and, in particular, the mentality underlying that censorship—why it is bad and what its implications are for the society.

As some of the chapters in this volume highlight, in many of our major First Amendment cases the Justices who were most sensitive to the need to devise a strong principle of free speech were appalled by the state of mind prevalent in the society that produced the frenzy of censorship. Holmes' description of the "perfectly logical" nature of "persecution" stems from this reaction. What is interesting, then, is to imagine "free speech" as not only protecting an especially valuable activity (i.e., "speech") but also as highlighting and preventing a very dangerous (even if "natural") state of mind that has all kinds of potentially negative effects on a society, not least on the intellectual and emotional character necessary for a well-functioning democracy. This conception of free speech transforms the human arena of "speech" into a zone where we demand of ourselves extraordinary tolerance, not because the "speech" is necessarily so valuable, but because overcoming the tendency to excessive intolerance—so widely problematic in a democracy—is itself so important.[15]

Stone: What is clear from all this is that the protection of free expression serves several important functions in a free and open democratic society. It facilitates the political process by enabling citizens openly to discuss and debate the merits of competing values and policies; it enables individuals to make a broad range of personal decisions—outside the political sphere—without undue government intervention; it constrains the danger that overbearing majorities will use the law to perpetuate their authority and to unduly constrain the freedom and autonomy of their fellow citizens; it protects the freedom of individuals to express themselves in ways that promote personal autonomy and human dignity; and it promotes an individual and societal sense of tolerance that is essential to a society that seeks to be open-minded, respectful of others, and tolerant of difference. The challenge, of course, is how to implement these complex aspirations in a workable legal doctrine.

But we are interested in this volume not only in how First Amendment jurisprudence has evolved in the United States but also in how the commitment to the principles of free expression have been embraced, modified, and pursued by other nations around the globe. Several of the chapters address this issue, exploring the meaning of free speech both in other nations and in international law. To what extent has the United States been seen as a model or as an outlier? Are the principles we have embraced on such issues as sexual expression, campaign finance regulation, terrorist speech, and hate speech serving as models for other nations, or have our principles and doctrines been challenged and even rejected, and if so, for what reasons? What can we learn from the differences that have emerged? Are we "right" because we have learned from our own experience and our own mistakes in the past? Are other nations being naïve because they overestimate their capacity wisely to regulate and to restrain free expression? Will they over time discover that they have made mistakes that will later come back to haunt them? Or have we learned the wrong lessons from our own experience?

Another set of issues that interests us concerns the rapidly evolving technology of free expression. How have the internet, social media, and the globalization of speech strengthened and/or weakened our own understanding of free speech? While vastly expanding the opportunities of individuals to participate in public discourse, contemporary means of communication have also arguably contributed to political polarization, foreign influence in our democracy, and the proliferation of "fake" news. To what extent do these concerns pose new threats to our current understanding of "the freedom of speech, and of the press"? To what extent do they call for serious reconsideration of some of the central doctrines and principles on which our current First Amendment jurisprudence is based? Should government have greater authority to censor "terrorist" speech, to punish knowingly and intentionally false "news," to insist that individuals be exposed to competing views and positions and thus not be permitted to lock themselves in an ever-worsening sense of intellectual and political tribalism? To what extent can government be trusted to deal with these concerns? To what extent can private entities like Facebook, Google, and YouTube be trusted to censor the speech on their sites? The chapters in this volume explore some of these critical challenges for the future—and for the present.

Bollinger: You've hit upon one of the greatest questions about the First Amendment, one that weaves its way through virtually all of the chapters that follow: Is the mission to keep the State out of public discussion of public issues? Or is there room for the government to be involved in structuring the public forum—to control private monopolization of ideas and opportunities for speech, to correct for the inequalities in the economic and cultural realms that then impact the public sphere, or to help us overcome our bad tendencies (e.g., only listening to what we agree with)? We know that this last century of free speech and press devised what was essentially a dual system of the press, one in which newspapers and print media were protected against any government interventions to expand speech, while broadcasters in radio and television were highly regulated by federal law and a federal agency as "public fiduciaries" with responsibilities to provide diverse and "fair" programming and discussions of controversial issues of public importance. This is, of course, a very complex and controversial area of the First Amendment, about which I have written with my own interpretation of what was going on.[16] The key point to be made here is that, while the broadcast model has been somewhat disfavored, for a variety of reasons, over the past two decades, the new issues you have just identified with the internet and social media are now beginning to renew its potential relevance.

Finally, the role of the First Amendment in an increasingly interconnected world is one of the most significant questions we will face in the decades ahead. The First Amendment experience of the last century can be seen as the gradual evolution of doctrine to ensure the creation of a national public forum that could provide citizens the opportunity to discuss and resolve what were increasingly national issues (regulation of a national economy, civil rights, environmental protection, etc.). The censorship of individual cities and states interfered with this trend—censorship anywhere effectively became censorship everywhere. The *New York Times v. Sullivan* decision to limit state libel actions and create a national standard under the First Amendment reflected this needed change.

Now with the powerful globalizing forces of open trade and investment, communications, and the movements of peoples, we are increasingly facing a set of issues that can only be addressed through collective action of citizens around the world. How we will develop the international norms of free speech and press needed to protect that process of discussion and decision is a profound problem, one which several of our chapters help us understand better. But we are living less and less in the contained world that was the premise of our thinking about the First Amendment over the course of the last century—one in which

American citizens exercised self-government and through that process directed our government to interact with the rest of the world, with First Amendment deference for "national security" and the conduct of "foreign policy." More and more we will have to conceive of the First Amendment as protecting the rights of American citizens themselves to interact with the larger world because that will be the only way we can resolve what are increasingly problems that transcend political borders.[17] The implications of the new reality of an interdependent world are only now being felt.

We are proud of the work of these authors and believe that together they provide both a sound introduction to the Free Speech Century and an indication of new horizons for freedom of speech and press as we look to the future.

PART ONE

THE NATURE OF FIRST AMENDMENT JURISPRUDENCE

1

Rights Skepticism and Majority Rule at the Birth of the Modern First Amendment

VINCENT A. BLASI

Learned Hand, Oliver Wendell Holmes, and Louis Brandeis all had the same problem. They were troubled—Holmes less than the others and later, but eventually—by the widespread and mean-spirited persecution of dissenters they observed as the United States entered World War I and then reacted to the Bolshevik Revolution. Today, most persons so troubled would think that constitutional rights, and particularly the freedom of speech, exist for the very purpose of countermanding zealous political majorities that deny or neglect the claims of dissenters. But Hand, Holmes, and Brandeis, each by his own distinctive path, came to the speech disputes of 1917–1919 with a well-developed regard for majority rule and jurisprudential commitments that denied the existence of natural rights and treated positive rights as exceptional, confined, and instrumental. Ruling that fundamental rights trump majority preferences was for them a heavy lift.

All three had played a key role, in one way or another, in discrediting the jurisprudence now known as "Lochnerism," the practice of the Supreme Court during the last years of the nineteenth century and early years of the twentieth of discovering controversial economic liberty rights in the majestic generalities of the Due Process Clauses of the Fifth and Fourteenth Amendments. Holmes' scathing dissent in *Lochner v. New York*,[1] eviscerating his brethren's holding invalidating a state maximum hours law, remains the *locus classicus* of the view that political majorities possess extensive power to regulate the leveraging of economic power. As a young New York lawyer, Hand authored the definitive law review article about the *Lochner* decision, a blistering critique.[2] Brandeis, a legendary advocate who devoted half of his working hours to pro bono representation, drafted and helped to get enacted several laws designed to constrain economic exploitation, then invented the "Brandeis Brief" as a means of defending them against Lochneresque constitutional challenges.[3] For Hand, Holmes, and Brandeis, invoking constitutional rights to invalidate laws passed by political majorities did not come naturally, to put it mildly. As a general matter, each considered such an exercise of judicial power to be historically tainted, dangerous, and presumptively illegitimate.

But when the coercive authority of the state is deployed not to prevent economic exploitation but rather to punish political dissenters in the name of civil order and national security, is there not a larger role for rights and a weaker claim for majority rule? Many legal analysts would contend that the text of the First Amendment, with its seemingly categorical injunction "no law abridging the freedom of speech," provides considerable warrant to limit the power of majorities to regulate speakers. However, a text that accords operative significance to terms such as "abridging" and "*the* freedom" (emphasis added) can hardly qualify as categorical in a strong sense, as would a constitutional provision that read, say, "no law regulating speaking." Moreover, the almost universally restrictive judicial interpretation of the freedom of speech in the decades leading up to 1917 meant that judges construing the First Amendment in that era could not help but be influenced by their understandings regarding the nature of rights and the claims of political majorities. It is no surprise, therefore, that Hand, Holmes, and Brandeis found it difficult to embrace the legal arguments of the speakers in the cases growing out of the 1917–1919 wave of repression, even as all three judges were appalled by the spirit of majoritarian intolerance that had taken hold of the country.

As is well known, they found a way. Brilliant minds have a knack for doing that—and make no mistake, these three judges really did possess extraordinary intellects, their celebrity notwithstanding. Each wrote a free speech opinion for the ages. For most beginning students, those opinions constitute the traditional path into First Amendment law and theory. Two features are most striking about the opinions viewed in tandem. First, it is noteworthy how all three judges went out of their way to avoid recognizing a free-standing individual right of expressive liberty that exists apart from and thereby limits the principle of majority rule. Second, despite that common ground, the theories embraced by the three judges differ radically from one another. I know of no better way to get to the heart of the question of how a robust right of free speech can be reconciled with the fundamental premise of popular sovereignty than to probe those differences. It helps, of course, that each line of reconciliation was articulated so powerfully by its judicial proponent.

Learned Hand

The way that Hand solved his problem was by conceiving of the freedom of speech as a majority-creating procedure rather than an individual right.

Anticipating an argument that Alexander Meiklejohn would make famous thirty years later,[4] Hand argued that collective self-criticism is the essential precondition that gives the phenomenon of consent of the governed its authority to coerce compliance. Only laws passed and public opinion generated in the face of what Hand termed "hostile criticism" can claim to embody the will of a governing majority, he maintained.

In *Masses Publishing Company v. Patten*,[5] one of the first judicial interpretations of the Espionage Act of 1917, Hand read the statute to prohibit only a statement that tells a person "it is his interest or his duty" to violate the law. Political advocacy, however critical and intemperate, that falls short of invoking a duty or interest to break the law is "part of that public opinion which is the final source of government in a democratic state." In Hand's understanding of "the normal assumption of democratic government," the "suppression of hostile criticism does not turn upon the justice of its substance or the decency or propriety of its temper." Neither does it turn on the predicted consequences of the speech. The antiwar advocacy under review in the *Masses* case involved sharp accusations that the War was being fought to serve the class interests of economic elites. The issue of the magazine in dispute included admiring portraits of draft resisters. Hand characterized such speech as of a sort that might "enervate public feeling at home," "encourage the success of the enemies of the United States abroad," and "promote a mutinous and insubordinate temper among the troops." However, because the speech amounted to political agitation rather than "direct incitement to violent resistance," it qualified as hostile criticism that serves the democratic function of forging majority will. As such, its predicted consequences were legally inconsequential, at least in the absence of a pellucid expression of congressional will to punish backed up by an invocation of the War Power.

In a later opinion and in letters to Holmes and the Harvard law professor Zechariah Chafee, Hand elaborated on his proposed legal test.[6] He reiterated his statement in *Masses* that he would make controlling not the literal meaning of the words used by the speaker but the message conveyed. He said that Mark Anthony would not escape punishment by his demagogic technique of literally admonishing against rioting to avenge Caesar's murder while unmistakably conveying the opposite message to his plebeian listeners. Hand gave two reasons that legal liability should be a function of the meaning conveyed by the speaker's words rather than either the predicted consequences of the speech or the speaker's illicit intent. First, the meaning conveyed by the speech is what matters most in determining whether it contributes to the hostile criticism that serves the process of constituting a legitimate governing majority. In this view, it is the value of the speech that is the most important variable in deciding whether it is protected. Second, a test that turns on what the speaker actually said rather than what he or she risked causing or intended can take the form of "a qualitative formula, hard, conventional, difficult to evade." A legal standard of that type, Hand surmised, "might be made to serve just a little to withhold the torrents of passion to which I suspect democracies will be found more subject than for example the whig autocracy of the 18th century."[7]

The two reasons are interrelated in that if the project is to secure a minimum of speech without which legitimate authority cannot be constituted, there is much to be said for a doctrinal safe harbor protecting the requisite speech unqualifiedly. A test that turns on predicted consequences or speaker intent is not well suited to providing such a safe harbor. Those phenomena are difficult to observe, measure, and prove. To identify them, a factfinder ordinarily must rely on speculation, inference, extrapolation, and generalization. What meaning a particular writing or speech conveys to its audience will not always be self-evident—interpretation and judgment cannot be eliminated from the process of applying a speech-protective standard—but the space for erratic or prejudicial assessment is smaller when the operative phenomenon is the operational meaning conveyed by a particular statement rather than its predicted consequences or the speaker's intent.

Hand's preference for a qualitative distinction between protected and unprotected speech was not driven solely by these practical concerns about the efficacy of a safe harbor and the risk of inconsistent or unpredictable application. He considered the distinction between the direct advocacy of law violation and speech falling short of such advocacy to be fundamental as a matter of democratic theory, as this passage in a letter to Zechariah Chafee makes clear:

> Any State which professes to be controlled by public opinion cannot take sides against any opinion except that which must express itself in the violation of law. On the contrary, it must regard all other expression of opinion as tolerable, if not good. As soon as it does not, it inevitably assumes that one opinion may control in spite of what might become an opposite opinion.[8]

Hand considered the commitment not to become "a State based upon some opinion, as against any opinion which may get itself accepted" to be "indubitably the presupposition of democratic states, however little they have lived up to it." In this respect, adherence to the principle of majority rule is a dynamic process, evincing a concern about inchoate, incipient, and potential majorities no less than current ones.

The clearest case of a state being "based upon some opinion, as against any opinion which may get itself accepted" would be if expressing a forbidden opinion were grounds for punishment simply on the ground of its being considered immoral or inconsistent with the polity's basic commitments or identity. But what if the opinion is punished not for being heretical in that way but because its dissemination is plausibly thought to be likely to lead to harms that the State has legitimate reasons to want to prevent? Does a state that punishes the expression of opinion on that ground thereby become a state "based upon some opinion"? Given the way he dismissed the relevance of the harms he conceded that the speech at issue in the *Masses* case might be expected to cause, it appears that Hand considered that kind of instrumental punishment of opinion to be a violation of democratic principle on account of its adverse impact on the hostile criticism that the creation of political authority depends upon.

Suppose, however, that a writer is punished for publishing an opinion that falls short of telling readers it is their duty or their interest to violate a law, but the basis for the conviction is that the writer published his or her piece for the very purpose of causing law violation? Should such a writing be considered part of the hostile criticism that democratic theory regards as integral to the creation of majoritarian political authority and therefore protected as a matter of first principle? In the same letter to Professor Chafee in which he introduced his "state based upon an opinion" taboo, Hand addressed this very question:

> There could be no objection to the rule of the Supreme Court, tendency plus a purpose to produce the evil, even though the words did not come to the objective [duty or interest] standard, if one were sure of the result in practical administration. The chance that the State would lose any valuable opinion by suppressing those whose purpose was to produce a violation of law, while they kept on the safe side of counseling it, seems to me much too thin for practical estimate.[9]

So at the level of basic principle, the requisite hostile criticism need not include the opinions of ill-intentioned speakers, even as it necessarily includes well-intentioned speech that very likely will cause harm. Hand's objection to punishing ill-intentioned speech was entirely practical: it would expose "all who discuss heated questions to an inquiry before a jury as to their purposes." And "it is precisely at those times when alone the freedom of speech becomes important as an institution, that the protection of a jury on such an issue is illusory." Only for that administrative reason would "the State lose any valuable opinion" by making the speaker's purpose disqualifying.

What is most revealing about these elaborations of his theory is that for the speech he would protect that others might not (hostile criticism likely to cause harm), and also for the speech he would permit society to criminalize that others might think does not justify punishment (direct advocacy of law violation that persuades no one), Hand's ultimate concern is whether regulation would cause society to lose any speech of genuine value. For him, both the justification for protecting controversial speech and the limits to that protection depend on categorical judgments regarding which kinds of speech as a general matter serve the democratic function of creating a governing majority. But Hand was no for-malist. He recognized that words and images are deployed to serve a multiplicity of functions, many of which have nothing to do with contributing to the hostile criticism that enables majority rule. He considered speech serving such extra-neous functions not to fall within the domain of the freedom of speech. One characteristically trenchant sentence making this point in his *Masses* opinion reveals how central it was to his analysis:

> Words are not only the keys of persuasion, but the triggers of action, and those which have no purport but to counsel the violation of law cannot by any latitude of interpretation be a part of that public opinion which is the final source of government in a democratic state.[10]

But why exactly is such counseling wholly lacking in the value that Hand ascribes to hostile criticism? ("Purport," by the way, does not mean "intention" but rather "meaning conveyed, professed, or implied.") If the speech he found lacking in democratic function consisted only of private, clandestine counseling of specific illegal acts such as murder—an example Holmes invoked—Hand's cat-egorical denial of protection might seem self-evident. But over the course of his-tory, much of the most consequential public political agitation has been interlaced with calls for illegal, forceful resistance, and not just in revolutionary scenarios. Think of abolitionism or the labor movement. Martin Luther King's "Letter from Birmingham Jail" is one of the classics of American political advocacy. It presents a moving, reasoned case for the violation of unjust laws. But it would be denied protection under Hand's test, or so it seems. Does that make sense?

Hand derived his preferred limit to the freedom of speech from the same source from which he derived his justification for that freedom: the requisites of majority rule. In a letter to Elliot Richardson written more than thirty years after he wrote the *Masses* opinion, Hand defended his refusal to ascribe democratic value to speech that counsels law violation:

> My reasons may sound didactic and too generalized; but here they are. Every society which promulgates a law means that it shall be obeyed until it is changed, and any society which lays down means by which its laws can be changed makes those means exclusive. . . . If so, how in God's name can an incitement to do what will be unlawful if done, be itself lawful? How do words differ from any other way of bringing about an event?[11]

Majorities must be forged and sustained by surviving hostile criticism, and so must their laws, but the authority thereby created is brought into existence to govern, if necessary by deploying the resources of the State to enforce compli-ance. This is the other side of the coin of democratic function.

Those who understand the freedom of speech in these terms might reasonably disagree about which types of dissenting speech are fundamentally inconsistent with submission to the authority of majority will, and in that respect not part of the very process that makes that freedom essential. At one extreme, some might conclude that the act of flag burning so diminishes the principal symbol of sovereignty as to compromise majority rule. At the other extreme, some might think that only the explicit and specific counseling of violence, perhaps only violence already planned in some detail and designed to be employed on a large scale, sufficiently contradicts majority rule as to fall outside the project of generating political authority by means of hostile criticism. The advocacy of nonviolent civil disobedience to be undertaken openly, with willing submission to punishment, for the purpose of reforming the law—Dr. King's definition of the concept— might readily be considered part of the process of identifying majority will, particularly in the context of massive denial of the right to vote. There is nothing inevitable about where Hand drew the line. What is most significant about his analysis in the *Masses* case is the considerations he took to be relevant in determining the boundary between protected and unprotected speech, considerations that derive from the notion of freedom of speech as a majoritarian procedure.

Oliver Wendell Holmes Jr.

The way that Holmes solved his problem was by conceiving of the freedom of speech as a salutary phenomenon that forces majority understanding and will to adapt to changing conditions.

So far as the freedom of speech is concerned, Holmes is best known for three formulations: (1) his "clear and present danger" test; (2) his limiting example of falsely shouting "Fire!" in a theater and causing a panic; and (3) the "marketplace of ideas" metaphor that has been universally attributed to him even though, ironically, he never used the phrase. Each formulation—the proposed doctrinal standard, the limit case, the suggestive metaphor—is about the role that time plays in human events. When exercising his rare gift for minting aphorisms, Holmes repeatedly spoke about time: "time has upset many fighting faiths";[12] "property, friendship, and truth have a common root in time";[13] "leave the correction of evil counsels to time."[14] The point of his book *The Common Law* is that legal doctrine is all about evolution and adaptation: "The life of the law has not been logic; it has been experience."[15] One might expect that a person who had conversations with John Quincy Adams and Franklin D. Roosevelt would see the world in terms of the passage of time.

His emphasis on the dynamic character of law and knowledge informed Holmes' rights skepticism and defiantly mundane conception of truth. Seldom has a serious legal thinker been so mocking of the concept of natural law, and by inference natural rights:

> There is in all men a demand for the superlative, so much so that the poor devil who has no other way of reaching it attains it by getting drunk. It seems to me that this demand is at the bottom of the philosopher's effort to prove that truth is absolute and of the jurist's search for criteria of universal validity which he collects under the head of natural law.[16]

He once defined truth as "the majority vote of that nation that could lick all others." He considered his own method of inquiry "the system of my (intellectual) limitations." What gave his convictions objectivity "is the fact that I find my fellow man to a greater or less extent (never wholly) subject to the same *Can't Helps.*" Rational justification and human dignity impressed him less than energy and force: "We do know that a certain complex of energies can wag its tail and another can make syllogisms."[17] This approach left room for a notion of rights, but only of a contingent nature:

> For legal purposes a right is only the hypostasis of a prophecy—the imagination of a substance supporting the fact that the public force will be brought to bear upon those who do things said to contravene it— just as we talk of the force of gravitation accounting for the conduct of bodies in space. One phrase adds no more than the other to what we know without it. No doubt behind these legal rights is the fighting will of the subject to maintain them, and the spread of his emotions to the general rules by which they are maintained; but that does not seem to me the same thing as the supposed *a priori* discernment of a duty or the assertion of a preexisting right. A dog will fight for his bone.[18]

As one might have predicted from this background, in Holmes' early skirmishes as a judge with the issue of freedom of speech he ruled consistently for the regulators. On the Supreme Judicial Court of Massachusetts he rejected a claim that the Boston Common must be made available on an evenhanded basis for speaking events.[19] He upheld a New Bedford law prohibiting police officers from participating in political campaigns.[20] As a Justice of the United States Supreme Court, Holmes wrote an opinion permitting a newspaper editor to be held in contempt of court for publishing an article and cartoon impugning the motives of judges in cases then pending,[21] and another opinion upholding the criminal conviction of a writer whose article extolling nude bathing was thought to encourage breach of the state's law against indecent exposure.[22]

Then came World War I and three cases in the spring of 1919 involving prosecutions of various speakers for statements critical of the War and the draft. Holmes wrote for the Court in each case, upholding convictions under the Espionage Act of 1917.[23] One of the unsuccessful appellants was Eugene Debs, the well-known leader of the Socialist Party, who a year later would receive almost a million votes for president running from his jail cell in the Atlanta Penitentiary. In those three opinions Holmes was at pains to reject the efforts of lawyers on both sides to frame the issue in terms of some fundamental principle, whether that be that speech rights in wartime are in effect suspended or that only speech that can be proved to have actually caused specific harm can be punished. He considered the issue of speech in wartime to be subject to the pragmatic, consequentialist approach he had attributed to the common law: "It is a matter of proximity and degree." Predictions of harm could be the basis for regulation, but they had to be more specific than broad, breezy generalizations about the "bad tendency" of certain ideas in the abstract. General criticism of the war and draft by speakers who were respected in certain quarters satisfied this specificity requirement, Holmes concluded for a unanimous Court.

In November of 1919 Holmes unexpectedly dissented from a decision upholding convictions under the Espionage Act of 1918 of five Russian immigrants for distributing pamphlets from a Greenwich Village rooftop criticizing President Wilson's dispatch of American troops to Russia to aid forces fighting against the Bolsheviks. When circulated, his proposed dissenting opinion so disturbed his colleagues in the majority that a delegation of them visited his home to implore him not to publish it.[24] Happily for posterity, the old soldier (age seventy-eight) held his ground and resisted their entreaties. And so the most quoted paragraph ever written about the freedom of speech entered the US Reports.[25]

Holmes began that paragraph, the peroration of his dissent in *Abrams v. United States*, by conceding the rational logic of persecution:

> If you have no doubt of your premises or your power and want a certain result with all your heart you naturally express your wishes in law and sweep away all opposition. To allow opposition by speech seems to indicate that you think the speech impotent, as when a man says that he has squared the circle, or that you do not care whole-heartedly for the result, or that you doubt either your power or your premises.

Then, true to his observation forty years earlier that law is more about experience than logic, Holmes shifted gears:

> But when men have realized that time has upset many fighting faiths, they may come to believe even more than they believe the very foundations of their own conduct that the ultimate good desired is better reached by free trade in ideas—that the best test of truth is the power of the thought to get itself accepted in the competition of the

market, and that truth is the only ground upon which their wishes safely can be carried out.

By framing the issue in terms of how best "safely" to achieve the "ultimate good desired," Holmes found his answer in the dynamic character of human understanding, a premise not only of the common law but also, in his view, of the constitutional regime. Far from being a repository of enduring principles, even the Constitution itself

> is an experiment, as all life is an experiment. Every year if not every day we have to wager our salvation upon some prophecy based upon imperfect knowledge.

If epistemic humility and adaptability sustained by the continuous competition of ideas is "the only ground" upon which the people's "wishes safely can be carried out," the freedom of speech takes on a special significance that sets it apart from other claims of right:

> While that experiment is part of our system I think that we should be eternally vigilant against attempts to check the expression of opinions that we loathe and believe to be fraught with death, unless they so imminently threaten immediate interference with the lawful and pressing purposes of the law that an immediate check is required to save the country.

This distinctive significance had escaped Holmes' notice in his earlier free speech opinions. The change of attitude was not fleeting. As Holmes would put the matter in another memorable dissent ten years later:

> If there is any principle of the Constitution that more imperatively calls for attachment than any other it is the principle of free thought—not free thought for those who agree with us but freedom for the thought that we hate.[26]

An important question to ask about these bursts of eloquence is whether they signal a change of view on Holmes' part regarding not only the importance of free thought and speech but also the nature of rights and the claims of majority rule. I think not. His concern remained collective instrumental efficacy, "the ultimate good desired," how "wishes safely can be carried out." Unpacking his market metaphor supports this reading.

Why exactly did Holmes believe that "the best test of truth is the power of the thought to get itself accepted in the competition of the market"? Market ordering has many defining characteristics. Markets decentralize and privatize decision making, nonprescriptively honoring and implementing preferences and judgments of all sorts. Markets reward participants who generate and master pertinent information. They respond to changing conditions and lessons learned, in this respect exhibiting a self-correction capacity. They encourage prudent risk-taking and punish both excessive caution and reckless undertakings. They demand skillful prediction. Depending on how they are organized, markets can be more transparent than rival mechanisms for allocating resources and distributing benefits and opportunities, thereby reducing corruption. They accept human differences regarding objectives, needs, wants, and valuation. By facilitating competition, markets identify and punish waste and obsolescence. They stimulate innovation.

Each of these potential advantages of market ordering conceivably could have purchase when the good that is being "traded" is ideas. Which did Holmes have in mind? I believe that the place to start in trying to answer this question is Holmes' oft-proclaimed interest in the work of Charles Darwin. *The Origin of Species* came out when Holmes was a Harvard undergraduate. It had an electrifying effect on the campus, and Holmes was in the middle of that. Later, when he returned home from the Civil War, Holmes joined a high-powered discussion group—other participants included William James and Charles Sanders Peirce—which self-mockingly called itself the Metaphysical Club. Its leader, Chauncey Wright, a thinker Holmes held in awe, at the time was engaged in an extended correspondence with Darwin. Scientific method was frequently discussed by the group.[27] The topic remained fascinating to Holmes all his life. When as a young man he first encountered the writings of John Stuart Mill, it was *A System of Logic*, Mill's spirited defense of induction, not *On Liberty*, which piqued his interest. In his later years, he corresponded regularly with the philosopher of science Morris Cohen.

Someone who brings a Darwinian perspective to the topic of market ordering is likely to be impressed by the way markets force adaptation to changing conditions. This includes attitudinal adaptation, which can be encouraged by having a plethora of points of view on offer. Adaptation also involves weeding out the fallacious and the obsolete. Holmes once explained his late-arriving regard for the freedom of speech in terms of such weeding out: "In the main I am for aeration of all effervescing convictions—there is no way so quick for letting them get flat."[28] Adaptation frequently demands the redirection of inquisitive energy, a corrective that can be stimulated by competition over ideas. Ordinarily, adaptation requires persons to overcome the forces of custom and inertia. By the way it can excite the passions and energize the will, sometimes even by the anger it generates, free speech can serve as a countervailing force. As with natural selection in biological evolution, adaptive change in the realm of ideas occurs mostly in populations rather than individuals, as demographic developments, most significantly generational turnover, change the mix, and new arrivals with different priorities deriving from different experiences exert influence enabled by the relative openness of market ordering.

I believe that Holmes came to value the freedom of speech largely for its capacity to generate new ways of thinking, discredit obsolete ideas, and alter priorities of inquiry. Those consequences are what he had in mind when he pronounced "the competition of the market" to be "the best test of truth." They are consequences in the large and over time, in effect public goods whose significance is reflected in a slightly different "test of truth" that Holmes articulated the year before his *Abrams* dissent: "a present or an imagined future majority in favor of our view." Characteristically, he saw the freedom of speech not as a source of individual understanding, assertion, or identity but rather a force—a force for collective adaptation. In that respect, he thought it served majority rule.[29]

Louis Brandeis

The way that Louis Brandeis solved his problem was to view the freedom of speech as an individual liberty important as such but especially important for its contribution to democratic character.

Brandeis' concurring opinion in *Whitney v. California*,[30] decided in 1927, contains his most intellectually ambitious account of the freedom of speech. The prestige of that opinion would be hard to overstate. In modern First Amendment adjudication, duels occasionally break out among the Justices over whose position can best claim support from Brandeis' reasoning in *Whitney*. As with most legal touchstones, the opinion's susceptibility to conflicting interpretations has enhanced its influence.

The four-paragraph segment of the opinion in which Brandeis spells out his general philosophy regarding free speech begins with a cascade of assertions regarding the beliefs of "those who won our independence," beliefs that have a suspicious congruence with those we know Brandeis held. Right away, a complex, interactive relationship between individual liberty and collective well-being is suggested:

> Those who won our independence believed that the final end of the state was to make men free to develop their faculties, and that in its government the deliberative forces should prevail over the arbitrary. They valued liberty both as an end and as a means. They believed liberty to be the secret of happiness and courage to be the secret of liberty. They believed that freedom to think as you will and to speak as you think are means indispensable to the discovery and spread of political truth.[31]

Deliberative government is a collective good. The development of faculties, presumably what Brandeis is referring to when he says that liberty is valued both "as an end" and as a means, occurs at the level of the individual. Similarly, courage and happiness are traits more often ascribed to individuals than to collectivities. But the discovery and spread of political truth sounds like a collective project. How did Brandeis sort out all these phenomena?

It may help in trying to interpret Brandeis to know that his observation about liberty being the secret of happiness and courage the secret of liberty was lifted from the Funeral Oration of Pericles, as rendered by Thucydides in his *History of the Peloponnesian War*.[32] Pericles attributed Athens' military success to the courage, awareness, and inventiveness that Athenians possessed as a result of their stimulating culture, which offered many opportunities for personal initiative and civic responsibility. His basic point was that individual, civic, and military flourishing are interconnected.[33]

In this regard, it is also noteworthy that throughout his *Whitney* opinion Brandeis seems unable to mention liberty without instantly invoking what it leads to: deliberative forces prevailing over arbitrary forces, happiness, and the discovery and spread of political truth. The list grows as the paragraph progresses:

> [Those who won our independence] knew that order cannot be secured merely through fear of punishment for its infraction; that it is hazardous to discourage thought, hope and imagination; that fear breeds repression; that repression breeds hate; that hate menaces stable government; that the path of safety lies in the opportunity to discuss freely supposed grievances and proposed remedies, and that the fitting remedy for evil counsels is good ones. Believing in the power of reason as applied through public discussion, they eschewed silence coerced by law—the argument of force in its worst form.

Order, stable government, the path of safety, the fitting remedy, nonarbitrary resolution of differences—this is a catalog of the most important goods that governments are instituted to provide, and they all flow from the freedom of speech, according to Brandeis.

Not only individual rights but also civic duties are part of this complex web of relationships:

> Those who won our independence believed . . . [t]hat the greatest menace to freedom is an inert people; that public discussion is a political duty; and that this should be a fundamental principle of the American government.

Like Madison before him and Meiklejohn afterward, Brandeis viewed the freedom of speech as generated in significant part by duties. Rights and goods that others think of as protecting individual choice or personal space—privacy, economic security, entrepreneurial opportunity, leisure time—Brandeis prioritized for their contribution to the discharge of the duties of citizenship. It may be revealing that in *Whitney* he defined "the final end of the state" to be to "*make* [not 'leave'] men free to *develop* [not 'exercise'] their faculties." For him freedom was serious business.[34]

Further evidence of this seriousness can be gleaned from the paragraphs that follow Brandeis' account of "the final end of the state." They are mostly about civic character, something that was much discussed in ancient Athens and Rome, as well as during the American founding, less so in Brandeis' time or today. In uncharacteristically soaring prose, first he proclaims:

> Fear of serious injury cannot alone justify suppression of free speech and assembly. Men feared witches and burnt women. It is the function of speech to free men from the bondage of irrational fears.

Then he comments on the character of the founding generation:

> Those who won our independence by revolution were not cowards. They did not fear political change. They did not exalt order at the cost of liberty.

Next, he explains how the clear and present danger test that he and Holmes had earlier embraced is best understood not as a standard marking the threshold of rational regulatory prediction of harm but rather the point when strong character cannot save the situation for lack of time:

> To courageous, self-reliant men, with confidence in the power of free and fearless reasoning applied through the processes of popular government, no danger flowing from speech can be deemed clear and present, unless the incidence of the evil apprehended is so imminent that it may befall before there is opportunity for full discussion.

In short, the freedom of speech is a remedy as much as a right, or rather a right that can best be justified and demarcated by appreciating its role in preserving civic order, identity, and aspiration:

> If there be time to expose through discussion the falsehood and fallacies, to avert the evil by the processes of education, the remedy to be applied is more speech, not enforced silence. Only an emergency can justify repression. Such must be the rule if authority is to be reconciled with freedom.

The key to understanding Brandeis, I think, is to realize that when he uses the term "reconciled" in this passage he means "integrated into" rather than "traded off against." In a republic, freedom of speech is not something that threatens majority rule but rather is a defining element of it. This is true because the ancient Greeks and the American Founders were right: a government based on popular sovereignty depends on the character of its people. Character is a public good, arguably the most precious. Not only does civic courage—the courage of the citizenry to confront unwelcome challenges, the courage to sustain commitment in the face of difficulty or disappointment—constitute the strongest check against evil ideas, it provides the energy of reform and aspiration. For all its dangers and excesses, free discussion is an indispensable ingredient of civic courage.

No one has better captured the essence of Brandeis than his former law clerk, Judge Henry Friendly:

> I go to the great words in the Gospel according to John: "the truth shall make you free." Surely this was the essence of Brandeis' teaching. He was the authentic child of the Aufklärung; he had none of today's doubts as to whether the truth could be ascertained. He did not believe with the evangelist that this truth could be found by abiding in the Word or in becoming the disciple of any leader. Neither did he think it came from intuition or from speculation in metaphysics. He thought it could and would come only from the relentless, disinterested and critical study of facts.[35]

A major reason Brandeis did not treat such concepts as rights, duties, and majority will as formally delineated and hermetically sealed is that he was skeptical of all abstractions. He worked from the ground up. He was not troubled, for example, by the accusation that many of the reforms he championed, maximum hour and minimum wage laws, for example, could be labeled "paternalistic." To him, understanding economic leverage and worker freedom of choice demanded more than a formal account of relationships and a derogatory label. Similarly, understanding democracy demanded as much attention to individual character and collective spirit, and how they interact, as to definitions of rights and powers.

When Brandeis said that the highest office in the land is "citizen"[36] he was not distinguishing individual rights from majority rule—precisely the opposite. Just as the Founders wisely "did not exalt order at the cost of liberty," Brandeis did not exalt liberty at the cost of order. Rather, he insisted that the liberties deserving of special constitutional recognition are *components* of political order. He came to that insistence not only by dreaming of an Athens that may never have been but also, and much more important, by spending most of his life tirelessly contending with various forces of political entrenchment and corruption. Brandeis' integration of individual liberty and majority rule embodied his credo that experience and responsibility are the best teachers. He valued the freedom of speech mainly for its function of broadening public understanding of and engagement with "supposed grievances and proposed remedies." He considered fact- and experience-driven independent judgment about public issues to be crucial for legislators, administrators, reformers, and other democratic actors, not least ordinary persons occupying "the highest office in the land."

Takeaway and Aftermath

At the dawn of the modern era of First Amendment interpretation, Hand, Holmes, and Brandeis were at pains to protect the speech of political dissent without undermining the claims of majority rule that were given short shrift in the *Lochner* case and its kindred decisions. They did so by conceiving of the freedom of speech as enhancing rather than confining the national experiment in republican governance. The clear implication of their efforts was that claims regarding the scope and depth of the freedom of speech should be evaluated with attention to how the communicative activity at issue fits into the larger constitutional design founded on the principle of popular sovereignty. The landmark First Amendment decisions of the following era—*Stromberg v. California* (1931) (display of red flag as a symbol of opposition to government),[37] *Near v. Minnesota* (1931) (anti-Semitic newspaper accusations of government corruption),[38] *Thornhill v. Alabama* (1940) (labor picketing),[39] *Bridges v. California* (1941) (contempt of court by publication),[40] *Chaplinsky v. New Hampshire* (1942) (face-to-face epithets),[41] *Valentine v. Chrestensen* (1942) (commercial advertising),[42] *West Virginia State Board of Education v. Barnette* (1943) (compulsory school flag salute)[43]—discharged that commission, granting or denying claims with consistent emphasis on the question of democratic function.

Barnette is a particularly instructive decision. The Court ruled that compelling children to salute the flag and pledge their allegiance to it violates a "right of self-determination in matters that touch individual opinion and personal attitude," a formulation that might suggest reliance on a notion of free-standing individual autonomy. But Justice Jackson's renowned majority opinion in *Barnette* did not simply assert the existence of this "right of self-determination." Rather, he described it as implementing the political community's decision to "set up government by consent of the governed." The Bill of Rights, he noted, "denies those in power any legal opportunity to coerce that consent." That an important mission of the public schools is "educating the young for citizenship" was deemed by Jackson to be a significant factor in the case, as was his judgment that "probably no deeper division of our people could proceed from any provocation than from finding it necessary to choose what doctrine and whose program public educational officials shall compel youth to unite in embracing." He questioned whether the worthy goal of inspiring civic commitment was truly served by the flag salute requirement: "To believe that patriotism will not flourish if patriotic ceremonies are voluntary and spontaneous instead of a compulsory routine is to make an unflattering estimate of the appeal of our institutions to free minds." In these respects, the *Barnette* opinion echoed Hand, Holmes, and Brandeis in conceiving of free and independent thought by individuals as both the starting point and the last line of defense of democratic governance.

In recent decades, though, some Justices, at times even a majority, have undertaken to conceptualize the First Amendment as embodying, in Justice Clarence Thomas' words, a "distinctly individualistic" notion of the freedom of speech, designedly independent of concerns relating to democratic function.[44] In a number of often quite important decisions, these Justices have invoked what might be described as "free floating" First Amendment principles, in Justice Stevens' disparaging characterization.[45] Increasingly, autonomy as a First Amendment concept has become a versatile, noninstrumental justification for invalidating a wide variety of laws that in the course of governance regulate or indirectly burden communicative activity.[46]

When the rationale for the freedom of speech becomes noninstrumental, decisions no longer have to be justified in the manner of Hand, Holmes, and Brandeis—that is, with reference to past experience, empirically grounded predicted effects, specific and broadly recognized commitments, or coherent fit within a larger political or social design. Abandoning such markers can lead to a dangerously *ipse dixit* jurisprudence. This is not to suggest that noninstrumental reasoning always has that quality, or that it must play no role in determining the meaning of the freedom of speech. Autonomy arguments anchored in historical conceptions of natural rights or carefully formulated ideals of self-authorship and personal responsibility might properly inform First Amendment interpretation if deployed in a disciplined, grounded, sparing manner. Noninstrumental reasoning becomes a problem, however, when it generates novel rights aggressively, especially if the principles invoked are discrete and "free floating," in effect justified by assertion alone.

This phenomenon is particularly evident in the Court's recent decisions dealing with laws regulating campaign finance. A Supreme Court ruling in 2011, *Arizona Free Enterprise Club PAC v. Bennett*,[47] provides a good illustration. Like some other states, Arizona attempted to make public financing of political campaigns a realistic option for candidates hoping to be truly competitive with privately financed opponents. The mechanism selected, which was adopted by referendum, was to give candidates who agreed to abide by prescribed spending limits an initial public subsidy, which then would be augmented by a second subsidy triggered whenever the candidate's privately financed opponent spent above a set level. The triggered second subsidy was capped, so that the publicly financed candidate still could be—and usually would be—outspent by the privately financed opponent, whose spending was not capped, and indeed could not be under the Court's 1976 holding in *Buckley v. Valeo*.[48] The point of the limited, triggered supplemental subsidy was to close, even if not eliminate, the spending gap between candidates, such that candidates could opt for public financing with somewhat less fear of being dramatically outspent by their privately financed opponents. Setting the initial subsidy much higher would, of course, serve that objective as well, but only by making the higher level of subsidy available to all publicly financed candidates, even those not facing flush privately financed opponents. Because universally available, noncontingent public financing at a moderate to high level would strain beleaguered state and municipal budgets, the triggering mechanism had become the strategy of choice among proponents of public financing for elections.

A closely divided Supreme Court ruled the Arizona scheme to be in violation of the First Amendment. The debate within the Court between Chief Justice Roberts for the majority and Justice Kagan for the four dissenters was conducted on both sides with great argumentative dexterity. For our purpose, what is striking about that debate is how difficult it was for the two sides truly to engage, despite their skillful lawyerly attention to each other's arguments. The reason is that they were miles apart in terms of what they took to be the most important considerations bearing on the First Amendment issue.

Justice Kagan wanted to contest the majority position by demonstrating how much the Arizona triggered-subsidy scheme advanced such democratic benefits as more overall speech for the electorate, a greater number of potentially viable candidates, a lower likelihood that claims and arguments made by one candidate would go unanswered by the opposing candidate for lack of resources, a reduction in the amount of time candidates needed to devote to fundraising, and more citizen trust that successful candidates would not enter office beholden to special interests. The Chief Justice, on the other hand, thought that the crux of the case was the burden placed on a privately financed candidate by the law's provision that additional spending by her would trigger the supplemental subsidy. Such a triggering, he maintained, would make the privately financed candidate an unwilling agent helping to generate the speech of her opponent, an unacceptable invasion of her personal freedom.

It is true that Chief Justice Roberts cited instances in which privately financed candidates limited or delayed their spending, and thereby their speaking, in order not to trigger the supplemental subsidy for their opponents, an outcome that deprived voters of speech that would have occurred but for the subsidy scheme. But he made no real effort to prove how common this phenomenon was in the face of the privately financed candidate's alternative possible response to an opponent's triggered subsidy of doubling down to maintain one's advantage. Nor did he explore whether the privately financed speech potentially deterred was more valuable to the electorate than the additional publicly financed speech generated by the subsidy scheme. In short, Roberts and the Court majority viewed the case as governed by a fundamental principle of individual liberty that takes priority over all the considerations invoked by Justice Kagan relating to democratic functioning.

Were the evidence more substantial or the empirical inference more plausible of perverse incentive effects, the holding in *Arizona Free Enterprise Club Freedom PAC* might have been supportable with reference to voter enlightenment, systemic fit, or some other consequence integral to majority rule. Since this was not so, it is no surprise that Chief Justice Roberts, skillful advocate that he is, chose to rest his case on a newly conceived principle of candidate entitlement not to have one's privately financed spending contribute by force of law to the financial viability of the opposing campaign. The principle sounds in personal freedom as an end in itself. In that regard it is noninstrumental and "free floating" in the sense sketched previously, and on that account difficult to reconcile with the priorities at least of Hand, Holmes, and Brandeis in their efforts to understand and elaborate the meaning of the First Amendment.[49]

Of the three, the thought of Justice Brandeis comes the closest to being reconcilable with the noninstrumentalist, "distinctly individualistic" notion of the First Amendment favored by Chief Justice Roberts, Justice Thomas, and others. Recall that in his *Whitney* opinion, a view he ascribed to "those who won our independence," Brandeis proclaimed that the "final end of the state [is] to make men free to develop their faculties." He said that liberty has value "both as an end and a means." In those two claims, the unit of reference is the individual and the good of individual liberty is formulated as partly intrinsic to personhood as such, not wholly derivative from social or political roles, prerogatives, or duties. That said, the most important and enduring contribution Brandeis made to the history of political thought was in the way he analyzed and articulated the *instrumental* value of individual liberty, leading him to conclude that "public discussion is a political duty" because "the greatest menace to freedom is an inert people." As elaborated earlier, for Brandeis, individual liberty, even intrinsic individual liberty, is conceptually integrated with democratic responsibility. That is not how the Chief Justice and Justice Thomas view the matter.

The implication of the Brandeis understanding for interpreting the First Amendment is not categorical but rather proportional. While there is a place in the American constitutional design for noninstrumental liberties, the existence and ambit of such intrinsic liberties must be construed with attention to how their recognition affects the instrumental liberties and prerogatives of self-governing citizens in a republic.[50] Hand and Holmes would surely agree, assuming that they even had to face the question given their skepticism (greater than Brandeis') about the very notion of "liberty as an end." A First Amendment jurisprudence of expansive, wide-ranging *ipse dixit* rights and free-floating principles, a jurisprudence in which consequences, duties, and matters of political design (including the claims of majority rule) play a subordinate role, fails to satisfy that requirement, and thus represents a departure from the teachings of Hand, Holmes, and Brandeis.

Every Possible Use of Language?

FREDERICK SCHAUER

One of the central questions in creating a constitutional jurisprudence of free speech is deciding what types of actions—what speech, to oversimplify—fall within "the freedom of speech" that the Constitution protects. If too little speech is covered, there is the danger that the constitutional guarantee will be ineffective in achieving its goals. But if too much speech is covered, then there is the danger that the constitutional guarantee will be ineffective because the protection given to the most important forms of speech will be diluted. This chapter explores how the Supreme Court—and Justice Oliver Wendell Holmes in particular—grasped the importance of this issue of "coverage" from the very beginning of the struggle to give meaning to the First Amendment.

1919

The year 1919 is likely the most significant year in the history of the First Amendment. Of greatest import is that 1919 was the year in which Justice Oliver Wendell Holmes Jr., in *Schenck v. United States*,[1] gave us the enduring idea that speech can be restricted on account of its alleged dangerousness only if the danger is "clear and present," and in which in the same opinion he offered the "falsely shouting 'Fire!' in a crowded theater" example that for a century has been a ubiquitous weapon in the speech restrictor's rhetorical arsenal. But 1919 was also the year in which the Supreme Court's refusal to reverse the Espionage Act conviction of prominent Socialist and 1912 presidential candidate Eugene Debs punctuated the repressive effects of the Red Scare,[2] and it was the year in which Holmes' eloquent dissent in *Abrams v. United States*[3] launched both the metaphor of the marketplace of ideas[4] and the important principle that speech was to be protected not because of the irrationality of restricting it but *despite* the rationality of recognizing that words could be the triggers to action.

33 not b/c it *does-t* makes sense L) even so, to restrict it still be protected

The *Schenck, Debs,* and *Abrams* decisions have become so prominent in free speech discourse that it is easy to lose sight of the fourth important Supreme Court free speech decision in 1919—*Frohwerk v. United States.*[5] Like Charles Schenck and Jacob Abrams, Jacob Frohwerk was a German immigrant, a Socialist, and a vehement opponent of American involvement in World War I. Based in Kansas City, Frohwerk was the editor of the *Missouri Staats-Zeitung,* the German-language newspaper in which he voiced his opposition to the war, at the same time expressing sympathy for those who had resisted the draft, whether for reasons of principle or simply in the service of self-preservation. For taking this public stand, Frohwerk was prosecuted, convicted, and sentenced to ten years' imprisonment under the Espionage Act. When his procedurally complex case arrived at the Supreme Court, it was again Holmes who wrote for the Court in upholding Frohwerk's conviction and imprisonment. For Holmes, the case was governed by *Schenck,* which had been decided just weeks earlier, and thus, for Holmes and his brethren, extensive justification for upholding Frohwerk's conviction and imprisonment seemed unnecessary.

Holmes and all of the other Justices believed that the outcome in Frohwerk's case had in effect already been decided in *Schenck,* but Holmes' brief opinion nevertheless emphasized the seeming obviousness of the result by observing that the First Amendment "cannot have been, and obviously was not, intended to give immunity for every possible use of language."[6] Although Holmes appears to have understood this observation as merely another way of stating in different words what he had said in *Schenck* about clear and present danger and what he had meant with *Schenck*'s "fire in a crowded theater" example, the exact statement in *Frohwerk* appears to say something different and broader. The observation that the First Amendment does not immunize "every possible use of language" raises not only the *Schenck* issue of whether some speech is sufficiently dangerous to justify restriction even in the face of the First Amendment's commands but also the question of just what uses of language are even *relevant* in the first place to the First Amendment. If we take the phrase "every possible use of language" literally, we can think of the language—the speech—that is used to make contracts, the language that testators use to write wills, the language that witnesses use when they are testifying in court, the language that is used to sell used cars and new securities, and much, much else. Holmes plainly had in mind the language that is employed in the "counselling of murder," but "every possible use of language" is far broader than even that. And in framing the issue in this way, Holmes, perhaps unintentionally because the matter would have seemed so obvious to him then, asked us to consider just which uses of language—and just which symbols, pictures, and other means of communication—trigger the rhetorical and doctrinal weaponry of the First Amendment, and, conversely, which uses of language have nothing to do with the First Amendment at all. As this chapter aims to show, this latter question—which uses of language are within the *coverage* of the First Amendment and which are not—is far more salient now than it was a century ago, but Holmes' basic insight as he expressed it in *Frohwerk* is as important today as it was then.

Frohwerk

Jacob Frohwerk was born in what was then Prussia in 1864 and, along with many other Germans, immigrated to the United States for reasons of expected economic opportunity. Frohwerk was eighteen years old at the time, and he traveled with his wife and brother, eventually winding up in Kansas City, Missouri. There he got a job with the *Missouri Staats-Zeitung*, where his responsibilities as one of two employees of the approximately one-thousand-circulation newspaper included soliciting advertisements, editing copy, and writing editorials. He apparently remained in this position for more than thirty years, and thus found himself among the large number of German-origin journalists and activists who were the targets of Justice Department scrutiny subsequent to the American entry into World War I in 1917. Frohwerk's antiwar editorials were conventional for the time, blaming the war on English empire-building and international cartels of bankers and munitions makers. But Frohwerk, along with Carl Gleeser (spelled in some records as Gleeson and in others as Glesser), the newspaper's owner and publisher, was prosecuted under the Espionage Act, chiefly on account of editorials sympathizing with (but not explicitly advocating) resistance to the draft. Gleeser pled guilty, was sentenced to five years' imprisonment, and testified against Frohwerk, who was found guilty in June of 1918 by the jury after all of three minutes' deliberation and then sentenced by the judge to imprisonment at the federal prison in Leavenworth, Kansas, for a term of ten years.[7]

Frohwerk appealed his conviction to the Supreme Court, but the brief filed by his attorney, Joseph Shewalter, who was himself a Socialist antiwar activist and writer of articles opposing the war,[8] was not so much a legal brief as it was a lengthy (334 pages!) antiwar rant. Frohwerk then retained a new lawyer, Frans Lindquist, but the case remained procedurally complex because no formal bill of exceptions—the document explaining exactly what had taken place at the trial and what errors were alleged to have been committed—had been filed in the case. As a result, the Supreme Court was forced to "take the case on the record as it is," in effect evaluating merely the sufficiency of the indictment and not the actual evidence adduced at trial. Given this procedural context, Holmes concluded that it was plausible that the jury had "found that the circulation of the paper was in quarters where a little breath would be enough to kindle a flame and that the fact was known and relied upon by those who sent the paper out." Relying on the outcome in *Schenck* but saying nothing at all about "clear and present danger," Holmes in his *Frohwerk* opinion appeared to rely heavily not only on deference to the jury's decision but also on the possibility that intent alone could justify the verdict of guilty. Frohwerk's conviction and sentence were accordingly upheld, although after the war ended the original ten-year sentence was subsequently commuted by President Woodrow Wilson and Attorney General A. Mitchell Palmer as being "grossly excessive," and Frohwerk in fact served slightly less than two years at Leavenworth before being released.[9]

On the Basic Structure of First Amendment Doctrine

In observing in *Frohwerk* that the First Amendment could not possibly reach to "every possible use of language," Holmes by all accounts did not intend to say anything of genuine importance to our understanding of the First Amendment. As he saw the matter at the time, the "every possible use of language" observation was just another way of restating the obvious. Lurking beneath this statement, however, and beneath Holmes' belief that this observation about the limited reach of the First Amendment was consistent with what he had said for the Court in *Schenck*, is an important and enduring difference between the assertion—almost an afterthought—that the First Amendment did not cover every possible use of language and the "clear and present danger" phrase, itself more of an afterthought or rhetorical embellishment than something intended to lay down a legal rule, that Holmes had used in *Schenck*.

To say that the First Amendment could not conceivably reach "every possible use of language" is to say that there are some uses of language that lie entirely beyond the grasp of the First Amendment's protections. At first this may also appear to be the conclusion of the premise that some utterances create such a "clear and present danger" that they can be regulated, but the seeming similarity between the two conclusions masks a crucial difference between how we arrive at those conclusions. And to understand this, we need to step back and look at how the courts, in general, view their role in evaluating the constitutionality of government action. Fourteen years before *Schenck*, *Frohwerk*, *Debs*, and *Abrams*, Holmes had delivered his famous dissent in *Lochner v. New York*.[10] In that case a New York restriction on the number of hours that a baker could work in a day or in a week was struck down by the Supreme Court, with Justice Peckham's opinion for a majority of the Court concluding that such a restriction interfered with the constitutionally enshrined freedom of an employer and an employee to make whatever contract for employment they wished—that freedom, according to Justice Peckham, being part of the "liberty" that was protected by the Due Process Clause of the Fourteenth Amendment. For Justice Peckham and the other Justices in the majority, the economic circumstances that would lead an employee to enter into an agreement to work for more than ten hours a day or more than sixty hours a week were of no constitutional consequence.

As Holmes saw it, the majority's conclusion, and its invalidation of a judgment made by New York's democratically elected legislature, amounted to the Supreme Court substituting its own laissez-faire economic and political philosophy for the somewhat different economic philosophy chosen by the legislature and, implicitly, by the people. For the Court to do so, Holmes believed, was ill-advisedly to install the Supreme Court as a super-legislature reviewing the policy judgments and economic philosophies of the people's elected representatives. "[A] Constitution is not intended to embody a particular economic theory, whether of paternalism . . . or of laissez faire."[11]

Holmes was in dissent in *Lochner*, but his views have subsequently been vindicated and enshrined into American constitutional law. Since the late 1930s, and the Supreme Court's eventual upholding of a host of (mostly state) regulatory mechanisms enacted during the New Deal,[12] the Court has taken the view that, in the normal course of things, state and federal laws, and the regulatory actions taken pursuant to them, will be upheld as long as they possess what has been called a "rational basis."[13] In practice, the rational basis standard is highly deferential, and a wide variety of laws, some paternalist and some not, some sensible and some not, have been upheld against constitutional attack.[14]

The First Amendment is plainly an exception to this baseline rule of deference, requiring something more than a mere rational basis to withstand a constitutional challenge. Indeed, one way of understanding the "clear and present danger" language from *Schenck* in 1919 is that laws or applications of those laws that restrict speech will be invalidated in the name of the First Amendment if the dangers to which they are addressed are only speculative (not "clear") or only distant in time (not "present"), even though legislative actions aimed at speculative or distant dangers will be upheld under the rational basis standard if their targets are not speech. Holmes himself probably did not at the time of writing the *Schenck* opinion understand "clear and present danger" in such a stringent way, and the phrase, by all accounts not carefully thought out, was likely meant only to suggest that speech having a tendency toward danger could be subject to regulation. But this was not the view that Holmes subsequently adopted in his *Abrams* dissent, where he much more clearly maintained the position that a mere "bad tendency," as it is sometimes put,[15] would be insufficient to justify prohibition. Thus, a retrospective and post-*Abrams* look at "clear and present danger" is consistent with understanding the clear and present danger idea as establishing that something more than a bad tendency—and something more than mere rationality—was required to justify a restriction on speech. To take a contemporary example, legislation regulating genetically modified organisms (GMOs) is almost certainly constitutional as satisfying the baseline rational basis standard, even though the dangers of GMOs, if any, are controversial, speculative, and, at best, distant. And this is but one example of the fact that legislative and administrative action is frequently—and constitutionally—based on a perception of harms, dangers, or other consequences that are neither clear nor present. But if legislation is aimed at speech and not food, then the First Amendment comes into play, and the constitutional hurdle is dramatically heightened, the heightening being embedded in the distinction between "rational," on the one hand, and "clear and present," on the other.

The clear and present danger standard is still with us. Its current version, dating from the Supreme Court's 1969 decision in *Brandenburg v. Ohio*,[16] requires that even speech advocating unlawful conduct, in order to be constitutionally regulable, must be directed[17] at producing "imminent" unlawful action under conditions in which the unlawful action is "likely." On one view, *Brandenburg* requires not only clear and present danger but also explicit incitement to probable imminent illegality, a test that appears to be even more stringent than clear and present danger. On another view of *Brandenburg*, explicit incitement to imminent illegality is sufficient to justify restriction, but so too is clear and present danger alone. And a third view is that both *Schenck* and *Brandenburg* are about advocacy, and potentially less relevant to instances involving the transmission of factual information involving no advocacy at all.[18] But although these various understandings of the *Brandenburg* test are important, especially now in light of current issues arising from the wide availability of bomb-making instructions and similar information now available on the internet and social media, for purposes of this chapter they are a side issue. For, however we understand the exact requirements of *Brandenburg*, it is plain that what it requires, and in what particular contexts it requires it, is far more than what is required by the baseline minimal rationality standard.

Indeed, it is a large oversimplification to understand *Brandenburg* itself as anything close to the only form of heightened scrutiny under the First Amendment. When the State attempts to protect reputation by creating remedies for libel and slander, for example, an elaborate series of tests, emanating originally from the 1964 case of *New York Times Co. v. Sullivan*,[19] sets the limits for what the State may do, those limits varying with the status of the allegedly defamed individual— public official, public figure, or neither—and, although less clearly, with the topic of the publication and with whether the defamatory statement was published in the media.[20] So too with remedies for invasion of privacy, where a different battery of rules, standards, tests, exceptions, and factors comes into play.[21] And when government seeks to regulate the speech used for commercial advertising, still another body of doctrine becomes applicable, a body of doctrine understood as imposing less stringent restrictions on regulation than *Brandenburg*, but nevertheless significantly more stringent, and thus significantly less permissive of regulation, than the largely toothless requirement of minimal rationality.[22]

The examples in the previous paragraph are merely examples, and current First Amendment doctrine contains myriad largely distinct rules and approaches for the public forum,[23] for speech by the government,[24] for so-called fighting words,[25] for the regulation of sexually explicit communication,[26] for prior restraints,[27] for the broadcast media,[28] and so on and on and on. But although in this sense *Brandenburg* is best understood as a metaphor and not a comprehensive approach to the First Amendment's requirements, it remains a valuable metaphor, serving as a useful placeholder for the basic idea that the First Amendment imposes on governmental action to restrict speech higher burdens of justification and more rigorous procedural and evidentiary requirements than those that are imposed on governmental action or regulation more broadly.

Distinguishing Coverage from Protection

Because governmental prohibition or other regulation of speech must thus meet one or more of the heightened standards just described, and because the regulation of nonspeech conduct will be evaluated under the far more deferential and permissive rational basis standard,[29] the question arises as to what forms of behavior (or what forms of restriction) qualify for what we might think of as the free speech exception to a general post-*Lochner* regime of deference to legislative, executive, and administrative decisions.

One possibility is that the just-described free speech exception applies to every form of conduct that would count as "speech" in ordinary language. But in saying that the First Amendment does not reach "every possible use of language," Holmes can best be understood as rejecting this possibility as unrealistic. In asserting that there are uses of language—"speech"—that the First Amendment does not even reach, Holmes might be seen as implying that some uses of language are not even entitled to any special constitutional solicitude and are thus to be evaluated under the extreme deference that Holmes had earlier urged in his *Lochner* dissent, and that we now understand as rational basis review. What must have seemed obvious to Holmes from the beginning was that the heightened standard of review required by the First Amendment could not conceivably be applied to that vast swath of human behavior that involves the use of language, and thus to the vast swath of human behavior that might qualify as "speech" in everyday talk.

This reading of the "every possible use of language" phrase is borne out not only by the actual practice of Holmes' time but also by Holmes' own decisions. Indeed, the very term of the Supreme Court that produced *Schenck, Debs,* and

Frohwerk provides numerous examples that implicitly support Holmes' assertion that not all uses of language qualify even for the weakened form of clear and present danger that Holmes employed in *Schenck* itself. In *Pittsburgh Melting Co. v. Totten,*[30] for instance, the Court upheld a requirement that certain forms of oleo oil could not be shipped unless marked as "not for food purposes," and it did so without even a suggestion that the government-mandated marking—with words, and thus with speech—created a First Amendment problem, or even a First Amendment issue. Similarly, in *Bliss Co. v. United States,*[31] the Court upheld a contractual provision prohibiting a government contractor—a manufacturer of torpedoes—from disclosing information about torpedo manufacture received from the government, and did so entirely as a matter of contract interpretation and patent law with not even a hint that there might be a First Amendment right to disclose the information. In *Watters v. Michigan,*[32] Holmes himself wrote for a unanimous Supreme Court in upholding a conviction for door-to-door solicitation without a license. The sole issue in the case was whether the Michigan law restricted interstate commerce, and again there was no suggestion of First Amendment relevance to a state law restriction on business solicitation. In *United Drug Co. v. Rectanus,*[33] the Court decided a case involving use of a trademark and did not even contemplate the possibility that a restriction on the words that constituted a trademark were within the reach of the First Amendment, and so too in *Westermann Co. v. Dispatch Co.,*[34] where liability was imposed for the unauthorized use of copyrighted advertising illustrations. In *Luckenbach v. W.J. McCahan Sugar Refining Co.,*[35] the Court upheld liability that was imposed based on the words in a contract, and in *International News Service v. Associated Press,*[36] the Court upheld, solely as a matter of the law of unfair competition, a restriction on the publication of news that had originally been obtained by the plaintiff, without any argument by the defendant that its First Amendment rights were implicated. In *United States v. Comyns,*[37] a criminal verdict for fraud by making intentionally false representations—with speech—about a future business arrangement was upheld with, again, no mention of the First Amendment. And on March 24, 1919, only two weeks after he wrote the Court's opinion in *Frohwerk,* Holmes delivered an opinion upholding against a property rights objection a size restriction on billboards,[38] even though such a restriction plainly regulated speech.[39]

When seen against the background of such cases, and of course countless others in which verbal or communicative conduct formed the basis for legal consequences without the "intrusion" of the First Amendment, Holmes' observation about "every possible use of language" can be seen—putting aside what Holmes might have had in mind—as making a very different point from his statement about "clear and present danger," whether as Holmes first intended it or as it has later been understood. The latter is about the standard to be applied in evaluating restrictions on those communications that are shielded, even if presumptively and not absolutely, and even if in various different ways depending on the nature of the speech, the speaker, the restriction, and the context, by the First Amendment. The former, however, is about the existence of a class of communications that do not receive the benefit of that shield at all—that are not in any way shielded by *any* First Amendment rule, test, principle, standard, or doctrine. Thus, we might say that the initial question is whether a communication is even *covered* by the First Amendment, and the subsequent question, the one to which "clear and present danger" or any other First Amendment–inspired standard is directed, is just what degree of *protection* is then available to those communications that are covered by the First Amendment.[40]

As with any rule, the first question is whether the rule applies, and the subsequent issue is what the rule directs with respect to the conduct to which it applies.[41] So too here, where the question of coverage is whether the rule that is the First Amendment applies at all, with the subsequent issue then being what degree of immunity or protection is available to the behavior to which the First Amendment does apply. The issue is slightly more complex in the context of the First Amendment than it might be for many other legal or other rules, because the First Amendment's stated domain of coverage—speech—is so broad as to be unmanageable and unrealistic. Holmes is thus best interpreted as having recognized that any sensible approach to the coverage of the First Amendment must take the domain of First Amendment coverage to be narrower than the domain of everything that can be labeled as "speech" or "language." As a matter of constitutional interpretation, we could reach this conclusion by saying that it is "the freedom of speech" and not "speech" that Congress (and, subsequently, state and federal governments generally) is prohibited from abridging according to the text of the First Amendment, or we might just get there as a matter of common sense, recognizing that a First Amendment so broad as to be relevant to all human conduct involving words, language, or communication would be a First Amendment that governed almost all of human action. Regardless of the route taken to this destination, it seems necessary, as Holmes recognized, to understand the coverage of the First Amendment as being substantially narrower than "every possible use of language."

Some Modern Examples

The distinction between coverage and protection is important for precisely the reason that Holmes first identified. Language is everywhere, and there are few forms of human behavior that do not in some way involve the use of language. If "every possible use of language" generated First Amendment–inspired scrutiny, even if not ultimate protection or immunity, the First Amendment would apply to a truly vast range of behavior and to an equivalently vast range of government regulatory action. Speech and language being so ubiquitous, such an approach would produce a constitutional environment in which the First Amendment dwarfed the remainder of the Constitution in importance.

In addition to the kinds of cases, noted previously, that surfaced in the Supreme Court's 1918–1919 term, many modern examples illustrate the same point. The Sherman Antitrust Act of 1890, for example, the law that still provides the foundation for American antitrust law, prohibits "contracts, combinations, and conspiracies . . . in restraint of trade or commerce."[42] But of course most contracts, combinations, and conspiracies are effectuated by means of language, and the exchange of price information among competitors can create antitrust problems even when there is no contract or other explicit agreement.[43] Whether it be a verbal agreement between competitors to fix prices or the contract by which a manufacturer imposes excessive resale conditions on a retailer, little of American antitrust law would remain if all such applications were invalid unless they satisfied the stringent requirements of some version of the clear and present danger standard, or even any other variety of heightened scrutiny. So too with almost all of the activities of the Federal Trade Commission in prohibiting false advertising and of the Food and Drug Administration in policing pharmaceutical advertising and labeling; so too with the laws prohibiting perjury, fraud, and misrepresentations in tax filings; so too with almost all of the law of evidence, which regulates what can—and cannot—be said by lawyers and witnesses in judicial proceedings; and so too with those aspects of tort law that might, for example, create liability on the basis of erroneous written instructions accompanying chainsaws, motorcycles, household cleaning substances, and countless other potentially dangerous (if not used or operated according to the instructions) products.

Although none of the foregoing examples would have even given pause on freedom of speech grounds in 1919, a few of them are indeed subject to controversy a hundred years later. Some advocates and theorists have argued that at least some Federal Trade Commission and Food and Drug Administration labeling and advertising restrictions are problematic under the First Amendment,[44] and others have offered similar objections to some aspects of the disclosure and preclearance requirements of federal securities laws.[45] But even in the face of such claims, most of which have yet to succeed, it is still simply fanciful to imagine that the First Amendment will be very much (if at all) applicable to the laws against perjury, to the law of evidence, to the law of wills and contracts, to products liability claims based on erroneous instructions for use, and to garden-variety (nonpolitical) criminal conspiracies or multiparty criminal activities. If one's job as a lookout in a bank robbery is to stand watch and to alert—with factually accurate words—the actual robbers to the arrival of the police, it is absurd to think that the lookout's use of words will place him or her behind even the weakest First Amendment shield, and the same can be said of the jewelry store employee who provides to robbers the accurate information about the combination of the safe or the procedures for disabling the alarm system.[46] It is not that in such cases there is a clear and present danger, although in some there might be. It is that the First Amendment does not even show up, and thus the regulatory or restrictive actions of government need not meet any higher constitutional standard than they would have to meet were words, speech, or communication not involved at all.

The importance of the clear and present danger idea, in both its 1919 and its 1969 incarnations, lies in its stringency, and even the multiplicity of other First Amendment rules and tests and doctrines impose barriers of at least some stringency on governmental restrictions of communicative activities. The result of this is that a large number of seemingly reasonable government restrictions are nevertheless unconstitutional under the First Amendment. Although it may have been (and probably was) unreasonable and irrational for the government in 1919 to worry that the unfocused ramblings of Frohwerk, Schenck, and Abrams (whom Holmes referred to as one of a group of "puny anonymities") would damage the war effort (although perhaps not so for Debs), it is hardly unreasonable or irrational today for the government to be concerned about political figures who publicly and falsely claim to have won high military honors,[47] about people who seek to disrupt military funerals with vitriolic anti-LGBT messages,[48] about the effect on the frequency of actual animal cruelty if films of puppy and kitten torture are free to be sold,[49] and about free access of convicted sexual predators to social media sites used by minors,[50] and yet all of these seemingly rational attempts at restrictions have been invalidated by the Supreme Court in recent years in the name of the First Amendment.

If the real bite of the First Amendment is thus not that it invalidates irrational or exaggerated or unreasonable restrictions (although of course it properly does) but rather that it invalidates even rational and reasonable restrictions in the service of deeper and longer-term First Amendment values,[51] then it becomes apparent that much of the existing and long-standing strength of the First Amendment is a product of the rigor of, broadly, either the clear and present danger idea or any of the other manifestations of heightened First Amendment scrutiny. And the importance of this conclusion in the current context is that this First Amendment rigor would likely be jeopardized if some number of the examples I have used were to have to pass through a First Amendment filter.

Assuming (and it is hardly a huge assumption) that the law of evidence, the prohibitions on perjury, the criminal prosecution of robbery lookouts, the illegality of price-fixing agreements, the authority of the Food and Drug

Administration to prohibit the mislabeling of prescription drugs, the ability of tort law to impose liability for injuries caused by following erroneous product instructions, the power of the Securities and Exchange Commission to require that sellers of securities not make false claims about prospective investments, and the authority of the Federal Trade Commission to sanction plainly untrue product claims are inevitably going to be upheld, then forcing such actions through the First Amendment filter will inevitably result in weakening that filter. If the filter must allow all of the foregoing examples of regulation to pass through it, then either the formulation or application of the filter, or of the various different filters, will be changed, creating a serious risk that the filter will no longer be able to block the kinds of rational but unconstitutional restrictions that characterize a large number of existing First Amendment controversies.

Although some of the dangers that these various regulations target are undoubtedly as clear and as present as are those implicit in the regrettably overused "falsely shouting 'Fire!' in a crowded theater" hypothetical, others are less serious and less immediate, even though they are widely accepted as the kinds of dangers with which government is and should properly be concerned. And thus, if responding to these speech-associated dangers is inevitable, and if those responses require a determination that these dangers are clear and present, or that in some other way they are very serious, the result is likely to be a weakening—a dilution—of clear and present danger or any other form of close First Amendment scrutiny, and thus a weakening and dilution of the strength of the First Amendment. It is of course possible that some of this risk could be alleviated by adding still more tests, doctrines, rules, and levels of scrutiny to the already complex edifice of First Amendment doctrine, but at some point the edifice may well become so complex that it loses its rhetorical and political effectiveness, possibly for judges but much more likely for the public and for the front-line and nonjudicial officials whose internalization and enforcement of First Amendment values are as important on a daily basis as is what judges do in the much smaller number of instances that actually reach the courts.

These worries are not new. Although it has now been more than forty years since the Supreme Court granted some but limited (and thus less than that embodied in the clear and present danger idea and the *Brandenburg* test) protection for pure commercial advertising,[52] Justice Powell early on worried that too much concern with, and too close scrutiny of, regulations of commercial advertising might result in "leveling" down the degree of protection available for more important political, social, and ideological communication.[53] His worry is well taken. As long as the kinds of uses of language discussed here are kept outside of the coverage of the First Amendment, the strength of the protection within the boundaries of coverage is not much in jeopardy. But if all of the examples of now-uncovered uses of language are understood to invite at least some First Amendment–inspired examination, then, on the assumption that this examination will still allow governmental regulation, reaching that conclusion may require just the kind of dilution or leveling that concerned Justice Powell. Perhaps the existing multiplicity of tests and standards will make such an outcome less likely than it would be if all ("clear and present danger") or nothing ("rational basis") were the only alternatives, but the risk remains that using First Amendment doctrines so widely may produce a First Amendment doctrine and culture that has less force when it is most needed than might otherwise be the case.[54] And although some of the past and well-advised broadenings of the coverage of the First Amendment—the inclusion of actions for libel, for example, or the inclusion of all but the most extreme pornography—appear to have produced little damage to core First Amendment values and protection, the lesson of such examples should not be taken too far. Many of the past broadenings, as with those just mentioned, have not resulted in dilution of the First Amendment because their consequence has been the invalidation of previously accepted restrictions. But the claim of dilution arises largely from the presence of restrictions that will not conceivably be invalidated. The dilution claim is thus a product of the combination of at least some First Amendment scrutiny with the inevitability that the scrutinized regulations will be upheld. When this combination exists, there are risks of dilution that do not arise when broadened coverage also produces increased protection, as it has in most of the historical examples of coverage expansion.

It is important in this context to distinguish the doctrinal from the cultural First Amendment. Although the risk of dilution plausibly exists even for judges, it is reasonable to expect judges, especially appellate judges, to understand complex categories and multiple levels of scrutiny. As a result, broadening the scope of coverage might not produce a weakening of the degree of protection for "core" speech as long as it is understood that speech on the periphery is protected to a lesser extent than that which is at the core. If, as is now the case, the weaker tests applicable to commercial advertising allow the Securities and Exchange Commission to sanction misleading securities advertising even as false or misleading noncommercial speech is fully protected, it is likely that judges, at least, will be able to apply the most stringent protection to core social, political, and ideological speech even while applying less stringent scrutiny to commercial advertising. But if, as seems increasingly the case, the First Amendment is understood by the public and by the political process as just another form of deregulatory rhetoric, there is a risk that being accused of hostility to the First Amendment will no longer be as stigmatizing as it has been in the past.[55] And if that is the case, then there seems again some risk that the fear of such stigmatization will be less even for those officials who would wish to control the kind of speech that lies at the center of what the First Amendment is all about.

All of this is, of course, speculative. In theory, one can imagine a genuinely controlled experiment designed to test the hypothesis that a doctrinal expansion of the coverage of the First Amendment would produce an increase in the prevalence of First Amendment rhetoric, and that such prevalence would make that rhetoric less effective when it most mattered. In practice, however, such an experiment would be impossible, given the vast number of variables at play. But to the extent that the story of the boy who cried wolf draws its force from the plausibility of its basic insight, there is some basis for believing that crying "First Amendment," just like crying "Wolf," may produce less of an urgent response when it really matters. Moreover, we might think of this as a problem of decision making under uncertainty. We are uncertain about the effects of a substantial broadening of the coverage of the First Amendment, with one possibility being that such broadening will bring increased protection for speech only remotely related to the core principles of freedom of speech with little or no negative effect on the degree of protection available for the speech much closer to the core. But the other possibility is that the increased coverage of the First Amendment will weaken the protection of what the First Amendment, historically, politically, and philosophically, is principally designed to do. Faced with such uncertainty, and recognizing that only one of the possibilities will jeopardize the core of the First Amendment, assuming the existence of the more dangerous possibility seems much the better course.

Ideally, judicial determinations of the coverage of the First Amendment would be guided by a deep and systematic application of the underlying purposes of the First Amendment, such that the First Amendment would be taken to cover those communications and restrictions that related in some way to the point of having the First Amendment in the first place, and to the underlying justifications for a principle of freedom of speech.[56] In practice, however, such determinations are made either on the basis of path-dependent historical practice (and thus of historical anomalies),[57] of almost intuitive and random perceptions of which communicative activities implicate the First Amendment and which do not,[58] or of vastly under and overinclusive presumptions and default rules that, again, tend to produce case-by-case, ad hoc, and often intuitive judgments of what is covered and what is not.[59] The existing approaches to determining coverage thus leave much to be desired, but part of the problem is the reluctance of the courts, especially, to carefully recognize the problem of coverage as a distinct question. Dealing with the question of coverage systematically and satisfactorily will accordingly involve, first and most important, recognizing that the question of coverage needs to be addressed separately from the question of protection.

Conclusion

Like his offhand remark about clear and present danger, and like his equally off-hand example of the false shout of "Fire!" in a crowded theater, Holmes' remark in *Frohwerk* about the inapplicability of the First Amendment to every possible use of language was plainly intended more as rhetorical flourish than as a canonical articulation of a legal principle. And although Holmes in 1919 may not have thought he was saying anything different in *Frohwerk* than he had said a short time earlier in *Schenck*, it is now clear that the casual statements in the two cases represent two quite different but equally important aspects of the structure of First Amendment doctrine. The better known of these aspects comes from *Schenck*, such that "clear and present danger" now not only is a part of legal doctrine but also has migrated into popular culture. But however important clear and present danger and its modern variants are and have become, the question of the initial applicability—the coverage—of the First Amendment is even more so, precisely because of the pervasiveness of language and the inevitability of regulation of much of its use. The First Amendment owes much of its strength to its focus, and, as Holmes wisely observed a century ago, that focus is and must be narrower than "every possible use of language."

In some number of non-American jurisdictions, Canada perhaps most prominently, the American concern with saying that some forms of communication—some uses of language—are outside of the reach of the First Amendment is treated with derision.[60] Why not recognize that all restrictions of speech, or communication, or expression implicate the concerns underlying speech protection and then, through the use of proportionality analysis, determine whether the extent of the regulation is proportional to the communicative interest involved? But it may be no coincidence that those jurisdictions with an expansive understanding of the coverage of the right to freedom of speech (or expression, or communication) turn out also to have a significantly less stringent degree of protection for the speech that is covered, and even for the speech that lies at the center of the principle of free speech. It is perhaps unreasonable to make a strong causal claim, but at the very least the existence in the United States of a limited domain of coverage and a high degree of protection within that limited domain suggests that this correlation reflects a causal relationship. If that is correct, then it may be that the willingness explicitly to limit the coverage of the First Amendment is a source of the First Amendment's greatest strength.

Rethinking the Myth of the Modern First Amendment

LAURA WEINRIB

There is an enduring origin myth about the emergence of free speech in America. It does not begin with the Framers of the US Constitution. The notion that the eighteenth-century drafters of the First Amendment dictated our modern speech-protective regime was dispelled decades ago. Rather, the myth is the one that generated this very volume, namely, that the triumph of free speech in America was a straightforward reaction to the repressive patriotism of World War I. On this generally accepted account, Justices Oliver Wendell Holmes Jr. and Louis Brandeis (aided by the thwarted district court visionary Learned Hand and by a handful of forward-thinking academics) spawned the contemporary commitment to free speech when they dissented from the convictions of antiwar agitators for condemning conscription and criticizing the war effort. Their stirring defenses of free speech prevailed in the marketplace of ideas, persuading their fellow Justices, as well as the American people, that the judicial protection of free speech was core to American democracy.

This myth, which introduces virtually every textbook and academic study on the modern First Amendment, presumes what I will call the *liberal* conception of free speech: free speech shields unpopular speakers and, in the interest of informed governance and pluralistic tolerance, exposes the polity to unconventional and even dangerous ideas. A core premise of this understanding is that the judiciary, because it is less susceptible to popular pressure than the political branches, is the institution best equipped to balance liberty against security and soberly to evaluate the State's asserted justifications for suppression. And so it falls to the courts to constrain overly zealous prosecutions and to invalidate unduly restrictive laws.

In reality, the roots of free speech in the United States are more complicated, and they are both more radical and more conservative than the traditional account allows. Yes, many interwar progressives believed expressive freedom was necessary to bolster and legitimate the exercise of state power. A handful even trusted the courts to demarcate the boundaries of protected expression. But most were harsh critics of the judiciary, and few were eager to invest courts with the authority to invalidate democratically enacted legislation. The shepherds of the modern First Amendment were a peculiar amalgamation of radical labor activists and conservative lawyers, not the New Dealers to whom we ordinarily ascribe the production of the postwar constitutional order.

To understand why this messier story has eluded us for so long, we need to shift our focus from antimilitarism to anticapitalism. At first cut, this means acknowledging that the defendants who lent their names to the seminal First Amendment cases during the war and its aftermath—such as Charles Schenck, Jacob Abrams, Benjamin Gitlow, and the Socialist leader and presidential candidate Eugene V. Debs—were first and foremost labor radicals, and they criticized the war because they believed that militarism served the interests of industry. But the relationship between class conflict and the early First Amendment was more fundamental than that. The radicals who promoted a strong vision of free speech during the 1920s, including the lawyers who litigated the cases in which Justices Holmes and Brandeis issued their celebrated concurrences and dissents, rejected the State's policing of property rights as much as its suppression of speech. When they demanded state neutrality in economic disputes, they wanted to protect the right of workers to engage in concerted economic activity, not merely to disseminate their views. And despite their own aversion to the courts, they hitched their state-skeptical agenda to a tradition of court-centered constitutionalism. The conservatives who embraced a powerful First Amendment a decade later, and whose support cemented judicial solicitude for expressive freedom, made a surprisingly similar calculation. A countermajoritarian right to free speech, they wagered, could also curb state meddling with business activity, including antilabor employment practices.

This chapter reviews the standard account of the origins of the modern First Amendment and explains why that account is inadequate. It then takes up, in turn, the radical and conservative free speech programs. Finally, it explores the implications of reorienting the history of free speech around class conflict for evaluating the trajectory of free speech in America today.

World War I and the Myth of the Modern First Amendment

The modern First Amendment, however disputed its principles and purposes, uncontroversially embodies two basic features: first, that the Constitution rarely permits government officials to prevent individuals from speaking or to penalize them for expressing their views, and second, that the judiciary is charged with ensuring that the political branches do not overstep their authority. The amendment does not restrict the private curtailment of expression, and it ensures only that government will not censor or suppress speech, not that speakers will have the resources to be heard. However natural they appear today, both of these components were contested in the formative years of the modern First Amendment.

For over a century after the First Amendment was ratified in 1791, public officials regularly suppressed speech they regarded as threatening, blasphemous, antisocial, and even uncivil, and the judiciary rarely intervened. Until the 1920s, the First Amendment was not considered binding on the states. Even with respect to federal law, courts seldom second-guessed government policies. Accounts of the World War I cases rightly emphasize the paucity of popular and political support for free speech. It is not the case, however, that censorship and suppression were universally accepted until Zechariah Chafee and (belatedly) John Dewey penned their trenchant wartime critiques. Debates over free expression had flared up with some regularity in the nineteenth and early twentieth centuries, albeit often in unfamiliar forms.

One such conflagration raged in the first half of the 1910s, even as Europe was plunged into war. As compared with its better-known counterparts, like the 1798 Alien and Sedition Acts and the controversial censorship and arrests of Union detractors during the Civil War, this Progressive Era conflict over free speech raised distinctive concerns. As an initial matter, the would-be speakers were workers, not antiwar protesters. Even more important is the nature of the expressive activity that labor advocates hoped to protect. Some of the silenced speakers advocated Socialist redistribution or revolution, in a manner that presaged subsequent controversy over Communist advocacy. Many, however, sought instead to organize workers into unions and to coordinate strikes and boycotts against recalcitrant employers. The concessions they demanded—increased pay, shorter hours, and improved working conditions—involved economic transactions that traditionally were regarded as private. And the police and hired security forces who quashed their organizing efforts invoked the property interests of employers and the liberty interests of strike-breaking employees rather than Cold War–era concerns about national security and subversion.

The effort to accommodate workers' concerted economic activity to the American tradition of free speech embodied in the First Amendment intersected somewhat awkwardly with the values of progressive reformers. The stumbling block was not the importance of vigorous debate. The Progressive Era was a time of rapid social and intellectual transformation, and many ideas that had seemed implausible or heretical at the end of the nineteenth century had rapidly gained acceptance. In other words, progressives understood that social and scientific progress required open discussion of ideas. At the same time, many progressives hoped to smooth rather than accentuate the divisions between social classes and regarded unions as a threat to public welfare. Opinions diverged regarding the extent to which strikes and boycotts deserved the same deference as the advocacy of unconventional ideas in leaflets or on street corners.

What labor unions and progressives overwhelmingly agreed on, however, was their distaste for the judiciary, which stubbornly adhered to a dogmatic conception of individual autonomy that critics considered untenable. In a period of rapid industrialization, the notion that workers could bargain individually for a living wage had come to seem hopelessly outmoded. Class warfare in the early twentieth century was real and often brutal. Striking workers were beaten, shot, and sometimes tortured. The most militant unions engaged in sabotage, property destruction, and intimidation. It was evident to contemporaries that laissez-faire capitalism offered no answer to rising income stratification and staggering poverty, or to the escalating class tension that resulted.

Different constituencies proffered different solutions. The menu of progressive proposals included workers' compensation, the minimum wage, and maximum-hours laws. Unions preferred to rely on the power of organized workers to withhold their collective labor and purchasing power. But all ran afoul of Progressive Era courts. Judges jailed striking workers for violating antipicketing ordinances or obstructing traffic. They issued injunctions against union activity—in the absence of courtroom testimony and upon unsupported employer predictions of economic loss—threatening the noncompliant with imprisonment for contempt. And they invalidated progressive measures regulating hours, wages, and working conditions on the grounds that they violated a constitutional liberty of contract purportedly contained within the Due Process Clause of the Fourteenth Amendment. That is, state and federal courts exercised what used to be called the "power to enforce constitutional limitations" to strike down reformers' hard-won efforts to ameliorate inequality through legislation.

Where unions reserved their worst vitriol for labor injunctions, it was the relatively less frequent exercise of judicial review, often associated with the Supreme Court's decision invalidating a New York maximum-hours law for bakers in *Lochner v. New York*, that most infuriated their progressive allies.[1] Progressive Era hostility to the courts was so acute that politicians campaigned on pledges to rein them in. No less respected a figure than former president Theodore Roosevelt complained that the courts were overreaching their constitutional authority and considered it "absolutely necessary for the people themselves to take control of the interpretation of the constitution."[2]

It is no wonder, then, that Progressive Era advocates of expressive freedom generally rejected judicial enforcement of the First Amendment as an appropriate avenue for achieving their speech-protective goals. Social reformers trusted in a strong state, and they sought solutions in the political branches. They urged legislatures and executive actors to refrain from criminalizing dissent or from prosecuting dissenters. Some also advocated new laws buttressing expressive freedom or allocating public space for community debate. But aside from a few lonely lawyers, hardly anyone favored a court-centered strategy for defending free speech. In the first half of the 1910s, academics, activists, and even a congressional commission concluded that courts impeded rather than enhanced free expression.

World War I posed a fundamental challenge for the dominant progressive conception of free speech. During the war, government actors and vigilantes worked together to enforce patriotism and conformity and to quash dissent. There were thousands of prosecutions, which continued after the Armistice, and juries readily delivered convictions. Major public figures were imprisoned for opposing conscription or American intervention in the war. Neither popular majorities nor government officials exercised the restraint upon which the prewar vision depended. Many progressives worried that patriotic fervor was being manipulated to target the very labor radicals whom they had defended on policy grounds before the war. Yet even the scholars and judges who were most anxious about the repression remained deeply suspicious of judicial review. In the agonized discussion of free speech in progressive journals and on the congressional floor, virtually no one endorsed judicial invalidation of the federal Espionage and Sedition Acts, which served as the basis for most of the notorious prosecutions.

In the traditional telling, the wartime repression was so extreme that a few pioneering progressives discerned a more enlightened path. The influential legal scholar Zechariah Chafee issued his path-breaking *Harvard Law Review* article, "Freedom of Speech in War Time," which misleadingly cast the convictions as a brash departure from America's First Amendment tradition. Other academics, including Harold Laski, issued similar critiques. With their prodding, Justices Holmes and Brandeis thought better of their own wartime acquiescence and, in the wake of the Armistice, began to write their iconic First Amendment dissents. And their reasoning was so persuasive, so obviously correct, that a majority of the Supreme Court remade the law to reflect it.[3]

On closer inspection, however, this pat narrative begins to unravel. To begin with, the rhetorical power of a Holmes dissent is hardly an adequate causal lever in the context of the pre–New Deal Supreme Court. After all, Holmes' stinging dissent in *Lochner v. New York*, lionized though it was by progressives, proved insufficient to move his fellow Justices to abandon liberty of contract—notwithstanding

Holmes' and Brandeis' steadfast reiteration of its premises in subsequent cases. Moreover, more than a decade passed between Justice Holmes' dissent in *Abrams* and the first Supreme Court decision invalidating a statute on First Amendment grounds. It was not until the late 1930s, when the Court issued its pivotal speech-protective decisions in such cases as *De Jonge v. Oregon, Hague v. CIO, Herndon v. Lowry,* and *Thornhill v. Alabama* (all of which involved radical advocacy or labor speech), that the contours of the modern First Amendment took shape. To be sure, there were incremental steps in the interim, including the 1925 decision in *Gitlow v. New York,* in which the Court assumed that the Fourteenth Amendment had "incorporated" the First Amendment's protection of free speech, thereby rendering it binding on the states. But there was little indication before the 1930s that free speech would become a core constitutional commitment, let alone a formidable constraint on government power.

Perhaps most significant, there was at best modest support during the 1920s for invigorated judicial enforcement of the First Amendment, even among the constituencies who ordinarily cheered Holmes and Brandeis on. After the Armistice, the realization that legislators and executive officials would overestimate national security concerns and either manufacture or capitulate to popular conformism highlighted the dangers of an unfettered state. Many prewar progressives (who increasingly adopted the label "liberal") emphasized the importance of free speech as a policy matter, as they had in the 1910s. Some thought judges could serve a moderating influence through their interpretation of state and federal statutes, by construing legislation to require clear evidence of incitement or unlawful purpose as a condition of conviction. Very few, however, believed that judge-made law should supplant an unambiguous statutory expression of political will. Justice Brandeis himself was famously reluctant to legitimate *Lochner*-era legalism by incorporating free speech and assembly, and he went along only because the "substantive" reach of the Fourteenth Amendment had attained the status of "settled" law, "despite arguments to the contrary which had seemed to [him] persuasive." Throughout the 1920s, esteemed progressive outlets like the *New Republic* declared that the legislatures, not the courts, were properly tasked with policing the First Amendment, and that civil liberties groups should be seeking the repeal of unjust laws, not their invalidation on constitutional grounds.[4]

To understand how the modern First Amendment ultimately prevailed, we need first to understand the change in attitude among the advocates and litigants who chose to pursue their free speech agenda in the courts. As it turns out, the protagonists are not, or at least not only, the progressive theorists and judges we ordinarily identify with the interwar First Amendment. Instead, the story begins with a group of lawyers and activists associated with the American Civil Liberties Union (ACLU). Their goal was not primarily opposition to militarism or even a generalized commitment to free speech. Rather, as one of the organization's founders put it in an early document: "We are frankly partisans of labor, [and] our place is in the fight."[5]

The Radical Roots of the Modern First Amendment

The ACLU features prominently, if not centrally, in most histories of the modern First Amendment. The organization's precursor, the National Civil Liberties Bureau (NCLB), litigated many of the best-known First Amendment cases during World War I. Scholars have rightly emphasized its founders' wartime defense of conscientious objectors, as well as its constitutional challenges to conscription and the Espionage Act. What has largely escaped attention, however, is the relationship between the interwar civil liberties campaign and the ACLU's staunch substantive commitment to a radical wing of the American labor movement. Already during World War I, the organization's leaders were most concerned to defend those individuals whose opposition to the war stemmed from their anticapitalism. When the war ended, and massive strikes in the coal and steel industries roiled the nation, their connection to labor radicalism only intensified, as the "union" in their organization's new title was meant to suggest.[6] At first blush, the ACLU's labor sympathies would seem to confuse rather than clarify its pioneering role in court-centered First Amendment advocacy. From the perspective of the organization's clients—who variously ascribed judicial antiunionism to psychological disposition, social pressures, or the constraints of classical legal thought—judges at best were unwitting tools of industry. Labor organizers and striking workers occasionally invoked the First Amendment as a shield against criminal prosecution, but they expected courts to rubber-stamp their convictions. Employers' reliance on injunctions after the war to thwart some of the most powerful labor actions only exacerbated union charges that judges were corporate stooges. Meanwhile, the Supreme Court issued a number of high-profile decisions restricting unions' rights to engage in strikes and boycotts. Although these cases are ordinarily classified under the rubric of "labor law" rather than freedom of expression, they sharply limited unions' ability to communicate with workers and consumers by picket sign or in print. That an interwar organization would have pursued vindication of labor's rights in the courts was practically unthinkable.

Still, there were few tenable alternatives to which they might have turned. Union leaders were hardly more sanguine about other officials than they were about judges. Police officers and state and national troops often intervened on behalf of employers in labor disputes. Politicians appealed to organized labor on the campaign trail, but once elected, they rarely acted to empower unions.

Labor leaders believed state institutions were stacked against them, and they insisted that meaningful legal protections accrued only to constituencies that had already proven their power.

On the whole, the ACLU's founders—many of whom had begun their careers as progressive reformers—came to share these views. A long stretch of "reactionary decisions" in litigated cases reinforced their conviction that "the status of civil liberty [was] hopeless so far as it is the concern of the courts of law."[7] At the same time, the war shattered their desire for a strong state. Cofounder Roger Baldwin, who spent time in prison for refusing compulsory military service, professed his "impatien[ce] with reform" and his determination to fight the "political state itself." Others within the organization shared Baldwin's conviction that the State served the interests of capital. According to an early pamphlet, "the property interests of the country [were] so completely in control of our political life as to establish what [was] in effect a class government—a government by and for business." Under the circumstances, it was hardly prudent to trust state institutions to protect labor's rights.[8]

Such attitudes infused the new ACLU when it was founded in 1920. The leaders of the fledgling organization claimed it as their mission to minimize violence in the massive class struggle they believed was on the horizon. To that end, they demanded government nonintervention in labor disputes. They hoped that free speech, defined capaciously, would avert the altercations that often led to bloodshed when officers ordered pickets to disband. To be sure, they also invoked and even pioneered the now-standard defenses of free speech: that open debate advances democratic legitimacy, encourages political participation, and produces better policy outcomes, among other virtues. Still, the organization's principal objective was not the freedom of leafletters and soapbox speakers to propagate their ideas. What the leadership desired was a right to remake the socioeconomic order by any peaceful means, including economic weapons such as boycotts and strikes.[9]

The ACLU did not presume, however, that what it called the *right of agitation* could be attained by judicial decree. The Supreme Court's wartime speech and labor cases stamped out any hope of securing new protections for constitutional rights in the short term; juries continued to return convictions, and "the power of injunctions . . . assail[ed] civil rights at every point." Like the radical labor groups it defended, the ACLU had concluded that rights could be secured only by "ceaseless agitation and sacrifice," and that they could be maintained only through "organized power."[10]

Reflecting backward, all of this is unfamiliar, even jarring. Like the progressives, radicals were acutely attuned to the class struggle and disinclined to rely on the judiciary to protect unpopular speakers from overeager majorities and their political representatives. But the radical conception of free speech seems even further from the modern First Amendment than its progressive counterpart.

Respectable outlets like the *Nation* warned that antilabor repression was "turning the thoughtful working people of the country into dangerous radicals and extreme direct actionists." Free speech, on this view, was an outlet for class aggression, an opportunity to vent grievances and thereby defuse them. For the ACLU's founders, by contrast, the right of agitation was essential to the revolutionary transformation of society that they awaited and endorsed.[11]

How, then, is this radical vision of free speech even relevant to the emergence of the modern understanding? Surely, one might reasonably suggest, the Justices who eventually embraced a strong First Amendment rejected the goals and the instruments of the early ACLU.

The admittedly reductionist answer is that the ACLU's staunch commitment to its substantive agenda made it more willing than progressives to reconsider its relationship to the courts. Over the course of the 1920s, a combination of state-sanctioned antiunionism and economic prosperity rendered fundamental social change a distant specter. The ACLU thus settled in for a long-term struggle and reluctantly adopted a more conciliatory posture that would attract progressive supporters, including a cadre of sympathetic lawyers.[12]

Early on, the ACLU recognized one productive potential of litigation: its ability to generate publicity for the civil liberties cause. In its first years of operation, the ACLU (drawing on Industrial Workers of the World [IWW] tactics of the prior decade) sent "free speech organizers" into centers of industrial conflict to provoke arrest, with the hope that passionate courtroom testimony and unjust convictions would move workers and their allies to repudiate a legal system that was rigged against them. Notably, this strategy yielded some of Holmes and Brandeis' most acclaimed opinions, including *Gitlow* and *Whitney*. The ACLU attorney who litigated those cases never expected to prevail on constitutional grounds; after all, he reasoned, judges attained their positions "by devoted service to important property interests." He nonetheless hoped that judicial defeat would sway public opinion. That ambition, it bears emphasis, appealed to progressives. In the mid-1920s, the *New Republic* expressed its unwavering aversion to constitutional test case litigation but accepted that criminal convictions were useful in "obtaining publicity" to bolster popular opposition to objectionable laws.[13]

Over time, however, the ACLU's consulting lawyers (including future Supreme Court Justice Felix Frankfurter) began to manifest ambivalence about "promoting propaganda by defeats in court." The impetus for reassessment was, in large part, an unanticipated development: every so often, the organization's lawyers won. The key to their successes was a two-pronged approach. In cases involving labor picketing and protests, they emphasized factual insufficiencies and procedural irregularities in lieu of attacks on the underlying laws. Simultaneously, the organization expanded its operations into areas that did not obviously implicate radical ends. For example, its foray into academic freedom was meant to appeal to influential liberals who were otherwise unfriendly to the organization's ventures because they "fear[ed] contamination with the defense of reds!" Once enlisted, those distinguished supporters often proved willing to provide written endorsements, which the ACLU (despite internal concerns about professional ethics) then circulated in newspapers and submitted to court.[14]

The ACLU's attitude toward the judiciary further evolved with the onset of the Great Depression and the subsequent election of President Franklin D. Roosevelt, which presented a fundamental challenge for the organization's understanding of civil liberties. For one, New Deal efforts to regulate labor relations introduced a strong role for the State in brokering disputes between workers and their employers that was at odds with the ACLU's State skepticism. In fact, the leadership was so concerned about administrative "inroads on the rights of agitation" that the ACLU initially opposed the New Deal's signature labor law, Robert F. Wagner's National Labor Relations Act (the NLRA or Wagner Act). After a contentious internal debate, however, the organization withdrew its negative statement. Eventually, it embraced the NLRA and became a vocal champion of the Senate's Civil Liberties Committee, launched by Wisconsin senator Robert La Follette Jr. to ensure that the labor rights it conferred were enforced and respected. Still, more than other New Deal organizations, the ACLU remained wary of state power.[15]

At the same time, the ACLU ran afoul of both labor leaders and liberals in its increasing openness to litigation as a civil liberties tool. Although it condemned antilabor injunctions, its assistance in framing and securing passage of the Norris-LaGuardia Act—a monumental labor law that curbed the power of the federal courts to enjoin strikes and picketing—had the counterintuitive effect of liberating the organization to pursue a more aggressive court-centered campaign for protecting free speech against other intrusions.[16]

At the beginning of the decade, the prospects for a First Amendment strategy remained dim. The ACLU regarded the Supreme Court's now-iconic decision in *Stromberg v. California*, which it helped to litigate, as a modest limitation on antiradicalism laws that offered "no hope for voiding the laws in principle." But by the middle of the decade, the ACLU's litigation focus was yielding notable results. The ACLU assisted the Communist-affiliated International Labor Defense (ILD) in challenging the specious capital sentences of the so-called Scottsboro boys, who were convicted in Alabama of raping two White women aboard a train. At the ILD's invitation, an ACLU lawyer argued and won two significant Supreme Court victories involving the defendants, including a major decision incorporating the Sixth Amendment right to counsel. Then, in January 1937, the Court followed suit by incorporating freedom of assembly. In *De Jonge v. Oregon*—which, like the Scottsboro cases, was argued by an ACLU attorney in cooperation with the ILD—the Justices unanimously overturned the conviction of a Communist Party organizer under Oregon's criminal syndicalism law, albeit on narrow grounds.[17]

In short, between 1920 and the mid-1930s, the ACLU helped to allay judicial hostility to radical litigants. Yet New Dealers, though they lauded the organization's victories, remained antagonistic toward the courts. After all, the ACLU's achievements were meager consolation for the more conventional uses of the judicial review to strike down social and economic legislation. Many of the New Deal's signature experiments to mitigate the effects of the Great Depression were invalidated on constitutional grounds, and liberals and labor advocates considered it a matter of time until the Wagner Act succumbed as well.

By early 1937, liberals were ready to act, regardless of recent First Amendment advances. As in the 1910s, there were vocal calls to rein in the power of the courts through constitutional amendment, jurisdiction stripping legislation, and other means. Most contemporaries assumed that eliminating judicial review of social and economic legislation would also curtail judicial enforcement of the First Amendment, but if doing so would empower state and federal legislatures to reduce unemployment and improve public welfare, they were willing to make the bargain. As one leftist legal organization put the point, "Judicial protection for civil liberties by means of the power to invalidate laws cannot be separated · from judicial protection for the selfish interests of large property." Preserving a role for the Court in protecting free speech would only serve to legitimate its enforcement of property rights. Besides, the courts' commitment to the First Amendment would cease as soon as speech threatened the existing order. "There can be no true enforcement of the Bill of Rights in the interests of persons instead of wealth except by the elected representatives of the people," the group concluded.[18]

Against this peculiar backdrop the deficiency of the standard etiology of the modern First Amendment is apparent. In 1937, two full decades after the first Espionage Act prosecutions made their way through the courts, many of the nation's most influential scholars and public figures regarded judicial enforcement of the First Amendment as unimportant, even undesirable. In articles and in congressional testimony, they clamored to voice their concerns about an excessively interventionist judiciary, not an overly permissive one. The priority among New Dealers was to rescue the nation from poverty and inequality, and their consensus was that judicial review was standing in the way. Put simply, the most vocal supporters of court-curbing measures in the mid-1930s were the liberals who ostensibly championed the Holmes and Brandeis vision and the labor leaders who were its purported beneficiaries.

As for the ACLU itself, its official assessment was ambivalent. In a statement, it acknowledged that the Court's "widening conception" of the Due Process Clause had produced occasional concessions to civil liberties but emphasized that the Supreme Court, like lower courts and even administrative officials, was more concerned about "protecting property than personal rights." In settling on a position, the organization surveyed a number of distinguished lawyers and public figures. Most preferred to preserve the judicial power to invalidate state and federal legislation under some circumstances. At the same time, all thought it acceptable to restrict the Due Process Clause to procedural matters as long as the courts retained authority to enforce the personal liberties contained within the Bill of Rights, including free speech. That is, where entrenched New Dealers expressed willingness to dismantle judicial review altogether, the ACLU's most trusted insiders and consultants prescribed a compromise position—broad deference to social and economic legislation coupled with a more searching review of incursions on personal rights—very much like the one that the Supreme Court itself would ultimately articulate in its famous fourth footnote of *United States v. Carolene Products*.[19]

Of course, New Dealers never succeeded in eliminating judicial review. Their failure was due in part to a major misstep by President Roosevelt, who introduced a disingenuous proposal to add Justices to the Supreme Court in lieu of a more straightforward alternative. Against a global landscape of rising totalitarianism, the so-called court-packing plan exposed Roosevelt to charges of executive aggrandizement and discredited his critique of judicial overreach. Even so, the president's proposal attracted substantial, if squeamish, support. The newly founded National Lawyers Guild, whose executive committee featured prominent liberals and radicals, was representative; although some members worried that the plan was "dangerous to Civil Liberties," the group's larger concern was the "unwarranted exercise of judicial power," and it advised Congress to pass it.[20]

Ironically, the group that most forcefully mobilized the ACLU's civil liberties victories to undermine the court-packing plan was the very organization that, by consistently privileging "concern for property" over "concern for liberty," had prompted liberal lawyers' defection to the National Lawyers Guild in the first place. It was the conservative American Bar Association (ABA)—not progressive scholars, silenced soapbox speakers, or even the ACLU—that cast an "independent judiciary" as indispensable to the "civil liberties of minority groups."[21] This enthusiastic endorsement of free speech among conservative lawyers and their clients reflected a marked about-face, and like the radicalism of the ACLU's early advocacy, it was an essential if unrecognized ingredient of the modern First Amendment.

The Conservative Roots of the Modern
First Amendment

The conservative relationship to free speech during the interwar period diverged from the progressive understanding as sharply as the ACLU's. Conservatives consistently rejected the progressive presumption that robust debate buttresses and legitimates a strong state, and they retained a strong emphasis on national security and public morals. Invoking the mantra that "liberty is not license," most thought the convictions in the Espionage Act cases were justified. After the war, as a strike wave and a spate of anarchist bombings raised the specter of a Bolshevik-style revolution on American soil, conservative eagerness to root out subversives only escalated.

Like the radicals and progressives, conservatives focused on labor organizing as much as revolutionary propaganda. Many supported outright bans on strikes and picketing; unable to amass legislative majorities, they mobilized instead for state criminal syndicalism laws, satisfied that such measures (which passed in dozens of states) would "shut up the agitators and keep them off the job."[22] The ABA's official journal went so far as to encourage the disbarment of lawyers who engaged in "extreme utterances and activities" on behalf of striking workers.

Of course, conservatives were predisposed to distrust state oversight, and they were enamored of judicial review. But as critics were quick to point out, their enthusiasm for constitutionalism only weakly encompassed expressive freedom. When conservative lawyers justified judicial power in the face of Progressive Era attacks, they emphasized property rights and liberty of contract more than free speech. A decade later, an ABA president proclaimed that "our constitution and laws and the courts that interpret them . . . preserve [our people's] liberties," even as he urged the arrest of agitators and clarified that there was "no place for so-called class consciousness in America." As John Dewey summed up the situation, the champions of laissez-faire resented government interference with business practices but were "almost uniformly silent in the case of even flagrant violations of civil liberties—in spite of lip service to liberal ideas and professed adulation of the Constitution."[23]

Still, outside the labor context, conservatives' devotion to constitutional limitations spilled over into the domain of personal rights. During the 1920s, they worried about the legislative expansion of state programs, as well as the sprawling administrative apparatus required to run them. Leaders of the American bar expressed approval of such cases as *Meyer v. Nebraska* and *Pierce v. Society of Sisters*, in which the Supreme Court, declaring that an "individual has certain fundamental rights which must be respected," constrained state power to dictate children's education. Similar sentiments drove many conservatives to endorse religious freedom claims and even—in the context of artistic censorship, sex education, and Prohibition—to oppose the deployment of state power "to enforce some particular rule of conduct, which those to whom it appeals describe as moral."[24]

In short, where progressives endorsed expressive freedom but not its state-constraining judicial enforcement, conservatives promoted judicial policing of state power, conditioned on generous deference to government regulation of speech. And that conservative combination of state skepticism and confidence in the judiciary, opposed as it was to progressive ideals, bore a striking kinship to the emerging understanding of the interwar ACLU—notwithstanding Roger Baldwin's emphatic effort to distinguish the right of agitation from the "right to exploit the American people without governmental interference."[25]

The New Deal only intensified conservative receptiveness to First Amendment claims. The change in attitude was multifaceted, but its core impulse was easy enough to explain. "Business interests" were "politically dominant" in the 1920s, as John Dewey observed, and "only those individuals who are *opposing* the established order ever get into trouble by using the right to free inquiry and public discussion."[26]

Over the course of the 1930s, Congress and the Roosevelt administration targeted a host of entrenched business practices, from lax financial reporting to union busting. At first, the old constitutional defenses appeared adequate to the task: the courts invoked the Commerce Clause and liberty of contract to strike down irksome legislation. As the decade wore on, however, appeals to private property no longer resonated as the anchor of American freedom, and so conservatives cast about for other arguments. The corporate media resisted regulation of advertising as an incursion on "freedom of the press." When a Senate committee investigating lobbying subpoenaed telegrams from opponents of the New Deal, a future president of the ABA decried the "attempt by congress to destroy the guarantees under the bill of rights," and he successfully resisted on Fourth Amendment grounds. Above all, the impetus for conservative awakening to the First Amendment was the New Deal assault on the judiciary itself. As liberal efforts to dismantle judicial review escalated, conservatives cast about for a cause that would rehabilitate the judicial reputation. They found it in free speech.[27]

It was the ABA that spearheaded the new approach. In the spring of 1937, an ABA committee considered how best to undermine support for the president's proposal. Its "best idea" was to air a series of radio programs spotlighting "famous case[s] in which personal rights have been upheld by the Supreme Court"—many of which had been litigated or promoted by the ACLU, with vocal opposition from the ABA. Meanwhile, the *ABA Journal*'s two issues on the court-packing plan heavily emphasized judicial protection of free speech, press, and assembly, boldly declaring that an independent judiciary was organized labor's "best friend."[28]

In the end, of course, momentum for court-curbing legislation was checked by another source. In March 1937, the Supreme Court unexpectedly rejected a constitutional challenge to a state minimum wage law. Just weeks later, in *NLRB v. Jones and Laughlin Steel Corporation*, it took the monumental step of upholding the NLRA as an allowable exercise of Congress' commerce power. In language that came close to endorsing a right of agitation, Chief Justice Charles Evans Hughes described the "right of employees to self-organization" as a "fundamental right."[29]

To conservatives, the so-called Constitutional Revolution was a "devastating destruction of constitutional limitations upon Federal power" unparalleled in American history. But if the spring 1937 decisions soured conservatives on the Hughes Court, they did not erode emerging support for the First Amendment. In a companion case to *Jones and Laughlin Steel*, the Associated Press argued that its statutory obligation to bargain with unionized workers ran afoul of "freedom of expression." Although the majority was not convinced, the Court's conservative Justices professed their commitment to the First Amendment's "cardinal rights." Indeed, with liberty of contract defunct, the First Amendment rapidly emerged as corporations' most plausible mechanism for challenging New Deal regulation.[30]

To be sure, many conservatives, including several on the Supreme Court, still doubted that the First Amendment extended to subversive speech, let alone labor picketing. The conservative Justices dissented in April when the Court overturned the conviction of a communist organizer for "inciting insurrection" in Georgia, and they dissented again in May when Justice Brandeis, writing for a bare majority in a labor picketing case, assumed in dicta that the right to publicize the facts of a labor dispute was within the scope of constitutionally protected free speech. But business groups were beginning to appreciate the importance of a consistent line (a lesson the ACLU, which vocally defended the speech rights of the Ku Klux Klan and Nazi Party, had long since learned). A March 1937 editorial in the journal of the US Chamber of Commerce argued that "tolerant 'conservatism'" required noninterference with Communist meetings. Over the ensuing years, influential industrialists cast free speech as a companion to "freedom of enterprise." The National Association of Manufacturers (NAM) launched a public relations campaign with the express purpose of promoting the "vital inter-relationship between private competitive business and personal and political freedom." A few years later, it felt it had managed to "link free enterprise in the public consciousness with free speech, free press and free religion."[31]

The ABA too adapted quickly to the new constitutional landscape. Its president from 1937 to 1938, Arthur Vanderbilt, had campaigned actively for free speech since at least the 1920s—and had even assisted the ACLU when Roger Baldwin was arrested in New Jersey for parading with striking workers—but he had long been a solitary voice within the bar. In the wake of the court-packing controversy, he pitched a committee on constitutional rights to the ABA's board of governors, but the "more conservative members . . . 'saw red' and voted the suggestion down." He tried again a few months later with the assistance of Wall Street lawyer Grenville Clark, after the latter, underscoring the outsized influence of the ACLU in advancing free speech, issued a plea to conservatives to take up the cause. It was Vanderbilt's successor as president, an unabashed conservative, who ultimately acted on their suggestion. As he emphasized in his inaugural address, vigorous enforcement of the Bill of Rights might mitigate the trampling of "well-worn shoes," but it would also come into play "when the crushed toes were encased in patent leather footwear of the wealthy, or the rights denied or the privacy invaded were those of the business corporation."[32]

Liberals greeted the announcement of the ABA's new Committee on the Bill of Rights with a mixture of celebration and cynicism. Zechariah Chafee, who agreed to serve on it, acknowledged public expectation that its principal concern would be "the right to be taxed low." But the choice of Grenville Clark to chair the Committee on the Bill of Rights—and, in turn, Clark's reliance for assistance on one of his firm's new associates, the future First Amendment luminary Louis Lusky—ensured that its interventions in service of the modern First Amendment would be forceful and effective. The committee's first act, at the invitation of the ACLU board, was to submit an amicus brief in a labor picketing case, *Hague v. CIO*. Although some within the ABA balked at the perception of assisting radicals, the organization's president assured them that none of its recent activities, including its "remarkably fine work" opposing the court-packing plan, had generated "such excellent public relations."[33]

The ACLU played a crucial role in facilitating conservative involvement in First Amendment advocacy. Freed by *Jones and Laughlin Steel* from the peril that a strong judiciary would dismantle labor's New Deal advances, the ACLU committed fully to a constitutional strategy for advancing the right of agitation. By the late 1930s, the organization was actively recruiting "outwardly conservative characters" as members and donors, and when the ABA's committee was announced, the ACLU pledged complete support. In controversies over the First Amendment rights of corporations, the ACLU sided with business groups and parted ways with the labor movement and New Deal administrators. And when the NAM (along with the Ford Motor Company and the white-shoe law firm that represented it) decried NLRB regulation of union-organizing campaigns as an abridgment of employers' free speech, the ACLU eventually, if equivocally, came to their aid.[34]

Although it is impossible to quantify the influence of the ACLU's approach, the organization felt sure it was instrumental. Even after the spring of 1937, liberal support for countermajoritarian constitutionalism was in scarce supply. Faced with unyielding opposition to judicial review, the Supreme Court might have adopted a more deferential posture toward clear legislative statements, as courts in many other democracies have always done. Instead, the ACLU's campaign for judicial enforcement of the Bill of Rights infused the Constitution with credibility. Almost alone among the New Deal's prolabor constituency, the organization counseled consistent adherence to the First Amendment, heedless of the beneficiary in particular cases. Industry advocates brandished the ACLU's endorsement of employer free speech in congressional testimony and press releases, along with legal briefs. And conservatives' cooperation, in turn, buttressed the respectability of the ACLU. Grenville Clark gleaned from insiders that the ABA's involvement in *Hague v. CIO* helped the ACLU to secure a First Amendment victory. By 1941, the ACLU could boast that its "battleground [was] chiefly in the courts," where "decisions in case after case [had] firmly established the interpretations of the Bill of Rights which the Union supports."[35]

The ACLU's erstwhile allies within the labor movement and the NLRB condemned the organization for privileging an evenhanded understanding of free speech principles over a pragmatic commitment to labor's rights. Indeed, the ACLU's alignment with conservatives during the late 1930s nearly tore the organization apart. But the ACLU leadership believed that protecting business speech, even when it seemed more economic than expressive, was the only way to ensure that picketing and boycotts would be protected too.

For a brief time, it seemed the gambit might work. In 1940, the Supreme Court held in *Thornhill v. Alabama* that labor picketing was shielded by the First Amendment. The implications of the decision were stunning. Even some labor sympathizers recoiled at the evident expansion of the First Amendment's scope. Earlier cases had deemed the legislative protection of labor activity constitutionally permissible, but *Thornhill* suggested that legislative restrictions on labor activity were constitutionally foreclosed. As one labor scholar posited, the "New Court" had merely replicated the errors of the "Old Court" by repackaging "substantive due process" in First Amendment guise.[36]

In the face of such criticism, along with the wave of disruptive labor activity that followed, the Supreme Court quickly tempered its bold pronouncement in *Thornhill* and carved out ample space for the State regulation of picketing and strikes. Within two decades, a steadily expanding First Amendment protected a broad range of communications and practices, from religious proselytizing to motion pictures to (some) sexually explicit speech, but the right of agitation, which the interwar ACLU had worked so diligently to construct, was utterly undone. The last straw fell in a 1957 case upholding an antipicketing injunction, and it is a bizarre historical quirk that the author of the majority opinion, who remained wary of judicial review throughout his tenure on the Court, was Justice Felix Frankfurter—a veteran of the interwar ACLU, an influential advocate of the Norris-LaGuardia Act, and one of the staunchest critics of the organization's increasingly court-centered First Amendment approach. As the dissenting Justices observed, Justice Frankfurter's opinion marked a "formal surrender" from the First Amendment protection of labor speech.[37]

But by then, free speech served other ends. In the frenzied middle decades of the twentieth century, the dominant understanding of the First Amendment was infused with an aspirational commitment to participatory democracy, minority rights, and peaceful social change. In the 1940s, the ACLU reported that "race relations . . . occup[ied] first place in the struggle for civil liberties," followed closely by religious freedom, immigration, and women's rights. The judiciary, imperfectly but more robustly than the political branches, carved out a sphere of expressive freedom that shielded the heroic champions of civil rights, along with antiwar protestors and anticapitalist ideologues. In their opinions, the courts cast expressive freedom as the central pillar of a constitutional democracy. And the ACLU, notwithstanding the excision of the right of agitation, never wavered in its devotion to the modern First Amendment.[38]

Reflections on the Future from the History of Free Speech

As a creation story, the myth of the modern First Amendment appears benign enough. America's commitment to free speech, in this airbrushed account, was born of error and repentance. When the hysteria of World War I receded, judges, scholars, and advocates at last understood that a strong First Amendment would preserve a platform for transformative political ideas. With Justice Brandeis, they came to recognize that "order cannot be secured merely through fear of punishment for its infraction; that it is hazardous to discourage thought, hope and imagination; . . . and that the fitting remedy for evil counsels is good ones."[39] And the strength of their convictions invested subsequent efforts to expand the First Amendment's reach with the authority of a storied past.

Much is lost in this traditional telling. It erases the labor-organizing tactics at the heart of the ACLU's interwar litigation strategy, along with corporate lawyers' effort to extract protection for newly imperiled business practices. It also elides a fierce debate about the role of the courts. In reality, there never was agreement on what function free speech should serve or which institution was best suited to enforce it. The liberal vision existed alongside distinct alternatives, both radical and conservative. The modern First Amendment was not reasoned from first principles. It was, rather, a compromise that served particular ends.

It is accordingly no wonder that the manufactured consensus of the twentieth century has begun to break down. The generation who came of age with McCarthyism and the Civil Rights movement took it on faith that the judicial enforcement of free speech was a shield against popular intolerance and the prerequisite for a robust and inclusive democracy. But as the chapters in this volume make clear, a heated debate has since emerged over the limits of the First Amendment and the extent to which the judiciary should determine its scope.

History cannot tell us how to resolve that debate. But in assessing the path forward, it is important to understand what the modern First Amendment was intended to achieve and what it has accomplished in fact. For many decades, both employer speech and labor speech received lesser First Amendment protection than the core political speech privileged by the liberal understanding. That arrangement has recently shifted. There has been little progress in extending First Amendment protection to the early ACLU's guiding ambition, the right to strike. Yet the Supreme Court seems ready to recognize a First Amendment right of public sector workers to refuse to contribute to union expenses, with potentially devastating consequences for America's already weakened labor movement.

From the standpoint of the interwar ACLU, then, the bargain turned out rather badly. The organization accepted protections for business speech to strengthen the case for labor speech. Now, labor's rights to picket and boycott are tightly hemmed in, and the expressive activity of corporations and antiunion workers has never been more secure. Nearly half of recent First Amendment victories have gone to businesses and trade groups challenging unwelcome regulatory interventions—a development that scholars have poignantly dubbed the "Lochnerization" of the First Amendment.

Looking forward, the future of the civil liberties settlement is uncertain. Over the past year, the president of the United States has launched an astounding assault on settled First Amendment precedent. A century after its founding, the ACLU has been a central pillar of the resistance. As in decades past, it has sought to preserve channels of protest by framing free speech as a neutral right enforceable by impartial judges. That approach has produced impressive results. Eighty years after the legal establishment hailed the judiciary as America's "greatest safeguard" against the "expansion of the executive power into dictatorship," liberals and conservatives have exhibited unusual unity in their shared denunciation of attacks on the courts.[40]

At the same time, a critique from the Left has re-emerged, and it has penetrated such disparate areas as campaign finance, hate speech, campus protest, and commercial speech. In a period of expanding income inequality, its exponents are asking whether an unflinching commitment to the First Amendment might prove inadequate or even counterproductive. They too might look to history for venerated antecedents. A well-known 1930s labor advocate who broke with the ACLU over its support for employer speech spoke for many New Dealers when he rejected the organization's vision of a neutral First Amendment. The marketplace of thought was "a *monopoly* market," he asserted, no better at producing an egalitarian distribution of ideas than of property or consumer goods. "We believe speech and the other civil liberties are meaningful only to men who dare to use them," he explained, "[a]nd that before 'daring' come bread and water, come roots in the community, comes respite from fear."[41]

In short, the myth of the modern First Amendment has always had its share of apostates. The dyed-in-the-wool New Dealers who parted ways with the ACLU at the end of the 1930s had fought tirelessly for free speech, but they feared judges would deploy the First Amendment to block democratic reform. And as Europe succumbed to totalitarianism, they worried that economic desperation might usher demagogues to power in America as well. As Wisconsin senator Robert La Follette Jr. framed the point in congressional testimony over the court-packing plan, "no kind of legal guaranty has ever been able to protect minorities from the hatreds and intolerances let loose when an economic system breaks down."[42]

4

The Discursive Benefits of Structure

Federalism and the First Amendment

HEATHER K. GERKEN

It might seem strange to write a chapter on federalism in a volume celebrating the birth of modern First Amendment doctrine. If anything, we imagine federalism and the First Amendment as competitors rather than complements. Everyone is familiar with the early role that states and local institutions played in facilitating dissent.[1] But decentralization's recent history has hardly been heroic given the tendency of local majorities to persecute minorities within their ranks. Jim Crow supplies the ugliest instance, but examples abound. That history may be why we typically don't associate state and local institutions that oppose national views with our storied tradition of dissent. Instead, federalism is typically understood as a threat to dissenters, one the First Amendment was designed to address.

In law, the distinction between federalism and the First Amendment looms so large that it is embedded into constitutional theory. Those interested in speech and dissent study the First Amendment. Those interested in the distribution of power study constitutional structure—federalism and the separation of powers. And thus the rights/structure divide was born. Even federalism's advocates have acquiesced to this arrangement. When it comes to dissent, federalism scholars don't offer much between the anodyne (laboratories of democracy) and the alarming (armed state rebellion). Otherwise, they emphasize the need for a floor of basic rights to protect dissenters, thereby reifying the assumption that rights, not structure, matter for those engaged in dissent.

It is a mistake to set federalism against the First Amendment whenever we think about dissent. Ours is not your father's federalism. Today, federalism can no longer shield discrimination from national norms. But it can play an important role in shaping those norms. That's because rights and structure serve as interlocking gears that move debates forward. Just as the First Amendment protects us against federalism's excesses, federalism compensates for the First

Amendment's shortcomings. The First Amendment is important, crucially so. But so are the "discursive benefits of structure"[2]—the ways in which federalism serves the same ends as the First Amendment. Federalism's discursive benefits would not be possible without a robust First Amendment, but federalism aids the First Amendment in facilitating debate and change.

The Limits of the First Amendment

It would be foolish to disregard the importance of the First Amendment to our democracy, especially in these trying times. The First Amendment guarantees the right to speak and associate, both core requirements for a well-functioning democracy. It shields dissenters against an overweening government and represents an important counterweight to state and local overreach.

The problem is that protest and debate are not always enough to effect change. To be fair, effecting change is far from the only end the First Amendment serves. But surely it is one of the most important. Democracy can't function if we lack the means necessary to change our minds and our policies.

One of the core functions/reasons for the First Amendment

When it comes to effecting change, a robust speech right is a necessary but not always a sufficient condition. That's because the real challenge for polit-ical outliers these days isn't getting their message out; it's getting their message across. There is, of course, a long-standing literature that makes this point.[3] But a simple example will do here. Think about the iconic image of the First Amendment: someone standing on a soapbox. A moment's thought should re-mind us that the soapbox is the least powerful perch in politics. We all know what those in the majority do when they see someone standing on a soapbox. They walk right on by. Dissenters can change minds only if the majority is willing to engage with them. Radio silence is one of the most powerful tools a majority possesses.

Given how hard it is to get one's message *across*, it's not a coincidence that our classic model of dissent is the iconoclastic outsider. The First Amendment confers a right to speak against a decision—not to change it, not even to influ-ence it. Participation, not power, is all political outliers can demand. That's pre-cisely why free speech is a private right. The moment a citizen ceases to speak for him- or herself and begins to speak for the State, First Amendment analysis shifts in profound ways.[4] The right to free speech is thus the right of the outsider. Even when dissenters are on the inside of a decision making process, we assume they lack the power to decide. They are *dissenters*, after all.[5] And given the many challenges associated with effecting change, what people gain from the First Amendment often has more to do with expression than efficacy.

definition of a dissenter

[margin note: Possible way to resolve this issue]

Scholars of dissent are familiar with the First Amendment's shortcomings, and the work of many has focused on giving dissenters something more. Some academics, for instance, have called for a more "institutional" First Amendment that lends greater protections to speech-facilitating institutions like universities, the media, and the like.[6] Others have insisted we need more public spaces for dissent.[7] Still others have urged the government to create more platforms for debate or more space for expression.[8]

Note that all of these proposals are aimed at producing more opportunities and more platforms for speech. That is all well and good, but it's not clear that these are the right solutions if one's focus is effecting change. To the contrary, given the proliferation of media outlets and platforms, it's relatively easy for dissenters to get their message out. The trouble is that these solutions may not help dissenters get their message across. Indeed, the vast array of information sources also creates the risk that dissent will be swamped by the many other media sites competing for our attention.[9] For every Wendy Davis,[10] there are thousands of protestors who can't find their way onto our screens.

[margin note: Something like the Climate change.]

What dissenters really need to get their message across are different forms of advocacy, different platforms for mobilizing, and different levers of change. As I discuss in the next section, that's where federalism comes in. It provides the "something more" that dissenters often need to effect change.

The Interlocking Gears of Rights and Structure

If we focus on getting one's message across, federalism supplies dissenters with a set of tools that the First Amendment cannot. That becomes especially clear once one recognizes that the term "federalism" should not be confined to the states, but should encompass substate, local, and sublocal institutions. What I've called "federalism all the way down"[11] includes not just states that depart from national views, but cities that favor transgender bathrooms, zoning commissions dominated by Greens, and school boards controlled by Darwin skeptics. All of these institutions create an opportunity for national minorities to constitute local majorities. *[margin note: Both sides of the coin benefit.]*

When political minorities can exercise control in some part of the system, they can do more than speak. They can "dissent by deciding,"[12] putting their ideas into policies. "Dissenting by deciding" thus offers dissenters a powerful tool to push change forward. That's why decentralization offers a much-needed complement to the First Amendment.

This may sound a bit abstract, so let me start with a real-world example: the marriage-equality debate. Proponents of marriage equality were dissenters for a long time. And they did just what dissenters do when exercising their rights

↗ but not enough.

under the First Amendment; [they protested, they marched, they wrote editorials and blog posts.] All of these activities were important.

If you think about the moment when the ground really shifted, however, it was when Massachusetts and San Francisco began issuing marriage licenses to same-sex couples.[13] The same-sex marriage movement took full advantage of the discursive benefits of structure,[14] and the debate changed as a result. The political center shifted when a dissenting view was converted into policy. Before then, lots of progressive pragmatists endorsed civil unions. When same-sex marriage became a reality, civil unions became the compassionate conservative's default.[15]

[The debate shifted for the American people as well. Same-sex marriage ceased to be an abstract idea the moment news agencies started beaming pictures of happy pairs of brides and grooms into our television sets. Until that moment, same-sex marriage was an issue debated by pundits. Now it was a reality.]   *Shift in the debate*

If we dig deeper, we can see that the same-sex marriage movement reveals other ways in which state and local decisions can jumpstart debates. The platform alone matters. Because of their real-world effects, decisions made by state and local governments, on average, get more publicity than protests or blogs or editorials. That was certainly true during the same-sex marriage debate. A debate that had been taking place in fairly elite circles was suddenly splashed across the front page of newspapers throughout the country and changed the way everyday Americans lived their lives.   *→ It's real policy. On the flipside, you have Alabama abortion laws.*

These state and local decisions also helped set the agenda.[16] Up until that moment, opponents of same-sex marriage did not need to engage with would-be dissenters to prevent same-sex couples from marrying. Once Massachusetts and San Francisco began to issue marriage licenses to same-sex couples, however, those in the majority had to do something if they wanted to return to their preferred status quo. That important fact is precisely what prompted Prop 8 and, ultimately, a debate that changed the minds of so many in California that a majority now support same-sex marriage.[17] The First Amendment cannot force engagement in this fashion. But "dissenting by deciding" gives dissenters a unique chance to shift the burden of inertia and force the majority to engage.[18]   *Makes it a real debate.*

"Dissenting by deciding" forces engagement not just by opponents, but by reluctant allies. Once same-sex couples could marry in San Francisco and Massachusetts, elected officials—who had preferred to duck the issue in the past—were forced to shift gears. Political leaders in states that didn't recognize same-sex marriage had to decide whether to recognize marriages blessed by those that did.[19] As a result, politicians who had been reluctant to join the fray could no longer sit on the sidelines. The same was true of the Obama administration, which had to decide whether to enforce the Defense of Marriage Act (DOMA) going forward. Note that in this instance, as with so many others, decentralization can beget centralization. The social movement that federalism (and the First Amendment) helped facilitate ultimately convinced five Justices to make marriage equality the law of the land.

There is another key difference between speaking and acting when it comes to dissent. When dissenters decide, they can put in place a real-life instantiation of their ideas. That means that dissenters are no longer confined to abstract arguments when they push their ideas. They can show that something does work rather than asserting that it will. At the very least, dissenting by deciding can put to rest the parade of horribles that is routinely trotted out against reform.

Here again, the same-sex marriage movement reveals the importance of this tool for change. For instance, California governor Schwarzenegger had offered dour predictions that there would be riots in the street if same-sex marriage were allowed.[20] What we saw instead was the not-so-riotous Gay Men's Choir serenading brides- and grooms-to-be.[21] The fact that opponents of same-sex marriage didn't show up to protest, let alone riot, told us a great deal about whether national change was possible. When surveyed, most people opposed same-sex marriage. But they didn't care enough about it to get on a bus and protest, a fact that mattered a great deal in thinking about the future of the movement. *Didn't care as much of pro-same sex marriage did.*

Still later, the real-world effects of San Francisco's decision continued to buttress the push for change. For instance, in the litigation that followed, the lawyers opposing Prop 8 could offer evidence of the positive effects same-sex marriage had on the lives of the couples who had managed to marry before San Francisco's activities were stayed. The lawyers weren't confined to abstractions and assertions. Instead, they could put a human face on the story they told to the court. *Also helps when it reaches national debate.*

Federalism and localism facilitate change in other ways. For example, decentralization allows dissenters to build their case for change one step at a time. The First Amendment, of course, technically lets you enter the so-called national conversation from the first moment you begin to speak. But it's very hard to have a national conversation without having a series of local ones first.[22] National movements rarely begin as national movements.[23] They usually begin small and grow into something bigger. That's why leaders of social movements have long used states and localities as sites for organizing and as testing grounds for their ideas. These local platforms don't just facilitate early mobilization, but also help connect nascent movements to the large and powerful policymaking networks that fuel national politics.[24] National policy, after all, is a *giant* gear to move. As with a clock, you need movement from lots of small, interlocking gears to move a bigger one.

Here again, the movement for marriage equality proves to be the rule, not the exception. An early part of this story, in fact, is embedded in a Supreme Court opinion, *Romer v. Evans*. During the early days of the equality movement, activists had been leveraging their voting power in liberal cities like Boulder and Denver to enact employment and housing protections for gays and lesbians. These decisions pushed the state majority to engage, passing an amendment to the state constitution that pre-empted these laws and required all efforts to protect people against discrimination based on sexual orientation to be passed statewide. That amendment, in turn, pulled the Supreme Court into the fray and led it to invalidate the amendment and thus gave the LGBT community its first Supreme Court victory a scant ten years after *Bowers v. Hardwick*.

Because of the high level of regulatory integration between the states and federal government, the discursive benefits of structure even help state and local dissenters influence *national* policymaking. State and national policymaking have become so deeply interconnected that one can't move without the other moving with it. That's obviously true of cooperative federal regimes, where states shape federal law as they implement it. Federalism thus puts skeptics inside the Fourth Branch.[25] When states and localities administer federal law, dissenters are decision makers, not just lobbyists or supplicants. They can help set policy rather than merely complain about it. They can control federal law from within rather than challenging it from without. And their actions can range from merely taking advantage of a gap in the law to outright civil disobedience. Cooperative federalism is thus paired with uncooperative federalism.[26] Cooperative localism[27] is paired with local resistance. Even in highly centralized, highly technocratic federal bureaucracies, we see state and local variation in carrying out routinized policy jobs.[28] The rebellion of the street-level bureaucrat is hardly confined to the street.

Even in areas where there are no formally recognized cooperative federal regimes established, outlier states can influence federal policymakers through the policymaking apparatus that federalism supplies. The federal government, for instance, generally depends on the states to determine who is married for purposes of federal programs. DOMA broke with that tradition. But when DOMA was invalidated by *Windsor*, states that issued licenses to same-sex couples were able to do what states do in so many other domains—tug the federal government along with them. State-recognized same-sex marriages became federally recognized ones. In the wake of *Windsor*, the federal government had to figure out how to work same-sex marriages into the federal regulatory system, thereby providing proof that the federal system could accommodate same-sex marriage.[29] It's precisely that type of forced engagement that federalism facilitates in an integrated regime like ours.

None of these observations is confined to the same-sex marriage debate. Want an example of state policymaking shifting the agenda? Look no further than state voter ID laws, which ignited the debate over vote fraud. Interested in the power that a real-life instantiation of an idea can have on policy debates? Consider how helpful it was that Massachusetts had enacted "Romneycare" before the debates over Obamacare began. If you care about the ways in which small movements turn into larger ones, consider the path the Christian Right took into politics. Activists began running for school boards and eventually emerged as a crucial force in the GOP. If you want to see a minority forcing a majority to engage, look no further than the sanctuary city movement or the debate over transgender bathrooms or local efforts to restrict abortion. As I've pointed out elsewhere, federalism—like the First Amendment—doesn't have a political valence. It can be used for progressive causes and conservative ones. The only question is who suits up and gets in the game.

So too there are many examples of state policymaking influencing national policy in formal or informal cooperative regimes. The Affordable Care Act (ACA), for instance, is a cooperative federal regime established by statute. Because of the influential role states play in administering federal health policy, state resistance to the ACA led to important modifications in its requirements and funding structure. We can also see the influence of state policy even where the federal government is nominally independent. For instance, when states like Colorado and Washington legalized marijuana, they effectively changed federal policy. Why? Because the federal government depends almost entirely on states to enforce its marijuana prohibition.[30] One scholar has gone so far as to suggest that this informal integration effectively gives states the power to nullify federal law.[31]

All of these examples involved dissenting positions. None of them could have emerged without a robust First Amendment to help marriage equality's proponents initiate and push forward the debate. But they also involved the use of structural arrangements—the gifts federalism confers on dissenters—to move a debate forward and force the center to engage.

Federalism, in short, doesn't just promote the same aims as the First Amendment; it also compensates for its shortcomings. It offers dissenters different forms of advocacy, different platforms for mobilizing, and different levers of change.[32] These advantages matter a great deal if your aim is to alter the status quo.

The converse is true as well. As with other democratic institutions, federalism requires a robust First Amendment to function. And where federalism fails dissenters, the First Amendment often succeeds. The opportunities for "dissenting by deciding" are catch-as-catch-can, emerging at different times and different places in the governance landscape. The First Amendment is a constant, allowing dissenters to speak and organize whenever they like.

So too the First Amendment allows dissenters to speak *however* they like. Federalism requires dissenters to pour their ideas into the narrow policymaking space available. It requires them to bargain and politic and strike deals. The First

Can say whatever they want.

Amendment allows dissenters the luxury of <u>ideological purity</u>, which can only be had outside the policymaking arena.

That's why the First Amendment and federalism work so well in tandem, and why both contribute to a well-functioning democracy. Dissenting speech leads to debate, which leads to organizing, which leads to policymaking, which in turn provides a rallying point for still more debate and organizing and policymaking. Because the push for change moves through both governance sites and media sites, social movements include pragmatic insiders, forging bargains from within, and principled outsiders, demanding more and better from without. The key point to emphasize, however, is that federalism—far from being the enemy of dissent—supplies the policymaking gears that are all but essential for any movement to move forward.

I don't want to be unduly sunny about it. The arc of the universe may bend toward justice,[33] but the gears of rights and structure can move backward, not just forward. Retrenchment happens at the state and local levels just as advancement does.

Nor is it easy to predict when federalism will succeed or fail as a tool for change. Federalism's influence on politics is as complex as politics itself. There is no more a recipe for success for federalism than there is for the First Amendment. To be sure, certain issues lend themselves more easily to "dissenting by deciding" than traditional dissent. But it's very hard to predict whether and when a political movement will take root. My point is simply that federalism and its homely cousin localism can be as important as the First Amendment in pushing debate forward.

Is the Game Worth the Candle?

Ardent supporters of the First Amendment may nonetheless remain skeptical of federalism even in the presence of a robustly enforced First Amendment. Here again, the ugly legacy of the Jim Crow era looms large, as states' rights were routinely invoked to undermine individual freedom.

Can also be dangerous

Note that it is precisely the advantage that "dissenting by deciding" confers—that it enables would-be dissenters to make policy—that is the source of an important worry. It's one thing to shield those who speak from the majority's reach. It's another to shield outlier *policies* from the majority's reach. Decisions can do damage that speech cannot. And while a well-functioning democracy requires institutional arrangements that facilitate change, a well-functioning democracy must also be able to enforce national norms. If states shield outliers from national norms, perhaps the federalism game isn't worth the candle.

Happily, "Our Federalism" is not your father's federalism. Today's federalism is sheared of sovereignty despite the best efforts of the Rehnquist and Roberts Courts. For every limit the Court has tried to impose on the national government, there is a ready workaround.[34] The nationalists have lost battles, to be sure—*Shelby County*[35] being the most heartbreaking defeat—but they are undoubtedly winning the war. Even *Shelby County* is easily remedied as a constitutional matter; we simply lack the political will to impose a constitutional solution.[36] That means that states cannot shield their discrimination from national norms, as they did during the days of Jim Crow. But they can help fuel the process by which those norms are constructed.

When federalism is sheared of sovereignty, its signature vices can become plausible virtues. The federal government can give would-be dissenters leeway to effect change without forfeiting control over national policy. States and localities don't protect outliers from national norms, but they do constitute sites for constructing those norms. The national government can thus police federalism's worst excesses while taking advantage of its best features, including the benefits it offers to dissenters. We can preserve appropriately majoritarian practices while still giving dissenters a better shot at democratic success. These facts ought to change our calculation as to whether the decentralization game is worth the candle.

Note here the contrast between the protections we afford to dissenters when they speak and those we should afford when they act. The First Amendment shields dissenters of every sort, and rightly so. But when dissenters put their policies into place, sovereignty does not protect them. Instead, their actions are protected by inertia, mutual dependence, and the give-and-take of politics. If the national government wants to bring resisting states to heel, it can. But such efforts require it to expend political capital and bureaucratic resources.

As a doctrinal matter, scholars of dissent who turn their attention to federalism must shift from thinking about notions like autonomy and rights to theorizing about politics, networks, and other informal sources of power. While such an approach does not offer the neatness associated with rights-based protections, it nonetheless brings forward topics that tend to recede into the background when we think about the First Amendment. Power relations tend to be understudied in the literature on the First Amendment. The role of groups is underplayed. And relatively little attention is paid to what takes place *inside* political structures. This means relatively little attention is paid to the institutions where power lies. The First Amendment is all about the road to the statehouse. But often our interest in the fate of dissenters seems to end at the statehouse door. Attention to the discursive benefits of structure would expand our vision not just of dissent, but of democracy.

Conclusion

It would be strange to close a piece in this volume without acknowledging the First Amendment's extraordinary import. Ours is a grand tradition, and it would have been impossible to write this piece in the absence of robust free speech protections. Far from trying to question the First Amendment's importance, I seek only to acknowledge that the Framers were right to think that structural guarantees matter just as do rights-based guarantees. Federalism could not function without the First Amendment. But the reverse may be true as well. Rather than thinking of the First Amendment and federalism as competitors, we should imagine them as interlocking gears, moving democratic debate forward.

PART TWO

MAJOR CRITIQUES AND CONTROVERSIAL AREAS OF FIRST AMENDMENT JURISPRUDENCE

Citizens United

Predictions and Reality

FLOYD ABRAMS*

Armed Nazis march in Charlottesville carrying flags emblazoned with swastikas and chanting fascist slurs ("Jews Will Not Replace Us") and slogans ("Blood and Soil") from the 1930s; religious zealots stand as close as they are permitted to churches as services proceed honoring American soldiers who died in combat in Iraq and Afghanistan, carrying placards denouncing the soldiers ("Thank God for Dead Soldiers") and all gay Americans ("God Hates Fags"); filmmakers create crush videos for sale that depict dogs savagely fighting each other to the death and women wearing stiletto heels stepping on and killing kittens and other small animals; a politician who has not been awarded any military medal wears and describes himself as having received the Congressional Medal of Honor, the nation's most treasured medal, which is given only to the bravest and most selfless American soldiers. All receive First Amendment–rooted protection.[1]

It would be easy to continue with examples of loathsome speech that is protected in this country that would be banned in most of the democratic world and as to which little or no claim can be made of public benefit.

Except one benefit. Every time such speech is protected by the First Amendment, we vindicate Justice Hugo Black's conclusion that "the very reason for the First Amendment is to make the people of this country free to think, speak, write and worship as they wish, not as the Government commands,"[2] and Justice Robert Jackson's observation that "the very purpose of the First

---

* The author thanks the Center for Responsive Politics for providing the data cited in this chapter with respect to donations by individuals, corporations, and other organizations including unions. The Center for Responsive Politics is not responsible for (and has not seen prior to publication) all analysis and commentary by the author. The author thanks Celia Belmonte for her substantial assistance in the preparation of the chapter.

Amendment is to foreclose public authority from assuming a guardianship of the public mind through regulating the press, speech, and religion."[3]

Fortunately, most of the speech the First Amendment protects is not at all as odious as set forth in the examples cited previously. Much of it is invaluable in a democratic society, such as political speech, speech that has repeatedly been recognized by the Supreme Court as requiring the highest level of protection from government, and, most particularly, advocacy about which candidate should be elected to public office. As the Supreme Court put it in a 1989 opinion, the First Amendment "has its fullest and most urgent application to speech uttered during a campaign for political office."[4]

That said, consider the following hypothetical: A generally liberal candidate is seeking and is expected to obtain her party's nomination for president. Political activists who are members of a conservative organization that believes the country would be ill served if she were elected prepare an hour-long documentary-like program that denounces her and seeks to make the case that she would be dangerous and unprincipled as president. They wish to have it shown on pay-per-view. The organization receives a portion of its funding from corporations. A federal statute makes it a crime for the film or, indeed, any such offering funded by corporate money to be shown on television, cable, or satellite within sixty days of an election or thirty days of a primary or political convention. Is that law consistent with the First Amendment?

My hypothetical is, of course, not at all hypothetical. It sets forth the facts of the highly controversial and often denounced Supreme Court opinion in *Citizens United v. Federal Election Commission,* 558 U.S. 310 (2010). That decision, rooted in the broad First Amendment protection afforded to political speech, basically held that corporations (and, implicitly, unions) could not be limited in their expenditure of money used to advocate the election or defeat of a candidate for federal office.

From the date of its issuance in 2010, the decision has been subjected to intense and often virulent criticism. It has been denounced by Justice Ruth Bader Ginsburg as the worst ruling of the Supreme Court since she joined it in 1993. It so offended Justice John Paul Stevens, the author of the ninety-four-page dissent in the case, that after his retirement, he drafted a constitutional amendment to overturn the ruling, one that would have been the first in American history to limit the scope of the First Amendment as determined by the Supreme Court.

Distinguished scholars also denounced the ruling. It so outraged Ronald Dworkin, a scholar and philosopher of enormous distinction, that he concluded that the Court simply could not have rendered the decision in good faith and that it must have resulted from its "instinctive favoritism of corporate interests" or of the Republican Party.[5] It so exasperated the nation's leading scholar on election law, Richard L. Hasen, that he described one line of the decision as reading "more like the rantings of a right-wing talk show host than the rational view of a justice with a sense of political realism."[6] It was denounced by American University professor (and now House Democratic representative) Jamie Raskin as "tilt[ing] the nation's entire political process toward the views of moneyed corporate power."[7] And it has so pained the public that polling data has consistently indicated that upwards of 80 percent of the public, on a totally bipartisan basis, disapproves of the ruling.[8]

Many aspects of the ruling were controversial, but the core of much of the distaste for the ruling stemmed from the sense, shared by many, that it was unjust and ultimately undemocratic for the nation's massive corporations to play a major role in deciding who would be elected. An earlier ruling of the Supreme Court, *Austin v. Michigan Chamber of Commerce*, 494 U.S. 652 (1990), written by Justice Thurgood Marshall, had offered support for just that view in affirming the constitutionality of a state law barring corporations from sending money to support or oppose candidates for state office. The law at issue was meant, Justice Marshall wrote, to prevent corporations from obtaining an "unfair advantage in the political marketplace" by using "resources amassed in the economic marketplace."[9] Doing so, he wrote, was a form of "corruption in the political arena: the corrosive and distorting effects of immense aggregations of wealth that are accumulated with the help of the corporate form and that have little or no correlation to the public's support for the corporation's political ideas."[10]

Do corporations have First Amendment rights akin to those of individuals? And if they do, can those rights be limited or overcome for what some view as the greater good of seeking to ensure democratic rule by avoiding political dominance by corporations?

The notion that corporations have significant First Amendment rights was not new. The majority opinion of Justice Anthony Kennedy in *Citizens United* cited twenty-five cases in which speech by corporations had been held protected by the First Amendment. It concluded that given the political nature of the speech effectively limited or banned by the statute, it could not withstand First Amendment challenge, and that neither could Justice Marshall's opinion in the *Austin* case, which *Citizens United* rejected as precedent.

Of particular support to Justice Kennedy's opinion was the Court's earlier ruling in the celebrated but also extremely controversial case, *Buckley v. Valeo*, 424 U.S. 1 (1976), to which I will return, that while individuals could be limited in the amount of direct contributions they made to candidates, they could not be limited in their own expenditure of funds in support of candidates for federal public office.

The public debate over the correctness of *Citizens United* (and of *Buckley*) continues to this day. Although my views in that debate may not be hidden in what follows—I represented Senator Mitch McConnell in *Citizens United* as *amicus curiae* and participated in oral argument in support of the proposition that the First Amendment had been violated—the focus of this chapter is not the correctness of the ruling but its consequences. During the case and in the years that have followed, predictions, often apocalyptic ones, have repeatedly been voiced about the impact of the case. Now, with two presidential and four congressional elections having transpired since the *Citizens United* ruling, it seems an appropriate time to compare those predictions with reality. I will turn first to the predictions made about the impact of the case and then to the reality of what has occurred.

The Predictions

One of the more modest expressions of concern about the impact of *Citizens United* is contained in Justice Stevens' dissent in the case. "Starting today," he wrote, "corporations with large war chests to deploy on electioneering may find democratically elected bodies becoming much more attuned to their interests."[11]

In their briefs in the case, the United States and its allies supporting the constitutionality of the statute at issue had gone further, offering even grimmer predictions about what would occur if corporations were permitted to spend great amounts in political campaigns. In one of the briefs submitted by the United States, it offered the following doomsday scenario to demonstrate the dangers of permitting unlimited corporate political expenditures. Fortune 100 companies, the government argued, had

> combined revenues of $13.1 trillion and profits of $605 billion. If those 100 companies alone had devoted just one percent of their profits (or one-twentieth of one percent of their revenues) to electoral advocacy, such spending would have more than doubled the federally-reported disbursements of all American political parties and PACs combined.[12]

Such an "amount of corporate cash pouring into the political system," the government urged, "could dramatically increase the reality and appearance of *quid pro quo* corruption."[13]

In one of the briefs of Senator John McCain, former senator Russell Feingold, and former representatives Christopher Shays and Martin Meehan, in support of the government's position, they offered the following similar scenario: "The tremendous resources business corporations and unions can bring to bear on elections, and the greater magnitude of the resulting apparent corruption, amply justify treating corporate and union expenditures differently from those by individuals and ideological nonprofit groups."[14] As such, the now former and current congressmen argued that significant

> corruption of the system . . . will result if campaign discourse becomes dominated not by individual citizens—whose right it is to select their political representatives—but by corporate and union war-chests amassed as a result of the special benefits the government confers on these artificial "persons." That concern remains a compelling justification for restrictions on using corporate treasury funds for electoral advocacy—constraints that ban no speech but only require that it be funded by individuals who have chosen to do so.[15]

Senator Chris Van Hollen, Representatives David Price and John Lewis, and former representative Michael Castle similarly lamented in their brief that, should the Supreme Court issue a ruling in favor of Citizens United, "we expect that, given the opportunity, many corporations would make vast expenditures from their general treasuries in an effort to influence federal election outcomes," and that such a ruling would thus "usher in a new era of corporate spending as a dominant force in politics."[16]

The Democratic National Committee (DNC) also weighed in, cautioning in its brief that

> spenders adjust to and function under rules that, if radically altered, have immediate and far-reaching effects on political competition. . . . Should the corporate sector as a whole be freed to make use of its large aggregations of wealth to influence voter choice, the very terms on which political parties compete to be heard will undergo dramatic, wholesale revision.[17]

Large elements of the press offered similarly cataclysmic predictions after *Citizens United* was decided. The *New York Times* foresaw that the effect of the ruling would be to "thrust politics back to the robber-baron era of the 19th century" by allowing "corporations to use their vast treasuries to overwhelm elections";[18] the *Washington Post* warned that "corporate money, never lacking in the American political process, may now overwhelm . . . the contributions of individuals";[19] and the *San Francisco Chronicle* declared that "voters should prepare for the worst: cash-drenched elections presided over by free-spending corporations."[20] In an article published on the *Huffington Post* in March 2010, former senator Bob Kerrey opined: "What does this ruling mean? Consider the influence of a single corporation like Exxon Mobil. . . . With $85 billion in profits during the 2008 election, Exxon Mobil would have been able to fully fund over 65,000 winning campaigns for U.S. House."[21]

In a foreword to Jeffrey D. Clements' 2012 book *Corporations Are Not People: Why They Have More Rights Than You Do and What You Can Do About It*,

Bill Moyers offered an impassioned post–*Citizens United* elegy to democracy in America:

> Rarely have so few imposed such damage on so many. When five conservative members of the Supreme Court handed for-profit corporations the right to secretly flood political campaigns with tidal waves of cash on the eve of an election, they moved America closer to outright plutocracy, where political power derived from wealth is devoted to the protection of wealth.[22]

He went on, "It is now official: Just as they have adorned our athletic stadiums and multiple places of public assembly with their logos, corporations can officially put their brand on the government of the United States as well as the executive, legislative, and judicial branches of the fifty states."[23]

Citizens United was decided in 2010, but the fiery debate over its consequences continues. Too much of that debate, however, is little different from that which occurred—or could have occurred—before its issuance or on the day after it was released. Have we learned nothing in the years that have followed? In fact, there is now a significant body of data that addresses the critical question of the consequences of the Supreme Court's ruling.

The Reality

What the data show is that the repeatedly expressed concerns about corporate dominance of the political process after and as a result of *Citizens United* were not only overstated but also simply insupportable. The predictions have not been borne out by reality. It is true that after and as a sort of follow-up to *Citizens United* so-called super political action committees (PACs) were established into which corporations and individuals could make donations used for political advocacy.[24] But it is not true that as a result corporations began to dominate the political process.

Let us begin by turning to the example cited by Senator Kerrey of potential donations by Exxon Mobil. It is indeed an elephantine entity with interests continuously affected by the policies adopted by political leaders up to and including the president. Given free rein by *Citizens United* to weigh in heavily in support of candidates who might view its needs favorably, how much did it contribute in a post–*Citizens United* world? According to Federal Election Commission records, in the overall 2016 election cycle—all federal elections from January 1, 2015, through December 31, 2016—Exxon Mobil contributed not a single dollar to any super PAC.[25] Not one. Nor did almost any other of the nation's largest corporations.

In fact, of the top ten corporate donors to super PACs, only one—Chevron— was in the Fortune 500 or the Global Fortune 500.[26] Chevron donated a total of $2,015,000 to super PACs during the entire 2016 election cycle.[27] A total of $37,641,619 was contributed by all top ten corporate donors. Here are their mostly unfamiliar names and the amounts they donated:

1. Starr Companies ($15,290,000)
2. Access Industries ($6,250,000)
3. Mountaire Corp. ($3,100,000)
4. Petrodome Energy ($3,000,000)
5. Rooney Holdings ($2,500,000)
6. Chevron Corp. ($2,015,000)
7. NextEra Energy ($1,750,000)
8. American Pacific International Capital ($1,300,000)
9. Devon Energy ($1,250,000)
10. Herzog Contracting ($1,186,619)

Corporate contributions to super PACs during the 2016 election cycle were far smaller than those of unions and other organizations. Here is their top ten list:

1. NextGen Climate Action ($32,556,885)
2. Priorities USA Action ($26,391,578)
3. National Education Association ($23,773,966)
4. Service Employees International Union ($23,274,845)
5. Senate Leadership Fund ($22,476,800)
6. One Nation ($21,700,000)
7. Laborers Union ($21,530,385)
8. Republican Governors Association ($20,725,000)
9. Carpenters and Joiners Union ($19,507,737)
10. AFL-CIO ($15,610,189)

And notwithstanding the government's ominous forecast of corporate dominance over the nation's politics, data published by the Federal Election Commission (FEC) shows that *individuals*, rather than corporations, contributed by far the most money to super PACs. In the entire 2016 election cycle, super PACs received a total of $1.8 billion. Of that amount, $1.04 billion was donated by individuals; labor unions and other organizations contributed $242 million; $85 million was donated by corporations.

The ten largest donations in the 2016 election cycle from individuals amounted to $376 million. Here are their names and the amounts they donated:

1. Thomas Steyer ($89,544,744)
2. Sheldon G. and Miriam O. Adelson ($77,900,000)

3. Donald S. Sussman ($38,645,000)
4. Fred Eychaner ($35,250,000)
5. James H. and Marilyn Simons ($25,025,000)
6. Paul E. Singer ($24,095,153)
7. Michael R. Bloomberg ($23,561,624)
8. Robert L. Mercer ($22,551,000)
9. Dustin Moskovitz and Cari Tuna ($19,915,000)
10. George Soros ($19,239,693)

The results in 2012 were similar. The top ten individual donors contributed a combined $201,972,439 to super PACs. The top ten corporations contributed $29,991,666.

To put into context the varying amounts donated by corporations, unions, and other organizations and individuals, the following is a list of the top thirty contributors from all sources to super PACs in the 2016 election cycle. Only one—Starr Companies—is a corporation.

1. Thomas Steyer ($89,544,744)
2. Sheldon G. and Miriam O. Adelson ($77,900,000)
3. Donald S. Sussman ($38,645,000)
4. Fred Eychaner ($35,250,000)
5. NextGen Climate Action ($33,041,885)
6. Priorities USA Action ($31,096,874)
7. Service Employees International Union ($27,046,869)
8. James H. and Marilyn Simons ($25,025,000)
9. Paul E. Singer ($24,095,153)
10. National Education Association ($23,999,966)
11. Michael Bloomberg ($23,561,624)
12. Robert L. Mercer ($22,551,000)
13. Senate Leadership Fund ($22,476,800)
14. One Nation ($21,700,000)
15. Laborers Union ($21,663,485)
16. Republican Governors Association ($20,725,000)
17. Dustin Moskovitz and Cari Tuna ($19,915,000)
18. Carpenters and Joiners Union ($19,507,737)
19. George Soros ($19,239,693)
20. Richard Uihlein ($19,128,500)
21. For Our Future ($18,161,392)
22. Jay R. and Mary K. Pritzker ($17,950,848)
23. AFL-CIO ($15,625,189)
24. Starr Companies ($15,290,000)

25. John Joe Ricketts ($14,453,829)
26. Haim Saban ($13,780,000)
27. Ronnie Cameron ($13,246,000)
28. Diane M. Hendricks ($12,970,900)
29. American Federation of Teachers ($12,343,256)
30. Environment America ($11,975,000)

These numbers do not include donations to political campaigns from corpo-rate PACs since that money comes from individuals employed by or otherwise connected with corporations rather than corporate treasuries. Indeed, for that reason, if corporate PAC donations were considered at all, they might well be deemed better described as individual rather than corporate in nature. But the amounts are, on any comparative basis to those previously outlined, on the small side—$1,868,796 from corporate PACs to presidential candidates in 2008,[28] $855,348 in 2012,[29] and $942,116 in 2016.[30]

When the 2012 election was over, Ezra Klein, writing in the *Washington Post*, offered a rare journalistic acknowledgment of error about journalistic overstate-ment of the likely impact of money on that campaign:

> It's hard to look at the 2012 election, with its record fundraising and the flood of super PACs and all the rest of it, and come away really persuaded that money was a decisive player. And yet the way we talked about money in the run-up to the 2012 election, we really suggested it would be a decisive player. In fact, we suggested, quite often, that it wouldn't just decide the election, but that it would imperil democracy itself. So I think we have some explaining to do.[31]

But little journalistic explanation followed. Indeed, the same overstate-ment (and sometimes misstatement) persisted in the 2016 campaign. On July 31, 2015, the *New York Times*, anticipating the first Republican debate, offered the editorial view that the debate might provide "entertainment and conflict" but that the forthcoming "circus will probably have little effect on the race" as compared to the likely impact of appearances of the would-be candidates be-fore the Koch brothers and others seeking their financial support.[32] Given the dominance—whatever else one thinks of it—of Donald Trump in that debate and the debates that followed, the emphasis by the *Times* on Koch contributions now seems outlandish.

A more perceptive contemporary analysis of the topic was offered on August 25, 2015, in an article by Jack Shafer in *Politico*. That article mused that it probably pleased Senator Bernie Sanders "each morning to wake up and realize . . . that Chief Justice John Roberts and Antonin Scalia didn't ruin the country in quite the way that progressive groups had feared in 2010" when *Citizens United* was released.[33] "The new order" supposedly created by *Citizens United*, wrote Shafer, hadn't, after all, "been enough to stop [Bernie Sanders] and Donald Trump from skyrocketing in [the] polls."[34]

So how much did *Citizens United* matter in our recent elections? Taking all available data into account, the following summary by Brooklyn Law professor Joel M. Gora seems correct in all respects:

> The predicted wave of corporate financial political intervention never materialized. Of all of the super PAC independent expenditure spending that escalated in the 2012 elections, very little of it came from corporate contributions. It was mostly contributed by individuals. Very wealthy ones to be sure, but ones permitted to do that going back to *Buckley*.[35]

To be sure, it is not as if nothing happened. On the financial side, those very wealthy individuals referred to by Professor Gora greatly increased their donations. While the total amount of individual donations in the 2016 presidential election was almost identical with that in pre–*Citizens United* 2008, the amount of donors has diminished while the amounts contributed by donors have significantly increased. As a result, although the total amount donated by individuals in the 2016 race was almost the same to the dollar as in 2008—$1,821,020,383 in the former and $1,811,175,217 in the latter—a study of donations in post–*Citizens United* America has concluded that "relatively few large donors [have] dominat[ed] campaign contributions since the *Citizens United* decision."[36] That shift, the study demonstrates, "has allowed a small group of political donors to account for a larger and larger share of the contributions total."[37] One hundred thirty-five donors gave more than $1 million to outside groups in the 2016 election; ninety-five did in 2012.[38]

Since so much money is now contributed by a shrinking group of individuals and, on any comparative basis, so little by corporations, it may well be that legal observers should focus less on *Citizens United*, which dealt with corporate donations, and more on the Court's decision in *Buckley v. Valeo*, which determined that individuals could not be limited in their expenditures supporting candidates for office. Like *Citizens United*, *Buckley* was extremely unpopular in the academic community. As Joel Gora, who argued the case challenging the statute for the American Civil Liberties Union (ACLU), put it, *Buckley* was routinely denounced in scholarly circles as a "derelict, a sport, a blemish on the law."[39] Some compared it to the worst rulings of prior generations—to *Plessy v. Ferguson*, 163 U.S. 537 (1896), for example, which had upheld racial segregation as constitutional. A distinguished attorney went further still in an article he wrote for the *New York Times* on the twentieth anniversary of *Buckley*, arguing that it was as indefensible and ultimately as evil as the racist pre–Civil War and possibly Civil War–causing *Dred Scott v. Sandford*, 60 U.S. 393 (1857) opinion.[40]

So let us return briefly to that case which concluded that individuals could not be limited in their expenditures for candidates for public office. In response to public outrage at what came to be known as "Watergate," a federal statute—the Federal Election Campaign Act of 1971, as amended in 1974—was adopted, which greatly limited a federal candidate's overall expenditures and set an extremely low limit on those expenditures, limited what a candidate could spend on his or her campaign, placed a ceiling of $1,000 on how much anyone could spend in support of a candidate, and placed enforcement of the law in the hands of a Commission chosen by politicians. The law was challenged by an extraordinary collection of individuals and organizations—by, among others, conservative Senator James Buckley and liberal Senator Eugene McCarthy; by the Mississippi Republican Party and the Libertarian Party; and by the New York Civil Liberties Union and the American Conservative Union. On the most important issues before it, the Court decided that there could be limits on direct contributions to candidates, but that when people were spending their own money, they could spend it as they liked and in any amount. The correctness of that apparent compromise by the Court is still much discussed in academic literature and is beyond the scope of this chapter.

The portion of the Court's opinion in *Buckley* that is most relevant is its answer to the basic question of what role the First Amendment plays with respect to expenditures citizens make on elections. Here are three things the Court said: Speaking very broadly, it observed that "[a] restriction on the amount of money a person or group can spend on political communication during a campaign necessarily reduces the quantity of expression by restricting the number of issues discussed, the depth of their exploration, and the size of the audience reached."[41] Then, responding to the argument that too much money led to too much "bad" speech in elections, it said that

> the First Amendment denies government the power to determine that spending to promote one's political views is wasteful, excessive, or unwise. In the free society ordained by our Constitution, it is not the government, but the people—individually, as citizens and candidates, and collectively, as associations and political committees—who must retain control over the quantity and range of debate on public issues in a political campaign.[42]

Most tellingly, the Court said this:

> The concept that government may restrict the speech of some elements of our society in order to enhance the relative voice of others is wholly

foreign to the First Amendment, which was designed to secure the widest possible dissemination of information from diverse and antagonistic sources and to assure unfettered interchange of ideas for the bringing about of political and social changes desired by the people.[43]

It is that conclusion, apparently written by Justice Potter Stewart for the Court, that those who object most to *Buckley* must be prepared to answer. And for precisely the same reasons, critics of *Citizens United*, which is, at its core, *Buckley* as applied to corporations, must do the same.

Finally, much has been written about "Dark Money." A total of $43,108,988, or 1.8 percent of the total $2,386,733,696 spent in the 2016 presidential election, came from Dark Money groups. Those entities are made up of political nonprofits—or "ideological nonprofit groups," as Senator McCain and others described them in their *amici curiae* brief,[44] which are under no legal obligation to disclose their donors—and, in certain situations, super PACs.[45] While super PACs are legally required to disclose their donors, they are considered Dark Money groups when they accept unlimited contributions from political nonprofits and shell corporations, which may not have disclosed their donors.[46] Of the $43 million, $21,611,752 was expended praising or criticizing Donald Trump. Hillary Clinton, in turn, was complimented or denounced in advertisements and the like that cost $16,173,988.

The $43 million figure is indicative that a considerable amount of money spent in the 2016 presidential election was publically unattributed. But that figure was less than 2 percent of the total dollars spent in the election, and *Citizens United* had nothing to do with the ability of groups to avoid disclosure. Many journalists and commentators have erroneously postulated that the Supreme Court in *Citizens United* produced an opinion that reflected an "unfortunate refusal to limit secret money."[47] In fact, the Court did just the opposite, ruling by an eight-to-one vote that the disclosure requirements of the campaign finance law at issue in the case were constitutional. Its opinion could hardly have been clearer, stating that "the First Amendment protects political speech; and disclosure permits citizens and shareholders to react to the speech of corporate entities in a proper way . . . [by] enabl[ing] the electorate to make informed decisions and give proper weight to different speakers and messages."[48]

Nor was it the *Citizens United* ruling or the Supreme Court that has permitted the nondisclosure of the identity of any contributors or the amount of their expenditures or contributions. It has been the Internal Revenue Service (IRS) and a complicit Congress that, in contradiction to the language of one section of federal law (Section 501(c)(4)), has permitted a significant amount of electoral expenditures to be made by tax-exempt "social welfare" organizations.

Moreover, as summarized by the Center for Competitive Politics in 2015, under Federal Communications Commission regulations, all broadcast and cable political advertisements must contain the name of the entity paying for the ad; all print political ads must contain the name of the payer; and "candidates, political parties, PACs, and super PACs at the federal level and in 49 states must disclose their expenditures, income, and donors."[49] Of the over $6.4 billion spent on federal races in 2016, $184 million was Dark Money, about 2.9 percent of total spending, and most of that came from organizations such as the National Rifle Association, the US Chamber of Commerce, the League of Conservation Voters, and the like. It may well be true, as noted earlier, that the IRS has erred in allowing the sources of donations to those organizations to remain undisclosed. But that failure can hardly be laid at the doors of the Supreme Court for its *Citizens United* ruling.

Reflections

A few additional thoughts may be in order with respect to this topic. The first is that while it is clear that corporations have thus far generally chosen not to exercise their First Amendment right articulated in *Citizens United* to spend large sums of money supporting candidates for public office, that need not be true in the future. I suspect it will be, though, for the same reason that I suspect they have not done so already—that is, the risk of public disapproval of their involvement. Michael Jordan has repeatedly, if possibly apocryphally, been quoted as explaining his former silence with respect to public issues by saying, "Republicans buy shoes too." The same reticence about being publicly affiliated with one or another political candidate may well act as a continuing deterrent to large corporations, which are dependent upon the goodwill of the public as a whole, becoming publically identified as being on one side or another of fiercely competitive electoral politics. The fact that public disclosure is required with respect to such expenditures, a requirement upheld in *Citizens United* by an eight-to-one vote, likely plays a significant role in this.

A second is that the extraordinary degree to which corporate donations trail behind those of unions, as well as of individuals, illustrates, not for the first time, how difficult it is to predict the on-the-ground impact of Supreme Court opinions. Critics of *Citizens United* as well as defenders of it—I have been one of the latter—had no idea that corporate donations would be lower than individual donations, let alone to such a startling degree. Nor did we anticipate that labor unions would outspend business corporations in the aftermath of *Citizens United*. My point is not just that a bit more humility might be in order when people comment on controversial Supreme Court opinions but that there should be recognition by all that in this area, as in so many others, predictions about the future are of only modest value.

A third observation is not one of surprise but regret. Where are the apologies of the newspapers that with absolute self-assurance pronounced that the impact of *Citizens United* would be new and near-total corporate hegemony over political life in the nation, or, more specifically, that asserted (as the *Washington Post* did) that corporate donations "may now overwhelm . . . the contributions of individuals"? Where are the apologies of the multiple drafters of constitutional amendments aimed at limiting the First Amendment by reversing *Citizens United* because of the newly augmented power it provided to corporate America to rule the nation? I do not suggest that the inaccuracy, as it turned out, of predictions of corporate dominance of the political process as a result of *Citizens United* requires abject public contrition by those who believed that would occur. As I observed earlier, predictions about the impact of Supreme Court rulings are, by their nature, often not borne out by later reality. And as I also acknowledged, it remains possible that the results thus far may not persist into the future. But it would be reassuring if some of those whose predictions, so firmly and authoritatively offered, of the baleful impact of the Supreme Court's ruling vindicating corporate free speech rights would acknowledge that, at least based on post–*Citizens United* elections to this point, they were—to choose a word—wrong.

Finally, there is no reason to expect the intellectual warfare that continues to rage years after *Citizens United* was decided to abate. Nor should it. At issue is not just the financing of political campaigns but the nature and scope of freedom of speech in the nation. While I differ with Justice Stevens about the Court's ruling in *Citizens United,* I share his view that the core issue to be considered is the same one that was at issue in *Buckley v. Valeo,* a case that did not even address the relevance of whether the speaker at issue was an individual or a corporation. Justice Stevens' view is that the *Buckley* ruling contained the "central error in the Court's campaign finance jurisprudence."[50] I disagree with the conclusion that the *Buckley* Court was in error. But I have no doubt that the ruling was and remains central to jurisprudence in this provocative and critical area of law.

On the Legitimate Aim
of Congressional Regulation
# of Political Speech

An Originalist View

LAWRENCE LESSIG

The First Amendment has become the tool by which democracy is protected from government. As it has evolved, one principal purpose has been to cabin the government's ability to use its power to dominate or direct democracy. Democratic will, on this account, must emerge free of the guiding hand of any current government.

To this end, the First Amendment has been held to limit the power of Congress and the states to regulate campaigns and campaign spending.[1] That doctrine, in turn, has evolved to produce a highly dysfunctional democracy. Yet at the core of this recent doctrine lies a conceptual confusion. That confusion is not the creation of the Supreme Court, and the Supreme Court could easily swat it away. If it did, the biggest complaint about the way the First Amendment interacts with our democracy could be removed.

We can see the confusion in a simple distinction—between (1) laws restricting political speech that aim to protect the public from speech deemed troubling and (2) laws restricting political speech that aim to ensure that representatives are not subject to improper influence. The Court, I will argue, has generally—and correctly—been skeptical of laws of the first type; it has been more accepting, though perhaps not enough, of laws of the second type. Yet the confusion comes from now separating carefully these two kinds of laws.

Austin v. Michigan (1990)[2] involved a law of the first type. Michigan had determined that corporations enjoyed an unfair advantage in the market for political speech.[3] Legislators feared the public would be swayed improperly by such corporate speech[4]—"improperly" because the wealth of Michigan corporations was due in part to the state.[5] The corporate form itself, Michigan claimed, was a subsidy.[6] Michigan corporations were thus using that state subsidy to steer the political debate. Such steering was thus "improper," Michigan claimed.[7] Banning corporate speech was the only proper response.

The Supreme Court agreed[8]—and improperly so. If the First Amendment means anything, it must mean that the government has no power to decide which political speech is dangerous and which is not.[9] It may well be that the people of Michigan were swayed by corporate political speech. Yet even if that's a problem, it is not the sort of problem the government should be allowed to solve. The people, in this sense, must learn to take care of themselves. And indeed, they *can* take care of themselves. To the extent they are exposed to speech from one side, they can expose themselves to speech from the other side. There is no need for the government's intervention. Even if there were a need, the danger of so enabling the government plainly outweighs any benefit.

And so the Supreme Court did ultimately hold, in one of the Court's most despised decisions in the modern era. *Citizens United v. FEC* (2010)[10] expressly overruled *Austin v. Michigan,* and held that the State has no power to limit the political expenditures of corporations or unions, at least so long as they are independent of the campaigns of candidates.[11] The government has no power, the Court in effect held, to protect the public from political speech, however "unfair" the source or overwhelming the quantity of that speech.[12]

Yet *Citizens United* did reaffirm the power of the government to police, in effect, the effect of "political speech" on the representatives themselves.[13] The Court confirmed that the State can regulate speech when the target of that speech is a representative, and the form is corrupting.[14] By "corrupting," the Court meant speech proposing or accepting a quid pro quo.[15] When a private party offers a specific incentive for a public official's action, or when the public official offers a benefit in exchange for a private incentive, that speech can, constitutionally, be regulated.[16]

Democracy needs this power. The public has no effective way to police the speech that its representatives are exposed to. It has no way, absent a law, to ensure that such speech doesn't influence representatives improperly. Reserving to the government the power to protect the political process is essential to the integrity of the political process. And as the Supreme Court recognized in the source of modern political speech jurisprudence, *Buckley v. Valeo* (1976),[17] it is essential to the public's trust of that process as well.[18]

Thus the distinction that opened this chapter: when Congress restricts speech to *protect the public* from the effect of political speech, its regulation is likely invalid. When Congress restricts speech to *protect representatives* from the effect of political speech, so long as it is a regulation of "corruption," its regulation is likely valid. (My emphasis on "restriction" is intended. I don't mean this analysis to reach beyond regulations that restrict speech, though I acknowledge the analysis might well be suggestive in the debate about speech regulation more broadly.)

From *Citizens United* to Super PACs

Almost immediately after *Citizens United* was decided, the DC Circuit extended its analysis from "political speech" through expenditures to "political speech" through contributions. In *SpeechNow v. FEC* (2010),[19] the DC Circuit held that if expenditures by independent political action committees could not, constitutionally, be limited, then contributions to independent political action committees could not, constitutionally, be limited either.[20] Despite the Supreme Court's long-standing distinction in the analysis of the regulation of expenditures and contributions, the DC Circuit held that the reasoning behind *Citizens United* erased any justification for upholding a limit on contributions to an independent political action committee (PAC).[21] And thus the "super PAC" was born.

The belief among most is that *SpeechNow* follows from *Citizens United*. That belief is a mistake, and is grounded in the confusion that I referred to at the start of this chapter. *Citizens United*, in my view, could well be correct, but *SpeechNow* plainly is not.

To see why, return to the distinction I introduced at the start, between speech affecting representatives and speech affecting the public.

"Contributions" occupy an ambiguous place within that distinction. Indeed, they are hybrids. A contribution can both affect a representative and affect the public. A contribution of $10 million to a super PAC certainly enables that super PAC to spend $10 million supporting or opposing a particular candidate. Under *Citizens United*, that aspect of the contribution should raise no legitimate regulatory concern.[22]

But a contribution can also affect a representative. Contributions to super PACs are public; representatives are intensely focused on who is giving to whom. Indeed, as former senator Evan Bayh described, this effect has become quite dominant in Washington today. In response to a question from a representative from the Cato Institute about whether money actually affected the political process, Bayh reported:

> [I have] never witnessed any bribery or that sort of thing during my 12 years in the United States Senate. [But] you bet people know when there are 10s or 100s of million dollars being contributed. And you bet they know which independent groups are gonna come to their defense or not when they're being subjected to these negative attack ads. So people aren't for sale. But it does in practical political terms warp the system. . . .

[W]e're seeing . . . the death of moderates. Because you tend to have the big money contributors on either side of the ideological spectrum. And the presence of that big money makes people less independent, less moderate, and much more likely to feel, in practical, political terms like, "They have to toe the party line," otherwise who comes to their defense when they're being subjected to a blizzard of highly negative attack ads?

[No doubt there is a distinction between direct contributions and contributions to independent political action committees. But] as a practical matter these days, it's a distinction without a difference. Someone can give you $2,500 contribution directly, that's one thing. If that same person is giving a $5 million contribution to an independent expenditure group, you're gonna find out one way or the other. . . . And so if that's gonna affect your thinking, it's gonna affect your thinking. It just is a practical matter as it is.[23]

Bayh is describing an effect on representatives flowing from a contribution. This effect, however, does not constitute "corruption," at least as the Supreme Court has defined it so far.[24] That's because, though a representative might notice and respond to such a contribution, the response is not *in exchange for* that contribution.[25]

Quid pro quo is thus the essence of individual corruption as the Court has described it so far. Though much of the history of democracy is filled with instances of quid pro quo bribery[26]—and some of the greatest innovations of American democracy have been bought through quid pro quo corruption (the Thirteenth Amendment, for example, was passed in the House because of a series of bribes made on behalf of supporters of the Amendment to lame-duck representatives keen to find their next gig[27])—it is relatively uncontested today that such deals do constitute "corruption." It is likewise not controversial that if the public believed their representatives were deciding matters because of promises of personal or political gain, that would weaken fundamentally the public's trust in representative government. For those reasons, the Court in *Buckley v. Valeo* (1976) concluded that large contributions "given to secure a political *quid pro quo* from current and potential office holders [undermine] the integrity of our system of representative democracy."[28] And not just actual contributions:

Of almost equal concern as the danger of actual quid pro quo arrangements is the impact of the appearance of corruption stemming from public awareness of the opportunities for abuse inherent in a regime of large individual financial contributions.[29]

Yet while quid pro quo corruption is undoubtedly "corruption," and thus undoubtedly properly regulable by Congress consistent with the First Amendment, why is it the only conception of "corruption" that might earn a First Amendment pass? Justice Breyer in his dissent in *McCutcheon v. FEC* (2015) listed many different conceptions of "corruption" and pressed the Court by asking why one was selected rather than any of the others.[30] His question was a fair one. If the State has the right to regulate the corrupting influence of its representatives, why is the State restricted in its understanding of what "corrupting" means?

This question is fundamental and, as of yet, unanswered by the Supreme Court. It is even more compelling once we introduce one more distinction: between the corruption of an individual and the corruption of an institution.

Individual versus Institutional Corruption

Individuals can be corrupt. Institutions can be corrupt too. An individual is corrupt when, for example, as with quid pro quo corruption, he or she decides a question based on an improper influence. An institution can be corrupt when it is structured to decide questions based on an improper basis.

The Supreme Court has never quite completely explained why it was improper for a representative to decide matters in exchange for personal or political gain. It didn't need to, so fundamental is that idea to our political tradition. But the question I want to press here is whether there's a way to understand institutional corruption that should also be uncontested or obvious within our tradition, and that should also secure the same license under the First Amendment as quid pro quo corruption has.

The answer depends on whether we can describe with confidence how the institutions of our representative democracy were meant to be structured, such that a deviation from that structure could be called "corruption."

The Founders gave us a framework for answering that question. In describing the institution of Congress—and I limit the analysis that follows to the legislative branch, excluding the president—the Framers distinguished sharply between the Senate and the House. Members of the Senate would be appointed by state legislatures.[31] They were thus to be "dependent" upon the states. But members of the House were to be elected by "the people."[32] Their election was to be frequent, and their districts kept small, so that they would be, as Madison described in Federalist No. 52, "dependent on the people alone."[33] And just to be crystal clear, Madison added, "by the people" meant "not the rich more than the poor."[34]

"Dependence" is a rich concept. It evokes the idea of an economy of influence. Not every influence is part of an economy. Thus, not every influence would be an improper dependence. Instead, "dependence" directs us to look for a kind of feedback and an understanding of how that economy is fed. For the House, the dependence was to be on "the people."[35] It was also to be exclusive.[36] Such an exclusive dependence could thus be "corrupted" if there were a different, and conflicting, dependence that competed with it.

Consider an example to make the point clear. A lawyer is dependent upon his or her client. Not exclusively so—the law requires the lawyer to operate within certain ethical boundaries, regardless of whether that benefits his or her client or not.[37] But subject to those boundaries, the lawyer's duty is exclusive.[38]

If, in the course of representing a client, a lawyer were to contract with someone with a conflicting interest to the client and steer the litigation against the client because of that interest, we'd have no difficulty understanding that arrangement as a corruption of the obligation to the original client.[39]

The same could be true within an institution. The Framers of our Constitution considered the British Parliament "corrupt."[40] That corruption was institutional. Because there were members of Parliament—elected from the "rotten boroughs"—who were dependent upon the king for their election, the institution of Parliament, these critics believed, was therefore corrupted. The Commons was to represent the people. Adding members to the Commons who were dependent upon the king corrupted that intended and exclusive dependence.[41]

From this perspective, an institution is corrupt at least when it manifests a dependence different from the dependence intended. It may be corrupt for other reasons as well—for example, its purposes may be corrupt. Think about the institution of the mafia, or a crime syndicate. But my point so far is just that there is at least one clear way that an institution could be considered institutionally corrupt: if it had an intended dependence that was then compromised.

Consider how this point relates back to the question of campaign contributions and campaign spending.

Bayh described the effect that contributions to a super PAC now have on representatives.[42] That effect, if believed, is dramatic. The mere recognition that taking a position could steer millions either for or against a candidate is obviously deeply salient to that candidate—and to the decision he or she makes about his or her positions. But does it effect an improper dependence?

The answer to that question depends on an understanding of campaign finance more generally. As most recognize, campaigns in America are privately funded.[43] That funding is either direct (a donation given to a campaign) or indirect (a donation given to a political action committee). Campaigns depend on funding. Members of Congress spend an extraordinary amount of time— between 30 percent and 70 percent of their time as representatives—trying to secure campaign funding.[44] That time evinces the dependence—but for the funders, those members could not be elected.

But members don't raise their money from "the people" randomly. They raise it from a tiny slice of the 1 percent. No more than one hundred thousand Americans give the maximum contribution to any candidate for Congress.[45] Those hundred thousand do not, whether Republican or Democratic, represent the views of "the people" upon whom the representatives are to be "dependent" exclusively. Instead, these funders constitute a different dependence: a dependence that conflicts with an intended dependence. And that conflict predictably corrupts the dependence that at least Madison expected our representatives would have.

Super PACS are just an extreme version of this dependence corruption. Indeed, as Bayh describes it, the system functions like a protection racket.[46] Congress members fear a super PAC will, in the final months before an election, spend a large amount against them.[47] To insure against that happening, the member allies with a super PAC that might support the member if he or she is attacked.[48] That alliance is a kind of insurance. And as with most insurance, the premium must be paid in advance. The Congressperson knows that if he or she is to induce the loyalty needed to insure the protection that might be needed, he or she must behave in a way that is attractive to the super PAC that might defend him or her.[49] That means the Congressperson must vote in the way the super PAC desires. Not a single dollar need be spent for the threat of this extraordinary intervention to affect the behavior of the representative.

But affect in what way? As Bayh argues, the most significant of these super PACs are at the extreme in our political system—either on the right or left.[50] And thus the effect of this implicit threat is to move the representative more to that extreme. The effect, in other words, is polarizing, and thus yet another influence within our democratic system that weakens the representativeness of the system.

With both direct and indirect contributions, we can thus see the elements of institutional corruption. If candidates for Congress are dependent upon funders, but those funders are not representative of the people, then the system has evolved a different, and conflicting, dependence within the economy of influence of Congress. That different dependence corrupts the intended dependence. That corruption is institutional; it exists whether or not there is any quid pro quo among the members.

This analysis hangs upon an understanding of "dependence." That concept, of course, is not absolutely precise. Any particular influence does not necessarily constitute an improper "dependence." Instead, the idea must tie to more systemic and regular influence, beyond the dependence intended. On this analysis, Congress would need an argument for showing why a particular pattern evinced an improper dependence. Consistent with First Amendment values, it would be appropriate for the Court to test that justification under some form of heightened review.

Does this mean independent expenditures are regulable too? Is this part of *Buckley v. Valeo* (1976)[51] therefore wrong? Not necessarily. If expenditures are irregular, not reasonably tracked by or consequential to candidates or campaigns, then it would be difficult to establish that they created an improper dependence. They could, but at least since *Citizens United*, the independent expenditures by corporations or unions have not constituted a significant part of the campaign spending.[52] That may change, but my point is just that, as the market has evolved so far, there is a clear dependence upon super PAC contributions, and not on independent expenditures.

If this approach is correct, then to remedy the corruption, Congress should be permitted to regulate to remove the improper dependence. One clear way would be through public funding of congressional elections. If Congress gave every voter vouchers to use to fund congressional campaigns, those vouchers would ensure that the "dependence" of the member reaches beyond the tiny slice of America that privately funds congressional campaigns today. Of course, voluntary public funding is already constitutional.[53] But this analysis suggests something more: if the private funding is itself institutionally corrupting, then mandatory public funding should, constitutionally, be allowed.

Likewise with contributions to super PACs: if members are dependent upon large contributions, not directly, but indirectly, then Congress should be allowed to restrict large contributions to undermine that dependence effect. If the limits were strict enough, then independent political action committees would not be biased in any suspect—meaning dependence-related—way. As with vouchers, the dependence would be diffuse. But without limits, the dependence is not diffuse, and that concentrated influence gives Congress a legitimate reason, grounded in the objective to avoid institutional corruption, for limiting such contributions.

Again, we are talking about *contributions* and not *expenditures*. If a conservative independent political action committee persuaded fifty million Americans to contribute $50 to a PAC, there would be no reason grounded in institutional corruption for banning that PAC from spending its $2.5 billion. That spending would be aimed at individuals. The First Amendment gives Congress no power to protect individuals.[54] The distinction at the start of this chapter would fit this difference in treatment.

But is this analysis right? Should the influence from this dependence—again, relative to the dependence intended by our Framers—be deemed "improper"? Should it be considered within the family of influences on representatives that justifies the Court in allowing Congress to regulate against "corruption"?

The answer to these questions turns on one's conception of "corruption." If "corruption" predicates only corruption of individuals, then the influence of a contribution to a super PAC cannot be corruption. By definition, as Justice Kennedy observed, with an independent expenditure, there could be no quid pro quo.[55] Quid pro quo is the only type of individual corruption identified by the Court as justifying restrictions on political speech.[56]

But why is the only democratically relevant corruption the corruption of individuals? Why isn't the corruption of an institution also relevant? If Congress can police influences on individuals that are presumptively corrupting of a deliberative process, why can't it police influences on the institution itself that more directly affect that deliberative process?

The answer to that question depends, of course, on the method the Court uses to determine the kind of "corruption" that should be amenable to regulation. For most Justices, that is simply a choice—whether they find the conception compelling, given our tradition and practice, as they see it.

In this chapter, however, I want to focus on the method that a certain kind of conservative Justice should admit—specifically, a Justice who practices originalism as a method for interpreting the Constitution, and cabining judicial discretion. What's the sense of "corruption" that such a Justice should admit? Should it be restricted to individual, quid pro quo corruption only?

Originalism and the First Amendment

Originalism is, admittedly, an odd framing for a First Amendment inquiry. Modern First Amendment doctrine was not crafted with the Framers in view.[57] The exception grounded in "corruption" was not crafted in light of the Framers' understanding.[58] So one might well question why the Framers' view about the meaning of "corruption" should be relevant to the inquiry at all.

But originalism is both a theory of meaning and a theory of judicial restraint. Its role, at least as some see it, is to vest decisions—especially decisions that go against a legislative majority—in an authority other than them.[59] Ed Meese, one of the clearest and strongest proponents of originalism as a method of constitutional interpretation, complained that judges treated the text of the Constitution like a picnic, where the Framers brought the words and the judges brought the meaning.[60] If we recognize—as everyone must—that the idea of "corruption" is multiple and varied, then for an originalist, one clear method for constraining his or her discretion would be to tie the idea of corruption to the conception the Framers would have had. If there was a kind of corruption that the Framers were especially exercised about, then such an approach should, at the very least, permit Congress to remedy that corruption too. At the very minimum, a reading of the First Amendment by an originalist should permit Congress to regulate according to a conception of "corruption" that was common or even dominant at the framing of the Amendment.

So what would the Framers have meant by the idea of "corruption"?

In an analysis of framing texts, I tried to determine this question. Drawing upon a database of texts published around the founding—including familiar works, like the Federalist Papers, as well as pamphlets, newspaper articles, and published speeches—researchers identified every instance of the use of the term "corruption."[61] They then coded those uses to determine the nature of the corruption being spoken of. Was the usage referring to individual or institutional corruption? Was it speaking of quid pro quo corruption or corruption of a different kind?

Thus, for example, the database included a writing, "Marcus II," published in the Norfolk and Portsmouth Journal in February 1788. Describing the positive effect that separating legislative from executive functions, the document states:

> But so long as the people's Representatives are altogether distinct from the Executive authority, the liberties of the people may be deemed secure. And in this point, surely there can be no manner of comparison between the provisions by which the independence of our House of Representatives is guarded, and the condition in which the British House of Commons is left exposed to every species of corruption.[62]

The researchers would thus code that writing by determining whether it was speaking of individual or entity corruption, and if entity, whether dependence corruption or not.

The results were quite striking. No doubt, the Framers spoke of quid pro quo corruption—but rarely. Of 325 uses identified, only 6 referred to quid pro quo corruption, and all 6 were referring to individual corruption alone.[63] By contrast, the majority of uses (57 percent) referred not to individual corruption, but to institutional corruption.[64] Of these, the largest single set referred to the corruption produced by an improper dependence.[65] In almost thirty cases, the Framers spoke of corruption in exactly this way—five times the frequency of any discussion of quid pro quo corruption.[66] If anything, if the Framers were concerned with "corruption," they were concerned *primarily* with "institutional corruption."

This fact has an important implication for an originalist interpreting the First Amendment. The Court permits the regulation of political speech when it is protecting *representatives* from improper influence, not when it is protecting *the public* from dangerous political speech.[67] The Court calls such speech "corruption."[68] So far, the Court has focused on the corruption of individuals only.[69] But the Framers were plainly focused beyond the corruption of individuals. They may well have been concerned about bribery or quid pro quo corruption, but their primary concern was the corruption of institutions.

That institutional corruption included at least a dependence within the institution that conflicted with the intended dependence of the institution. Thus, to declare a dependence corrupting, we must first identify the dependence intended.

For the House, the intended dependence was clear. The Framers meant the House to be dependent upon "the people alone."[70] And synthesizing the Seventeenth Amendment, that same standard should now apply to the Senate too.[71] Now that the Senate is also directly elected, it should also be true for the Senate.[72] For both bodies, the intended dependence was to be exclusive and general.

Yet today, for both bodies, a separate and conflicting dependence has emerged—a dependence upon the funders of campaigns. That dependence exists with direct donations. It exists in an extreme way with super PACs. And thus, from the perspective of institutional corruption, there is a corruption of the process of influence that flows from this dependence by representatives upon their funders.

For most Justices, such an argument is just persuasion. I've sketched a plausible account of institutional corruption and suggested why the Court should admit institutional corruption as one of the types of corruption that should justify restrictions on political speech targeted at representatives.

For originalists, this argument should have a special purchase. If originalism is a tool of both meaning and restraint, then the question for the originalist becomes just this: What justifies judicial invalidation of laws targeting institutional corruption when it is clear that at the very least, that corruption more than individual corruption was the corruption the Framers were focused on? What justification, in other words, does the originalist have for looking beyond the Framers' understanding of "corruption" when determining the meaning of corruption that they will apply to the First Amendment?

The originalists have not answered this question, in part because no litigant has yet framed it like that. But so framed, the answer for an originalist should be clear: whether or not *Citizens United* is correctly decided, *SpeechNow* is not consistent with originalism. The originalist should thus permit Congress to regulate to avoid dependence corruption, at the very least by limiting contributions to independent political action committees.

The Classic First Amendment Tradition under Stress

Freedom of Speech and the University

ROBERT C. POST

The First Amendment was ratified in 1791, and ever since, Americans have enjoyed a robust civic culture that celebrates freedom of expression. But courts played virtually no role in protecting free speech rights before the 1930s. As late as 1907, Justice Oliver Wendell Holmes could easily summarize the dominant doctrinal view of the First Amendment as having the "main purpose" of preventing "all such previous restraints upon publications as had been practised by other governments," and not of preventing "the subsequent punishment of such as may be deemed contrary to the public welfare."[1]

The Emergence of the Classic First Amendment Tradition

Holmes' narrow view of the First Amendment evolved during the twentieth century due to altered understandings of self-government.[2] The nation began to equate democracy with "the organized sway of public opinion."[3] The efforts of the Wilson administration to control public opinion by prosecuting those opposed to World War I prompted American jurists to rethink the role of courts in protecting freedom of speech. As Learned Hand wrote to his friend Zechariah Chafee, "any State which professes to be controlled by public opinion, cannot take sides against any opinion except that which must express itself in the violation of law. On the contrary, it must regard all other expression of opinion as tolerable, if not good."[4]

When the Supreme Court at last began actually to protect First Amendment rights in the 1930s, it explicitly theorized First Amendment rights in terms of the political value of self-government. In the early and decisive case of *Stromberg v. California*, for example, the Court proclaimed that "the maintenance of the opportunity for free political discussion to the end that government may be responsive to the will of the people and that changes may be obtained by lawful means, an opportunity essential to the security of the Republic, is a fundamental principle of our constitutional system."[5] A decade later the magnificent opinion by Justice Roberts in *Thornhill v. Alabama* affirmed that

> those who won our independence had confidence in the power of free and fearless reasoning and communication of ideas to discover and spread political and economic truth. Noxious doctrines in those fields may be refuted and their evil averted by the courageous exercise of the right of free discussion. Abridgment of freedom of speech and of the press, however, impairs those opportunities for public education that are essential to effective exercise of the power of correcting error through the processes of popular government.[6]

The classic First Amendment tradition thus protected speech insofar as it was deemed necessary for the formation "of that public opinion which is the final source of government in a democratic state."[7] The corollary of this conceptual framework was that speech deemed irrelevant for the free formation of public opinion was not protected by the First Amendment. Only two years after *Thornhill*, for example, Justice Roberts could hold for a unanimous Court that "the Constitution imposes no . . . restraint on government as respects purely commercial advertising,"[8] evidently because such advertising was regarded as exogenous to the discovery and spread of political and economic truth.

Over the years, the Court developed core First Amendment rules that give content to the right to participate in the formation of public opinion in the public sphere. Here are three such rules that are essential to modern First Amendment jurisprudence:

Rule 1: "It is axiomatic that the government may not regulate speech based on its substantive content or the message it conveys. . . . When the government targets not subject matter, but particular views taken by speakers on a subject, the violation of the First Amendment is all the more blatant. Viewpoint discrimination is thus an egregious form of content discrimination."[9]

Rule 2: "We have therefore been particularly vigilant to ensure that individual expressions of ideas remain free from governmentally imposed sanctions.

The First Amendment recognizes no such thing as a 'false' idea. As Justice Holmes wrote, 'when men have realized that time has upset many fighting faiths, they may come to believe even more than they believe the very foundations of their own conduct that the ultimate good desired is better reached by free trade in ideas—that the best test of truth is the power of the thought to get itself accepted in the competition of the market.' "[10]

Rule 3: "It is . . . a basic First Amendment principle that 'freedom of speech prohibits the government from telling people what they must say.' . . . 'At the heart of the First Amendment lies the principle that each person should decide for himself or herself the ideas and beliefs deserving of expression, consideration, and adherence.' "[11] " 'The essential thrust of the First Amendment is to prohibit improper restraints on the *voluntary* public expression of ideas. . . . There is necessarily . . . a concomitant freedom *not* to speak publicly, one which serves the same ultimate end as freedom of speech in its affirmative aspect.' "[12]

First Amendment doctrine incorporates these three very stringent rules because they enable the First Amendment to serve "as the guardian of our democracy."[13] The First Amendment underwrites democratic legitimacy insofar as we are free to influence public opinion and insofar as we believe that the State is responsive to public opinion.[14] If these two conditions hold, we can believe that our government is also potentially responsive to us.[15] The three essential rules of First Amendment jurisprudence are designed to safeguard the first of these conditions.

The three rules thus apply to the set of communicative acts judged necessary for the formation of public opinion. I shall call this set "public discourse." In the context of public discourse, the rule against content discrimination ensures that persons set the agenda for government action rather than the reverse. The State cannot rule out topics or viewpoints that persons wish to place on the national agenda. The rule establishing the equality of ideas stands for the proposition that every democratic citizen has an equal right to influence the contents of public opinion. As John Rawls once put it, in public debate "there are no experts: a philosopher has no more authority than other citizens."[16] The equality of ideas flows from the premise of political equality, not from any postulated epistemological equality, which would be incompatible with the very concepts of truth and falsity.[17] Finally, the rule against compelled speech prevents forms of coercion that would interfere with the ability of persons to imagine that the State is potentially responsive to them. We are not the free authors of our own government if we are compelled to participate in the formation of public opinion in a manner that is contrary to our own will.

The Classic Tradition under Siege

When persons participate in the formation of public opinion, they are sovereign. They decide the destiny of the nation. The three essential rules of First Amendment jurisprudence define and codify this sovereignty. But, as Alexander Meiklejohn famously noted, in a democracy "the governors and the governed are not two distinct groups of persons. There is only one group—the self-governing people. Rulers and ruled are the same individuals. We, the People, are our own masters, our own subjects."[18]

Meiklejohn's insight is fundamental. The people could not be sovereigns if they could not also sometimes be subjects, for there would then be nothing left to govern. That is why classic First Amendment doctrine does not and cannot apply to "speech as such."[19] Almost all human action is communicative, and if First Amendment rights were interpreted to endow persons with sovereignty every time they spoke, the People would be constitutionally prohibited from almost all forms of regulation. They would pro tanto lose their sovereignty.

The Court stumbled across this dilemma in 1976 when it reversed its own precedent and extended constitutional protection to commercial speech.[20] The commercial marketplace exists through acts of communication, and if all such speech were protected by the three essential rules of First Amendment doctrine, the people would be stripped of the power to regulate their own economic circumstances. The Court thus very self-consciously created forms of protection for commercial speech that are far less strict than those accorded to public discourse.[21] It said that commercial speech could be compelled,[22] for example, and that the State could engage in content discrimination by suppressing "misleading" advertisements.[23] In the commercial marketplace all opinions are not equal; some are downright fraudulent.[24]

The classic First Amendment tradition has in the past two decades come under severe strain because the Court seems to have lost track of *why* the First Amendment protects speech. It has begun to apply First Amendment doctrine to all kinds of communication that have nothing to do with the formation of public opinion.

A clear sign of this confusion is judicial efforts to extend to the professional speech of doctors the same protections that it accords to the formation of public opinion. As the Third Circuit recently opined in a case involving a statute regulating the speech of physicians, "Speech is speech, and it must be analyzed as such for purposes of the First Amendment."[25] Taken literally, the Third Circuit's approach would transform every malpractice case involving communication— every failure to warn, every misleading medical opinion—into a question of constitutional law.

The same tendency to overreach has become visible in the context of commercial speech.[26] The overextension of First Amendment doctrine has led to repeated condemnations of modern First Amendment decisions as creating "the New Lochner,"[27] as establishing the rationale for striking down ordinary commercial regulations.[28] In this chapter, I shall illustrate this contemporary failure to appreciate the fundamental purpose of the First Amendment by examining recent controversies about freedom of speech and universities.

Freedom of Speech within Universities: Misapplying the Classic First Amendment Tradition

The Contemporary Controversy

One hears now everywhere the cry that First Amendment rights are at risk because universities have failed to protect freedom of expression. Within weeks of her confirmation, the new secretary of education, Betsy DeVos, proclaimed that "the real threat" in modern universities "is silencing the First Amendment rights of people with whom you disagree."[29] And in September Attorney General Jeff Sessions complained that "freedom of . . . speech on the American campus is under attack."[30] Universities, Sessions announced, should abide by "what the late Justice Antonin Scalia rightly called 'the first axiom of the First Amendment,' which is that, 'as a general rule, the state has no power to ban speech on the basis of its content.' "[31] Certainly, Sessions asserted, failure to comply with such "free speech rights" was "not an option" for public universities, "but an unshakable requirement of the First Amendment."[32]

Controversies currently roiling American campuses are characterized as pitting "a sharp increase in attention to students' psychological health" against "a somewhat diminished concern—sometimes bordering on outright skepticism—about the right to free speech."[33] They are said to reveal "an 'apparent chasm' between free speech advocates and student activists."[34] Efforts to curb microaggression are resisted as "nothing less than an attack on free speech"[35] and as provoking the question of whether "racist expression should be allowed as long as it's cloaked in the First Amendment."[36] "The 'safety'-crusaders who equate words with violence" are charged with nullifying "the First Amendment on account of feelings."[37] Cancellations of university speakers are condemned as inconsistent with "the First Amendment."[38] The upshot is the enactment of statutes like the Campus Free Speech Protection Act of Tennessee, which provides:

(a) The general assembly finds and declares that public institutions of higher education in Tennessee are not immune from the sweep of the First

Amendment to the United States Constitution . . . which guarantees freedom of speech and expression.
(b) It is the intent of the general assembly that the public institutions of higher education embrace a commitment to the freedom of speech and expression for all students and all faculty.[39]

On one side of the spectrum, the president of the University of California system, invoking "First Amendment protections," complains that "we have moved from freedom of speech on campuses to freedom from speech."[40] On the other side of the spectrum, right-leaning commentators argue that "pro-life speakers are unwelcome, and conservatives are demonized, even banned from campuses for believing that ideas written into America's Constitution have meaning in modern America. Farewell 1st Amendment and the remainder of the Bill of Rights."[41]

The organization that is most influential in advocating the application of First Amendment jurisprudence to universities is the Foundation for Individual Rights in Education (FIRE). "The mission of FIRE is to defend and sustain individual rights at America's colleges and universities. These rights include freedom of speech, legal equality, due process, religious liberty, and sanctity of conscience—the essential qualities of individual liberty and dignity."[42] FIRE's mission statement explicitly notes the following:

> Why is free speech important on campus?
> Freedom of speech is a fundamental American freedom and a human right, and there's no place that this right should be more valued and protected than America's colleges and universities. A university exists to educate students and advance the frontiers of human knowledge, and does so by acting as a "marketplace of ideas" where ideas compete. The intellectual vitality of a university depends on this competition— something that cannot happen properly when students or faculty members fear punishment for expressing views that might be unpopular with the public at large or disfavored by university administrators.
> Nevertheless, freedom of speech is under continuous threat at many of America's campuses, pushed aside in favor of politics, comfort, or simply a desire to avoid controversy. As a result, speech codes dictating what may or may not be said, "free speech zones" confining free speech to tiny areas of campus, and administrative attempts to punish or repress speech on a case-by-case basis are common today in academia.

> What is the First Amendment?
> The First Amendment to the United States Constitution is the part of the Bill of Rights that expressly prohibits the United States Congress

from making laws "respecting an establishment of religion," prohibiting the free exercise of religion, infringing freedom of speech, infringing freedom of the press, limiting the right to peaceably assemble, or limiting the right to petition the government for a redress of grievances. The protections of the First Amendment are extended to state governments and public university campuses by the Fourteenth Amendment.[43]

FIRE aggressively proclaims that First Amendment protections of free speech ought to apply within the domain of universities. The assumption is apparently that First Amendment protections attach to speech, and that speech occurs within universities.

The Classic First Amendment and the Campus

The question I wish to explore is what it might mean to apply the classic First Amendment to universities. The purpose of classic First Amendment principles is to protect the process of self-government. But speech within universities does not serve this purpose. It serves the purpose of education, which requires an entirely different framework of speech regulation and protection. Speech within campus is ordinarily protected according to principles of academic freedom, as distinct from freedom of speech.

Consider, for example, speech within a classroom. Classroom communication is not about influencing public opinion; it is about educating students. When students express themselves in a classroom, they are not acting as sovereign agents of self-government. They are acting as students who are tasked with learning from their instructors. The plain implication is that their speech may be regulated in ways that facilitate their education.

It is for this reason that the three cardinal rules of First Amendment jurisprudence are manifestly inapplicable to student speech in the classroom. First, content discrimination is rampant in all classrooms. Students must address the subject under class discussion rather than whatever happens to be on their minds. If I am teaching a class on the Constitution, my students cannot ramble on about the World Series. Second, all ideas are not equal within classroom discussion. Each student should be respected, but the function of classroom conversation is to instruct students in the art of distinguishing good from poor ideas.[44] No competent teacher would conduct a class on the premise that all ideas were equal. Third, compelled speech is normal within classrooms. Students are called on to answer questions and required to take examinations.

Consider other important First Amendment doctrines. To preserve equality of participation within public discourse, the First Amendment precludes the State from regulating public discourse by suppressing speech that is offensive or outrageous or abusive.[45] But no competent teacher would permit a class to descend into name-calling and insults. Even if the object of classroom education is to expose students to ideas that they might not otherwise encounter and that they might find disturbing or threatening, it is nevertheless inconsistent with learning for students to experience this encounter in settings in which they are personally abused or degraded.[46] Competent teachers therefore insist on respect within the classroom to promote the effectiveness of the educational experience. Personal insults and incivility are inconsistent with deliberation and learning.

A similar analysis applies if we focus on the speech of professors within the classroom. The three essential rules of First Amendment jurisprudence do not apply to professorial communication in the classroom. The mission of the classroom is instruction, and professors are regularly judged on the competence of their performance in successfully educating students. Universities routinely engage in content discrimination in assessing professorial classroom communication. If I am supposed to be teaching constitutional law, I can't spend my classroom time talking about auto mechanics. Universities also assess the quality of the ideas conveyed by professors. If a mathematics professor continuously gets her equations wrong, her competence will be called into question. Universities also compel professors to show up to class, to teach, and therefore to speak. Within the classroom, university professors do not have freedom of speech, as measured by the classic First Amendment tradition.

Professors do, however, have *academic freedom* within the classroom.[47] The scope of academic freedom is not determined by First Amendment principles of freedom of speech, but by the requirements of professional competence. Professors are free to teach in ways that are required by the educational mission of a university and that are thus conceptualized as professionally competent.

The function of higher education is ordinarily said to be the inculcation of what Cardinal Newman called "real cultivation of mind."[48] As the American Association of University Professors put it in its classic 1915 *Declaration of the Principles on Academic Freedom and Tenure*, the purpose of university education is "not to provide . . . students with ready-made conclusions, but to train them to think for themselves, and to provide them access to those materials which they need if they are to think intelligently."[49] This training can occur only if students and faculty in a classroom are "free . . . to express the widest range of viewpoints in accord with the standards of scholarly inquiry and professional ethics."[50]

Independence of mind is not a form of information that can be handed from teachers to students. It is instead a characterological trait that students must be inspired to embrace. The hope is that students who witness actual independence of mind will be moved to internalize autonomous thinking as a form of living. As Richard Rorty puts it, "Students need to have freedom enacted before their eyes by actual human beings" if higher education is to achieve its purpose of be-coming a "provocation to self-creation."[51]

No doubt much of higher education requires the transmission of information and skills. But if our most important goal is to inspire a mature independence of mind, professorial speech within a classroom must be given great latitude. Professors must be allowed to demonstrate their own independence. As the 1915 *Declaration* reasons:

> No man can be a successful teacher unless he enjoys the respect of his students, and their confidence in his intellectual integrity. It is clear, however, that this confidence will be impaired if there is suspicion on the part of the student that the teacher is not expressing himself fully or frankly. . . . It is not only the character of the instruction but also the character of the instructor that counts; and if the student has reason to believe that the instructor is not true to himself, the virtue of the in-struction as an educative force is incalculably diminished. There must be in the mind of the teacher no mental reservation. He must give the student the best of what he has and what he is.[52]

Academic freedom of teaching is thus quite encompassing. But it does not derive from, nor is it homologous with, the classic First Amendment tradition. Freedom of teaching is not about self-government; it is about education. That is why the three essential rules of First Amendment jurisprudence do not apply to professors in the classroom.

It is also why professors who bully, abuse, degrade, or demean their students risk being found professionally incompetent in achieving the university's mission of education. Professional ethics require professors to "demonstrate respect for students as individuals and adhere to their proper roles as intellectual guides and counselors."[53] They also require professors to "avoid any exploitation, harass-ment, or discriminatory treatment of students."[54] Professors must walk a narrow and difficult line between maintaining student trust and identification and pro-voking students to consider new, unfamiliar, and perhaps even threatening ideas.

If the classic First Amendment tradition does not apply to speech in the class-room, it also does not apply to the professional research of faculty. The mission of universities includes the expansion of knowledge. Universities are not especially concerned with the kind of knowledge that derives from immediate sensory ap-prehension; nor do they typically dedicate themselves to the production of the charismatic knowledge characteristic of art. Instead, universities seek to advance the *expert knowledge* produced by what we call *disciplines*.[55] One cannot know whether cigarettes cause cancer merely by smoking; one cannot measure climate change by taking the temperature on a winter's day; one cannot know the half-life of plutonium-230 merely by staring at a lump of metal. To know or even to formulate these questions, one must understand the practices of disciplines like medicine, climatography, or nuclear physics.

Universities provide an institutional home for such disciplines. Other organizations like private corporations may create knowledge, but *only* universities reproduce, refine, and conserve the practices, beliefs, and methods of knowing that define the disciplines that certify expert knowledge. Universities are the only major institutions that systematically train the experts on whom we must inevitably rely in deploying disciplinary knowledge.[56] We depend on doctors to create vaccines to immunize us against Zika; we rely on engineers to build bridges. We do not crowdsource such questions or decide them by public opinion polls or by popular vote. We use universities to train engineers and to educate doctors in their respective disciplines.

Disciplines may be defined as "communities of the competent."[57] In contrast to public discourse, which postulates the democratic equality of all citizens, disciplines are inherently hierarchical. To speak with authority within a discipline requires training in relevant beliefs, practices, and methods of knowing. It takes long years of preparation to become an authority within a discipline. That is why disciplines subject new devotees to long and arduous apprenticeships in the course of graduate education. Disciplines are grounded on the premise that some ideas are better than others; disciplinary communities claim the prerogative to discriminate between competent and incompetent work.

Healthy disciplines also require freedom of inquiry. As Thomas Haskell writes, "*The price of participation in the community of the competent is perpetual exposure to criticism.*"[58] The reason for this price is not complicated to discern:

> The function of seeking new truths will sometimes mean . . . the undermining of widely or generally accepted beliefs. It is rendered impossible if the work of the investigator is shackled by the requirement that his conclusions shall never seriously deviate either from generally accepted beliefs or from those accepted by the persons, private or official, through whom society provides the means for the maintenance of universities.[59]

The freedom of inquiry characteristic of a disciplinary community differs starkly from the classic First Amendment tradition. The distinction is often carelessly ignored, probably because of the old saw that "it is the purpose of the First Amendment to preserve an uninhibited marketplace of ideas in which truths will ultimately prevail,"[60] and that the First Amendment advances "knowledge . . . by fostering a free marketplace of ideas and an 'uninhibited, robust, wide-open debate on public issues.' "[61] But these bromides about the marketplace of ideas are quite misleading.

Disciplines do not create expert knowledge through a marketplace of ideas in which content discrimination is prohibited and in which all ideas are deemed equal. No professionally edited journal runs on the principle of the marketplace of ideas. Instead, disciplinary journals authorize experts to make judgments of quality that acknowledge the possibility of critique and discovery. The marketplace of ideas is inimical to such judgments.

The marketplace of ideas prohibits such judgments because each person is endowed with an equal right to influence the content of public opinion. As Michael Walzer writes, "Every citizen is a potential participant, a potential politician. The potentiality is the necessary condition of the citizen's self-respect."[62] If the value of political equality entitles all to participate in the marketplace of ideas, disciplinary debates are not subject to this value. Disciplinary disputes occur among those who are already trained within existing disciplinary practices. Authority and competence matter within disciplinary debates.

Disciplines thus live in the tension between freedom of inquiry and judgments of competence. Disciplines that do not allow freedom of inquiry wither and atrophy; but disciplines that do not evaluate the quality and merit of disciplinary work disintegrate and become incoherent. The three essential rules of the classic First Amendment apply to the marketplace of ideas precisely because it is not afflicted by any such tension.

It would make no sense, therefore, to apply these three rules to university regulations of faculty research. In pursuing their mission to advance knowledge, universities regularly and routinely exercise content and viewpoint discrimination. Universities offer grants to research projects they consider likely to be productive; they do not operate as passive marketplaces of ideas. Universities hire faculty based on considerations of content, focusing on areas they believe especially important to the development of disciplinary fields. Universities continuously assess the competence of faculty. They do not consider all ideas to be equal. If there were no such thing as a false idea, there would be no such thing as a true idea, and the entire aspiration of disciplines to produce expert knowledge would collapse. That is why history professors who deny the Holocaust are not hired or promoted. Universities also compel speech. The rule is publish or perish. Universities hire and promote faculty based on their certification as experts, and consequently faculty must demonstrate their expertise by speaking.

The classic First Amendment tradition is thus a very bad guide to the way that universities actually control the professional speech of faculty. Within universities, research faculty are not entitled to classic First Amendment protections for speech. They are entitled instead to *academic freedom* of research.[63] Academic freedom of research is, in the words of the *Declaration of the Principles on Academic Freedom and Tenure*, the freedom to pursue the "scholar's profession"[64] according to the standards of that profession. The *Declaration* asserts that the "liberty of the scholar within the university to set forth his conclusions, be they what they may, is conditioned by their being conclusions gained by a scholar's method and held in a scholar's spirit; that is to say, they must be the fruits of competent and patient and sincere inquiry."[65] Academic freedom, the *Declaration* precisely notes, upholds "not the absolute freedom of utterance of the individual scholar, but the absolute freedom of thought, of inquiry, of discussion and of teaching, of the academic profession."[66]

The classic First Amendment tradition protects the right of *individuals* to speak. This is because democratic legitimation attaches to individual persons. But the freedom of inquiry that is relevant to a university's mission of research attaches instead to disciplinary communities. It is designed to allow such communities to develop autonomously according to their own internal logic.

To get a concrete sense of what this might mean in practice, consider the case of a young assistant professor who is denied tenure because a university has judged his work to be incompetent. If the professor sues for damages, a court will rule in his favor if it believes that his work was not substandard when measured by relevant disciplinary criteria. But a court will rule in the university's favor if it concludes that the professor's work was indeed substandard when assessed by pertinent disciplinary criteria. In effect, therefore, a court will not protect the right of the professor to publish what he individually wishes to say; it will not protect the professor's right to freedom of speech. It will instead protect the integrity of relevant disciplinary standards.

The Source of the Confusion

When seen from this angle, it seems so obvious that speech within universities cannot be governed by classic First Amendment doctrine that we may ask how constitutional First Amendment rights could ever have come to be confused with the regulation of speech within universities. Why do people now complain, as they so often do, that universities are denying First Amendment rights? I suggest that confusion occurs in circumstances where the educational or research functions of a university are neither salient nor well theorized and where academic freedom is thus not a very useful concept.

Disputes over invited speakers, for example, often involve uncertainty over the educational and research missions of the university. Such speakers are responsible neither for disciplinary competence nor for competence in teaching. Their research does not add to the productivity of the university, nor are they expected to establish long-term relationships with students that can inspire the development of intellectual independence. Outside speakers thus appear almost as strangers to the essential missions of the university. It is not clear how academic freedom applies to them. It is a small step from this ambiguity to the conclusion that outside speakers should be regarded as participants in public discourse and therefore accorded full First Amendment rights.

But this conclusion obscures the essential logic of how outside speakers actually enter university environs. Universities are not public fora. Whatever happens under the aegis of a university must be justified by reference to the university's twin missions of research and education. This means that outside speakers are invited to universities *because* they serve these missions. Universities betray their fiduciary responsibilities to the extent that they expend resources on speakers who fail to serve these missions.[67] It follows that although the conceptual framework of academic freedom has not been elaborated to include outside speakers, the scope and bounds of the proper regulation of the speech of outside speakers must nevertheless be justified in terms of their contribution to the twin missions of the modern university.

Exactly how outside invited speakers contribute to the educational or research missions of a university is a complicated question. Relevant circumstances and distinctions proliferate indefinitely. So, for example, consider the case of a faculty member who invites an outside speaker to lecture in her class because she believes that the speaker will contribute to her research or to her pedagogical responsibilities. If the university administration believes that the outside speaker is inconsistent with the research or educational functions of the university, there is a conflict between faculty and administration about how to attain university goals. Principles of academic freedom require the university administration to give great (if not decisive) deference to the judgment of faculty in such contexts.[68] First Amendment free speech principles have little to do with the matter.

Outside speakers are often invited in ways that do not implicate the academic freedom of faculty. Especially difficult cases often arise in the context of student-invited outside speakers. Students are accountable neither for the research mission of the university nor for its educational responsibilities. It is puzzling, therefore, how to analyze student-invited speakers in terms of the purposive goals of the university.

We must begin our analysis from the premise that universities are not Hyde Parks. Unless they are wasting their resources on a frolic and detour, they can authorize students to expend university resources to invite speakers[69] *only* because it serves university purposes to do so. In the case of student-invited speakers, universities delegate to students the determination whether particular speakers serve university educational or research purposes. Outside speakers are not selected at random, even by students. Students invite speakers because they believe the speakers have something worthwhile to say. The first two cardinal rules of First Amendment jurisprudence are thus inapplicable, because students exercise content (and perhaps viewpoint) discrimination, and they also determine that certain ideas are more worth hearing than others.

Yet content and viewpoint discrimination, as well as judgments of value, are acceptable in universities, so long as they serve educational and research purposes. The difficulty is that universities typically undertheorize the relationship between student-invited speakers and its own education and research mission.[70] Universities might support student-invited speakers because they wish to empower students to pursue research interests different from those offered by faculty. Or universities might support student-invited speakers because they wish to create a diverse and heterogeneous campus climate in which students can learn the democratic skills necessary to negotiate a public sphere filled with alien and cacophonous voices. Universities may wish to educate students in practices of citizenship by encouraging a wide variety of student groups to invite outside speakers to recreate within the campus a marketplace of ideas.

As universities clarify *why* they authorize student-invited outside speakers, they will concomitantly clarify the circumstances in which the communication of such speakers is and is not appropriate. The First Amendment rights of invited speakers are irrelevant to this clarification. The question is how policies that authorize students to invite speakers to campus do and do not advance institutional purposes of education and the expansion of knowledge. It is mistaken to invoke freedom of speech principles to pre-empt this inquiry.

Apart from the question of invited speakers, recent years have witnessed controversies about the regulation of student speech that occurs off campus and that does not arise in the context of university activities. Often the rationale given for such regulation is the protection of the campus "environment" from hostile racist or misogynist influences.[71] But as the connection between off-campus student speech and the campus environment grows more tenuous, this rationale becomes more difficult to credit. Freedom of speech principles become a concomitantly more attractive lens of analysis.

In such circumstances, analysis must begin from the premise that if student speech has literally no connection with a university's mission, either positive or negative, then a university cannot justify regulating that speech by a purposive account of its own goals.[72] The fact that universities are nevertheless reaching out to regulate off-campus behavior suggests that they in fact do believe that it somehow relates to their educational mission. I suspect that this is because a new definition of educational goals is now emerging. Student pleas for "safe spaces" and for expurgated environments reflect a desire for universities to adopt an educational commitment that can properly be called in loco parentis.

If universities were indeed to formulate their educational mission in this way, they would accept the obligation to educate the *entire* student, not just those aspects of students that directly interact with the university environment.

Just as parents assert control over every dimension of their children's lives, so universities under an in loco parentis conception of their educational mission would not compartmentalize distinct aspects of their students' lives. They would seek comprehensively to educate persons who are students. Hence, if universities adopt an in loco parentis conception of education, they might be justified in asserting jurisdiction over all aspects of student speech, including speech off campus and seemingly unrelated to university matters.[73]

This comprehensive educational ambition was rejected by most universities in the 1960s. Its resurrection now is neither well understood nor widely accepted. University efforts to regulate student speech based on this account of their educational mission are hotly disputed.[74] Ultimately, however, this controversy cannot be resolved by the classic First Amendment tradition; it can be settled only by clarifying the educational mission of universities, which is a challenge well worth meeting.

Public Universities

I have so far discussed freedom of speech in the context of universities in general. But public universities are state institutions that must abide by the First Amendment. It is therefore tempting to believe that ordinary principles of freedom of speech should (at a minimum) apply in the context of public universities.

Public universities, however, no less than private ones, are designed to serve particular purposes. All government institutions established to achieve particular goals must regulate speech as necessary to achieve those goals, on pain of becoming ineffective.[75] That is why, in the context of higher education, the Court has explicitly announced that "a university's mission is education" and that the First Amendment does not deny a university's "authority to impose reasonable regulations compatible with that mission upon the use of its campus and facilities,"[76] which includes "a university's right to exclude . . . First Amendment activities that . . . substantially interfere with the opportunity of other students to obtain an education."[77]

If state universities could not regulate speech as required to achieve their mission, they would be forced to abstain from content discrimination; they would be compelled to treat all ideas equally; they would be disabled from compelling speech. Neither private nor public universities could function under such severe constraints. Public universities, no less than private ones, must evaluate the competence of both students and faculty; they must compel students and faculty to speak; they must routinely and pervasively engage in content discrimination. FIRE and overblown public rhetoric notwithstanding, it makes little sense to apply core First Amendment principles of freedom of speech to public universities.

The constitutional question for public universities is thus whether and how communicative restraints are necessary to realize the twin objectives of research and education. The fullest account we have of the relationship between freedom of expression and the achievement of these objectives is contained within the long and distinguished tradition of *academic freedom*, which starkly contrasts with ordinary principles of First Amendment doctrine. Academic freedom turns on judgments of competence, whereas ordinary First Amendment principles forbid such judgments. Academic freedom protects the autonomy of a profession, whereas First Amendment rights protect the freedom of individuals. Because public universities must achieve the purposes for which they are created, First Amendment doctrine as applied to them is best conceived within the functional framework that informs principles of academic freedom.

First Amendment restraints on public universities are therefore most difficult to understand when the requirements of academic freedom are most obscure. Many contemporary controversies involving freedom of expression on university campuses simply do not implicate academic freedom, as it is traditionally understood. In such circumstances First Amendment analysis must revert to first principles. It must begin from the premise that public universities may regulate speech as necessary to achieve their institutional objectives.

This raises the constitutionally difficult question of how the mission of public higher education is to be understood. It is true that the Constitution contains no explicit account of this mission, but whenever speech is regulated within the context of a government institution, this same basic constitutional question of mission is raised.[78] In the context of public universities, we can make it visible in a relatively simple case. Suppose students march through campus chanting, "No means yes; yes means anal."[79]

Traditional principles of academic freedom do not tell us much about how to handle such a demonstration. It is clear that such a demonstration could not be excluded from a public park, because it would be protected by the cardinal rules of First Amendment jurisprudence. The march would be deemed public discourse and immunized from regulation despite its offensive and outrageous nature. But because public universities are not public parks, and because they are dedicated to the mission of educating their students, the constitutional inquiry whether student demonstrations of this nature seriously interfere with the educational mission of a public university cannot be evaded.

Ordinary First Amendment doctrine concerning offensive or outrageous speech is not helpful with regard to this inquiry, because such doctrine is rooted in the requirements of self-governance in the context of a heterogeneous nation.[80] Instead, a court must determine the nature of a public university's educational mission and the extent to which student demonstrations of this kind obstruct that mission.[81] These are no doubt truly difficult issues, but classic First Amendment doctrine does not help us resolve them.[82]

Conclusion

Modern debates rely heavily on the constitutional rhetoric of freedom of speech because in recent years so many have contended that First Amendment protections ought to be applied to "speech as such"[83] rather than to public discourse. This tendency derives from a failure to understand the *purposive* nature of First Amendment rights. Because communication inheres in all aspects of life, this failure poses a great threat to the classic First Amendment tradition. The predictable overextension of First Amendment rights will in the long run prove unsustainable. We ought to stop traveling down that path while there is still time. Contemporary controversies about the regulation of speech within universities well illustrate the danger.

Keeping Secrets

DAVID A. STRAUSS*

Late on an October night in 1969, at a time when people were demonstrating against the Vietnam War in American cities, Daniel Ellsberg stuffed his briefcase with papers and walked out of the office building where he worked, past a security guard who should have inspected the briefcase but didn't. Ellsberg was an employee of the RAND Corporation, a contractor that was working for the US Department of Defense. The papers in Ellsberg's briefcase were part of a seven thousand page document entitled *History of U.S. Decision Making Process on Vietnam*. It was classified top secret. Ellsberg spent the next several hours making photocopies of the pages he'd taken; he used a photocopying machine at a friend's advertising agency. Then he returned to his office, early in the morning, and put the documents back in a safe. He did the same thing on another night, and another, for weeks, until he had several photocopies of the entire document.[1]

History of U.S. Decision Making Process on Vietnam came to be known as the Pentagon Papers, and Ellsberg's late night copying led to one of the most important First Amendment cases in history. After trying, and failing, to get members of Congress who opposed the Vietnam War to publicize the Papers, Ellsberg eventually—in February 1971—gave them to a reporter for the *New York Times*. The *Times* spent weeks reviewing the Papers. Then on June 12, 1971, the *Times* published the first of a series of excerpts from the Papers. The *Washington Post* published excerpts on June 18. The federal government filed suit to enjoin the publication of the Papers, and the case reached the Supreme Court before the end of June.

The stakes were potentially very high, on both sides. The Pentagon Papers contained details of diplomatic negotiations, intelligence operations, and

* I am grateful to Lee Bollinger and Geoffrey Stone for very helpful comments, and to the Burton and Adrienne Glazov Faculty Fund for financial support.

military strategy. [The government asserted that publishing the Papers would cause irreparable harm to national security.]Allies would be unwilling to trust us with secrets; our battlefield opponents in the Vietnam War would gain an advantage; intelligence sources would be compromised; American lives would be lost. But at the same time, the Vietnam War was a consuming issue in national politics. Much of the material in the Papers reflected directly, and adversely, on the wisdom, candor, and morality of the US government's policy and could critically influence the national debate on Vietnam.

On June 30, the Court held that the publication of the Papers could not be enjoined.[2] Justice Potter Stewart's opinion laid down a standard that a majority of the Court agreed had to be met: [a court may not enjoin the publication of documents like the Pentagon Papers unless they will "surely result in direct, immediate, and irreparable damage to our Nation or its people."[3] Ellsberg's disclosure of the Papers was entirely unauthorized and, according to the government, a crime. But the Supreme Court held that once the *Times* and *Post* got hold of the Papers, they had a nearly absolute right to publish them.[4]

Doubts

The Pentagon Papers case—officially, *New York Times Co. v. United States*—has stood, since then, as a cornerstone of the American law of freedom of expression. But the ground underneath that cornerstone—never quite as secure as it might have seemed—has shifted in recent decades. There is a legitimate question whether the First Amendment principles that the Pentagon Papers case established should still govern issues about the disclosure of government secrets and, if not, what should replace those principles.

The Pentagon Papers Paradox

Every government has to be able to keep secrets. Sometimes those secrets are about matters in which the public has little or no legitimate interest—private individuals' tax returns, for example, or the identities of undercover law enforcement agents. But sometimes, as in the case of the Pentagon Papers, there may be legitimate interests both in secrecy and in public knowledge. [Disclosing some information—it might be a planned government policy, or internal deliberations of government officials, or intelligence that the government has learned—might both interfere with the government's ability to do its work and, at the same time, inform citizens about a critical issue of public policy in a way that makes it possible for the people to hold the government accountable.] Paradox

This conflict, between the government's need to keep secrets and the people's need to know what the government is doing, involves values that are at the heart of democracy—and of the First Amendment. The central purpose of the First Amendment is to allow free debate about government policy.

When the government withholds information that can be used in that debate, it undermines, to that extent, the system that the First Amendment is supposed to protect. But the government may have legitimate reasons to withhold such information.

How should this conflict be resolved? The Pentagon Papers case held that, once the information was in the hands of the *Times* and the *Post*, they could not be stopped from publishing it. The *Times* and *Post* had a nearly absolute right to publish the information that they had. But the Supreme Court did not hold that the public had a right to that information in any other sense. It did not hold that Ellsberg was entitled to do what he did. The government's criminal prosecution of Ellsberg himself fell apart, but the government has successfully prosecuted employees for disclosing classified information. The First Amendment generally allows a government employee who discloses information without permission to be fired. In some circumstances, the government can impose financial penalties on employees for unauthorized disclosures even of unclassified information.[5]

If Ellsberg had not leaked the Papers, there would have been no way for the *Times* or the *Post* to get them. No one could have forced the government to hand over the Papers. The Freedom of Information Act (FOIA) gives individuals the right to demand records from the federal government in some circumstances, but classified documents are exempt. So while the Pentagon Papers case ringingly endorsed the right of the *Times* and the *Post* to publish the Papers, free from government interference, once they had them in their possession, nothing in the Supreme Court's decision entitled the newspapers to get them from the government in the first place.

These are the First Amendment principles about government secrets that the Pentagon Papers case has given us. Looked at from one angle, the Pentagon Papers system is irrational. Whether critical information reaches the public depends on the fortuity of whether there is someone, like Ellsberg, who is willing to run the risk of being a leaker. Under the Pentagon Papers case, the government can do what it wants to prevent the leak. It can carefully select who has access to the information, monitor those who do, and threaten them with serious consequences if they leak. If the government succeeds, the secrets remain secret, even if the public interest in disclosure is great. But if, despite the government's efforts, there is a leak, and the information reaches the newspapers, there is almost no way to prevent it from being publicized throughout the world, even if the government had no legal obligation to make it public in the first place.

An orderly society, one might think, should have a means of deciding what information may be kept secret and what information should be made public. Some adjudicator, a court for example, should hear arguments on both sides and make a decision about whether the government's interest in secrecy outweighs the public interest in disclosure. If the decision were that the government is entitled to keep the information secret, then the government really would be able to keep it secret. Not only would it be able to prevent its employees from disclosing the information and punish them if they did, the government could, contrary to the holding of the Pentagon Papers case, get a court order forbidding publication by the newspapers or anyone else. But if the decision were that the interest in disclosure outweighed the government's interest in secrecy, then the government would be required to release the information officially, no leaking needed.

No adjudicator is perfect, so undoubtedly there would be mistakes in a system like this. But, one might say, how can it be worse than a system in which everything turns on whether there is an Ellsberg—that is, an Ellsberg who has good judgment about what should be leaked—and a careless security guard? The Pentagon Papers case put the Supreme Court's imprimatur on a system in which the vital and difficult choice between the government's claims to secrecy and citizens' claims to knowledge is resolved by the happenstance of whether someone leaked.

And yet: that system seems to have worked. We can only say "seems" because, in the nature of things, we cannot know. We don't know whether it would have been better on balance for there to have been more leaks or fewer over the last several decades. There are too many uncertainties and contingencies to have definite conclusions about any of this. But there does seem to be a general sense that the system worked reasonably well. For what it's worth, there is evidence, for example, that, despite the government's claims during the Pentagon Papers litigation, disclosing the Papers did not seriously harm the national interest.

It is hard to believe that *exactly* the right amount of leaking and publication has taken place since the Pentagon Papers decision. Undoubtedly there have been some secrets that should have come to light because they would have informed the public debate without causing serious damage to the government. And it is likely that some leaks actually did damage legitimate government interests to a degree that outweighed their value in political debate. But while of course there have always been complaints from government officials about leaks and complaints from the media about secrecy, there do not seem to be signs of deep dissatisfaction with the Pentagon Papers solution—at least until recently.

There is also a plausible explanation of why the Pentagon Papers solution worked. It is illustrated by the leak of the Papers itself. Leaking is costly and risky. Ellsberg spent night after night sneaking the Papers out of his office and standing over the photocopying machine. He knew he was putting himself in legal jeopardy. His leak was the opposite of a casual or thoughtless act. Maybe more important, he understood the significance of the material he was leaking. He helped prepare the Papers, and he had been involved in decisions about national security policy for much of his career. He was in a position to know both the risks of leaking—to himself and to national security—and the rewards. [If a person in that position leaks, there is reason to think that the leak is justified— not in every case or in every respect, of course, but as a general proposition.] → not malicious

On the receiving end, the editors at the *Times* and the *Post* who published the Papers also did not act casually or thoughtlessly. [They reviewed the Papers and decided not to publish parts that they thought would jeopardize national security] Media outlets like the *Times*, the *Post,* and major TV networks will—when presented with leaked information—give government officials an opportunity to persuade them not to publish. Under the Pentagon Papers case, the final decision to publish rests with the media outlet. But that decision will be the result of a process that takes into account the government's interests in secrecy, as well as the public's interest in disclosure.   b) just w/o g'vt regulation

So—one could say—the Pentagon Papers decision really did leave us with a reasonable process. If there is a leak, quite possibly there *should* have been a leak, given the leaker's knowledge and incentives. And if there is publication, it is the product of a decision by editors who want to see themselves as acting in the public interest. Obviously the rationality of this process can be overstated. Leakers can act out of spite or vanity, or they might know less about the importance of the material they are leaking than they think they do. Editors have abundant commercial motivations that might cause them to act in ways inconsistent with the public interest. But the process is not as irrational as it might at first seem.

The New World

That arguably satisfactory equilibrium may no longer exist. In particular, some of the protections of secrecy that are built into the Pentagon Papers system have eroded, or even disappeared. Today, if you want to leak, you do not have to sneak a briefcase past a security guard or spend nights at the photocopying machine; Edward Snowden allegedly downloaded 1.7 million documents onto a handful of thumb drives.[6] Paper copies of the Pentagon Papers were locked in file cabinets and accessible only to people who could physically grab them; digital records can be transmitted with a few keystrokes by anyone who has credentials (or by someone who hacks in, but that is a separate issue from leaking).

Partly because the government expanded the national security establishment dramatically after September 11, many more people have access to those digital records. During the period when he was downloading documents, for example, Snowden, an employee of private firms that contracted with the government, decided that he would like to have access to more documents than his IT job gave him. So he changed jobs and went to work for a different private contractor (apparently accepting a pay cut) so that he could get hold of still more hundreds of thousands of documents.[7] And unlike Ellsberg—who knew what was in the Papers and had an idea about how damaging they might, or might not, be—the people who have access to secret government records today are more likely to have only a vague sense of what is in those records and how significant their disclosure would be. Snowden leaked because he was concerned about government surveillance programs. But Snowden, unlike Ellsberg, was not deeply knowledgeable about the materials he was leaking. He had no particular background or training that would enable him to evaluate either whether the government was acting wrongly or how damaging the release of the information might be. He had access to all that information not because he was an expert but because he was an IT guy.

The limits provided by mainstream media outlets like the *Times* and *Post* have also eroded, or disappeared. Anyone can post material on the internet. Sites like WikiLeaks serve as aggregators and have their own agendas.[8] WikiLeaks did, at one point, ask a US official if there was material, in a batch of documents that it was planning to disclose, that would harm specific individuals.[9] But it showed no sense of an institutional obligation systematically to consult with officials about the release of government secrets. Beyond that, it is now much easier for entities operating entirely outside the United States—most of WikiLeaks infrastructure is outside of the United States—to obtain and circulate damaging information.[10] So even if the First Amendment permitted the government to enjoin publication of some information, the government might be unable to do so.

These changes have the effect of making leaks more likely, more extensive, more highly publicized, and potentially more damaging. But the harm is not only the risk of excessive disclosure. There is a backlash too that creates a risk of too little disclosure. The government can no longer count on the built-in limits that existed at the time of the Pentagon Papers—the difficulty and cost of leaking, and the willingness of the media to cooperate to some degree with the government. Whether information is kept secret or is revealed to the world might depend entirely on whether a marginal government employee has been deterred by the existing penalties for leaks.

In these circumstances, the government—even if it is operating in good faith, with a proper respect for the importance of keeping the public informed—is likely to be more aggressive in dealing with leaks. Because the other checks have eroded, it has become more important, as far as the government is concerned, to prevent leaks, including by punishing leakers to deter them. The threat of criminal prosecution may be the only way to prevent the worldwide disclosure of information.

The Obama administration, for example, is said to have punished more people for leaking classified information than all previous administrations combined.[11]

James Risen, a *New York Times* investigative reporter, called the Obama administration "the greatest enemy of press freedom in a generation." Bob Schieffer, a CBS Washington correspondent, is quoted as saying: "Whenever I'm asked what is the most manipulative and secretive administration I've covered, I always say it's the one in office now. . . . This administration exercises more control than George W. Bush's did, and his before that." It is unlikely that the Obama administration was just more authoritarian or paranoid than its predecessor (which was in turn more so than its predecessor, and so on), or that the Obama administration had a perverse interest in antagonizing the *New York Times* or CBS News. The more likely explanation is that things have changed in a way that has made damaging leaking more likely, and the government has responded in the way that it thought it needed to, in order to protect its interests. And it is possible, of course, that the government has—or will, at some point in the future—overreacted and deterred leaks to a degree that is damaging to democracy.

It would be magical thinking to suppose that the Pentagon Papers equilibrium was ideal—that it produced just the right amount of publicity for just the right government secrets. But there is good reason to think that the new world is worse. Government officials always complain about leaks, and for obvious reasons it is difficult for anyone on the outside to evaluate just how damaging an unauthorized disclosure is. In general, only the officials who have access to sensitive information will be in a position to make an informed judgment about how much damage, if any, was done, at least until a long time has passed. But the Obama administration—which in other contexts showed no lack of respect for free expression, and which had generally good relations with the mainstream press—thought that leaks were enough of a problem to justify an unprecedented level of enforcement. And many of the leaks in recent years, like those of Snowden and Chelsea Manning, were of such a large scale, and were so indiscriminate, that it's plausible to think there was a genuine problem that went beyond a few specific cases. Responsible members of the media, meanwhile, are concerned about the government's reaction. All of this suggests that, because it is so much easier now to acquire secret information and transmit it widely, the Pentagon Papers system is no longer working very well.

Are there ways in which the law, including the law of the First Amendment, might be adjusted to deal with the erosion of the checks that at least seemed to make the Pentagon Papers system bearable? These issues are, of course, fraught with uncertainty, both empirical and normative. Just as it is hard to know whether the Pentagon Papers equilibrium was satisfactory, it will be hard to gauge the effects of any changes in the law; beyond that, there is no consensus on what the right amount of disclosure is. The government has to be allowed to keep some secrets; it is very likely that some things the government wants to keep secret should, in fact, see the light of day; but we don't know exactly where the line is and would not be confident in our ability to get there even if we did.

A New System?

In these circumstances, maybe the best we can do is to try to find ways to modify existing laws and institutions to recreate something like the balance that the Pentagon Papers system struck—to replace the limits that have eroded because of changes in the way information is kept and transmitted. At least three possibilities seem to be worth considering. One would be to try to use the courts to address directly, perhaps under the First Amendment, the question of when information should be disclosed. A second would be to insist, either as a matter of constitutional law under the First Amendment or by changing applicable statutes, that the limits on disclosures by people who have access to sensitive government information be more discriminating—that those limits try to distinguish between acceptable and unacceptable leaks. In principle, that would enable more vigorous enforcement against leakers, and even against the media, but only in circumstances in which the leaks were damaging. A third possibility would be to provide more extensive protection to more responsible media outlets while allowing the government to take action against others.

1. *A new bargain: a First Amendment right of access to government information, coupled with more limits on unauthorized publication.* Rather than relying on a balance of competing forces, as the Pentagon Papers solution does, this approach would have courts decide when information should be made public. Authorized disclosures could, in general, then be publicized by anyone. But any unauthorized disclosures, including by the press, would be unlawful and could be enjoined or could result in criminal prosecutions.

This would be an effort to rationalize the system, so that the information that should be publicized is publicized and information that should not be isn't. Media outlets, or anyone else, could sue the government to force it to disclose information; a government employee who thought information should be disclosed could sue instead of leaking. If the government claimed that disclosure would be harmful, a court would evaluate that claim. But in return, some of the protection that the Pentagon Papers decision gave the media would be weakened: the government could take action against anyone who published unauthorized disclosures.

The underlying idea is that there would be a new bargain between the media and the government. The media would have a more robust right to force the government to disclose information. They would not have to rely on fortuity of a leak. The media could be confident that information they received in this way is accurate and complete; there is no assurance of that when information is leaked. So media outlets would be spared the cost of confirming the information conveyed in a leak and the risk that they would convey distorted information. Leakers, of course, often have motives other than the disinterested desire to inform the public about important facts. In the current system, the media can be used as a way of carrying out the private agenda of a leaker. If the decision to disclose secrets were made by a court, instead of by a leaker, there would be less risk of that.] Gain this.

In exchange for those benefits[the media would accept that the government will be able to take stronger actions than it can now against unauthorized disclosures by the media. Those actions could include what the Pentagon Papers case almost always forbids, an injunction against the publication of information that the government was entitled to keep secret. It could also include, for example, requiring reporters to disclose the sources of unauthorized disclosures. The First Amendment, as currently interpreted, does not forbid the government from doing that, but the government pays a political price because media outlets object so strongly. An explicit judicial decision that certain information should not be disclosed would also help legitimate more extensive enforcement by the government.] Lose this.

The first part of this system—a right to sue the government for access to information—exists in limited form today, but under FOIA, not the Constitution. Current First Amendment rights of access are very limited. FOIA is a statute, so Congress controls what is disclosed, and, as I mentioned earlier, classified information is exempt from disclosure. In principle, courts can review whether information is properly classified, but courts give great deference to the government's classification decisions. A First Amendment disclosure regime could use FOIA as the starting point, but the First Amendment right would be more expansive.

The idea of a First Amendment right of access to government information is not new, but there are obvious problems, many of which already exist under FOIA. It is time-consuming for government agencies to comply with broad requests for information. There are difficult issues (which also arise under FOIA and elsewhere) about sharing highly sensitive information with judges so that they can evaluate the competing claims. Agencies' responses to requests may not be complete, and it will be hard for courts to make sure that they are.

Most important, courts might make the wrong decision—in either direction—about whether information that the government wants to keep secret should be disclosed. Answering that question—that is, deciding just how risky it might be to disclose information—might require a court to consider a lot of contextual information that it cannot easily gather or evaluate. Insufficient disclosure seems like a greater risk than excessive disclosure, because the government has obvious advantages in a dispute about whether information should become public. Damage to national security, or to other important government interests, often seems more concrete and threatening; benefits to public debate are generally more speculative and remote. Also, because the government has more information, and usually more credibility, it will be hard to refute the government's claims about the damage that a disclosure might cause. It will obviously be difficult for a media outlet to argue that secret information should be released when, necessarily, it does not know very much about what that information is. Those are the reasons that the FOIA right of access is not so robust, at least when national security information is at stake.

Structural difficulties

Beyond that, some of the same changes in the media ecosystem that undermine the Pentagon Papers model also make a judicially enforceable right of access less workable than it might have been a generation ago. Major media outlets today face greater competition and, as a result, are stretched thinner financially. Litigation is expensive, especially when the government is determined to resist a claim, and it is far from clear that many media outlets will have the resources, or the commitment, to assert a right to disclosure in court.

The question, though, is not whether a system that coupled a First Amendment right of access to government information with more extensive enforcement against the media would be ideal; it is whether such a system would be superior to what we have now, with the Pentagon Papers balance upset by changes in the way information is kept and circulated. Of course, even with a new system of this kind, there would still be leaks, and there would still be unauthorized publication. But if the First Amendment right of access were taken seriously by courts, a government employee or whistleblower would not have to reveal vast quantities of information. It would be enough to leak something that would give someone—a media outlet, a public interest group, or anyone who could support litigation—an idea about what demand to make of the government in court. There would also be incentives for both sides to settle to avoid an adverse decision. The government would be more confident that, by agreeing to disclose a certain amount, it could limit further disclosures; the media would know that they could publish free of any fear of enforcement action.

The specifics would have to be worked out. Exactly what criteria would courts use in deciding whether the First Amendment required disclosure? What kinds of enforcement actions against unauthorized publication would be permitted, and upon what kind of showing? Would this system require a specialized court, both so that secrets could be disclosed, securely, to the judges and so that the judges would have the background and training needed to evaluate whether public disclosure was warranted? But it does not seem obvious that such a system would be worse than what we have now.

Incentives still but worth exploring?

2. *Better-defined, and more balanced, prohibitions against disclosure.* The most important criminal statute forbidding leaks is the Espionage Act of 1917.[12] That statute makes it a crime to transmit "information relating to the national defense" to "any person not entitled to receive it" if the person who has that information "has reason to believe [it] could be used to the injury of the United States or to the advantage of any foreign nation"[13] Other statutes contain more specific prohibitions, for example, on disclosing classified information related to communications and cryptography,[14] and on disclosing the identity of covert agents.[15]

None of these statutes is designed to deal generally either with leaks or with the publication of leaked information by a media outlet. Espionage, of course, is different from a leak to a newspaper: espionage is a clandestine disclosure of information to a foreign power for it to use, not a disclosure intended for publication. The wording of the Espionage Act, though, seems broad enough to reach disclosures to news media, and lower courts have held both that a leak to a publication violated the Espionage Act and that prosecuting the leaker under the Espionage Act did not violate the First Amendment.[16]

It is generally assumed that the Pentagon Papers decision forbids the government from prosecuting media outlets for publishing leaks, except perhaps in extraordinary circumstances. The Supreme Court did not actually say that; its opinions were limited to the issue before it, which was whether a court order could enjoin the Papers from publishing. In fact, Justice White, who agreed that a court could not order the *Times* and *Post* to stop publishing, suggested in his opinion that the newspapers might nonetheless be prosecuted under the Espionage Act.[17] Historically, "prior restraints" have been a central concern of the First Amendment, so there was a basis for Justice White's suggestion that speech that could not be enjoined (an injunction is a prior restraint) could nonetheless be punished (criminal punishment comes along after the fact). But today, it is hard to explain why that distinction should matter. A "prior restraint" like a court order does not physically restrain someone from doing something; a person who violates a court order will be punished afterward for contempt of court. There are some differences between being punished for contempt of court for violating a court order and being punished for violating a criminal statute—among other things, a defendant in a criminal prosecution is entitled to a jury trial, unlike a person charged with contempt of court. That difference loomed large when the distinction between prior restraints and criminal prosecutions was originally emphasized, centuries ago, but it matters much less today. There are some other differences as well, but after the Supreme Court's ringing endorsement of the First Amendment rights of the *Times* and the *Post* in the Pentagon Papers case, it would have been very surprising if the Court had allowed the editors to be sent to jail, and the general understanding of that case is that it would not have allowed criminal prosecutions either.[18]

This just heightens the paradox of the Pentagon Papers solution, however. At least under lower court decisions, an individual who leaks information to a reputable newspaper reporter might be punished under the Espionage Act, a statute designed to deal with spies and traitors. But a media outlet that discloses that information to the world has a First Amendment right to escape punishment. Of course, a government employee or contractor who is entrusted with sensitive information is not in the same position as a reporter who gets a leak; the reporter has not breached an implicit or explicit promise to the government to keep the secrets. But as far as the public interest is concerned, the question is why it makes sense to threaten serious punishment to prevent information from being leaked and then allow the same information to be published widely, once a media outlet has come into possession of the leak.

All of this—coupled with the fact that there is no general antileaking statute— suggests that we need a better-designed system of prohibitions against leaks. The statutes that enact these prohibitions will be shaped by First Amendment principles. Apart from the Pentagon Papers case itself, and a decision upholding the statute that forbids the disclosure of the identity of covert agents,[19] the Supreme Court has not said much that bears directly on when the First Amendment permits prosecutions for revealing sensitive national security information. So there may be room to work out a sensible balancing of the interests if, as I've said, the Pentagon Papers settlement no longer holds. And, as always in this area, a balancing of competing important interests is the order of the day: too much disclosure and too little disclosure are, each in its own way, damaging to the foundations of democracy.

A new system of prohibitions should have three features:

(a) It must not be too sweeping or draconian. Sometimes leaks are good; we do not want a system in which there are never any unauthorized disclosures. We don't have that kind of confidence in the government's decisions about what information to keep secret. If we did, the Pentagon Papers case would have come out the other way. But the nature and amount of unauthorized disclosure will be determined not just by the scope of a statute—that is, by what the statute criminalizes—but also by the punishment that the statute threatens. Severe punishment will cause individuals to steer clear of any disclosure that might possibly be seen, after the fact, to be illegal, even if it actually is not.

So unlike the Espionage Act, for example, a criminal statute that is well designed to deal with leaks should not treat them all alike. Particularly damaging ones might be punished more severely than leaks that are unlikely to be damaging. To some extent our current system does that, through the exercise of discretion by prosecutors and sentencing judges (and sentencing guidelines). But explicit norms would be better than a system that depends entirely on the discretion of individual officials.

Beyond that, a system of criminal prohibitions has to take into account the possibility that the government will sometimes not act in good faith and, in fact, might sometimes engage in a systematic effort to suppress speech—including leaks—not for legitimate reasons but because the speech is politically threatening. The First Amendment exists, after all, partly to deal with just that possibility. Sweeping laws and, perhaps even more so, the threat of severe punishment lend themselves to government efforts like that. In principle, the rules against selective prosecutions by the government—against, for example, using prosecutions as a weapon against political enemies—can provide a safeguard against actions like those, but selective prosecution claims are notoriously hard to establish.

(b) There should be a defense for whistleblowing or a leak reasonably intended to disclose wrongdoing, but it should be designed in a way that encourages leakers to be careful about exactly what they leak. One of the things that makes the outcome of the Pentagon Papers case so appealing is that Ellsberg was a conscientious leaker. He knew what was in the Pentagon Papers; he was in a good position to determine how damaging, if at all, his leak would be; and he deliberately withheld some of the materials because he thought their disclosure would be too harmful to the government's legitimate interests.[20] By the same token, one of the things that is so troubling about more recent leaks, like Snowden's and Manning's, is that the leaks disclosed large amounts of information, assembled relatively indiscriminately, and the leakers did not have the expertise or knowledge to evaluate how damaging their leaking might be.

It would be a mistake to suggest that a government employee or contractor, no matter how knowledgeable or expert, should routinely appoint himself or herself the ultimate judge about what government secrets should be disclosed. One of the changes that has undermined the Pentagon Papers equilibrium is precisely that so much more highly sensitive information can now be leaked by employees and contractors who are not very familiar with it—and some of those individuals, just as a matter of probabilities, will have bad judgment about when a leak might be appropriate and how damaging a leak will be. There are, in any event, whistleblower provisions already built into the law, although they seem to be of limited value in dealing with leaks.[2] But it is still worth trying to differentiate among leakers in deciding what should be punished, so that a carefully limited disclosure that reveals illegality or the abuse of power is not treated in the same way as a massive and indiscriminate leak.

(c) There should be restrictions on the media, linked to the restrictions on leakers. This is, of course, a break with a central principle of the Pentagon Papers settlement, according to which leaks can be punished but subsequent publication by a media outlet cannot. But, to reiterate, what made that settlement plausible was the self-restraint and public spiritedness of the major media outlets, who were the only ones able to reach large numbers of people. So the object of a criminal prohibition should be to encourage anyone who might publicize a leak to exercise the same kind of discretion and concern for the public interest.

It might even make sense to impose the same standards on media outlets as are imposed on leakers. Disclosing secret information would be unlawful, but the definition of that category of information would not be too broad, and the punishments would not be uniformly harsh. A reasonable claim that the information that was publicized revealed wrongdoing should cause a publication to be treated differently from one that disclosed information indiscriminately. This kind of linking of the media outlets to leakers might even be accomplished through established criminal law principles, like the law of conspiracy (especially if the media outlet had some role in encouraging or facilitating the leak) or accessory after the fact.

As a practical matter, the government is unlikely to try to prosecute media outlets like the *Times* and the *Post*. Established publications like those will be careful about what they publish. They will have the resources both to examine material before they publish it, so as to reduce the chances that they are damaging legitimate government interests, and to defend themselves if they should be prosecuted. And of course the political costs to the government of proceeding against an established media outlet will ordinarily be very great. President Nixon, by all accounts, despised the *Washington Post* in particular, but his Department of Justice did not take Justice White's suggestion that it could prosecute the *Post*'s editors.

Protect these too ←

The bigger concern is with media outlets that are less well established, that lack resources, that have a more aggressive orientation than the *New York Times*, but that are still more or less responsible organizations. Outlets like those can flourish today in a way that was unthinkable when the Pentagon Papers case was decided, and that is potentially a very valuable contribution to the system of free expression. The Pentagon Papers settlement, with its lack of restrictions on publication by media outlets once they got hold of leaked information, made sense because of the self-restraint of newspapers like the *Times* and the *Post*, and the tendency of the people in charge of those newspapers to share the general outlook of government officials in many respects. Seen from another angle, though, those are potential weaknesses. The people who run established media outlets might be too deferential to the government, especially if they are generally sympathetic to an administration and think well of its officials.

In those circumstances, especially, there is an important role for media upstarts who will publish information that might otherwise not see the light of day. For those less well-established outlets, the threat of a criminal prosecution is a death threat; they might be unable to survive the initiation of a prosecution, even if they would have prevailed in the end. Ideally one would like to trust the discretion of government prosecutors, but of course the point of a constitutional protection like the First Amendment is that one cannot always trust the government not to overreact or act in less than good faith. So there are real dangers. It does not seem tenable, though, to disable the government from acting against outlets that undermine the national security by recklessly, or in furtherance of a hostile agenda, publishing information that should be kept secret.

3. *A differentiation among media outlets?* That last point raises the possibility of making a distinction, for First Amendment purposes, among media outlets. The Pentagon Papers equilibrium made sense to the extent that newspapers like the *Times* and the *Post* could be counted on to act responsibly. If you wanted to re-create that equilibrium, one obvious step would be to provide a stronger set of First Amendment safeguards for media outlets that resembled those newspapers in that way.

There are equally obvious problems with taking this step. Having the government distinguish between responsible and irresponsible speakers seems antithetical to the First Amendment. At the limit, it invites a Potemkin system of free expression: disclosures and dissent from tame, established speakers will be tolerated, creating the appearance of a robust system of free speech, while the speakers who might truly challenge the status quo will be more easily silenced. And drawing a line like this among speakers is hard to reconcile with established First Amendment principles. A few early cases suggested that the protections for allegedly defamatory speech derived from *New York Times v. Sullivan* would apply only to the institutional press, not to all speakers, but the Court has repeatedly refused to make any such distinctions, in part because there is no apparent way to draw such a line.[22]

Nonetheless, it might be necessary for the government to operate with a distinction between responsible media outlets that are committed in some way to journalistic professionalism and other outlets that are not—and to be more willing to take enforcement actions against the latter. State "shield" laws that protect reporters from having to disclose their sources distinguish between journalists and others; there seems to be no consensus on what the definition should be, but those laws have to draw some such distinction or they would make too many criminal investigations impossible. Also, the same forces that undermined the Pentagon Papers settlement—it is much easier both to gather information and to publicize it than it was a decade or two ago—enable irresponsible speakers to invade individuals' privacy and threaten their security,[23] and that will create pressure for legislatures and courts to distinguish legitimate journalists from others.

At the very least, such a distinction, even if it could not be reduced to a rule enforceable in court, might guide the discretionary decisions that are a critical part of law enforcement and that the government will unavoidably make in dealing with leaks. In other contexts, prosecutors properly consider whether someone has generally acted responsibly and make decisions about whether to bring a prosecution partly on that ground. Even when First Amendment values are at stake—for example, when the government decides which media outlets will be given passes to official press conferences or have access to government facilities—the government makes such distinctions. There are obvious risks of abuse, when those judgments are influenced by the editorial positions of the particular media outlet or government officials' perception of whether they are getting fair coverage, and there is no question that those abuses have happened. There are also plenty of borderline cases, of semi-established outlets that have a fair claim to be treated like insiders. And a system like this will, other things equal, favor the established and traditional press over innovators. But there does not seem to be a plausible alternative.

Similar norms might apply—with similar risks—when the government is deciding how to enforce whatever prohibitions exist against publishing leaked information. In fact, the alternatives seem worse, so far as the values of free expression are concerned. In principle, the government's policy could be that it does not care whether a disclosure is made by the New York Times or by WikiLeaks; it will treat them both the same. But an unauthorized disclosure in the New York Times is more likely to have been vetted by editors both to ensure its accuracy and to minimize the damage it causes to legitimate public interests, so deterring or punishing the New York Times is likely to accomplish less and to do more harm. For all the obvious dangers, on balance this kind of differentiation among media outlets seems like the better way to proceed.

Conclusion

The Pentagon Papers case was a celebrated chapter in the history of the First Amendment, and the principle established by that case has become foundational. The government may keep its secrets, even if they concern matters of great public interest, by prohibiting people within the government from leaking them. But once they are leaked, a newspaper may not be enjoined from publishing those secrets, except in extraordinary circumstances. Abstractly, that principle seems hard to justify. Information should either be secret or be disclosed, one might say, and it does not make sense to have everything turn on the fortuity of whether the information has been leaked. But, while it is difficult to judge these matters with confidence, the system put in place by the Pentagon Papers decision seems to have worked in the past.

Today there is reason to think it is no longer working as well. There are more people in a position to leak information; it is easier to leak; and it is much easier to leak large amounts of highly sensitive information, as recent events have demonstrated. At the same time, the ability to spread that information throughout the world is not limited, as it was at the time of the Pentagon Papers case, to a handful of newspapers and television networks, run by people who took seriously their obligations to protect national security. We should consider some changes to the Pentagon Papers settlement to adapt to these new circumstances. A First Amendment right of access to government information, coupled with stricter limits on publication, is one possibility; more carefully designed prohibitions on both leaking and publication, treating careful and reasonable efforts to expose wrongdoing differently from more indiscriminate leaking in both contexts, is another; and a formal or informal differentiation among media outlets is yet another.

The issues are riddled with uncertainty, both empirical and normative. It is hard to know how well any system is working, or will work, and hard even to know what the right balance is in principle. But the stakes are great, on both sides, and the world has changed in ways that make it important to rethink the way we deal with this problem.

The First Amendment

An Equality Reading

CATHARINE A. MACKINNON*

Once a defense of the powerless, the First Amendment over the last hundred years has mainly become a weapon of the powerful. Legally, what was, toward the beginning of the twentieth century, a shield for radicals, artists and activists, Socialists and pacifists, the excluded and the dispossessed, has become a sword for authoritarians, racists and misogynists, Nazis and Klansmen, pornographers and corporations buying elections. In public discourse, freedom of speech has gone from a protection for dissenters from dominant power to a claimed protection of those with dominant power, of their hierarchical position, of hierarchy itself. It has gone from an entitlement of structurally unequal groups to expose their inequality and seek equal rights to a claim by dominant groups to continue to impose their hegemony.

[handwritten margin note: Used against its intended purpose]

In the speech itself, socially dominant groups promoting ideologies of social supremacy have solidified and enhanced their power through inaccurately but successfully positioning themselves as socially marginal powerless dissenters, or minimally as debaters just expressing ideas. As much public speech, from White supremacy through pornography to election rhetoric, has escalated in its abusiveness, markedly on social media, First Amendment law has increasingly blatantly sided with dominant status and power—economically wealthy and upper-class, White racist, and masculinist gendered voices. Voices challenging inequality, on campuses and in media, as well as on streets, in communities, and in courts, continue to be effectively muted and exposed to further abuse and

* The insightful contributions of Lori Watson, Max Waltman, and Lisa Cardyn are gratefully acknowledged, with the expert assistance of the University of Michigan Law Library and the support of the Cook Fund. This chapter is dedicated to the memory of Thomas I. Emerson.

This is what the First Amendment should be protected.

silenced through subordinating attacks, verbal and otherwise, in the name of freedom of speech.] How did this happen?

In law, the doctrinal pivot of this twisted development contains a vicious irony. The very First Amendment doctrine that has supported intensifying hierarchies of power in its results has its foundation in the application of a purported equality principle. Starting in the 1970s, the First Amendment began to build a doctrine of content neutrality, extended (where applicable) to viewpoint neutrality, that was said to be predicated on equality. Neutrality has become its principal tool, overwhelming even its few substantive recognitions. In fact, content neutrality, like gender neutrality or colorblindness under the Equal Protection Clause, is predicated on the abstract Aristotelian notion of formal equality, which can distinguish sameness from difference within a narrow range, one thing from another, but has proven incapable, absent the injection of substantive direction—considered nonneutral, hence nonprincipled—of reliably distinguishing social dominance from subordination: inequality as hierarchy.[1]

An inadequate theory of power, resulting in an incapacity to identify substantive inequality when it animates First Amendment cases—indeed, a resistance to identifying it—is thus a major part of the underlying story. Being unable to tell the difference between relative power and powerlessness—for instance, being unable to identify the deployment of racial and/or gender-based terrorism through historically unambiguous means, a determined blindness to reality—has become firmly entrenched in the First Amendment, and social discourse invoking it, as the virtue termed "neutrality," with the inevitable result of reflecting and reinforcing existing unequal social arrangements, namely, structures and practices of inequality, sometimes taking aggressive forms. The First Amendment, firmly ensconced within the liberal tradition, more or less exclusively recognizes power as residing in the State, which it sees as power's fountainhead. In liberalism, because power, rendered "coercive power," is seen as emanating from the State, and society absent intrusion by the State is deemed free, freedom—here freedom of speech—becomes about protecting existing social arrangements, which includes inequality of power in society, when the State intervenes to address it by means of, for example, civil laws against discrimination. As a result, statutes that aim (for example) to protect disempowered or discriminated-against social groups from inequality imposed through speech or expressive conduct, violent or otherwise, because they are statutes, turn those harmed by such conduct into actors with power, as if they *are* the State, rather than recognizing the statutes as attempted legal interventions on behalf of subordinated social groups in an attempt to shift or mitigate their inequality, or to shield them from its violent excesses. Society is overwhelmingly not grasped as a locus or source or fountainhead of power, hence of its inequality.

The absence of a substantive notion of equality is—in the guise of equality, no less—embedded in the First Amendment's doctrinal illusion of content neutrality (when few if any of its outcomes are neutral as to content), and in its associated doctrine of viewpoint neutrality (when viewpoints are typically present but buried), which is systematically implemented to protect "speech" that promotes substantive social inequality as it currently exists. In the law of freedom of speech, it also converts practices of inequality into expressions of the idea of inequality, transforming actionable discrimination into speech protectable from viewpoint discrimination. Opposition to discriminatory practices becomes censorship of thoughts or ideas on one side of a discussion. The crucial debate and judicial decision in this respect occurred from the mid-1980s to the late 1990s concerning the creation of civil claims for harms done through pornography recognized as sex discrimination.

Neutrality as a doctrinal approach can be seen to support the status quo distribution of power—that is, inequality, enforced by practices of discrimination, including expressive ones—under the First Amendment just as effectively as it largely does under the Equal Protection Clause, where neutrality became the mainstream doctrine during the same time period. Substantive inequality is all but invisible in First Amendment doctrine and commentary, although it is vividly visible in the facts of many First Amendment cases, if read through a substantive inequality lens. Discrimination, including through expressive acts of the powerful and advantaged, silences the speech of disadvantaged and subordinated groups, promotes their disadvantage, and actualizes their subordination. Realization of the potential role of the First Amendment in promoting substantive equality requires asymmetrically exposing harms of discrimination done by expressive means, permitting their careful restriction, and supporting expression by subordinated groups against their inequality.

I.

In the First Amendment dissents of the early twentieth century that became the North Star for its authoritative interpretation, alignments of power and powerlessness were, substantively speaking, correctly identified. Those the Court's dissenters sought to protect authentically needed their speech protected, for the reasons the Court's dissenters said they needed it. The defendants were principally critics of the State, needing protection from the State, the primary agenda of which was to protect itself through statutory prohibitions on dissent. As came to be recognized, the State did not need the protection the Supreme Court majorities of the era said it did; the people challenging the State did. This eventually resulted in the invalidation or vitiation of most of the statutes under which these defendants were prosecuted and the installation of the dissents as guiding precedent.   ↳ like Holmes' dissents

The vaunted tradition of speech-protective First Amendment case law, beginning in Justices Holmes and Brandeis' dissents[2] and growing through those by Justices Black and Douglas,[3] arose to protect political advocacy critical of the government from the power of the government to silence it through criminal law: censorship. The cases involved verbal opposition to governmental ideology or state policies, such as opposing the draft or enlistment in the military or advocating a change in the form of government, under state or federal criminal statutes. The principal concern of the statutes was "serious injury to the State," as to which, given the importance it was granted, a serious risk was enough. → "gravey issue

The vindicated dissents against the convictions of Abrams and Gitlow turned largely on a comparison of the powerlessness of the defendants with the powerfulness of the State; the defendants' advocacy should be protected, they argued, largely because it was relatively weak. The *Abrams* dissent would have allowed "the surreptitious publishing of a silly leaflet by an unknown man."[4] Dennis and his colleagues were described in the dissent as "miserable merchants of unwanted ideas; their wares remain unsold. The fact that their ideas are abhorrent does not make them powerful."[5] Communists "*as a political party* . . . are of little consequence."[6] The powerlessness of the speakers, hence of the speech, relative to the power of the State—the inequality between the parties—became baked into the First Amendment paradigm as a strong rationale for protecting the less powerful, as well as cogent evidence that there could be no "clear and present danger that this advocacy will succeed."[7] The Court's dissenters in these cases, laying the foundation of modern First Amendment law, clearly saw who needed protection and why in who had power and who did not. The relation between the parties was not expressed as an inequality, although it was one. The Supreme Court sustained this same substantive recognition of relative powerlessness as justifying First Amendment protection as late as 1982, invalidating a federal law compelling disclosure of campaign contributions applied to the Socialist Workers Party because it would likely devastate "a minor political party which historically has been the object of harassment by government officials and private parties."[8] History and substance—context, that is, the reality of less relative power—counted, as did discriminatory harassment.

Reality also mattered when the Supreme Court upheld a group defamation statute that embodied considerations of social inequality, although again the term was not used. The opinion for the Court by Justice Frankfurter in *Beauharnais v. Illinois* upheld a statute that prohibited portrayals of " 'depravity, criminality, unchastity, or lack of virtue of a class of citizens, of any race, color, creed or religion' " that " 'exposes the citizens of any race, color, creed or religion to contempt, derision, or obloquy or which is productive of breach of the peace or riots.'"[9] Finding the statute to be "specifically directed at a defined evil,"[10] the Court extended libel doctrine from individuals to groups, recognizing the status, opportunity, resource, and dignitary differentials of substantive inequality, refusing to deny that the legislature might believe "that a man's job and his educational opportunities and the dignity accorded him may depend as much on the reputation of the racial and religious group to which he willy-nilly belongs, as it does on his own merits."[11] This is equality thinking. Really, the statute prohibited practices of discrimination known to enact and promote substantive social inequalities on the concrete grounds the statute listed.[12]

Ominously, dissents by Black and Douglas condemned the Illinois law as censorship by transforming performances of bigotry into protected discussions of matters of public concern.[13] They also distinguished between *Chaplinsky's*[14] application of "fighting words" to individuals and to groups, not grasping that inequality is inherently collective even when visited on individuals, that all groups are made up of individuals, and that harm on group grounds exponentially expands harm to individuals. The liberals abstracted away the speech interest from its role in violent inequality, defending those with power—Whiteness was already supreme—as the conservatives, with the state legislature, aimed to protect the targets.

A watershed ruling in which the liberals' abstract speech template prevailed, as it has to this day, was *New York Times v. Sullivan* in 1964.[15] Cloaked in a vindication of the speech rights of equality seekers against racist officials, this decision actually empowered the media to publish inaccuracies. The *New York Times* had run a civil rights fundraising ad for Black leaders that described racist misbehavior by Southern White police officers. Based on inaccuracies in the ad, the *Times* was successfully sued for libel by the police commissioner under state law. In the Supreme Court, the newspaper successfully argued that more than inaccuracies should be required to sue for speech, establishing First Amendment hegemony over the law of libel, requiring for the first time not mere falsity, but "reckless disregard of whether it was false or not" to establish libel of public officials. Thereafter, a libel claimant has had to show that the publisher of defamation of a public figure knew the truth but ignored it.

The submerged substantive alignment pitted the Civil Rights movement against the police, but the case played out through its formal legal parties: the supposedly vulnerable mainstream media against the all-powerful state common law of libel. The civil rights speech at the case's factual foundation ignored, the Court proceeded as if the underlying substantive inequality between assertion of civil rights and official Southern police suppression of their pursuit—the equality content of the speech—was irrelevant, and placed a powerful entity, a mainstream media outlet, a colossus actually, in the victimized position of the powerless speaker in need of protection against the powerful state, represented by libel law. The *Times'* lawyer, Herbert Wechsler, had created "neutral principles of constitutional law"[16] in opposition to *Brown v. Board of Education,*[17] which combined explicit formal equality logic with an implicit substantive shift assuming the inherent equality of Black and White children—one greatly protested by Wechsler.[18] Ignoring the content of the speech made it unnecessary for the law or the public debate to consider whether the mighty power to publish defamatory falsehoods that publishers, which today include internet service providers, gained in the case might, as or more often, find the inequality shoe on the other foot. Thus was the speech of equality entirely sidelined as the law of libel was drastically weakened as a tool against published lies.

A similar elision of the content of substantive inequality occurred in *Brandenburg v. Ohio,*[19] another landmark speech case in which inequality drove the facts but was entirely ignored in the decision. There, a leader of a Ku Klux Klan group was convicted under a criminal syndicalism statute that was struck down, doubt was cast on *Abrams* and *Schenck,* and the new "incitement" test was created for measuring the relation between speech and the harm it caused.[20] The First Amendment's free speech guarantee, *Brandenburg* held, allows restriction of advocacy of force only where "such advocacy is directed to inciting or producing imminent lawless action and is likely to incite or produce such action."[21] The substance of the Klan's White supremacist advocacy—"derogatory of Negroes and, in one instance, of Jews,"[22] including the threat of violence in a speech on film stating that if existing government "'continues to suppress the white, Caucasian race, it's possible that there might have to be some revengeance taken'"[23]—with the Klan's well-known history of acting on such threats,[24] was ignored. A second speech contained the virulent "'Personally, I believe the n---er should be returned to Africa, the Jew returned to Israel,'"[25] quoted by the Court without noting the role of mass deportations in genocide, the ultimate substantive inequality. Legally protecting the White supremacist point of view, as this decision did, was not seen as state action on one side, the hierarchically dominant side, of a political issue or debate that has another side, the subordinated substantive inequality side. Conforming to the prior First Amendment template, the injury to subordinated peoples was reconfigured as injury to the State, such that advocating violent means to political and economic change "involves such danger to the security of the State that the State may outlaw it."[26]

Thus was the stage set for the rulings, and abdications of rulings, in a situation a step closer to genocide, that put an even finer legal point on the same substantive conflicts over inequality and their evasion under the First Amendment. In 1978, the Seventh Circuit, in an opinion on which certiorari was denied, invalidated a local ordinance against dissemination of materials that promoted hatred on the basis of race, national origin, or religion, and permitted Nazis to march in brown uniforms with swastikas flying in a town of seventy thousand inhabitants, of which forty thousand were Jewish.[27] Upholding the ordinance was seen to express "ideological tyranny";[28] the Nazis and their beliefs were not seen as ideologically tyrannical, nor was officially permitting their expression. Authoritatively allowing their bigotry (they marched in Chicago instead) was thus rendered neutral. The court asserted that permitting unpopular views "distinguishes life in this country from life under the Third Reich,"[29] eliding the fact that the substantive views it was officially permitting were those that characterized—as authoritatively articulated and actualized in—the Third Reich.

["Content control" was regarded by the Seventh Circuit as an intrinsically "slippery and precarious path," exemplifying "the essence of forbidden censorship."[30]]

It paraded the cherished truism that "under the First Amendment there is no such thing as a false idea."[31] The decision distinguished facts from what were rendered Nazi beliefs, for instance, "that black persons are biologically inferior to white persons . . . [and] that American Jews have 'inordinate . . . political and financial power' in the world and are 'in the forefront of the international Communist revolution.'"[32] Actually, these statements are factual in form. In reality, they are false. The idea that they are true is a false idea, which leaves "under the First Amendment" as a stand-alone *ipse dixit*, such that no idea in factual form, however false, can attract legal action.

Further false statements in factual form that provide the basis for prejudice and stereotype include that homosexuals are pedophiles who are coming for your children, that Muslims are terrorists, that Black men are lazy and violent, that Black women are promiscuous, and that women are men's biological and intellectual inferiors. Belief in such lies, and actions predicated on them, is a real engine of substantive inequality. In the Skokie case, the consequences of the march, termed "symbolic," were instead reduced to psychological "offensiveness" and "trauma" within the heads of the target population, connections with inequality to the point of genocide ignored. The Nazis were termed "dissidents," unjustifiably conflating them with the dissidents of the past free speech tradition, the role of anti-Semitism in American life, not to mention the world, ignored.

Justice Blackmun, one of the Court's most substantive thinkers, dissented from the denial of certiorari, joined by Justice White, perhaps its sharpest legal mind, together refusing to forget who Nazis, in reality, were. The majority's refusal to review the decision, they noted in understatement, was in "some tension with *Beauharnais*," and considered that the question whether "there is no limit whatsoever to the exercise of free speech" should be examined in circumstances in which the proposed demonstration "just might fall into the same category as one's 'right' to cry 'fire' in a crowded theater."[33] At least someone imagined that if speech could present a clear and present danger to the State, it might, in some circumstances, realistically endanger a historically subordinated group.

While their dissent grasped that the Nazis were moving to impose on Jews on US soil the very substantive inequality that this country had overthrown in a war in Europe, equality as an interest protected by the ordinance, challenged by the Nazis, defended by Skokie on behalf of its Jewish citizens, and violated by the Seventh Circuit and the Supreme Court majority in the result was, as such, unstated.

[handwritten margin note: That context matters in some cases]

These milestone free speech cases thus achieved their speech protections by submerging powerful evidence of substantive inequality, frequently protecting and furthering it. The cases were predicated on facts in which bigoted expression was sought to be protected or racist acts were opposed by law, yet were resolved without even legally noticing these realities, almost as if it was crucial to the legal posture of principle to ignore on what side of an inequality line the free speech decision came down. Well past when it was justified by the facts of the cases, the decisions acted as if the power alignments in the litigation were what they had been in the (then-established) tradition of the syndicalism and communism dissents: the State, embodied in a statute or ordinance representing the powerful suppression of speech on one side, and powerless dissenters subject to prosecution or state restraint—now the Klan or the Nazis, their allegedly unpopular speech being suppressed—on the other.

Subsequent cases often construed situations in which the State was involved on this same abstract model, as if the State held a monopoly on power and those whose "speech" it was restricting had less or little or none, regardless of whether the State was no longer protecting itself but was seeking to protect some people in society from other people, whose biases represented structural social dominance. It was as if, when arguable expression was restricted, that situation was reflexively rendered an expression of the dominant power of the State over powerless people, rather than an attempt by the State to support social equality in civil society for disadvantaged groups. The State was not seeking to protect itself or its own power in *Beauharnais, Brandenburg,* or *Collin v. Smith,* nor was the State the target of the potential violence sought to be addressed. The target was African Americans, formerly legally enslaved and still structurally subordinated across American society, and Jews, including many who had survived the Nazis when six million of them within memory had not.

In this light, the speech-protective tradition of the First Amendment was hijacked, substantively speaking, for dominant interests, first for powerful media, then for organized terrorist groups. This could happen not because these entities were powerless, but because they were not: the decisions track the substantive status quo distribution of power. Both the mainstream media and these racist groups had already established social hegemony. And despite the racism in the facts, nothing in these cases, legally speaking, was seen to be about equality. In other words, the early dissents represent an unrecognized First Amendment equality tradition all but demolished and certainly dishonored by the doctrine of tacit inequality that inverted and replaced it.

II.

Equality as such entered the First Amendment canon unannounced. In *Schacht v. United States*, the US Supreme Court held that a statute that prohibited the unauthorized wearing of an American military uniform, here in a "theatrical production," would have been facially constitutional, but "leav[ing] Americans free to praise the war in Vietnam but [sending] persons . . . to prison for opposing it, cannot survive in a country which has the First Amendment."[34] The notion that prohibiting all speech of a certain content—content here being wearing a uniform for artistic purposes—is acceptable to the First Amendment, but selecting a preferred point that could be made while prohibiting its opposite was not, was subsequently construed in equality terms as permitting a neutral regulation but not a viewpoint-based one. The notion that all unauthorized wearing of American military uniforms could constitutionally be prohibited was regarded as "*neutral*,"[35] although actually the American military uniform conveys a message replete with content and can never be truly content neutral. Uniforms exist to convey a message. The notion embedded in this case clearly aspires to the contentlessness, hence putative neutrality, of formal equality: treating likes alike, unlikes unalike, "affect[ing] alike all persons similarly situated."[36]

The subsequent decision in *Police Department of Chicago v. Mosley*[37] in 1972 made what it called an equality consideration explicit in a First Amendment context, invalidating a Chicago ordinance prohibiting picketing within 150 feet of an open school, except for peaceful labor picketing.[38] The Court assumed all picketing could be prohibited but found unconstitutionally unequal "under the Equal Protection clause, not to mention the First Amendment"[39] allowing, based on content, some peaceful pickets but not others. Considering equality within the First Amendment thus became the formal equality distinction between some First Amendment restrictions and others.[40] As equal protection has been largely confined to the formal equality straightjacket, the First Amendment has increasingly been restricted to content and viewpoint neutrality. The extended results of viewpoint neutrality, which has become a doctrinal obsession, have reinforced power and status as they exist.

Formal equality thus became the standard First Amendment notion of content neutrality, termed "protection against governmental discrimination based on speech content."[41] This abstract prohibition against distinguishing between some speech and other speech without strong reasons is aimed against the government prohibiting the expression of some points of view as more offensive than others, or granting the content of some views a forum because it finds them acceptable but denying a forum to others "to express less favored or more controversial views."[42] Given some merit in this sensitivity, entirely missed is the fact that neither governmental favor as such nor offensiveness has anything to do with the ways in which the substance of inequality is largely promoted through verbal and other expressive conduct. Karst perceptively noted, "The formal equality of 'content-neutral' procedural rules . . . may conceal a hidden inequality"[43] but did not disclose substantive inequalities concealed. The article thinks substantively but speaks abstractly.

On this reading of the tradition, courts have spent much of the intervening decades since *Mosley* trying to justify, or criticizing the justification of, distinctions between some restrictions and other restrictions, or explaining why restricting some expressive materials is acceptable and others not, when in fact they all have content, and most ineluctably convey points of view that often go unrecognized as such. For instance, the Supreme Court permitted the conviction of David Paul O'Brien for burning his draft card, which he burned to protest the draft, to stand under a statute that prohibited destroying draft cards.[44] The case became the standard for permitting prohibitions of expressive acts. Destroying one's draft card may have a number of meanings, all with content, however, and it is virtually impossible to express a point of view favorable to the selective service system by burning its registration vehicle. The act may have been prohibited for reasons other than its content, but its prohibition is far from viewpoint neutral.

The absence of a substantive equality approach has been as damaging to equality interests in the First Amendment area as it has been under the Equal Protection Clause.[45] In *Boy Scouts of America v. Dale*,[46] for one example, the Supreme Court used formal equality logic to entrench a substantive inequality when it disallowed a New Jersey public accommodation statute that prohibited sexual orientation discrimination as applied to the Boy Scouts because it could "significantly burden the Boy Scouts' desire to not 'promote homosexual conduct as a legitimate form of behavior.' "[47] Purporting to be neutral as to the Boy Scouts' (then express) homophobia,[48] the Court failed to see what the statute saw: substantively, guaranteeing gay rights is guaranteeing equality rights, while permitting homophobia as a basis for a public policy under the guise of protecting its free expression, there expressive association, is not. In other words, substantive equality guarantees are not neutral as between equality and inequality. First Amendment content neutrality permits substantive inequality to be official policy.

Under the First Amendment, the expressive dimension of being gay also lost under formal equality's content neutrality, which was not neutral at all. A substantive equality approach would have protected it. Formal equality, seeking outcomes on no one's side, is actually not possible in real inequality situations; it tilts toward power winning because neutrality favors nonintervention, meaning not disrupting the status quo that power has established. At best, it can go either way. It is thus not an equality rule, being indifferent between (substantive) equality and inequality. First Amendment neutrality has thus become a shibboleth for fairness in the guise of equal treatment while overwhelmingly siding with inequality in substance, as well as the form in which the ever-elusive holy grail of high groundlessness is sought, when what is actually needed is an injection of context, substance, and history: inequality's reality. What happens under the First Amendment now that gay and lesbian rights have some constitutional dimension[49] is an open question. The neutrality fixation provides no confidence as to the answer, since not disturbing what power has wrought always looks more neutral than equalizing it does.

A substantive equality recognition has sometimes overcome First Amendment neutrality before and after *Mosley. Pittsburgh Press Co. v. Pittsburgh Commission on Human Relations*[50] held that the state interest in preventing sex discrimination at work outweighed the First Amendment commercial speech interest in publishing sex-segregated ads, a result Karst found "unfortunate."[51] Similarly, the Supreme Court in *Roberts v. United States Jaycees*[52] held that states have a "compelling interest in eradicating discrimination against its female citizens"[53] on the basis of sex, as embodied in a Minnesota human rights statute, that outweighed any First Amendment right of expressive association that would have kept the Jaycees an organization confined to " 'young men.' "[54] The Court recognized that "acts of invidious discrimination in the distribution of publicly available goods, services, and other advantages cause unique evils that government has a compelling interest to prevent—wholly apart from the point of view such conduct may transmit. . . . Accordingly . . . such practices are entitled to no constitutional protection."[55] Recognition that acts of discrimination, apart from the viewpoint conveyed, are not constitutionally protected, despite the occasional hat tip, has largely remained a principle confined to this case.

Against this backdrop, the trajectory of academic freedom, a right of "special concern" to the First Amendment,[56] traces the same arc of powerlessness to power, with the same reversal in inequality's substance at its factual core. Initially a liberatory shield against imposition of orthodoxy on dissenters following the McCarthy era's suppression of the expression of teachers on the left, assertion of academic freedom has increasingly become a sword in the hands of sexual harassers and racists asserting it against students who claim their equality rights based on race and sex are being violated.[57] The law on this tension is unsettled, with Supreme Court auguries pulling in both directions, leaving unclear outcomes regarding academic misogyny and racial bigotry in educational relationships and environments that violate equality guarantees on campuses. Neutrality is not, however, encouraging.

The application of abstract equality formalism with the sidelining of historical reality came to a head in *R.A.V. v. City of St. Paul*,[58] in which a young man was accused of burning a cross on the fenced yard of an African American family's home under a statute that prohibited such acts and flying swastikas, when the actor reasonably knew the act would "'arouse anger, alarm, or resentment in others on the basis of race, color, creed, religion or gender.'"[59] Interpreted by the State as a subcategory of "'fighting words,'"[60] the inequality grounds were rendered "'specified disfavored topics'"[61] by the Supreme Court majority. In contending that the law "goes even beyond mere content discrimination, to actual viewpoint discrimination,"[62] opining that under the statute those arguing in favor of equality were permitted to use statements that "insult, or provoke violence," but those arguing against it could not, the Court obscured the fact that these grounds list the substance of substantive equality, while supporting discrimination on those grounds violates equality rights. Precisely what the Supreme Court found violated the First Amendment was what a substantive equality analysis would support: opposition to "'bias-motivated'" hatred and fighting words "'based on virulent notions of racial supremacy.'"[63]

Under this doctrine, when a viewpoint is seen, and law based on it is found to violate the First Amendment, is thus when substantive inequality is exposed and explicitly opposed as such by public policy. But a ground of inequality is not a viewpoint; it is a cultural artifact that is a basis for assigned systemic advantage and disadvantage, a foundation for social stratification. Discrimination is not a viewpoint either, although it contains one as most acts do; it is the imposition or enactment of an inferior or endangered status on a socially systematic but arbitrary ground. Where equality is social policy, it is also an illegal practice. Cross burning is not a discussion any more than rape or segregation is, although all three are communicative and actively subordinating. The hostility of the *R.A.V.* majority to equality as a basis for social policy is itself a viewpoint, one contrary to any serious legal prohibition on inequality, indeed contrary to the history of the Fourteenth Amendment, which opposed discrimination on the basis of race in substance, even if its jurisprudence today often does not. The *R.A.V.* list of "disfavored topics" actually lists the grounds of substantive inequality.

The exception for some inequality that the *R.A.V.* majority made for Title VII, while welcome, was incoherent. As the dissent accurately noted, the federal Title VII hostile work environment regulation "focuses on what the majority would characterize as the 'disfavored topic'" of sexual harassment.[64] Because a general ban on harassment would cover it, they noted, proscribing this subcategory would violate the First Amendment. However, sexual harassment does "'itself inflict injury,'"[65] and so comes within Minnesota's construction of the statute's fighting words.

Just over a decade after *R.A.V.*, *Virginia v. Black*[66] upheld an anti-cross-burning statute, providing an exceptional substantive, if tacit, First Amendment equality ruling. Contextualizing Virginia's prohibition on cross burning "with intent to intimidate"[67] in the history of the reality of cross burning—Ku Klux Klan terrorism, heralding lynching and other torture and murder[68]—the practice was accurately if minimally characterized as a virulent and unambiguous "symbol of hate."[69] This outcome was seemingly acceptable to a majority of the Court under the First Amendment because the concrete ground for the inequality that the cross burning effectuated did not say "race"; the law only said "cross burning." Apparently, if the Skokie ordinance had only prohibited all swastika flying and brown shirt jackboot marching, it would have been constitutional.

Not permitted, in other words, in prohibiting the imposition of an inequality by specified means, is an express recognition of the substantive grounds of that inequality. The grounds must be censored. Opposing inequality is unequal, a neutrality violation. Allowing it to be imposed is not, nor is prohibiting its imposition, so long as the grounds on which it is imposed are not mentioned. Cross burning can be prohibited as in *Virginia v. Black* because anyone can say anything on any side of anything about anyone by burning one. Never mind that, in reality, cross burning only expresses one side of one thing by some people only over and against certain others. Prohibiting the racist inequality that cross burning constitutes and promotes and threatens was thus able to be treated not as a prohibited viewpoint discrimination by the sleight of hand of prohibiting cross burning the act, although the only viewpoint that cross burning expresses is virulent White supremacy, a race-based point of view. A substantive equality principle, by contrast, stands squarely against White supremacy and favors opposing it, as, in one of its rare substantive moments, does the Equal Protection Clause. The prohibited word "race" may not be statutorily uttered.

Viewpoint neutrality is not waning; it is metastasizing even as suspicion that domestic racist terrorism simply is not real to Supreme Court majorities in prejudice or portent grows upon reading the 2011 decision in *Holder v. Humanitarian Law Project*. There, a federal statute prohibiting core political speech, including support for groups on the congressional terrorism watch list that includes counseling them in nonviolent resolution of conflict, survived First Amendment strict scrutiny[70] for the first time since the beginning of the last century. This terrorism, replete with viewpoint, is apparently real.

III.

An obligato tracking these developments during the same time period is the First Amendment's law on pornography. Beginning with obscenity, a doctrine under which more writers and artists than pornographers were early prosecuted,[71] it morphed into rulings on indecency, child pornography, animal cruelty videos, and violent video games. Obscenity law exhibited no more awareness of the inequalities in its facts than have other First Amendment areas. Contrary to the unsupported conventional wisdom invoked by Justices Souter and Ginsburg, dissenting in 2008, that "as a general matter pornography lacks the harm to justify prohibiting it,"[72] the exploitation by pornographers of vulnerable and abused populations acquired for use to make pornography is well documented,[73] facially abusive treatment of women is frequently clearly visible in the materials,[74] and the empirical record of harm done in its making is massive and increasingly decisive,[75] as is the evidence of harm done to others as a result of its use by consumers.[76]

From an equality perspective, given this evidence, obscenity law, followed by indecency legislation, provides a major exercise in missing the point. *Roth*,[77] permitting a federal statute prohibiting mail of "obscene, lewd, lascivious, or filthy . . . or other publication of an indecent character"[78] in 1957, defined obscenity as a category outside constitutionally protected speech that appealed to the "prurient interest" in sex and was "utterly without redeeming social importance."[79] There was nothing on the inequalities required to produce the materials or the harms imposed and promoted through its use. *Redrup v. New York* in 1967,[80] under which scores of obscenity decisions were overturned, spelled the end of First Amendment restrictions on written materials and established the basic framework of what, refined, became the *Miller* test for obscenity in 1973.[81] *Miller*,[82] recognizing no harms or the inequalities based on gender, age, race, and wealth on which the exploitative sex industry depends, has also proven essentially unenforceable[83] as the pornography industry has, among its other effects, habituated massive populations to its abuse of women,[84] creating the "community standards," also known as rape culture,[85] under which it has exploded exponentially.[86] Despite pornography presenting much abuse, obscenity law contains no prohibition on violent depictions: "speech about violence is not obscene."[87] The one recognition of harm in the obscenity tradition occurred in 1968 in upholding a statute that restricted children's access to obscenity that was " 'harmful to minors.' "[88] The Court neither provided nor required evidence of that harm nor said what it was. →Just took it to be.

In sharp contrast, the law against child pornography prohibits sexual material made of children on the express observation that it requires and constitutes child abuse, a harm presumed rather than specified or required shown.[89] This, despite being a content prohibition and a viewpoint restriction, for materials that are as much "speech" as any pornography is, is criminalized based on its content: content that promotes the view that sex between adults and children is desirable for, and desired by, both. If there is merit to the view that "adult speech refers not merely to sexually explicit content, but to speech reflecting a favorable view about being explicit about sex and a favorable view of the practices it depicts,"[90] the same is no less true of pornography of children. The child pornography prohibition was nonetheless extended to buyers and collectors on the accurate analysis that purchase and possession create and stimulate the market that caused the abuse required to make it.[91]

Although the distinction between child and adult is not termed an inequality in this doctrine, it is one. Age provides a hierarchy of adults over children—physical, economic, and political, and in social status, psychological development, and access to speech and its credibility. The child pornography prohibition is tacitly based on the substance of this inequality: the powerlessness of children relative to the adults who pimp, manipulate, and sexually use the children to make pornography for adult sexual and financial (sometimes exchanged) profit. In practical effect, these decisions were significantly undercut by the ruling in *Ashcroft v. Free Speech Coalition* in 2002, which permitted virtual child pornography and computer-generated images of children engaged in sexual activity, invalidating their federal prohibition.[92] Justice Rehnquist's dissent realistically noted that, with emerging technology, it would become increasingly hard to tell the difference between real and virtual children, making many prosecutions for child pornography difficult to impossible.[93]

What may have been the tipping point of adult pornography regulation, foreshadowing *R.A.V.* in viewpoint discrimination's ascent under the First Amendment, was the Seventh Circuit's *Hudnut* decision in 1986. This facial case challenged the legal attempt to squarely recognize the substantive inequality between the sexes in and of pornography, defined as "'sexually explicit subordination of women, whether in pictures or in words'" that also included a range of sexually objectifying and abusive presentations, providing civil causes of action for four acts of sex discrimination proven connected to its making and use.[94] The Seventh Circuit invalidated the ordinance as viewpoint discrimination under *Mosley*, citing in support *Brandenburg* that "the ideas of the Klan may be propagated"[95] and *Collin v. Smith* for the permissibility of Nazis marching through a Jewish community.[96] Despite accepting the premises of the ordinance that, as that court put it, "pornography is an aspect of dominance. It does not persuade people so much as change them," is "not an idea," and perpetuates subordination that "leads to affront and lower pay at work, insult and injury at home, battery and rape on the streets,"[97] the panel concluded that "this simply demonstrates the power of pornography as speech," as well as, and hence, its value as speech.[98] In defining pornography as sex discriminatory, the court found that Indianapolis "has created an approved point of view" and no successful rationale for the law could "be limited to sex discrimination."[99]

Why sex discrimination was necessarily inadequate was unclear. The actionable civil injuries of discrimination—coercion, force, assault, and trafficking—were not points of view but acts, discriminatory when proven sex based. The definition made materials that constitute inequalities, that actively subordinate, actionable through these four causes of action only. Yet these same harms, rendered nonneutral by the opinion, provided a protective First Amendment mantle for pornography. The Supreme Court summarily affirmed.[100] This terrorism, apparently, was not real.

How far existing First Amendment doctrine denies, through being conceptually prevented from seeing, the harms of pornography can be focused by asking whether a prosecution for a "snuff" film, in which a person—for this purpose, an adult woman—is murdered to make a sex film,[101] would be constitutional. Is snuff protected speech? Much would depend on the law under which it was prosecuted, but the lack of a law designed to face this most brutal reality of the pornography industry makes part of the point. Snuff is likely not obscene because a jury is unlikely to concede that it "appeals to the prurient interest in sex" under *Miller*,[102] although it obviously does or no such market would exist. Such films are usually sexually violent, which (again) obscenity law is not designed to cover.[103] "Incitement to imminent lawless action"[104] is not likely provable here, because while a snuff film may stimulate desire for the acts it presents and inspire copying, acquisition and use are typically deeply clandestine, such acts may not be imminent, and the violence of most immediate concern—that required to make it—has already occurred. Unless someone fights back, snuff is not "'fighting words.'"[105] Snuff is not child pornography if the murdered person had reached the age of majority, or looks as if they could have.

Would a film of a murder committed so the killing could be filmed as sex be judicially rendered "about" the "topic" of sexual murder, per the *R.A.V.* approach, "a distinctive idea, conveyed by a distinctive message"?[106] Snuff is definitely "'sexually explicit subordination'"[107] that typically includes women being dismembered or tortured to death in a sexualized context, but restricting that was deemed "thought control,"[108] despite pornography of torture (when sadomasochism) being constitutionally criminal.[109] Snuff is not likely terrorism as defined,[110] although members of the same group as the person sexually murdered for the film might well be intimidated or coerced upon encountering it.[111] A snuff film definitely falls within the 1949 standard in *Giboney v. Empire Storage & Ice Company*,[112] being "an integral part of conduct in violation of a valid criminal statute,"[113] here murder (or conspiracy to murder, a federal crime[114]). The creation of adult pornography is thus "'intrinsically related' to the sexual abuse" of those who are used to make it,[115] giving the speech at issue "a proximate link to the crime from which it came."[116] But most pornography violates valid laws against prostitution and often rape, without that having been noticed, or—having been noticed—having been incoherently repudiated.[117] Going back yet further in the First Amendment tradition, Holmes' dissent in *Abrams* is suggestive: "I do not doubt for a moment that by the same reasoning that would justify punishing persuasion to murder, the United States constitutionally may punish speech that produces or is intended to produce a clear and imminent danger that it will bring about forthwith certain substantive evils that the United States constitutionally may seek to prevent."[118] If persuasion to murder as an act post "speech" can be constitutionally criminalized, might a sex film of murder that required committing one as an act ante "speech" be as well?

The Court's decision on animal snuff in *United States v. Stevens* offers close parallels but little encouragement.[119] Animal crush and human snuff are both clandestine and highly profitable. Too, as Justice Alito noted in dissent, before Congress passed the law against the animal crush and cruelty films the *Stevens* decision invalidated, the underlying conduct in the videos could be prosecuted but, without an inside witness, had proven nearly impossible; the videos provided both a prosecutable crime and evidence for the underlying conduct.[120] As the market in child pornography was recognized to stimulate the abusive acts if possession and viewing were permitted,[121] the *Stevens* decision put crush videos back online.[122] Justice Alito observed that "crush videos present a highly unusual free speech issue because they are so closely linked with violent criminal conduct."[123] Actually, it is not at all unusual for pornography of adult women to be linked with violent criminal conduct. Women in pornography are often coerced; someone (usually someone else) is paid for the sex acts depicted, making it prostitution, which is criminal conduct.[124] Rape or torture, which are acts of violence, are not uncommon, and pornography is an industry of organized crime,[125] a violent industry. What is unusual is recognizing the link between the "speech" and the violent criminal conduct. Justice Alito saw that the materials in *Stevens* were like those in *New York v. Ferber*[126] in containing "speech that itself is the record of sexual abuse,"[127] and so are not constitutionally protected for the same reasons. His dissent gets at much of the substance of the inequality between humans and nonhumans without recognizing it as such. Human snuff raises the question whether adult women would be treated any better than animals by the Court, should a statute against similar atrocities be enacted for their protection.

Given the Court's determined protection of sexually abusive materials, hope that the harm done by speech recognized as violent was further dimmed by the 2011 *Brown v. Entertainment Merchants Association* decision, which declined to permit California to restrict the sale of violent video games to adults. The interactive training effects of the video games, in which users perform the motions of maiming, killing, torture, and rape, like pilots learn to fly planes in flight simulators (termed "target practice" by Justice Breyer in dissent),[128] were dismissed by the majority as the same as reading a book or watching a movie.[129] The sexual content of the violent video games was distinguished from its (presumptively nonsexual) violence, although the California law was limited to "killing, maiming, dismembering, or sexually assaulting an image of a human being."[130] A snuff film presents these same acts actually being done as sex to a real human being. If violence against a person is an ultimate act of inequality, no glimpse of any " 'actual problem' in need of solving"[131] can be discerned in *Brown*.

A video game may be closer to being "about" its contents than a snuff film is. Still, the tendency of this Supreme Court majority to make anything that contains words or images or symbolism or meaning into "speech", containing an "idea about" its presentations was apparent in its description of the danger posed by the California law, which was described much as cross burning in *R.A.V.* had been: "the *ideas* expressed by speech—whether it be violence, or gore, or racism—and not its objective effects, may be the real reason for governmental proscription."[132] One would think what a law does would be at least as important as what the Court imagines it was passed to do. One also wonders about this Court's response to direct-feed webcam prostitution, in which the consumer orders what he wants for masturbation for real-time viewing on his computer screen from the prostituted person, adult or child, live on the other end of a video camera, typically run by a pimp. Does putting prostitution into this artifact form, conveyed and consumed digitally on a screen while being performed live simultaneously, render it "speech" too? Who is speaking? Is this "ideas about" prostitution? As Andrea Dworkin put the point:

> We are told all the time that pornography is really about ideas. Well, a rectum doesn't have an idea, and a vagina doesn't have an idea, and the mouths of women in pornography do not express ideas; and when a woman has a penis thrust down to the bottom of her throat, as in the film *Deep Throat,* that throat is not part of a human being who is involved in discussing ideas.[133]

In the weaponization of "speech" for unequal ends that has increasingly occurred over the past seventy or so years—prominently for White supremacist and male-dominant sexual ends—the social and legal dynamics and discourses are tightly linked, with the role of pornography arguably pivotal. Both the public discussion and the arc of the law have gone from obscenity wars, which were mainly about literature or birth control and homosexuality, not pornography at all, to affirmatively protecting a burgeoning industry of abuse, as if the same interests were at stake. The pornography industry does not produce art or literature, nor are pornography pimps artists or literary writers; pornography is a technologically sophisticated form of trafficking in women and children with profits to match.[134] In this area, the same First Amendment reversal from protecting the powerless to protecting power has occurred. The past place and mantle of relatively powerless legitimate literary and artistic actors subjected to the narrow-minded moralistic might of state censorship has been usurped by powerful exploitative actors of international organized crime, more potent in the lives of the most vulnerable women and children than the State is in protecting them.

The urgency to reconfigure acts as speech, bigotry as neutrality, is driven by the need to protect sellers and buyers of sexual violation and exploitation in the form of pornography, which requires a foundation of sex, racial, and class inequality and sexual acts against women and children to make it. Once neutrality is law, discrimination is rendered a point of view; discrimination in this form becomes invisible and nonactionable. Any ground given in restricting anything considered "speech" risks restricting pornography as an underlying target of protection, making the pursuit of substantive equality in this field impossible.

Pornography, the most mass of media, is the original fake news: it is lies, pure and simple, about women's and children's sexuality, in particular presenting them as desiring to be violated by acts the consumer is aroused by imposing, hence seeing being imposed. The original alternative facts were then invented and circulated by public relations firms hired by pornographers[135] to persuade a credulous and desensitized public to the conventional wisdom that exposure to pornography, which vast numbers were using, does no harm, in the sense of doing no damage to those affected by the consumers who are affected by the pornography. No such methodologically valid facts exist. Social discourse has become accustomed to hearing only what supports an abusive unequal sexuality and status for over half the population, this industry having conditioned its sexual pleasure to it. The authoritarian sexuality purveyed by pornography, on which ejaculatory entertainment vast swaths of the electorate are hooked, is not politically neutral, and far less is it gender neutral.

It becomes difficult to avoid the suspicion that First Amendment law has been constructed over the past half century or so in the increasingly long shadow of pornography—that is, to ensure that pornography remains protected, or at least not to risk reraising the contentious question of its protection. Understandings and evidence of harm must be trivialized and suppressed, causation made linear, and governmental intervention in "speech" made "neutral" when all this is orchestrated precisely to preserve these particular materials from accountability for the harms of inequality they require and do, so sexual use of the materials, hence the people, can continue. And although this conclusion is repudiated by the R.A.V. majority,[136] it seems increasingly clear that doing real harm is indeed protected speech so long as it is done in the guise of conveying a viewpoint favorable to the doing of that harm. Examining the viewpoint contortions, such as discriminating against antidiscrimination law based on its content, with doctrine framed so that none of pornography's massive record of harm is even legally relevant to its adjudication, it is difficult to avoid the conclusion that the First Amendment is construed as it is so men can have their pornography.

IV.

A First Amendment substantive equality standard predicated on proof of harm could begin from the understanding in *Schenck* that "the most stringent protection of free speech would not protect a man . . . from an injunction against uttering words that may have all the effect of force."[137] Further confining prohibited abuse and harassment by expressive means to specific hierarchical grounds of historic inequality provides a far more predictable and administrable test than the empty, generic, abstract sameness-and-difference formal equality model now applied to any distinction with content, which in reality is most distinctions. Equality, substantively, is a limiting principle, keeping the slippery slope from sliding beyond the protection of groups historically subordinated on concrete well-established grounds.

In a substantive equality framework, the *New York Times* decision would have restricted the use of state libel law when attempted to be applied to limit equality seeking through speech. The speech at issue there promoted equality, a legitimate and compelling state interest. A constitutional right to publish equality advocacy that exposes racist officials suppressing civil rights activities, who then attempt to punish that expressive exposure through suit for nonmaterial inaccuracies, provides a kind of retaliation claim. In the Skokie case, the expression at issue targeted the very group that those who sought the permits had slated for extinction in a genocide. Substantively grasped, the treatment of Jews could become a principle for recognizing expressive harm.

Until very recently, the closest to a harm test the Supreme Court has come in the First Amendment area, other than possibly *R.A.V.*'s exception for Title VII, is *Brandenberg*'s "incitement" test. Had the inequality that animated the facts in that case been noticed, incitement would apply not only to advocacy of violence in linear causal relation, immediate and lawless, but also to advocacy that mobilizes pre-existing established powerful forces—attitudes and behaviors—against specific unequal groups. Instead, the pre-existing First Amendment template of protecting the State from damaging speech was inaptly applied to vulnerable social groups. Even then, the State is treated better. The State was protected from clear and present danger; the Klan's targets were protected only from "imminent lawless action,"[138] ignoring both the power of the State and the potency of White supremacy. Then in 2011 a harm too great—honestly, a harm real even to the privileged—was encountered: foreign terrorism. Despite the Court's observation in *Brown*—"Last Term, in *Stevens*, we held that new categories of unprotected speech may not be added to the list by a legislature that concludes certain speech is too harmful to be tolerated"[139]—*Holder v. Humanitarian Law Project*[140] did just that. Disallowing material support of specified foreign terrorist organizations under federal statute, including funding rendered speech, as well as political speech itself, despite being part of no "long . . . tradition of proscription,"[141] was upheld,[142] sparing us the usual litany of speech platitudes, including neutrality. There was no waiting around for the violence to happen this time.

If the tipping point on racist hate speech was *Collin v. Smith*, on pornography it was *Hudnut*—both Seventh Circuit decisions that the Supreme Court let stand. As to pornography's unequal harms, if no existing First Amendment test fully encompasses them, the Court's approach to child pornography in *Ferber* and *Osborne* at least begins with the harm done to those violated in the making, and grasps possession and use as creating a demand for that abuse. Child pornography is not, it seems, a discussion of ideas, despite conveying "a favorable view of the practices it depicts."[143] Facing the age inequality that is exploited could support extending prohibition, actualized overwhelmingly through voluntary compliance, from the children in the materials to those on whom the materials are used, or who are targeted and groomed for sexual abuse through the stimulation and conditioning tools provided to user adults by the materials. The contortions over morphing[144] and apparent children—adults in age who "look like" children, who have no rights at all in this setting—could be avoided, the real damage done by virtual, morphed, and pandered materials encompassed. The equality approach of the ordinance litigated in *Hudnut*, subject only to summary affirmance in the Seventh Circuit and hence accessible for deployment elsewhere, addresses these and other relevant harms done through both adult and child pornography in a human rights context. Free expression appears to have survived the criminalization of child pornography, as the American Civil Liberties Union (ACLU) and others in vociferously opposing the *Ferber* law darkly predicted it could not,[145] through a de facto partial substantive equality approach.

Canada has adopted substantive equality in its constitutional freedom of expression provision. Building on its explicit rejection of formal equality and embrace of substantive equality,[146] the Supreme Court of Canada has upheld a hate propaganda prohibition largely on an equality rationale in a case involving teaching anti-Semitism to schoolchildren.[147] Parliament's distinctive obscenity law, which prohibits "undue exploitation of sex, or of sex and any one or more of . . . crime, horror, cruelty and violence,"[148] was saved on equality grounds from attack as a violation of freedom of expression.[149] After ten years of litigation, one defendant was convicted of snuff-themed verbal and visual pornography sexualizing the torture and murder of women, a conviction upheld on appeal. However, since 1994, no published Canadian obscenity case has prosecuted for nonviolent adult pornography, suggesting that the equality principle of substantive hierarchy needs further constitutional backbone. Meantime, free speech appears robust in Canada. In the United States, the tired canard that truth will triumph in the marketplace, so nothing that can be considered expression should be restricted, was well addressed by John Stuart Mill in a less commonly quoted passage in *On Liberty*: "It is a piece of idle sentimentality that truth, merely as truth, has any inherent power denied to error of prevailing against the dungeon and the stake."[150] Knowing that the dungeon and the stake are also sexual preferences and sexual practices, a reality clearly evidenced in pornography, extends the literal accuracy of this observation.

Adherence to a wooden reductive analysis that nothing anyone says is responsible for events in the real world, much of the mainstream media's underlying position, inhibits addressing, for example, terrorism domestic and foreign, since belief in certain views obviously motivates lethal actions that actualize and further those views, without in any way reducing the responsibility of criminals who commit criminal acts. The attacks of September 11, a democratized experience of harm that is real to people to whom little else appears to be, may have slightly dented this liberal article of faith, yet the cry of "censorship" from the left and "PC" from the right remain reflexive whenever "speech" and harm are observed linked. In contrast, a First Amendment that sustained its original insights into dissent and powerlessness, building into them a modern understanding of substantive equality, would open expression to the unequal instead of confining its protection largely to the powerful, especially those for whom speech is their principal form of power.

10

Does the Clear and Present Danger Test Survive Cost–Benefit Analysis?

CASS R. SUNSTEIN

The constitutional guarantees of free speech and free press do not permit a State to forbid or proscribe advocacy of the use of force or of law violation except where such advocacy is directed to inciting or producing imminent lawless action and is likely to incite or produce such action.
—Brandenburg v. Ohio, 385 U.S. 444 (1969)

Each agency must . . . propose or adopt a regulation only upon a reasoned determination that its benefits justify its costs.
—Exec. Order No. 13,563, 76 Fed. Reg. 3,821 (Jan. 18, 2011)

The Cost–Benefit State

Imagine that a coal company is emitting harmful pollutants—particulate matter, greenhouse gases, ozone. Imagine too that if public officials direct it to reduce its emissions, it will face high costs, perhaps in the tens of millions of dollars. Imagine finally that the benefits of emissions reductions would be mostly felt in the future, in the form of reductions in premature mortality in a decade or more, and a small (but far from zero) reduction in climate change. Imagine finally that the monetized benefits of emissions reductions, with the appropriate discount rate, would dwarf the costs. On those assumptions, is there any doubt that regulation would be a good idea, even though the principal benefits would not be enjoyed for several years? (This is not meant to be a difficult question. There is no such doubt.)

Now suppose that the Department of Homeland Security and the Federal Aviation Administration are considering a new policy to reduce the risk of successful terrorist attacks at airports. They are contemplating the use of a new security scanner that will (according to experts) prove more effective in detecting potential weapons, including small or novel kinds that terrorists might use in the future. The economic cost of the new scanner is high—at least $2 million for each. Federal officials concede that they cannot say, with confidence, that the new scanner will save lives; they cannot even say that it is more likely than not to do so. But they believe that it will reduce the risk of a successful terrorist attack. Would it be a mistake to mandate the scanner? (This is meant to be a difficult question. The answer is not obvious. But mandating the scanner would not be a clear mistake.)

Accounting

The two cases just given are standard. Federal regulators often act without the slightest hesitation even though the benefits of their action will not be immediate; indeed, such benefits might occur many years in the future (as in the case of climate change[1]). Federal regulators also act without much hesitation when reasonable people think that the chance of producing any benefits at all is under 50 percent. Consider, for example, regulations designed to reduce the risk of a nuclear power accident (improbable but potentially catastrophic) or another financial crisis, for example, by increasing capital and liquidity requirements. Of course, regulators will not impose costs for no benefits. Instead, they will think about the expected value of regulatory requirements. If a mandate will have a one in x chance of producing \$500 million in benefits, it might be worth proceeding even if x is pretty big—and if the potential benefits are (say) \$5 billion, a chance of one in twenty would justify a quite costly regulatory mandate.

The American regulatory state has become a *cost–benefit state*,[2] at least as a general rule. In deciding whether to impose regulatory controls, officials ask whether the benefits would justify the costs, as mandated by Executive Order 13563 and its predecessors.[3] (It is true that some statutes forbid executive branch officials from making cost–benefit analysis the rule of decision,[4] but even when this is so, such officials are required, by executive order, to provide an accounting.) Sometimes this inquiry presents difficult challenges, because quantification of various costs and benefits is difficult. Importantly, administrators have various tools for handling those challenges.[5] Whether or not those tools are sufficient, the most general point is that in deciding whether to proceed, they need not be much moved by learning that the benefits would not be imminent, or even that they are not likely to occur at all. The question is *the expected value of proceeding*. A lack of imminence suggests that the discount rate will greatly matter,[6] and of course a low probability of obtaining benefits must be recognized, and it will drive the expected value way down. But these are points about the magnitude of the benefits, which may nonetheless be high, or at least high enough to justify proceeding.

Precautions and a Principle

In the regulatory context, some people reject cost–benefit balancing in favor of some kind of Precautionary Principle, calling for regulation even when it cannot be said, with anything like certainty, that precautions will actually eliminate harm.[7] On one view, the proponents of an activity face the burden of proof. They must show that they are not threatening to harm people, and until they meet that burden, they are forbidden from engaging in risk-creating activity. Suppose, for example, that new foods contain genetically modified organisms, and that genetically modified organisms may create risks to human health and the environment. If so, many people would understand the Precautionary Principle to ban the marketing of such products.

The Precautionary Principle plays a role in many nations, and some version of it can be found in American law as well.[8] It is generally understood to be far more proregulatory than cost–benefit balancing, and those who endorse it do so in part for that reason. No nation has become a Precautionary State, but there are good arguments for taking regulatory steps to reduce low-probability risks of harm, certainly if those steps are not especially costly.[9]

Especially to those who favor cost–benefit balancing, the Precautionary Principle is highly controversial, in part because it seems to require steps that impose risks of their own—and thus violate the Precautionary Principle.[10] If, for example, nuclear power plants are banned on precautionary grounds, nations might have to rely on fossil fuels, which emit greenhouse gases, and thus create serious risks. If foods with genetically modified organisms are banned, more expensive foods or more dangerous foods might be marketed instead. To the extent that the Precautionary Principle forbids the very steps that it mandates, it is paralyzing, even incoherent, and cost–benefit analysis is a preferable approach.

Some people endorse a more limited idea, the Catastrophic Harm Precautionary Principle, which supports regulatory restrictions in cases in which catastrophic harm cannot be ruled out.[11] The basic claim here is that even if a harm is unlikely to occur, and even if it will not occur imminently, sensible regulators might be willing to proceed. It makes sense to prevent low-probability risks of catastrophe. Airports might be made more secure against the risk of terrorism even if terrorism is unlikely. In the regulatory context, no one seriously questions that possibility.

The Costs and Benefits of Speech

Is speech different? How?

For purposes of analysis, I am going to use a broadly welfarist framework, suggesting that we should focus on the real-world consequences of various approaches.[12] If, for example, an approach to free speech would seriously harm people's capacity to learn about values or facts, it would be exceedingly hard to defend. (Think: dictatorships.[13]) If an approach to free speech would allow significant numbers of people to be killed, it would have a big strike against it. (Think: free speech absolutism.) It should be readily acknowledged that welfarism raises many questions and doubts. For one thing, it needs to be specified; are we speaking of some form of utilitarianism, or something more capacious?[14] Perhaps more fundamentally, we need to know *what kinds of welfare losses count*. Suppose that certain forms of speech make people sad or mad. May they be regulated for that reason? The standard forms of welfarism must count sadness and anger as hedonic losses, but a system of free speech could not stand as such if it did so as well: if speech could be regulated whenever it made people sad or mad, we would be regulating a lot of speech. (I am not going to count sadness and anger as losses here.)

For those who reject welfarism, and think that (for example) a deontological approach to speech would be preferable, my focus will seem quite misplaced. Notwithstanding this point, I believe that a broadly welfarist approach to free speech has considerable appeal, and that we can make considerable progress on the clear and present danger test without running into murky philosophical waters. The proof, of course, lies in the pudding.

Speech and Conduct

At least in principle, current thinking about costs and benefits would seem to apply to speech no less than to conduct. Suppose that we had a perfect technology for making predictions about the probability that certain causes, including speech, will produce certain effects. Suppose that the technology demonstrates that a specified kind of speech—promoting, say, terrorism—is more likely than not to produce serious harm in the form of successful attacks, resulting in a specified number of deaths, not in a month, but in two years. Or suppose that the likelihood that speech will cause harm is just one in five—but that if the harm occurs, it will be very grave. In such cases, it would seem odd to say that regulation is off-limits.

Of course, a full evaluation would require attention to the benefits of the speech, not only its costs. With respect to the assessment of benefits, there are special challenges, perhaps especially for speech that combats a tyrannical or unjust status quo, and that promotes, purposefully or otherwise, violence as a form of resistance. But we could easily imagine cases in which the benefits of speech that has a high expected cost would also be relatively low—so that the outcome of cost–benefit analysis is not at all favorable to protecting such speech.

In fact, it is not necessary to use our imaginations. Terrorist organizations are engaged in incitement and recruitment activities every day.[15] Their initial weapon is speech. On the internet and elsewhere, they call for acts of murder and destruction. Let us simply stipulate that however hateful, most or many of these statements cannot be said to be more likely than not to produce imminent lawless action. In such cases, there is no clear and present danger as that phrase is generally understood. Instead, they create a nonquantifiable risk that such action will occur at some point in the unknown future. On standard regulatory principles, government is nonetheless permitted to take action, at least if the benefits of allowing the speech do not exceed the costs. (I will turn to the question of benefits in due course.)

Those principles are hardly foreign to free speech law. Some form of cost–benefit balancing played a role in *Dennis v. United States*,[16] a decision that is generally treated as a dinosaur, or an object of ridicule, in constitutional law circles. The case involved an alleged conspiracy by members of the Communist Party hoping to overthrow the US government. The Court said that it was "squarely presented with the application of the 'clear and present danger' test, and must decide what that phrase imports." In that sense, it purported to apply rather than to reject that test. The Court explained:

> Obviously, the words cannot mean that, before the Government may act, it must wait until the putsch is about to be executed, the plans have been laid and the signal is awaited. If Government is aware that a group aiming at its overthrow is attempting to indoctrinate its members and to commit them to a course whereby they will strike when the leaders feel the circumstances permit, action by the Government is required. . . . Certainly an attempt to overthrow the Government by force, even though doomed from the outset because of inadequate numbers or power of the revolutionists, is a sufficient evil for Congress to prevent. The damage which such attempts create both physically and politically to a nation makes it impossible to measure the validity in terms of the probability of success, or the immediacy of a successful attempt.[17]

At that point, the Court referred to Judge Learned Hand's formulation for the court below, a form of cost–benefit balancing in accordance with which, "in each case, [courts] must ask whether the gravity of the 'evil,' discounted by its improbability, justifies such invasion of free speech as is necessary to avoid the danger."[18] The Court adopted this standard as its own, on the ground that it "takes into consideration those factors which we deem relevant, and relates their significances. More we cannot expect from words."[19]

Not coincidentally, Hand's free speech formula is similar to the famous Hand formula for negligence, celebrated in (and actually helping to spur) the economic analysis of law. Hand's negligence standard calls for cost–benefit analysis:

> Since there are occasions when every vessel will break from her moorings, and since, if she does, she becomes a menace to those about her; the owner's duty, as in other similar situations, to provide against resulting injuries is a function of three variables: (1) the probability that she will break away; (2) the gravity of the resulting injury, if she does; (3) the burden of adequate precautions. Possibly it serves to bring this notion into relief to state it in algebraic terms: if the probability be called P; the injury, L; and the burden, B; liability depends upon whether B is less than L multiplied by P: i.e., whether $B < PL$.[20]

For speech, Hand was singing the song of contemporary American regulators, and in *Dennis*, the Court embraced the idea as a rendering of the clear and present danger test. But today, almost no one likes that idea. Why not?

"More Speech, Not Enforced Silence"

1. *Counterspeech.* In their great free speech opinions, Oliver Wendell Holmes Jr. and Louis Brandeis rejected cost–benefit balancing. Brandeis offered the most elaborate explanation. In his view, "only an emergency can justify suppression."[21] That conclusion undergirded his own understanding of the clear and present danger test, which (contrary to *Dennis* and Hand) required a showing of imminence. In his account, "no danger flowing from speech can be deemed clear and present unless the incidence of the evil apprehended is so imminent that it may befall before there is opportunity for full discussion. If there be time to expose through discussion the falsehood and fallacies, to avert the evil by the processes of education, the remedy to be applied is more speech, not enforced silence."[22] As he put it, that is "the command of the Constitution," and it "must be the rule if authority is to be reconciled with freedom."[23]

Some of this is mere rhetoric on Brandeis' part. There are plenty of ways to reconcile authority with freedom, and the clear and present danger test is merely one. The *Dennis* approach may or may not be underprotective of speech, but it is surely an effort at reconciling authority and freedom. Perhaps it is not the best one. At one point, Learned Hand himself offered a radically different route, one with great contemporary relevance in light of the rise of terrorism. In his view, the free speech principle does not protect explicit or direct incitement to violence, even if no harm was imminent.[24] If you are merely agitating for change, the government cannot proceed against you, but if you are expressly inciting people to commit murder, you are no longer protected by the Constitution. What matters is what you are saying, not whether it will have bad effects. Hand greatly preferred his approach to the clear and present danger test, which he thought squishy and susceptible to biased assessments by federal judges. As he wrote:

> I am not wholly in love with Holmesy's test and the reason is this. Once you admit that the matter is one of degree, while you may put it where it genuinely belongs, you obviously make it a matter of administration, i.e. you give it to Tomdickandharry, D.J., so much latitude . . . that the jig is at once up. Besides their Ineffabilities, the Nine Elder Statesmen have not shown themselves wholly immune from the "herd instinct" and what seems "immediate and direct" today may seem very remote next year even though the circumstances surrounding the utterance be unchanged.[25]

Of course, cost–benefit analysis has been criticized on similar grounds, though modern economic strategies can greatly reduce the problem. By contrast, Hand defended his exemption of incitement as a "qualitative formula, hard, conventional, difficult to evade."[26] Hand's test would of course allow punishment of terrorist speech if and to the extent that it qualifies as incitement. (Note that Hand's test was hardly a cost–benefit test, because it embodied a categorical distinction; he preferred it in part for that reason, a point to which I will return.)

Whether or not it is right to exclude incitement as Hand understood it, Brandeis' approach cannot simply be read off the Constitution, and we cannot see the *Dennis* approach as necessarily or inherently incompatible with it. To be sure, the First Amendment protects "the freedom of speech," but you can embrace that form of freedom while agreeing—or even insisting—that on a certain showing of harm, regulation or subsequent punishment is acceptable. Brandeis' judgment on behalf of his understanding of the Constitution's command depends on arguments of his own, not a mere announcement.

2. *Imminence.* Brandeis does offer an argument, and it is an exceedingly famous one to boot. The argument is essentially a defense of the imminence requirement: if there is time to avert the evil through discussion, then the remedy is not forced silence, but counterspeech. Instead of censoring speech or threatening to punish it, government should attempt to rebut it. If people defend overthrow of the government, or claim that women should be subordinate to men, or attack racial minority groups, their arguments should be rebutted. For reasons elaborated by John Stuart Mill,[27] that process of rebuttal has numerous advantages; it corrects error, opens up possibilities, sharpens thought even when it does not change it, undoes complacency, and helps societies to move in the direction of truth.

These are appealing ideas, but on reflection, they are a bit of a mess, certainly as a defense of the clear and present danger test in genuinely hard cases. Suppose that a speaker is saying something that is 40 percent likely to result in the death of a hundred children, not imminently but in the next two years. By emphasizing the potential value of discussion, Brandeis is fighting the hypothetical. He is assuming or stipulating that because there is no emergency, speech can provide the remedy. Maybe so, but that is simply a way of denying the predicate of the question, which seems to deserve a real answer.

The regulatory analogy is helpful here. It is true that with respect to Brandeis' central concerns, speech is unique; for (say) pollution, the harm that regulators seek to address is unlikely to be addressable (merely) through discussion, if only because we are not dealing with speech. To be sure, you could say that the right approach to pollution is the system of free speech; people could say to polluters, "Stop polluting!" At the same time, that is hardly likely to be sufficient. To stop environmental harm, we need action as well.

But to tighten the analogy, that harm might well be addressable through some other means, short of regulating the underlying conduct. If the harm is prema-ture mortality or climate change, a less-than-imminent harm might well turn out to be preventable at some point before it actually occurs. For climate change in particular, adaptation, or some unforeseen technological fix, might prevent the harm in (say) 2040. That possibility raises a fair question, often offered by objects of regulation: *Why should we impose expensive precautions today?* Whenever the issue involves health and safety, it is possible to think that interim steps will pre-vent the feared harms from coming to fruition. Would it not be better to delay costly measures until tomorrow, or the day after?

Actually, no. The best answer, of course, is suggested in *Dennis* itself: if we do not act now, it might turn out to be too late in the future. An ounce of preven-tion might well be worth a pound of cure. Regulators should certainly consider the possibility that the harm can be averted through other means, but there is no reason to foreclose regulatory action merely because of that possibility. As always, it is part of the analysis; if the probability of averting the harm is 50 per-cent, the benefits should be discounted accordingly, taking into consideration the costs of the steps that avert the harm. A complete analysis would consider the full set of costs and benefits, with reference to the appropriate discount rate and estimates of all relevant probabilities—but (and this is the central point) it would hardly lead to Brandeis' approach. The upshot is that the imminence requirement is difficult indeed to defend, unless it is a rough-and-ready way to instantiate the idea that the harm must be likely. Brandeis might be thinking that if the harm is not imminent, it is simply too speculative to say that it is likely, and that nonimminent harms are unlikely to occur so long as discussion is available. But purely as a matter of logic, that cannot be true.

3. *Likelihood.* So much for the imminence requirement. What about the idea that harms must be *likely*, taken by itself? We could imagine a free speech regime that requires a showing of likelihood but that says nothing at all about imminence: a likelihood ten years hence is the same as a likelihood tomorrow. But as in the regulatory context, this is a puzzling view. A small risk of catastrophe deserves more attention than a large risk of modest harm; at least as a first approximation, expected value is what matters.[28] What is so magical about a probability of more than 50 percent? Why should that be the threshold?

At its origin, the idea of a "clear" danger almost certainly meant something far more modest, now lost to history. When Holmes first announced the clear and present danger test, he did not intend anything especially speech protective.[29] And when he used the word "clear," he might well have meant not "more likely than not," but something more akin to "real rather than fanciful." On that view, the word "clear" was intended to clarify the word "danger" in a modest way, by signaling the simple fact that the government must actually be able to point to one. That would bring free speech law closely into line with regulatory standards, where fanciful risks also cannot be regulated (because regulation would fail cost–benefit balancing); and of course such a test would be a far cry from current law.

As a matter of current understandings, however, this point is moot. In *Brandenburg v. Ohio*,[30] the Court read "clear" to mean "likely." That interpretation has been unchallenged for decades. What I am suggesting thus far is that the unchallenged interpretation seems very hard to defend, because cost–benefit balancing is better. Indeed, the difficulty of defending it becomes only clearer when we expand the viewscreen. In regulation, as noted, the expected value of the harm is only one part of the picture; the benefit of the underlying activity matters as well. We might be dealing with socially beneficial activity, and it might cost (say) $900 million to regulate it, or we might be dealing with activity from which society does not much benefit, and it might cost $1 million to regulate it. It much matters with which we are dealing.

Shouldn't the same be true for speech? And once we start thinking in terms of both benefits and costs, we will be refining the framework in *Dennis*, in a way that makes that framework compatible with regulatory approaches more broadly. In the cost–benefit state, why would that be a mistake?

Defending Likelihood and Imminence

I now turn to three possible defenses of the clear and present danger test, taking them in ascending order of persuasiveness. The first is that in light of the insuperable difficulties of quantification, cost–benefit analysis is not feasible in this domain. The second points to the pervasive risk of institutional bias, arguing that the clear and present danger test is a second best, designed to counteract that bias. On that view, the test is actually what cost–benefit analysis calls for, because it responds to the danger of inaccurate case-by-case assessments. The third, and the most convincing, justification is that in the real world, the cases for which the clear and present danger test fails did not exist in the last half of the twentieth century, or at least could not easily be identified if they did exist. If the second and the third justifications are put together, the clear and present danger test looks pretty good.

A reasonable conclusion is that the clear and present danger test is hard to defend in principle or in the abstract. But the difference from the more general regulatory context is that it is hard to list real-world situations in which speech should be regulated because it produces nonimminent, low-probability harms. Because of the rise of terrorism, however, the first half of the twenty-first century might be different from the second half of the twentieth on that count.

Challenges of Quantification

In the world of regulation, it is often possible to quantify both costs and benefits. For example, an energy efficiency regulation might be anticipated to cost $200 million per year. It might save consumers $80 million per year and also reduce air pollution by specified amounts, with monetizable effects. If so, the aggregate benefits are far higher than the aggregate costs. Analysis of this kind is standard for federal regulations.

The whole exercise is far more challenging for speech, and in some ways, it is neither feasible nor attractive. Suppose that a speaker is calling for violent acts to resist what he sees as oppression. Suppose that the acts will result in some number of deaths. We might enlist the usual number of the value of a statistical life, which is $9 million,[31] and multiply that times the number of lives at risk, discounted by the probability that the bad outcome will occur. But there are multiple uncertainties here. How many lives are at risk? Is $9 million the correct number in this particular context? What is the probability? Perhaps analysts can produce lower or upper bounds, which might make the analysis more tractable. But the guesswork here is substantial.

Valuation of the benefits of speech is even more difficult. Suppose that we are dealing with pro-Communist speech, racial hate speech, Nazi marches, terrorist recruitment, celebration of terrorist attacks, or calls for overthrow of a government. What is the benefit of that speech? Can we quantify it?

One way to answer that question would require us to probe some deep questions. We might protect speech because it protects autonomy, because it serves the goal of arriving at truth, because it is a safety valve, because it is indispensable to self-government, or because it promotes social welfare. These are, of course, among the largest issues in free speech theory. If we believe that even one of these things is true, or that all of them are true, we will not have made much progress toward valuing benefits. If we are serious about costs and benefits, the valuation exercise requires quantification. For pollution reduction, it is usual to begin by asking about the real-world effects (reduced mortality, reduced morbidity), and then to quantify them (five hundred premature deaths averted, two thousand nonfatal cancer cases averted), and then to turn them into monetary equivalents (usually with resort to the idea of people's willingness to pay). For speech, steps of that kind are both difficult and (to put it mildly) not self-evidently attractive.

To value speech, we would hardly want to rest content with asking speakers how much they would be willing to pay to retain their right to say what they want (or how much they would demand to give up that right). That would be patently inadequate, a kind of category mistake. The value of the right to take part in a political protest—say, by people objecting to police brutality or the practice of abortion—is not properly measured by asking speakers how much they would pay for it. One reason is that even if the answers to such questions are in some important sense relevant, the value of speech is not captured by its value to speakers; the audience matters as well, and it is probably what matters most. Free speech is for listeners even more than speakers.[32]

To assess the value of speech to listeners, would it make sense to ask (a random sample of) people how much they would be willing to pay to hear certain speeches? To ensure that certain speakers are allowed to speak? In a nation that values freedom, those are terrible questions. One reason is that speech is supposed to affect, and not simply to track, people's values and preferences. Economic analysis of willingness to pay does not adequately capture what matters. (Of course, some people think that the same is true for pollution, but at least the theoretical justification is well developed in that context.) Another reason is that people's judgments about the value of speech may well depend on whether it pleases them, which would produce a distorted assessment of the benefits of speech; whether speech is valuable does not depend on whether it pleases people.

For these reasons, the usual approach to valuing costs and benefits fails in this context. It presents insuperable empirical problems, and even if these could be surmounted, there are serious normative objections to using that approach. But what is the implication of these conclusions? *Dennis* did not purport to use economic analysis of any formal kind; it endorsed something far looser and more intuitive, designed to specify or soften the clear and present danger test in circumstances in which the danger was neither clear nor present. The basic idea is that if speech has a positive probability of causing or contributing to egregious harm, government is not powerless to prevent it. We can take this idea as a form of rough-and-ready cost–benefit analysis or as a version of the Catastrophic Harm Precautionary Principle. And indeed, it is written as the former. The basic point is that the difficulty of quantifying costs and benefits is neither a convincing objection to the *Dennis* approach nor an adequate defense of the clear and present danger test.

Institutional Bias

An alternative view is that the clear and present danger test is an excellent response to a pervasive institutional risk, which is that the government's own assessments will be systematically skewed, above all because its own self-interest and the interests of powerful private groups are so often at stake. The risk, in other words, is that while invoking a risk of harm, and speaking of expected value, public officials are actually trying to insulate themselves from criticism. Their real concerns are about protecting their own power and legitimacy, rather than protecting the society from danger. Our own history speaks volumes here.[33] Internationally, one can readily think of examples from Russia, China, Cuba, and Turkey.

Suppose, for example, that some protesters, objecting to what they see as racist violence by the police, demonstrate noisily in a large city, or that other protesters, skeptical of what they see as an overreaching national government, are vigorously objecting to recent legislation. Public officials might complain about a risk of violence, but their actual goal (whether conscious or not) might be to insulate themselves from criticism. Their interest in precautions, and their assessment of costs and benefits, will be systematically self-serving—an unreliable and even dangerous basis for authorizing action. Any Precautionary Principle, with respect to the harms stemming from speech, would put democracy itself at immediate and severe risk. Cost–benefit analysis might seem much better, but it suffers from precisely the same vice, which is that it enables untrustworthy officials to invoke a seemingly neutral and abstractly appealing standard in defense of outcomes that actually violate that very standard. On welfarist grounds and in principle, the clear and present danger test might not be close to perfect. But in the real world, it is incalculably (so to speak) preferable to what would emerge from open-ended balancing by unreliable balancers. In short, it considers the risk of manipulation and biased judgment by those actually charged with assessing the costs and benefits.

In the regulatory context, a similar argument is not unfamiliar. A standard claim, especially within the business community, is that government regulators typically overstate the benefits and understate the costs of what they do.[34] Whether or not that is true, the proper response, if it is indeed true, is to put in place institutional safeguards that correct mistaken judgments.[35] We might, for example, allow assessment by some kind of independent entity within the executive branch or insist on judicial review of the agency's analysis. As in the context of regulation in general, so in the free speech context: *the most natural response to institutional bias is to create safeguards to combat it.* Federal judges need not defer to whatever legislative and executive officials think; they could force them to meet a (high) burden of proof. On this approach, some version of the *Dennis* test would be firmly in place, but with strong judicial efforts to reduce the risk of bias. Other institutional safeguards might be put in place to reduce that risk, in the form of independent analysts within the legislative or executive branches, whose job would be to monitor the assessment of both costs and benefits.

The upshot is that the risk of institutional bias is entirely real, but the more direct corrective is not to jump from a cost–benefit test to a clear and present danger test, but to increase the likelihood that the proper test will be properly applied. The institutional defense of the clear and present danger test is forceful but incomplete. It identifies the right ailment, but it does not offer the most obvious cure. The most that can be said is that if the right cure is unavailable, it might be a second best—but it cannot, on its own, produce a full-scale defense of the test.

As It Happens

Here is a final argument on behalf of the clear and present danger test. In my view, it is basically convincing—or at least it has been convincing—for most of the time in which the test has held sway. The problem is that it depends on empirical assumptions that will not always hold, and that probably do not hold today.

The central claim is that in the world in which we live, the cases that confound the clear and present danger test exist rarely or not at all. I have pointed to situations in which harm is neither likely nor imminent, and when speech causes a one in x risk of harm in a distant future. But the stubborn fact is that in such cases, the costs of allowing the speech have turned out to be low (in reality), and those costs can be avoided or minimized without restricting speech—as, for example, by taking strong (and not unduly costly) steps to avert violence. Suppose, for example, that a number of people call for violent acts in circumstances in which the clear and present danger test is not satisfied—to overthrow the government, to kill police officers, to have some kind of revolution. If such calls in fact produce violent acts that could not be prevented through other means, then the argument for speech regulation would be difficult to avoid; the clear and present danger test would be responsible for tragedy. But (the argument goes) there are essentially no such cases.

On this count, the regulatory context is altogether different. It is easy to find cases in which regulation is important or even critical to prevent harms even if they would not occur imminently. For situations of low-probability risks, it is more difficult to find examples, but it is plausible to think that in the context of climate change and financial stability, numerous actions have been justified and desirable even if the harms were not "likely." A clear and present danger test would make no sense for regulation in general; it would impose high net costs. The same cannot be said in the context of speech. And that is, in a nutshell, the central defense of the clear and present danger test.

We would need a lot of detail to know for sure, but for the decades in which the clear and present danger test has held sway, this defense is plausibly convincing. Defenders of *Dennis* would be hard-pressed to point to situations in which their preferred approach would have prevented serious harm. But of course everything depends on assumptions about the state of the world. We could easily imagine a nation, facing a high degree of volatility and serious risks of speech-induced violence, in which the argument for the *Dennis* approach would be quite strong. (From the standpoint of the British, would that be the situation in the American colonies in the years immediately preceding the American Revolution?) And in an era of international terrorism, the argument for something like *Dennis* might well be stronger. At the very least, some people think so.

Is it? That is, of course, an empirical question. To put it in sharp relief, suppose that within the next (say) ten years, there is a significant chance (say, at least 50 percent) of two or more serious terrorist attacks in the United States, each producing a loss of at least two hundred lives, with proliferating harms of high magnitude. Suppose too that if relevant terrorist recruitment speech is banned, half of those attacks would be prevented. If so, the cost–benefit calculus might well come out favorably to regulation—and the *Dennis* approach might well be better. At least this is so if we believe (as I do) that the benefits of terrorist recruitment speech are essentially zero.

I do not mean to press any empirical claims here. But with this sketch of the best arguments for the clear and present danger test, we can see that under imaginable assumptions, it would have unacceptably high net costs. If the risk of institutional bias could be cabined, and if the test would allow horrifying acts to occur, then *Dennis* would be better. It is hard to say that the clear and present danger test has caused mischief over the last fifty years. But it is not implausible to say that it will cause mischief over the next fifty. In the context of terrorism, whether that possibility justified something more like *Dennis*, or perhaps akin to Hand's incitement test, is at least a question worth asking.

Has not failed, but might in the future

Conclusion

The modern regulatory state uses cost–benefit analysis as its standard rule of decision, and it would not make much sense to say that the regulatory choices of the Environmental Protection Agency, the Department of Transportation, and the Department of Health and Human Services should be based instead on the clear and present danger test. Reasonable people have contended that cost–benefit analysis fails to take sufficient precautions against risks; almost no one argues that such balancing generally produces excessive regulation (even if it might do so in particular cases).

In principle, some form of cost–benefit balancing might well seem preferable to the clear and present danger test in the context of speech as well. A natural objection involves valuation: What, exactly, are the costs and the benefits of speech that (say) calls for some kind of political revolution? That is an excellent question, but at least in some cases, it is unnecessary to resolve difficult valuation questions to say that the balance comes out unfavorably to speech, even though no danger is clear and present.

The best justifications for the clear and present danger test point to institutional biases and to the possibility that the cases that confound that test are not likely to arise in the real world. It need not be emphasized that public officials will often find a danger even when there is no such thing; their own desire for self-insulation will pervert their judgments. It is true that institutional safeguards could reduce or perhaps eliminate this problem, which makes it important to contend that as opposed to the clear and present danger test, *Dennis* responds to a generally nonexistent problem.

In the United States from the period between 1960 and 2001, that conclusion seems right. But it is less obviously right today. The clear and present danger test is not a test for all seasons. In imaginable times and places, it rests on doubtful assumptions. Even in the face of international terrorism, it would be reckless to say that we would be better off without it. But it is not reckless to say that that is a perfectly fair question to ask.

PART THREE

THE INTERNATIONAL IMPLICATIONS OF THE FIRST AMENDMENT

Reflections on the Firstness of the First Amendment in the United States

ALBIE SACHS

[Writer's note: This text was written as if with sad foreboding just days before the extremely distressing events of Charlottesville, Virginia, in early August 2017. I have left it unaltered save for some clarifications and small style changes.]

It was Justice Frank Jacobucci of the Canadian Supreme Court who introduced me to the concept of the "firstness" of the First Amendment to the US Constitution. It was 1994 and at the time I was waiting to hear whether I would be appointed to the South African Constitutional Court. Our Judicial Service Commission had sent ten names to President Nelson Mandela, from which he had to choose six.[1] I was one of them—on tenterhooks. Having been invited to receive an honorary degree from York University in Toronto, I had arranged a visit to the Canadian Supreme Court to help me get at least an initial feel of what it might be like if I was indeed appointed. Ours would be a completely new court interpreting a totally new Constitution. We would need all the ideas we could get from all over the world. Frank was pointing out that the Canadian Supreme Court's philosophy was rather different from that of the US Supreme Court. American judges, he told me, centered their Constitution on the notion of free speech. To them, government was the foe that needed to be guarded against, not the friend that had to be prevented from taking wrong steps[2]—hence his reference to the firstness of the American First Amendment.[3]

His words made me reflect on what rights were being placed first in our new South African constitutional democracy. There was no doubt about the importance of freedom of speech. Apart from living under draconian legislation to suppress meaningful political dissent to apartheid, we had suffered the stings of an extensive network of laws to crush free expression.[4]

A history of censorship

In my own case, I was one of thousands of people who had received banning orders that expressly forbade me to write anything for publication, even to be on the premises of a publisher.[5] It was a criminal offense for anyone to be in possession of anything I had prepared for publication or to communicate to anyone else any statement made by me.[6] My doctoral thesis at the University of Sussex, which had been published by Heinemann in London and the University of California Press in Berkeley,[7] had been banned not once, but three times—banned because I was banned, expressly banned as a title, and banned because it quoted the words of Oliver Tambo and Nelson Mandela, who were also banned people.[8] For years the book was smuggled into South Africa under a false cover and avidly read by law professors and students, maybe even by a judge, until, that is, change came and it lost its forbidden-fruit luster. At every level government had gone out of its way to protect us from dangerous ideas. For decades, the Publications Control Board had decided not only what books we could read but also what films we could see and what plays could be put on.[9] We chortled when the children's book *Black Beauty* was banned.[10] But it wasn't funny.

Since the 1950s, the African National Congress (ANC) struggle slogan had been "Freedom in Our Lifetime,"[11] and freedom of speech was high up on the list of freedoms to which we aspired. But it was not number one. Number one was equality. We had been fighting against a system of White overlordship commonly known as apartheid. Achieving equality and human dignity lay at the core of our endeavor. Freedom of speech was fundamental for securing democracy and important in itself as an aspect of affirming human dignity. But it was not the first right to spring out of the blocks.

Those of us in the struggle who went to work on the text and timbre of our new Constitution felt that we should root it in our history just as the American drafters had done with their Constitution. It had been no accident that in the United States the First Amendment had related to prohibiting abridgment of freedom of speech, on the one hand, while simultaneously guaranteeing free exercise of religion on the other.[12] The colonists had fled from religious persecution in England.[13] They had resisted the imposition of an established religion[14] and had fought against authoritarian controls by the imperial government intended to suppress any form of rebellion against the Crown.[15] Equality and human dignity had not been foundational principles.[16] Indeed, many of the founding fathers were slave owners.[17] Very few would have favored rights for women, and Native Americans were virtually excluded from the purview of the Constitution altogether. Where the shoe had pinched the most had been in relation to British imperial control of expression and belief. If ever there was an original "Original Intent," this was it. Having free speech and freedom of belief was more than just a right to be guarded against governmental control. It was a proclamation of identity, a statement of what it meant to be a free American rather than a colonial subject, a Declaration of Independence coming from the heart and conscience of each born American. *a response to their conditions.*

Yet our trajectory toward constitutionalism had been very different. Our primary goal had been to destroy the system of racial supremacy and create an open and democratic society freed of racism. Our Constitution opens with a ringing Preamble relating to our history and goals.[18] It then sets out its founding values: human dignity, the achievement of equality, and the advancement of human rights and freedoms; nonracialism and nonsexism; supremacy of the Constitution and the rule of law; and multiparty democratic government to ensure accountability, responsiveness, and openness.[19] And then come the cornerstone provisions of the Bill of Rights.[20]

The South African Bill of Rights does not, as in the United States, come as a set of Amendments attached to an already-adopted Constitution structuring government. On the contrary, our Bill of Rights comes before the chapters dealing with the institutions of democratic government.[21] We can in fact speak of the firstness of our founding values and Bill of Rights. The Bill of Rights declares its own primacy. It opens with the statement: "The Bill of Rights is a cornerstone of democracy in South Africa. It enshrines the rights of all people in our country and affirms the democratic values of dignity, equality and freedom."[22] Although all three values are clearly overlapping and interdependent, it should be noted that freedom is not first in the triad, but third. Then, though not too much should be read into the sequence in which protected rights are proclaimed, it is notable that clauses dealing with equality, human dignity, life, freedom and security of the person, and privacy and freedom of religion, belief, and opinion come before the one concerning freedom of expression.[23]

At the same time, it is also clear that freedom of expression is given great constitutional amplitude and attended to with unusual detail. The reach of protection is wide. It explicitly includes (1) freedom of the press and other media, (2) freedom to receive or impart information or ideas, (3) freedom of artistic creativity, and (4) academic freedom and freedom of scientific research.[24]

Yet the clause expressly declares that these rights do not extend to (1) propaganda for war; (2) incitement of imminent violence; and (3) advocacy of hatred *→ "hate speech"* that is based on race, ethnicity, gender, or religion and that constitutes incitement to cause harm.[25] Furthermore, it must be pointed out that like all other rights in the Bill of Rights, the residual affirmatively protected rights of freedom of expression may themselves be limited in terms of a law of general application to the extent that the limitation is reasonable and justifiable in an open and democratic society based on human dignity, equality, and freedom.[26] A noncontroversial example of such a permissible limitation would be a legislated prohibition on the media against mentioning the names of children involved in court cases to protect their identity.[27]

As drafters, we could only do our best to capture all the competing considerations. Yet like all freedoms, freedom of expression by its very nature resists being put into a neat definitional box. Even if we denied it the quality of firstness, we had no doubt about its pungency and pervasiveness for the whole constitutional project. The right to think, know, and express yourself went well beyond being simply a claim that every individual might have against an overbossy state. It was fundamental to the enjoyment of all other rights. It gave meaning to your rights to vote, to have your dignity respected, to conscience, to health and gender equality, to be a child, to speak your language and follow your faith, to fair labor practices, to a fair trial, to silence and conscience, and freedom from violence from the State or private sources or from detention without trial—indeed, to all the rights protected by the Constitution. In that sense, freedom of expression has become constitutive of our new citizenship, a key ingredient of the open and democratic society promised by the Constitution. And any perceived threats from government to impose restrictions on reporting by the media or to wrap governmental activity in secrecy are met with vociferous public outcries. For their part, the courts are extremely reluctant to impose prior restraint on the publication of defamatory reports.[28]

It is in this respect that resounding notes struck in two cases by the US Supreme Court generations ago continue to reverberate in our country. It's not simply a question of text or doctrine or whether freedom of speech comes first or eighth in the list of protected rights. It's about what it means to live in an open and democratic society, and more particularly, the role of the judiciary in keeping the society open and democratic. Thus, the constitutional imaginations of many of my generation had been strongly inspired by decisions of the US Supreme Court dealing with free speech. The first was the Pentagon Papers case, where the US Supreme Court tore a big hole in the veil of secrecy that the US administration had been seeking to place over the conduct of the Vietnam War.[29] The second was the *Sullivan* matter,[30] which dramatically extended free speech doctrine to effectively outlaw public officials from using civil remedies under the law of defamation to suppress critical voices in the United States, which was at the time a pervasive practice in countries like Singapore,[31] Kenya,[32] and Malaysia.[33] For those of us about to become judges in our new democracy, these decisions shone like lanterns to illuminate the role that judges should play in keeping society open and strengthening democracy.

In both cases, the specific context in which doctrine was developed in the Supreme Court seemed to us to have been important. It was not only the unpopularity of the Vietnam War in large sections of American society and internationally that had been significant, but also the secrecy that was being used to keep important information out of the national debate.[34] It was not only truth that was the casualty of war, it was critically relevant information. The British tradition of deferring to the royal prerogative and the protection of governmental secrecy in "the national interest" had taken strong root in even the most democratic of the former British colonies and had remained strong in the United Kingdom itself.[35]

These US Supreme Court decisions in favor of openness had a reverberation well beyond the United States. They challenged undue judicial subservience to executive fiat in favor of open, deliberative, and participatory democracy.[36] *Sullivan* ended the possibilities of racist officials in the South being able to se-cure huge damages awards from racist judges and juries in cases they brought against critics of Jim Crow. Of particular importance was the Court's acknowl-edgment of the chilling effect generally on investigative journalism produced by the threat of huge damages awards being based on inaccuracies in otherwise damning reports of governmental misconduct.[37]

The US Supreme Court's approach to freedom of information and free speech during that period was later to become a source of immense inspiration to the emerging generation of constitution makers and judges in our new democracy. At the same time, there were aspects of First Amendment free speech rights that we found to be quite alarming. Having just begun to emerge from a society based on racial persecution, it was shocking to think that self-proclaimed Nazis could freely conduct a march in the center of a suburb with a very large Jewish pop-ulation, including thousands of Holocaust survivors, because of a court ruling that a city ordinance intended to prevent them from doing so denied them their First Amendment rights.[38] In our view, an open democratic society would in-deed have a legislative duty to protect the victims of racist horror from gratui-tous insults of that kind. We noted that, given its particular history, post-Hitler Germany had made Holocaust denial a criminal offense.[39] What Holocaust deniers like David Irving[40] could utter freely in the United States would send them to jail in Germany.

Similarly, it was shocking to discover that, in the name of freedom of expres-sion, the judiciary would not restrain the placing of a burning cross, the insignia of the Ku Klux Klan, on the pavement across the way from a home occupied by a Black family in a White neighborhood.[41] I remember my progressive friends in America being absolutely shocked at the time—and we shared their shock. It was hard for us to accept that what seemed to be an absolutist approach to free speech could sanction a profound undermining of the equality principles in the Constitution. In our thinking, equality could not be understood without regard to respect for human dignity. Speech that profoundly undermined the dignity, even the safety, of people who historically had been treated as less than human not only threatened the very fabric of our democracy but also induced an intol-erable degree of continuing pain and undermined the right of those targeted by it to freely express being who they were.

Our Constitutional Court was appointed after the first democratic elections in 1994 and began hearing cases a year later. Interestingly, I was one of the Original Intenders of our Constitution who found ourselves on the Constitutional Court interpreting provisions we had helped formulate. Not once in our decisions did we ever refer to what our actual original intent had been.[42] To be candid, there had been so many drafts and counterdrafts that I couldn't have remembered even if I had tried. But as a matter of principle, our starting point was that the Constitution was a public document that spoke for itself through its text and values, to be interpreted in its historical and social context as a transformative instrument that would progressively enable the country, as promised by the text, to overcome racism and sexism and achieve meaningful equality in conditions of freedom and accountability. The only Original Intention of which I can be sure we all had was that the tree we were planting would grow with time and circumstance.

As it turned out, we were frequently called upon to uphold the importance of freedom of expression as a fundamental element of our democracy. We struck down laws that permitted prepublication censorship[43] and the criminalization of the possession of erotic photographs.[44] We also declared that though it was reasonable and justifiable in an open and democratic society for a law to limit the right of soldiers to strike, it would not be reasonable and justifiable to limit the right to freedom of speech involved when a soldiers' trade union sought to canvas soldiers' views with regard to representing them in negotiations on their pay and working conditions.[45] At the same time, we upheld the criminalization of film and photographs depicting child pornography, even if the images had been produced by computers without the involvement of actual children.[46] The Court's rationale was that in our open democratic society it was reasonable and justifiable to protect the rights of children in general through suppressing the development of a culture of adult predation.[47]

Many of us were wondering when the first case would be brought to our Court urging us to develop our common law in line with our Constitution by applying the freedom of speech principles laid down in *Sullivan*. Would we agree that "public officials" can only recover for falsehoods that injure their reputations when spoken with "actual malice,"[48] meaning with knowledge of falsity or reckless disregard of falsity? Would we go along with *Gertz* and extend this doctrine to "public figures," as well as public officials?[49]

Our common law of defamation at that stage in effect held that the onus was on the maker of a statement calculated to lower the public esteem of any person to prove that the statement was true and that its communication was for the public benefit.[50] I don't recall the facts of the alleged libel in the matter that eventually reached us; save to say that they were not symptomatic of any pattern of civil court processes being used abusively to suppress dissent. What

I do remember, however, is that my starting point was that the Constitution required us firmly to encourage free speech and serious and penetrating investigative journalism, while not losing sight of the way in certain countries powerful press conglomerates had undermined genuine public debate by relentlessly and recklessly destroying the reputations of personalities who had happened to incur their disfavor. I also realized that the fact that free speech was now firmly protected in our Constitution would require us to take a robust look at common law doctrine that had evolved in a society far more hierarchical than the open and democratic one now being envisaged.

After hearing extensive argument from counsel and having conducted deliberative workshops among ourselves, we concluded that while we should embrace the broad free speech values of *Sullivan*, we should not follow it doctrinally.[51] In the first place, the basic principles of balancing interests should be the same whether the plaintiff was a public official or not. Second, while we substantially relaxed the burden of proof on defendants who published statements that were untrue, we did not go as far as letting them off the hook completely if the plaintiff could establish malice and actual knowledge of or reckless disregard for the truth of the statement.[52]

One of the features of our Constitution is that it requires the courts to interpret all legislation and develop the common law in a manner that promotes the "spirit, purpose and objects of the Bill of Rights."[53] In doing so, we are expressly authorized to have regard to foreign law and, more generally, required to have regard to the values of open and democratic societies.[54] This meant that we could both comfortably look at the US Supreme Court's decision in *Sullivan* and at the same time feel no need to limit our Constitutional Court gaze to public officials or figures. The fact that the allegedly defamatory statement related to the reputation and dignity of someone who was a public official would, of course, be highly relevant to the balancing of interests in a particular case, since a healthy democracy facilitated the strictest scrutiny of those exercising public power. But it would not be determinative of our jurisdiction.

The appropriate balance required by our Constitution in relation to untrue statements, we believed, would be achieved by allowing publishers of inaccurate defamatory statements about public (or private) figures to establish a defense that they had taken reasonable measures to verify the accuracy of the impugned statements.[55] Our thinking was that this formulation would not have an unduly chilling effect on the publication of critical information on the one hand, while on the other it would place an onus on the press to train its journalists well and introduce appropriate forms of fact checking.[56]

For what it is worth, visitors to our country comment on how freely the media today reveal damaging information about leading public figures.[57] South Africans speak their minds freely, openly, and even raucously. At the same time we have respected press ombudsmen (so far only men) who receive complaints about inaccurate reporting and who, I believe, have responded diligently, required corrections and apologies, and helped significantly to develop a culture of responsible journalism.[58] I should add, however, that there are important public figures who argue that self-regulation by the press is inadequate, and that a state media appeals tribunal should be established to achieve effective remedies for inaccurate reporting.[59]

When it comes to artistic expression, our country must be among the most open in the world. A painting depicting the president in a Leninist posture with his penis exposed provoked huge public controversy.[60] But the argument has not been so much about the lawfulness of this and other similar works as about their propriety. I personally have, both on and off the Bench, written strongly in defense of parody, satire (drawing strongly on the US Supreme Court decision in the "Pretty Woman" case[61]), and cartoons, and generally about the importance of humor as an elixir of democracy in our society.[62] At the same time, I have urged artists as creative persons with humane souls not to engage in using imagery that evokes stereotypical and demeaning echoes of past and continuing human abuse.

The question of obscenity has not been fully litigated upon. At the time when our Court started, there were hot debates internationally over the question of obscenity. On the one hand there was a powerful movement that criticized puritan censure or taboos on any public exhibition of naked bodies. Frequently, the public prohibition of nudity was accompanied by hypocritical lasciviousness on behalf of the lawmakers themselves. I remember reading that in the United States where the law came down heavily on what was called "obscenity," the annual expenditure on strip clubs was six times that of the spending on symphony concerts, theaters, and art galleries put together.[63]

On the other hand, people like Catharine MacKinnon were pointing out that the true offense was not nudity as such but the way in which women's bodies were being objectified and demeaned for the sake of male pleasure.[64] In the one case that came before us the Court struck down a regulation that prohibited the sale of liquor on premises where there was nudity.[65] The Court followed the "high art" road and held that the regulation was overly broad because it would prohibit the sale of liquor during the intermission of a play in which nudity served a manifestly artistic purpose.[66] The majority of the court, myself included, took the antipuritan side. Still, I regretted the fact that the Catharine MacKinnon argument was not raised at all in the case.

The most difficult free speech issues in our country, however, have not related to criticism of public officials or to obscenity. They have arisen from what is frequently referred to as hate speech. The term has been used in relation to homophobia, anti-Semitism, Islamophobia, and xenophobia, but its main relevance here has been in relation to race. The central tension has been between the urgent need to open up our society from the draconian and ubiquitous restrictions of the past, on the one hand, and for the law to promote social cohesion by preventing inflammatory, racist abuse that could tear the country apart and undermine the foundations of our new democracy, on the other.

This tension was highlighted but not resolved in a Holocaust denial case brought to the Court by the Jewish Board of Deputies against a Muslim community radio station that had broadcast a program in which a United Kingdom academic had said that only one million Jews had died in the Nazi camps and that they had died from disease.[67] The Jewish Board of Deputies had approached the Broadcasting Complaints Commission seeking revocation of the radio station's license to broadcast.[68] The radio station relied on free speech rights, claiming that the violation had been charged under a regulation referring to "the likelihood of prejudicing relations between sections of the population," which was void for vagueness and overly broad.[69]

The Court pointed out:

> Freedom of expression, especially when gauged in conjunction with its accompanying fundamental freedoms, is of utmost importance in the kind of open and democratic society the Constitution had set as our aspirational norm. Having regard to our recent past of thought control, censorship and enforced conformity to governmental theories, freedom of expression as the free and open exchange of ideas was no less important than it was in the United States of America. It could actually be contended with much force that the public interest in the open marketplace of ideas was all the more important because our democracy was not yet firmly established and had to feel its way. It was necessary therefore to be particularly astute to outlaw any form of thought control however respectably dressed.[70]

Freedom to speak one's mind was now an inherent quality of the type of society contemplated by the Constitution as a whole and was specifically promoted by the freedoms of conscience, expression, assembly, association, and political participation, protected by the Bill of Rights.[71]

At the same time, having come out so strongly in favor of free speech, the Court went on to state that the pluralism and broad-mindedness that were central to an open democratic society could be undermined by speech that threatened democratic pluralism itself.[72] The Constitution declared that South Africa was founded on the values of human dignity, the achievement of equality, and the advancement of human rights and freedoms.[73] Open and democratic societies permitted reasonable proscription of activity and expression that posed a real and substantial threat to such values and to the Constitutional order itself. The right to freedom of expression could not be said automatically to trump the right to human dignity.[74] The Court noted: "How these two rights are to be balanced in principle and in any particular set of circumstances is not a question that had to be decided in that matter. What is clear though . . . is that freedom of expression does not enjoy superior status in our law."[75]

The Court accepted that appropriate regulation of broadcasting in the public interest served an important and legitimate purpose in a democratic society.[76] There is a critical need for the South African community to protect human dignity, equality, freedom, the healing of the divisions of the past, and the building of a united society.[77] The Court continued:

> South African society is diverse and has for many centuries been sorely divided, not least through laws and practices which encouraged hatred and fear. Expression that advocated hatred and stereotyping of people on the basis of immutable characteristics is particularly harmful to the achievement of these values as it reinforces and perpetuates patterns of discrimination and inequality. Left unregulated such expression has the potential to perpetuate the negative aspects of our past and further divide our society.[78]

Having pointed to these competing constitutional considerations, however, the Court decided that it was not called upon to make a definitive ruling one way or the other on the Holocaust denial statement. This was because it found that the wording of the relevant regulation on which the complaint had been brought was grossly overbroad in its reach and needed to be replaced by a fresh regulation neatly tailored to preserve the legitimate public interest.[79]

The area in which the theme of hate speech has been most vigorously debated has related to social media, where the tendency is for wounding or inciting statements quickly to go viral. Until now, the criminal law has not been used as a weapon to punish hate speech, however it might be defined. The media are encouraged to go in for responsible self-regulation. Allegations of hate speech can be reported to the Equality Courts, which have been set up with a view to encouraging reconciliation and apology where possible, but also to impose fines.[80] Thus, a White woman in Durban who complained on Facebook that Black families crowding the beach on holidays had left litter behind "like monkeys" was directed to appear before the Equality Court and ordered to pay a substantial fine to a nongovernmental organization (NGO) that promoted constitutionalism.[81] The case aroused huge public interest.[82] One proposal that has been made is that the NGO should use the money in a restorative-justice way to enable Black kids who have never seen the sea to spend a holiday there, possibly with some form of appropriate and voluntary participation by the defendant.

unlike
US

As noted earlier, the Constitution expressly excludes certain forms of hate speech from its protection.[83] Thus, Parliament is completely free to adopt legislation outlawing advocacy of hatred that is based on race, ethnicity, gender, or religion and that constitutes incitement to cause harm. As far as I am aware, no court of appeal, including the Constitutional Court, has yet ruled on the full import of this provision. The principal debate that is emerging is about what is meant by "harm." Does it imply physical harm, or does it extend to harm to the dignity and sense of self-worth of people affected? The current tendency appears to be for trial courts to locate the notion of harm in the context of our history, which would give special weight to the moral and spiritual harm caused by the challenged advocacy. In any event, the categories of speech identified by the Constitution as not meriting protection do not define the outer reaches of permissible legislative restraint on hate speech. And it must be stressed that even the protected body of free expression is subject to such reasonable limitation as would be justifiable in an open and democratic society.[84] This allows restrictions on hate speech such as xenophobia and homophobia, which have been included in the remit of the Equality Courts.

In making any inquiry in regard to what would constitute a reasonable and justifiable limitation on protected free expression, our courts would inevitably notice how varied the responses of open and democratic societies have been to hate speech. I suspect our judiciary would give great weight to the history of the particular country concerned, the context in which the relevant constitutional provision was adopted, and the manner in which its interpretation has evolved since. Such a survey of legal responses around the democratic world would, I am sure, show that the First Amendment is probably only the first in the United States, with its particular history, culture, and current makeup. But the fact that in the rest of the world the First Amendment is not the first does not mean that it is the last. Again, I would suspect that the survey would show that two strong contradictory developments have taken place—while there has been a vast extension throughout the globe in relation to freedom of expression generally, there also has been a notable and distinctive move toward outlawing racial abuse, whether on the sports field or in public discourse or in social media. The tension between these two developments arouses fierce public debate in all continents.

Two recent decisions by judges in South Africa illustrate well how strong that tension can be. They were both handed down while I was finally revising this chapter. The first concerned an attempt by a body to get a court order restraining the South African National Gallery from permitting a performing artist, who happened to be transgender and White, from wearing apparel with the words "Fuck White People" written on it and sitting in front of a painting with the same words on it.[85] The Judge refused to grant the injunction, saying that in the context of a gallery performance the expression did not violate the Equality Act, which gave explicit exemption to serious artistic expression.[86] I should mention that the Constitutional Court has held that the fact that Whites had historically been, and largely continued to be, the beneficiaries of a system of race privilege did not mean that they could never find themselves in a vulnerable position as a minority being discriminated against unfairly.[87] Accordingly, by a majority of ten to one, the Court struck down a municipal regulation that allowed for court processes to be issued for nonpayment of municipal water and electricity bills against householders in upmarket and overwhelmingly White areas, while suspending the operation of such processes in desperately poor African townships.[88] The lone dissenter happened to be myself—though I agreed with the general principle enunciated, I felt that it was not unfair for what was then a largely White municipal council to temporarily suspend summonses in areas where grossly underserved communities had developed a culture of nonpayment as an act of resistance, and now needed time to enable a culture of civic inclusion and mutual responsibility to develop.[89] It might have been a rule-of-law issue, I held, but looking at equality law substantively, on the facts it was not an equality one of unfairly targeting the Whites, who were not being singled out for disparate and unfair treatment.[90] As I have said, my colleagues favored an unequivocal determination that the equality provisions furnished equal protection in terms of law enforcement to everyone, whether former oppressor or oppressed.

The second matter concerned a statement in a column by a prominent journalist, who was later appointed an ambassador, that in terms of his African culture he wished to declare that it was not OK to be gay.[91] The judge to whom the matter had been referred by the South African Human Rights Commission decided that under our law it is not OK to say that to be gay is not OK.[92] I have not seen the text of the judgment, but newspaper reports indicate that it was based on the provisions of the Equality Act, which were themselves based on various provisions in the Constitution. Sentencing will take place some time in the future.

A measure is now before Parliament to make hate speech a criminal offense, as well as to require courts to impose more serious penalties in hate crime cases where the victims have been targeted because of the group to which they belong, whether that be due to their race, gender, sexual orientation, or religion.[93] While there has been widespread support for regarding the context of such group hate as an aggravating factor in the case of crimes of violence, many doubts have been expressed about the wisdom and efficacy of attempting to curb hate speech as such through the blunt instrument of criminal law.[94] One intermediate proposal that is being considered is to allow the courts to impose injunctions against repeat users of hate speech who could then become criminally liable for violation of the court orders. More moderate solution.

Conclusion

I understand that early this century the Supreme Court held that there was all the difference in the world between planting a cross in someone's front lawn and burning a cross in a field some miles away.[95] Thus, the State could not ban cross burning as a general matter, any more than it could ban flag burning as a general matter; yet it would be constitutional to forbid cross burning in circumstances that constituted the equivalent of a threat—for example, such an act in the front lawn of an African American family moving into a formerly all-White neighborhood.

It is not for me to comment on whether the Court's approach to the First Amendment was right or wrong. My remit has been to write on how the First Amendment has been perceived abroad, and more particularly in my country, South Africa. As far as perception is concerned, I think that a South African lawyer would regard such an approach as being more protective of individual property and personality rights than of the rights of all Black people in the country not to be reminded of the epoch of lynching and White supremacy, and the rights of all Americans to live in a society where the equality thrust of the Fourteenth Amendment was taken seriously.

In this respect, a progressive American friend of mine whom I respect very much has suggested that the national contexts make a difference here: Nazism in Germany was pervasive, as was Apartheid in South Africa. In the United States, on the other hand, slavery was limited to states in the South, although de jure discrimination against African Americans extended far more broadly.

As an outsider I would readily acknowledge that my understanding of the American legal system and of American history is distinctly lacking in nuance, and that American jurisprudence is far richer and more textured than most non-Americans would allow—messages lose their intricacy as they cross the ocean. Yet I cannot help thinking that the core problem is not derived from the formal, legalized structures of racial domination, which were abolished, but stems from the covert culture of racism that survived after abolition and desegregation. Lynching had profound free speech implications. Its objective was precisely to terrorize people, to shut them up with a view to preventing them from asserting their Reconstruction rights under the Constitution.[96] And the Ku Klux Klan was set up in Indiana,[97] not just the South, while lynching took place in Midwest Ohio[98] and West Coast California,[99] as well as in the South. Using the language of today, one could say it appeared to be a very American form of lawless civil society speaking power to truth. And viewed with the lenses of South African legal culture, the cross burning in the field would be quite different from the American flag burning outside the Supreme Court, and, as a general matter, would call for a very different legal response.

Where I can go along with my American interlocutor, however, is in relation to the importance of national contexts with regard to legal culture. To Americans, the firstness of the First Amendment is axiomatic. It is seen as a source of enlightenment, as being the most constitutive and defining element of the whole constitutional order. The legal cultures of Germany and South Africa, however, have a profoundly different foundational element. It is not free speech, but human dignity. What is axiomatic to an American lawyer could be problematic to us. What is axiomatic to us could be problematic to an American. The conclusion to the debate over the First Amendment, then, is inconclusive—a mutually respectful "so be it."

With one last double exclamation, that is: an unrestrained hallelujah and a sad lament.

The hallelujah is for the manner in which an activist US Supreme Court in the Pentagon Papers case blasted a hole in the apparently impregnable wall of state prerogative and secrecy. That breach helped reconfigure the imaginations of jurists throughout the world to promote democratic accountability in the North, South, East, and West.

The lament is for the same Court in the same country with the same Constitution coming out with the even more judicially activist decision in the *Citizens United* case.[100] This time the Court tore a rent in a long-standing, bipartisan, and carefully constructed legislative net designed to restrain the rampantly distorting effect that the deployment of huge corporate moneys was having on the maintenance of democratic integrity. To an outsider it was as if, having lived and achieved international luster by the sword of the First Amendment, the one-time glow around the US Supreme Court was now dying as a result of its use.

How I wish it were not so.

Freedom of Expression Abroad

The State of Play

TOM GINSBURG*

This chapter examines the global constitutional history of freedom of speech in the era of modern national constitutions. Since 1789, nation-states have increasingly memorialized their fundamental laws in a single constitutional text, which sets up fundamental institutions and also provides for limitations on public power in the form of rights. These documents provide powerful symbolic affirmation of the core ideas that animate governance across time and space, even as their actual implementation varies widely with social and political conditions.

Freedom of expression is at the core of liberal constitutional democracy, both conceptually and empirically. Constitutional democracy presumes a set of meaningful political choices, implemented through elections that produce a government limited by law. While some have tried to reduce the essence of democracy to elections, in fact it also depends on a set of legal freedoms and institutions that make meaningful choice possible. Without robust freedom of expression, alternative policies cannot be offered. Without the ability to express criticism of policies and leaders, democratic accountability fails. Without the ability to speak, political organization is hampered and elections cannot provide for meaningful choices. And without the ability to call attention to the violations of constitutional rights, their protection becomes unlikely.

[handwritten margin note: Why liberal democracies need freedom of speech.]

In this chapter, I demonstrate that freedom of expression is also empirically at the core of constitutional democracy. I first show that rights to speech and free expression are the most popular rights found in national constitutions, so prevalent as to be considered almost definitional to the form. So important is freedom of expression that countries that make no attempt to actually provide it to citizens still make a point of paying lip service to the concept: even North Korea

* Thanks to Ilayda Gunes, Odysseas Theofanis, and Sophia Weaver for research help.

makes a constitutional promise of freedom of speech.[1] Ironically, the guarantee of freedom of expression has become almost nonnegotiable for nation-states, even though they often severely infringe its exercise in practice.

Next I show that although robust rights to freedom of expression have spread around the world, they are naturally more limited than the rights appear on paper. Courts have engaged in a vigorous practice of borrowing concepts from each other in adjudicating cases. American jurisprudence, though somewhat exceptional in many ways, has been quite influential, including the *Schenck v. United States* case to which this volume is dedicated.[2] By articulating the idea that an interference with speech ought to be allowed only if it prevents a "clear and present danger," Justice Holmes set in motion a jurisprudence that has spread across the globe. His opinion provides a textbook illustration that the influence of legal cases goes far beyond the details of who won or lost.

In the final section, however, I demonstrate that rights to free speech are under some pressure in many countries. This is true, almost by definition, of those countries that have witnessed constitutional backsliding and erosion, such as Turkey and Hungary. But more worryingly, several established democracies have seen challenges to freedom of speech and expression. We may be witnessing a test of the conceptual centrality of free speech to democracy.

Freedom of Expression at the Constitutional Core

Modern constitutions emerged in the late eighteenth century, with the drafting of fundamental charters in the American states and a few other jurisdictions around the world. Freedom of speech, of course, was at the core of the enlightenment ideals of that era, and so it naturally found expression in constitutional texts.[3] "The free communication of ideas and opinions is one of the most precious of the rights of man" reads the French Declaration, before going on to guarantee citizens the freedom to express themselves within the boundaries of the law.

The first national constitutions triggered a wave of diffusion, as both successful and failed liberal revolutions mimicked the constitutional form. The US Constitution was particularly influential, inspiring drafts in Latin America and elsewhere.[4] The idea of a constitutional bill of rights, though obviously contested at home, quickly became part of the standard repertoire of constitutions. This universality of the idea of rights, however, contrasted with the particular choices made in any given constitution-making context. There is not one bill of rights, but many, and each country has a distinctive set. Drafters, after all, are engaged in a process of specifying the rules of self-government of a *particular* people, and thus make choices from a broad conceptual menu about what features, including rights, to put into a national constitution. This variation is helpful because it allows us to determine which ideas are central and which are less so.

Together with my colleagues at the Comparative Constitutions Project, we have analyzed what we see as the "core" parts of constitutions, that is, the essential features that appear in the vast majority of constitutions around the world. We contrast these with more peripheral provisions, or optional features, such as, for example, a national motto (found in less than 20 percent of constitutions since 1789). To illustrate, virtually every constitution contains rules defining who are nationals or citizens of the country, but relatively few have provisions for a countercorruption commission, a relatively recent development. Virtually every constitution provides for rules about how the head of state is selected and how the constitution is to be amended.

Rights in general tend to be core. Table 12.1 lists the rights that are found in more than three-fourths of historical constitutions, along with selected other topics, and shows trends over time. (The number of new constitutions produced in any given era fluctuates with the number of countries and their overall stability.) We include any topic that was found in more than three-fourths of constitutions in any given era, even if the overall number was lower for the whole sample. By this metric, freedom of speech is indeed one of the very core provisions found in national constitutions, along with guarantees of equality and property. It is more popular in national constitutions than other liberties that are often considered core to the enterprise of constitutional democracy, such as religious freedom or the right to life. A constitution that does not provide for freedom of expression barely deserves the name.[5]

As Table 12.1 indicates, different rights provisions of constitutions go in and out of the "core" over time. There has been, however, a gradual consolidation of the features found in many constitutions. In particular, the "Age of Rights," as Louis Henkin put it, has seen a great expansion in the number and popularity of rights in national constitutions.[6]

Furthermore, the table indicates that other provisions closely related to freedom of speech, such as freedom of the press, are also quite prevalent. We also ask in our survey of constitutional texts whether there are limitations on censorship, and provide that data in the last line of the table even though it does not meet the criteria of having been a "core" provision in any given era. Interestingly, as Figure 12.1 indicates, explicit provisions on censorship reflect a flatter pattern over time, having been more popular in the nineteenth century than today. Among these rights, one might view freedom of expression as having strongly individualist overtones, as compared with press freedoms and the associated limitation of government censorship.

Table 12.1. **Core Rights Provisions over Time (by Fraction of Constitutional Texts with a Given Right)**

	Pre-1900 (181 New Constitutions)	1900–1945 (118 New Constitutions)	1946–1989 (328 New Constitutions)	1990–Present (164 New Constitutions)	Total (791 New Constitutions)
Equality guarantee	.71	.80	.90	.99	.86
Right to property/freedom from expropriation	.86	.81	.75	.91	.81
Freedom of speech or expression	**.59**	**.80**	**.84**	**.93**	**.80**
Freedom of religion	.41	.83	.86	.88	.76
Freedom of assembly	.46	.83	.78	.93	.75
Freedom of association	.39	.77	.81	.95	.73
Right to privacy, incl. home or letters	.62	.73	.71	.89	.73
Freedom of opinion/conscience	.41	.62	.66	.87	.65
Freedom from unjustified restraint	.58	.53	.66	.73	.63
Freedom of movement	.44	.55	.59	.93	.62
Freedom of the press	**.56**	**.48**	**.44**	**.71**	**.58**
Right to petition	.77	.69	.45	.49	.57
Prohibition vs. slavery*	.57	.35	.38	.65	.47
Freedom from torture	.27	.23	.43	.84	.45
Right to life	.19	.32	.45	.79	.44
Right to counsel	.11	.17	.48	.76	.41
Freedom from cruel or degrading treatment	.15	.23	.41	.79	.40
[Limitation of censorship]	.51	.44	.28	.41	.38

* Answer choices "prohibited with exceptions" included in the data for this variable.

Source: Data from the Comparative Constitutions Project, http://www.comparativeconstitutionsproject.org, and Tom Ginsburg and James Melton, *Writing Rights* (forthcoming).

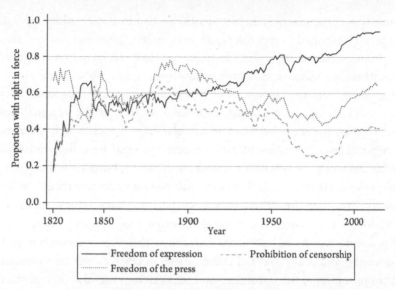

Figure 12.1. Popularity of Different Expression-Related Rights over Time.

Among the mechanisms by which many rights became more popular were the so-called International Bill of Rights, the Universal Declaration of Human Rights, and the two major International Covenants.[7] These documents, along with regional treaties like the European Convention of Human Rights and the American Declaration of Human Rights, had a powerful focal effect on drafters of national constitutions, consolidating their choices. In other work, my coauthors and I show that those rights included in the Universal Declaration, like freedom of expression, became more popular after its adoption, while those rights that were left out (say, a right to petition) became less popular.[8] Article 19 of the Universal Declaration mentions freedoms of expression and opinion, but does not mention freedom of the press or freedom from censorship, and this may have contributed to the rising popularity of the former pair of freedoms relative to the latter two among constitution makers. Regardless of the mechanism, freedom of expression is clearly at the core of national constitutional drafting practice.

The Influence of "Clear and Present Danger" and the Conceptual Migration of Free Speech

Of course, this only refers to the *form* of constitutions rather than to their implementation. Agreement on the normative level does not in itself say anything about practice, as the example of North Korea cited in the introduction demonstrates. The practical impact of any constitutional provision depends on the meaning ascribed to it in the practices of courts, governments, and civil society. In this section, I argue that the meaning of free speech is, in many contexts, transnationally produced, as doctrines flow from country to country.

A growing literature canvasses freedom of speech around the globe.[9] Because it is a fundamental human right, embodied in each of the regional human rights treaties, the scope of freedom of expression is increasingly determined at a regional level.[10] Another literature focuses on what are called transnational judicial dialogues, conversations among courts across borders in their jurisprudence, in which they consider how to handle certain issues that recur in different contexts.[11] Together these literatures suggest that the interpretation of the scope of freedom of expression is increasingly transnational, in which courts can and do borrow doctrines and learn from each other. This phenomenon is in part the product of dramatically lowered communication costs, as well as a recognition that countries face similar problems and thus can be a useful source of information. (The United States is distinctive in that the practice of borrowing is very controversial among Justices of the Supreme Court.)

One important adjudicative technique in this regard is the idea of proportionality. In both the Inter-American and European regional human rights systems, restrictions on speech must be limited to those "necessary in a democratic society."[12] This means that they must be directed toward certain designated purposes, such as national security, public order, or protecting the rights of others. The courts have developed the idea that, even if the aim is valid, the restriction must be reasonable and proportionate to the social goal; typically it must be the least restrictive means of meeting the goal.

The idea that the interference with rights should be as minimal as possible echoes Holmes' famous "clear and present danger" phrase from the *Schenck* case. That case, of course, concerned an antiwar activist who condemned the draft and was subsequently punished. While Holmes upheld the conviction on the ground of wartime exigency, his conceptual leap was to examine the "proximity and degree" between the speech in question and the substantive harm to be avoided. Tightening the required link between advocacy and harm shifted the focus from the State interest to the liberty of the speaker. While American courts continued to use various balancing techniques for much of the twentieth century, the notion of clear and present danger implies maximizing the realm of expression in the course of the balancing exercise. This position, which the Supreme Court finally embraced half a century later in the "imminent lawless action" test of *Brandenburg v. Ohio*,[13] would certainly *meet* the proportionality test. Proportionality and the Holmes approach bear much in common, notwithstanding different intellectual histories and trajectories.[14] Both provide a tool for assessing government actions in ways that both recognize the need for regulation and strive to maximize liberty.

Freedom of speech is now the topic of a global conversation, at least for many jurisdictions. Rather than try to capture the entire scope of freedom of speech globally, I want to give a flavor of the phenomenon, with reference to the clear and present danger test. Accordingly, I identify several jurisdictions in which this test has been used. The exercise illustrates a more general point, which is that the particular details of who wins or loses in legal cases are not all that matters. Although much social science analysis of law focuses on the votes in particular cases, a complete understanding requires knowing what ideas are being deployed and developed by judges, and how these ideas spread.

South Korea

In South Korea, the test played an important role in the country's democratization. In 1990, just two years after the formation of the Constitutional Court, a case was brought challenging the scope of the National Security Act (NSA), which had been used during the authoritarian period to suppress political expression and organization. The 1980 version of the Act criminalized anyone who "praises, encourages, or sympathizes with the activities of an anti-state organization or its members, or any person who receives orders there from; and any person who by any means whatever benefits an anti-state organization."[15]

In its decision, the country's new Constitutional Court held this provision to be vague and overbroad, and to threaten constitutional guarantees of freedom of the press and speech, freedom of academic study, and freedom of conscience.[16] Noting the continuing confrontation with North Korea, the Court did not actually strike down the law, but ruled that the provisions could be applied only in the case of danger of actual security risks. The Court restricted interpretations of the law and asked lower courts to balance the proximity of danger with the constitutional position on freedom of expression. In particular, the Court held that the law could only be used to punish activities posing a substantive danger, so merely "encouraging" or "sympathizing" without a showing of substantive danger could not be prosecuted. However, a dissenting opinion by Justice Byon Chong-soo called for the Court to require a higher standard of "clear and present danger" before a prosecution could be upheld in an NSA case.[17] Justice Byon characterized the majority test as one of "bad tendency," consciously modeling his decision on Holmes' opinion in *Schenck*.[18] Following this decision, the National Assembly amended the law to apply only where the person charged had *knowledge* that his or her actions might endanger the existence or security of the State or the "fundamental order of liberal democracy," which is, of course, a far cry from clear and present danger.[19]

[handwritten margin note: Not true freedom of speech, but the author blames this on their conflict w/ North Korea.]

[Prosecutions under the Act have continued.[20] South Korea continues to be very aggressive with regard to speech that demonstrates sympathy with North Korea.] While the clear and present danger test is said to have had some influence in particular cases, there are dozens of prosecutions every year. Perhaps this is not surprising given the continuing tensions on the Korean peninsula.

Israel

Like South Korea, Israel has confronted the need to balance national security with civil liberties. In the famous case of *Kol Ha'am v. Minister of Interior*, the Supreme Court had to confront a decision of the government to close a newspaper because of articles that allegedly would have incited violence.[21] In adopting a balancing test in the interpretation of rights, Justice Shimon Agranat (who was born in Louisville, Kentucky and attended the University of Chicago Law School) cited classic American cases including *Schenck*, *Abrams v. United States*,[22] and *Whitney v. California*.[23] Agranat imported a "probable danger" doctrine, a modified version of clear and present danger, while also introducing other elements of free speech doctrine into Israeli law. More generally, in laying down a general approach to rights adjudication in Israel, Agranat also established a pattern whereby foreign law citations would play a prominent role in Israeli jurisprudence.[24]

The phenomenon of transnational borrowing is heavily associated with Chief Justice Aharon Barak, who has referred to American cases in illuminating the task of the judge in balancing civil liberties and national security.[25] During his time on the Court, the Judges generated a "constitutional revolution" by reading into two Basic Laws a power of judicial review over legislation, and extending the Basic Law on Human Dignity and Liberty to create an entire catalog of rights. This was accomplished largely through a macro-comparative syllogism: (1) Israel is a constitutional democracy; (2) constitutional democracies have judicial review and extensive rights; (3) therefore, Israel should actively adopt rights through judicial examination of and incorporation of doctrines that come from abroad. A huge fan of balancing tests, Barak has been central to the global phenomenon of judicial dialogue and of advancing the proportionality doctrine.[26] And, more generally, the integration of Israeli legal education with that of the United States has led to an active exchange, manifesting itself in citations to US cases, including in freedom of expression cases. This has naturally led to instances in which US jurisprudence is rejected, as well as accepted.[27] Holmes and his test, in short, are not infrequent visitors to Israel.[28]

Japan

In contrast with Israel, Japanese courts are not always vigorous participants in this transnational citation conversation. But the clear and present danger idea has made its appearance at times. In a 1975 case on a Public Safety Ordinance, Judge Kishi's concurring opinion refers to the US Supreme Court idea without specifically citing *Schenck*.[29] A 1995 case does the same.

Although freedom of expression law in Japan bears a superficial resemblance to that of the United States, the Japanese Supreme Court has *never* found violations of the right to freedom of expression. In one famous case, the Ministry of Education reviewed a history textbook to approve its use in public schools, and rejected it for its negative portrayal of Japan's actions in World War II. It insisted, for example, that the phrase "invasion of China" be replaced with the euphemism "advance into Asia." Professor Ienaga, the author, brought a claim based on academic freedom and freedom of speech. While the district court found that the screening system itself was constitutional, it found the system too invasive in this case. However, the Supreme Court reversed and remanded, the Ministry changed its rules, and Professor Ienaga was denied standing. Obscenity restrictions have also been upheld, as in the case of the publisher of a translation of *Lady Chatterley's Lover*, whose prosecution was upheld on a wide reading of "public welfare" justifications.[30] And government workers have been successfully prosecuted for private political speech while off duty.[31]

Other repressive measures that have been upheld are restrictions on advocacy during the implementation of a postwar Emergency Food Supply Order.[32] A farmer had claimed that government officials lied to him, and he called on farmers not to sell their rice to the government as required by the Order. After he was convicted of the crime of "advocating illegal conduct," the Court upheld the conviction without inquiring into the connection between the advocacy and the purported harm to society. This might have been an instance for applying a version of the clear and present danger test, but it was not utilized.

Numerous commentators have urged the Court to make more use of the clear and present danger test.[33] Several statutes criminalize advocacy of illegal action, and in interpreting these, the Court has taken a broad view of government power. In one case when left-wing students called for "storming the Prime Minister's house," they were successfully prosecuted under the Subversive Activities Prevention Act, though they were nowhere near the house at the time.[34] It is perhaps no surprise that the United Nations has criticized Japan for infringements on freedom of expression, and that the country ranks low in indices of press freedom, as I discuss further later.

Hungary

Hungary's Constitutional Court was once considered one of the most important and powerful courts in the world.[35] In the early years after democratization, the Court led the country's liberalization through a vigorous human rights jurisprudence and liberally cited foreign cases, including American ones.[36] Free speech cases were among those with the highest number of citations, and an important early decision incorporated the clear and present danger test into Hungarian law.[37] The case concerned hate speech regulations, criminalized in the criminal code. The Court ruled that hate speech had to be tolerated unless it was an act of instigation, drawing on subsequent development of the American framework to emphasize the link with imminent lawless action. In its later jurisprudence, the Court has not always followed a balancing approach, sometimes preferring a more absolutist approach.[38] But it has on occasion explicitly invoked the clear and present danger test in striking down government legislation, mostly in the hate speech context.[39]

[handwritten margin note: borrowed from US jurisprudence]

Europe

Freedom of expression is protected under Article 10 of the European Convention of Human Rights. Perhaps unsurprisingly, the clear and present danger test first announced in *Schenck* has also made its appearance in various cases at the European level. One case involved the United Kingdom, another liberal democracy that has grappled with threats of war and terrorism. In 1974, its courts faced a case remarkably similar on its facts to *Schenck*. An antiwar activist was distributing pacifist literature to soldiers who were to be posted to North Ireland. The courts convicted her under the 1934 Incitement to Disaffection Act, and she appealed to the European Commission on Human Rights (a now-disbanded body that used to screen applications for admissibility before sending them to the European Court of Human Rights). She also invoked the clear and present danger doctrine, saying that she had not posed any risk. In rejecting her application, the Commission noted that the "necessary" prong of Article 10(2) of the European Convention of Human Rights implied a social need that "may include the clear and present danger test and must be assessed in the light of circumstances of a given case."[40]

The European Court of Human Rights later had to grapple with security-based infringements on freedom of expression in a series of cases involving Turkey, beginning with *Zana v. Turkey* in 1997.[41] That case involved a Turkish statute that made it a crime to publicly praise or defend an act punishable as a serious crime. Zana, former mayor of a Kurdish city, made a statement to reporters while in prison, in which he condemned a massacre but expressed support for the Kurdistan Workers' Party (PKK) terrorist group that had carried it out. In examining the case, the Court took a contextual approach and found that the statement, in light of his position, could be found by authorities as "likely to exacerbate an already explosive situation" in Southeast Turkey.[42] Framing the question in the Holmesian way led, as in *Schenck*, to upholding a restriction.

Over the next few years, a series of cases came before the Court in which Turkey was alleged to have violated Article 10. In sixteen out of eighteen cases in 1999 and 2000, the Court found that Turkey was in violation. In these decisions, the Court consistently framed the question as whether the impugned publication or statement would lead to violence or have a serious impact on national security or public order, and found such a connection lacking. *b) similar to clear & present danger test*

In two of the cases, however, the Court found that the restrictions (involving letters and commentary in a newspaper in the Kurdish region) were justified as punishing the incitement of violence.[43] Several dissents disagreed with that conclusion. One of them, written by Judge Bonello, relied heavily on Holmes' opinions in *Schenck* and *Abrams* and Brandeis' opinion in *Whitney v. California* in finding that the statements did not create a risk at all, "let alone a clear and present danger."[44] He noted that "punishment by the national authorities of those encouraging violence would be justifiable in a democratic society only if the incitement were such as to create 'a clear and present danger.' When the invitation to the use of force is intellectualised, abstract, and removed in time and space from the foci of actual or impending violence, then the fundamental right to freedom of expression should generally prevail."[45]

This test was not generally followed in subsequent cases. In other parts of its vast case law, the European Court has upheld restrictions on speech that are seen to incite violence and hatred, and in so doing it has not required a tight link between expression and outcome in this regard. In part, these decisions are seen as deferring to the "margin of appreciation" given to state authorities under prevailing European Convention jurisprudence. States can adopt a clear and present danger test, but need not do so to conform with European law.

Summary

This thumbnail account of the journey of "clear and present danger" around the world illustrates the central power of the test, and the conceptual framework that it embodies, in the judicial imagination. Sometimes evoked to limit government action and sometimes to uphold it, clear and present danger stands for something bigger than its actual application: the idea that judges should be able to review and consider government action that interferes with the core constitutional liberty of freedom of expression, and should do so weighing the harms and benefits in a way that gives scope to the liberty. While it has been replaced by other adjudicative techniques in many jurisdictions, its impact, at least as loosely understood, lives on.

The Illiberal Turn

It has often been noted in recent years that there are signs that the "Third Wave" of constitutional democracy, which began with the democratization of southern Europe in the 1970s and accelerated with the end of the Cold War, may have crested. While the number of democracies remains far greater than the number of dictatorships, the gap is shrinking. The "new democracies" of Hungary and Poland have seen significant backsliding, and there has been a severe decline in countries like Venezuela and Turkey, which have returned to authoritarianism even as elections continue. Furthermore, and perhaps more worryingly, there are concerns about a decline in the *quality* of democracy within the core countries, the rich industrial democracies of the world. The election of Donald Trump, with his frontal challenges to traditions of accountability, has prompted hand-wringing, even as it has triggered vigorous and even vicious battles in the media. New illiberal parties are on the rise in Western Europe.

The causes of this phenomenon are complex and beyond the scope of this chapter, but candidates include the rise of social media, growing social anxiety, and increased economic inequality. One important factor is that authoritarian regimes are, with growing confidence, articulating an alternative view of freedom of expression. In China, Russia, and even more tolerant places like Singapore, governments push the view that freedom of expression is not generative, but dangerous. These regimes see freedom of expression as posing risks to social harmony and threatening the deference to the state they seek to inculcate. To be sure, there is not a monolithic view among such countries. In Singapore, the emphasis is on intercommunal harmony. In China and Russia, the focus is on political stability, broadly conceived. What all these countries have in common is an emphasis on hierarchy and the protection of state interests. One can view our current situation as one in which there are two opposite poles to which countries are drawn: a wide-open American view of free expression and a restrictive authoritarian view.

What do these trends mean for freedom of expression and its trajectory? This section provides an early assessment of an ongoing phenomenon. It focuses on four of the countries canvassed before: Hungary, Turkey, Japan, and Israel.

The Challenge to Expression in Backsliding Democracies

As noted earlier, Hungary was one of the poster children of constitutional democracy in the 1990s, with a Constitutional Court that was widely celebrated for its activism and leadership of democratic transition.[46] In 2010, however, the Fidesz party came back to power by trouncing the beleaguered and weakened Socialist Party. Although Fidesz won only 53 percent of the vote, it secured 68 percent of the available legislative seats thanks to an electoral system designed to prevent legislative fragmentation and divided government. Once in power, Fidesz quickly exploited its two-thirds majority to draft a wholly new constitution. (Hungary had never had a post–Cold War constitution, but had massively amended its Communist-era document.) The new Constitution had many ramifications. It created a media council, made up entirely of Fidesz appointees, that formulated content-based regulations and initiated registration requirements. It also increased the size of the Constitutional Court, allowing Fidesz four immediate appointments. And the government passed a series of laws designed to undermine judicial independence, including lowering the mandatory retirement age, with the effect of firing the Chief Justice.

Later, the Constitution was amended to permit the punishment of statements that harm the dignity of others, including those that violate "the dignity of the Hungarian nation." The idea that the *majority* has a dignity interest underpinned a criminal ban on denying the inhuman actions of fascist and communist regimes. Hate speech toward minorities, on the other hand, appears to be on the rise and is tolerated by officials. In other legislative moves, the country banned the making of false videos or recordings, even if not distributed, in the name of protecting human dignity. Defamation actions are regularly brought against journalists and even ordinary citizens for Facebook posts.

"Good" but used to attack the others not in control the opposition.

The Constitutional Court struck down some of these early restrictions on free speech, such as the ban on totalitarian symbols. But lower courts did not follow the constitutional jurisprudence. In *Fratanoló v. Hungary*, the European Court of Human Rights heard a challenge to one of the lower court decisions, and found that restrictions on symbols could be justified only if "there was a real and present danger of any political movement or party restoring the Communist dictatorship."[47] This promising decision suggested that the Constitutional Court might be a site of resistance to Fidesz, in that it had support from the European Court for its approach. By 2015, however, critics claimed that the Constitutional Court had become completely loyal to the ruling party through a series of appointments. In 2016, the government sought to close down the Central European University, ostensibly because of foreign funding. Clearly, freedom of expression in Hungary is under significant threat today, and the tight link required by a test like clear and present danger is nowhere to be found.

Turkey has gone further and seen a complete slide into dictatorship as far as freedom of expression is concerned. While the country was never a paradise for freedom of expression, it did feature a vibrant press. No longer. It has now jailed more journalists than China. President Recep Tayyip Erdogan is an aggressive user of libel actions and has jailed critics on Twitter and other social media critics, including cartoonists and someone who posted a comparison of him to the

Gollum character from *Lord of the Rings*. Newspapers have been closed, and so-cial media shuttered.

Other countries have seen similar kinds of backsliding and to some extent provide a reminder of why freedom of expression is so critical to the vibrancy of constitutional democracy. The range of techniques is remarkable: Poland's gov-ernment has sought to limit journalists' access to parliament, and to take direct government control of the hiring of chiefs of state broadcasting organizations. Although at this time these moves have not been successful, in part because of strong criticism from the European Union, they illustrate the ways in which po-tential authoritarians learn from each other.

Some more subtle than others.

The Challenge to Expression in the Constitutional Core

More surprisingly, a set of established democracies have seen some challenges in terms of freedom of expression, especially in the years since September 11. I will focus on two countries in particular, Japan and Israel. Both are clearly estab-lished constitutional democracies, with guarantees of freedom of speech that are encapsulated in a constitutional text (Japan) or judicial practice (Israel). Yet the freedom of expression has come under threat from governments in both places.

Japan

Japan is a constitutional democracy, but one in which the government plays an active role in managing the information environment. The regulation of textbooks on history has already been noted. The media, on the other hand, is subject to soft constraints rather than overt censorship. The media in Japan has long operated under the so-called *kissha* club system. This system is a kind of information cartel, whereby reporters receive collective access to in-formation from the government agencies that they cover. But there are many reports of instances in which reporters delay distribution of information to avoid losing access. There have also been a number of recent instances in which newspapers fire or demote reporters who write articles critical of the government. As a result, there is a tremendous amount of self-censorship about sensitive topics.

In addition, there is no independent media regulator in Japan. Article 4 of the Broadcast Act requires broadcasters to "not harm public safety or good morals," "be politically fair," "not distort the facts," and "clarify the points at issue from as many angles as possible." In 2016, the minister of communications stated pub-licly that the government had the right to shut down broadcasters who violated these standards. The government characterized this as a mere restatement of the law; civil society actors perceived it as a threat. The ruling party and government officials have criticized broadcast officials about allegedly "distorted" reports.[48]

The Abe government represents a faction directly (and in his case literally) descended from the militarists of World War II. It has proposed to amend the Constitution of Japan to emphasize that freedoms and rights are accompanied by duties and obligations, and must be exercised in ways that do not violate the public interest and public order.[49] It specifically would append to Article 21's simple and unqualified guarantee of "freedom of speech, press and all other forms of expression" a significant limitation clause: "Notwithstanding the foregoing, engaging in activities with the purpose of damaging the public interest or public order, or associating with others for such purposes, shall not be recognized." While much attention, in Japan and abroad, has focused on proposals to amend the famous Article 9, which contains the "peace" clause that forever renounces war, the arguably more insidious constitutional proposals are those that would undermine Japan's democratic quality by limiting the public sphere.

[handwritten margin note: undermines very purpose of the freedom right to speech]

The Abe government's proposal to amend the Constitution has not yet succeeded. But resistance has not deterred government efforts to limit freedom of expression. It has passed a series of acts in recent years that seem to inhibit public discourse. In 2014, a new State Secrets Law took effect, punishing leakers of government secrets, and including journalists who "instigate" leaks. The UN Special Rapporteur on Freedom of Expression has also criticized the country for its Broadcast Law, which includes "political fairness" as one of the criteria the government can consider in suspending broadcast licenses for violations of fairness.[50]

In June 2017, the Diet passed a controversial "anti-conspiracy" bill that the Japanese Bar Association says may curb civil liberties across the country. The nominal excuse is the need to be on the lookout for terror in advance of the 2020 Olympic Games, but critics fear it may be used to limit peaceful protests. The law criminalizes planning and conspiracy to commit a wide range of offenses, including stealing forest products and copyright violations, and also prompted a statement by the UN Special Rapporteur on Privacy.[51] All these legislative changes confront a political culture in which the press has been free but information cartelized.

Israel

Facing significant security challenges, the Israeli government and courts have long had to balance national security and individual liberties. In recent years, some critics have noted the government's use of the national security concerns to promote a distinctly nationalist vision of the society. The government is seeking to limit criticism in the public sphere. It has passed a controversial nongovernmental organization (NGO) bill, requiring registration and reporting of foreign funding. It has made it a civil offense to call for a boycott against the country. It has criminalized the advocacy of military desertion and any commemoration of the Day of Independence as the *Nakba*, the term used by Palestinians to denote it as a disaster. The minister of culture has introduced a "loyalty in culture" bill to ban artists who express ideas that are defined as disloyal to the State and has sought to defund artists whose work she disapproves of.[52]

In addition, the Ministry of Education has banned certain books from school curricula because they depict romantic relationships between Jews and Palestinians, and has sought to introduce a "code of conduct" to prevent academics from expressing views in the classroom on public issues.[53]

Even parliamentary speech is being constrained: in 2016, the Knesset passed a law allowing members of parliament to be expelled for incitement, racism, or advocacy of struggle against the State. These terms are of course open to interpretation, and seem to be targeted against minority Arab lawmakers. Clear and present danger this is not. Meanwhile there has been significant media consolidation. In a telling sign, the Economist Intelligence Unit ranks Israel as a "flawed democracy" chiefly on the basis of its poor score on civil liberties. In 2016, Israel ranked eighty-fifth for civil liberties, clustered around lower-ranked "flawed democracies" such as Sri Lanka and Malaysia, as well as higher-ranked "hybrid regimes" such as Mali and Honduras.[54]

Conclusion

Ideas about free expression go to the core of the project of liberal constitutional democracy, and indeed are fundamental to its survival. This fact is reflected in part in the near universality of freedom of expression in national constitutions, as the concept has spread around the world at a normative level. At the level of practice, however, the situation is more complicated.

It is well known that rights jurisprudence spreads across borders, as concepts developed in one jurisdiction can be utilized, and transformed, in others. This process is no doubt accelerating in an era of expanded access to foreign legal materials. The test announced in the *Schenck* case, namely, that government regulation of speech is appropriate only in the face of a clear and present danger, marked an important conceptual leap in the way judges think about rights. It shifted the presumption toward maximizing liberty, even as it provided a language that regulators could use to justify their restrictions. Courts around the world have used that conceptual framework, and sometimes even borrowed the language formulated by Holmes and developed in later US cases such as *Abrams*,

Gitlow, Dennis, and *Brandenburg.*[55] Other tests are sometimes used, but <u>it is often recognized that some link between speech and harm is required.</u>

Ideas about democratic governance spread across borders, but so do techniques to undermine it. There is an alternative authoritarian discourse about expression, which is that it is dangerous and needs careful control. In the last few years, in a series of democratic countries, there have been attempts to restrict speech and expression for narrow and partisan political needs. Some of these attempts, such as those overseen by Viktor Orbán in Hungary and Recep Tayyip Erdogan in Turkey, have been quite successful. Others have been limited or effectually staunched. Perhaps the most worrying development, however, is the potential degradation of freedom of expression in well-established, long-enduring democracies like Israel and Japan. Neither country has seen the kind of democratic collapse that we have observed in less established democracies, and I do not think either is likely to do so. But the constraint of freedom of expression should be troubling, and suggests there is a continuing need for vigilance to protect and preserve this core constitutional right in the core constitutional democracies.

13

Hate Speech at Home and Abroad

SARAH H. CLEVELAND*

*Any advocacy of national, racial or religious hatred that constitutes incite-
ment to discrimination, hostility or violence shall be prohibited by law.*
—International Covenant on Civil and Political Rights,
Article 20(2) (1966)

Ideas are fought with ideas and reasons.
—Colombian delegate to negotiations on the Convention on the
Elimination of All Forms of Racial Discrimination, Article 4 (1965)

The United States' best-known constitutional protection internationally is
surely the First Amendment. Around the world, the United States is perceived
as protecting freedom of expression and the press first and foremost, among all
rights. And whether admired for its purity and idealism or dismissed as naïve
and *sui generis*, the United States' approach to free speech is globally examined,
critiqued, and debated. It is the United States' most prominent constitutional
export, informing the drafting of foreign constitutions, statutes, and judicial
interpretations, and undergirding the protection for freedom of expression in
the international and regional human rights systems.

This chapter could focus on the many areas in which international and regional human rights law have substantively converged with the US protection
of freedom of expression. But I will focus on the area where the chasm between
US and international approaches is the greatest—the area of hate speech. I argue
that while the international community has been much more willing to restrict
expression that is hateful and discriminatory, in the name of protecting other
rights, the United States' commitment to free expression in a democracy and its
suspicion of government regulation have vitally shaped global norms regulating
hate speech. Even in this contested realm, the United States' commitment to free

---

* I am a member of the UN Human Rights Committee, but the views in this chapter are personal
and do not necessarily reflect the position of the Human Rights Committee.

speech has helped secure freedom of expression as a fundamental human right, shaped negotiations over the content of that right, and informed ongoing global interpretations of freedom of expression. From a platform firmly rooted in the First Amendment, the United States, in turn, has zealously promoted protection of freedom of expression internationally, including in the context of hate speech, while distancing itself from aspects of international law that diverge from the First Amendment.

Hate Speech in the Human Rights System

If the dawn of the modern First Amendment came with the trilogy of Supreme Court decisions in 1919, the dawn of freedom of expression in international human rights law came midcentury. In January 1941, President Franklin Delano Roosevelt pronounced the "four essential freedoms" that should be the foundation of the postwar era, including, first and foremost, "freedom of speech and expression."[1] The US president's vision began to be implemented with the adoption of the United Nations Charter in 1945 and then with the 1948 Universal Declaration of Human Rights, a nonbinding pronouncement of the human rights to be protected in the postwar order.

Drafted under the skilled chairpersonship of Eleanor Roosevelt and adopted unanimously by the General Assembly in December 1948, the Universal Declaration of Human Rights incorporated President Roosevelt's four freedoms into its preamble, and also proclaimed in Article 19 that "everyone has the right to freedom of opinion and expression."[2] Thereafter, the UN Commission on Human Rights and Eleanor Roosevelt worked to codify the Declaration's rights into binding treaty law. This effort ultimately came to fruition when the International Covenant on Civil and Political Rights (ICCPR) was adopted in 1966, with Article 19 again proclaiming the right of everyone to "freedom of expression, including the freedom to seek, receive and impart information and ideas of all kinds, regardless of frontiers." Freedom of expression is also protected in all regional human rights systems.[3]

Hand in hand with this international movement to protect freedom of expression, however, came a parallel movement to promote racial and religious equality and prohibit racial or other hatred, discrimination, or violence. The atrocities of the Nazi regime, including its comprehensive use of propaganda to disseminate racial and religious hatred and violence, with devastating human consequences, cast a long shadow over the construction of the postwar human rights regime. Joining the United States and other advanced democracies around the negotiating table for that system were representatives of the Soviet Union and Soviet bloc states, which had suffered the greatest human losses to the Nazis and were staunchly opposed to granting freedom of speech to Nazi and Fascist movements. The negotiators also increasingly included representatives of post-colonial states, which sought to combat the discriminatory ideologies of colonial subjugation.

Perhaps not surprisingly in this context, equality and nondiscrimination were the only human rights expressly set forth in the UN Charter. Concerns about advocacy and incitement to discrimination also began to emerge in human rights law. Thus, in 1948, the Genocide Convention obligated states to prohibit "direct and public incitement to commit genocide,"[4] and the Universal Declaration of Human Rights prohibited discrimination, including "any incitement to . . . discrimination."

One of the most contentious provisions of the ICCPR was Article 20, which accompanies the Article 19 protection of freedom of expression and requires states to "prohibit by law" "any propaganda for war" and "any advocacy of national, racial or religious hatred that constitutes incitement to discrimination, hostility or violence." The 1965 Convention on Racial Discrimination went further, providing in Article 4 that states shall make punishable "all dissemination of ideas based on racial superiority or hatred, [and] incitement to racial discrimination."[5] In the regional human rights systems, the European Convention and the African Charter allow, but do not require, states to prohibit hate speech, while the American Convention obligates states to prohibit "incitements to lawless violence or . . . similar illegal action" motivated by discrimination.

Taken together, these instruments make clear that international and regional human rights law diverges sharply from modern First Amendment norms in allowing, and at times requiring, states to prohibit and even criminalize certain forms of hateful speech. In the rest of this chapter, I explore this divide and the extent to which US engagement has helped steer the international system in a direction more compatible with the First Amendment.

Evolving US Doctrine Regarding Hate Speech

During the period from 1946 to the mid-1960s, when the foundational human rights instruments were developed, the United States' own position on restricting extremist speech was in flux. Justice Holmes' dissent in *Abrams v. United States*[6] had interpreted his "clear and present danger" test to preclude regulation of "opinions that we loathe," "unless they so imminently threaten immediate interference with the lawful and pressing purposes of the law that an immediate check is required to save the country." But this was a dissenting view. In 1927, for example, the Court upheld a statute on the ground that merely "advocating" violent means for political and economic change involves such danger to the security of the State that the State may outlaw it.[7] Over the next several decades, the Court began applying the "clear and present danger" test in a range of cases, including in *Cantwell v. Connecticut*,[8] which upheld the ability to play an inflammatory religious message on a public street. But in 1951, at the height of the McCarthy era, the Court applied a loose interpretation of that test to uphold the conviction in *Dennis v. United States*.[9]

During most of this period, the First Amendment was not understood to apply to common law defamation, libel, slander, or other forms of "low value" speech. In 1942, for example, the Court in *Chaplinsky v. New Hampshire*[10] upheld a conviction for calling a police officer a "damn fascist," on the grounds that such face-to-face "fighting words" necessarily "inflict injury or tend to incite an immediate breach of the peace" and did not implicate the First Amendment. In *Terminiello v. Chicago*,[11] the Court overturned the conviction of a Fascist orator under an ordinance criminalizing speech that "stirred people to anger, invited public dispute, or brought about a condition of unrest." The majority found the ordinance unconstitutionally overbroad, since it was precisely a function of free speech to invite "dispute" and "unrest." In dissent, Justice Jackson pointed out that the incendiary speaker had used epithets like "slimy scum," "snakes," and "bedbugs" to attack Communists, Jews, and other groups; that the speech had provoked a "surging, howling mob" in protest; and that it had thus posed a "clear and present danger." Then, in its 1952 decision in *Beauharnais v. Illinois*,[12] the Court upheld a criminal fine under a state law that prohibited publications portraying "depravity, criminality, unchastity, or lack of virtue of a class of citizens, of any race, color, creed or religion, [which exposed them] to contempt, derision or obloquy." Beauharnais was the president of a White supremacist organization whose leaflets promoted segregation laws with the caption "Preserve and Protect White Neighborhoods!" The Court treated the statements as unprotected libel directed at a racial group, because the law was rationally related to the goal of combatting racial violence.

Twelve years later, though, in *New York Times v. Sullivan*,[13] the Court cast doubt on *Beauharnais*, when it began subjecting state libel laws to First Amendment scrutiny, in light of "the profound national commitment to the principle that debate on public issues should be uninhibited, robust, and wide-open." Then came the Court's landmark decision in *Brandenburg v. Ohio*,[14] in 1969, which finally crystalized the Court's modern distinction between mere advocacy of violence (which is protected by the First Amendment) and incitement to imminent lawless action (which is not). *Brandenburg* involved televised speeches of a Ku Klux Klan leader delivered to hooded Klan members, some of whom were armed, and who burned a cross. The speeches included statements such as "Send the Jews back to Israel" and "Bury the niggers," and warned of possible "revengeance" at some point in the future. The Court held that such speech could not be prohibited, "except where such advocacy is directed to inciting or producing imminent lawless action and is likely to incite or produce such action." In short, the modern First Amendment test is not whether a speaker calls for violence, or even whether violence might occur. The speaker must seek to produce lawless action that is imminent, and such action must be likely to occur.

Current Holding. ⭐

By the time of the infamous planned Nazi march in the Chicago suburb of Skokie, Illinois, in 1977, it was well established that the First Amendment protects speech that is hateful and racially offensive, as long as it does not incite to imminent violence.[15] The Skokie ordinances prohibiting the march were based on the law upheld in *Beauharnais*, and were similar to some modern international human rights law prohibitions on hate speech. They prohibited granting parade permits to activities, inter alia, inciting "violence, hatred, abuse or hostility," and "dissemination" of materials "promoting or inciting group hatred," due to religion, race, or nationality.[16] Though the march would grievously offend the Jewish community of Skokie, many of whom were Holocaust survivors, there was no claim that the march would constitute incitement to immediate violence. Suppressing the march thus was unconstitutional viewpoint discrimination under the First Amendment.

A decade and a half later, in *R.A.V. v. City of Saint Paul*,[17] which involved burning a cross on public property, the Court struck down a law making it a misdemeanor to place a symbol on public or private property, including "a burning cross or Nazi swastika," which would "arouse anger, alarm or resentment in others on the basis of race, color, creed, religion or gender." The Court reasoned that while the human rights aims of the city were compelling, by only addressing harm based on "race, color, creed, religion or gender," rather than all such harms, the ordinance was an overbroad content-based restriction on speech. Showing "special hostility" to particular harms was "precisely what the First Amendment forbids." The Court, however, later upheld a state statute that prohibited burning a cross with intent to intimidate in *Virginia v. Black*,[18] holding that "true threats," which seriously express an intent to commit unlawful violence against particular individuals, are not constitutionally protected. Threats communicated by cross burning, in light of their "long and pernicious history as a signal of impending violence," could be specially punished as a "particularly virulent form of intimidation." The plurality nevertheless carefully distinguished such intimidation from the constitutionally protected use of cross burning to express the racist ideology of the Ku Klux Klan.

In short, as the US debate over regulation of extremist and hateful speech has evolved, the overarching question under the First Amendment has been when, if ever, governments *may* prohibit hateful speech. The modern Court's answer has been that such authority is limited to laws that are narrowly tailored and applied in circumstances that constitute incitement to imminent lawless conduct or violence. By contrast, international human rights law recognizes that there are circumstances when governments may prohibit extremist speech and asks the additional question of when governments *must* prohibit such speech to protect others from discrimination. Although the approach to that question varies and has evolved over time, human rights law generally has insisted that such speech must be prohibited in circumstances broader than those where regulation is allowed under the First Amendment.

Part of the explanation for the divergent US approach may be methodological. The doctrinal inquiry in the United States for whether hateful speech may be regulated is decidedly linear and unipolar. If one point of view is allowable (such as the promotion of racial equality), then the opposing viewpoint cannot be prohibited (such as the promotion of racial superiority). To do so is to impose intolerable content- and viewpoint-based restrictions on the latter speaker. The harmful content of the viewpoint is irrelevant, so long as the speech does not intentionally incite to immediate violence.

The international approach to limitations on human rights in general, however, including regulating freedom of expression, is multipolar and focuses on a variety of potential harms and social values. The relevant inquiry is whether a restriction is necessary for respect of the rights or reputations of others, the protection of national security, public order, or public health or morals. Human rights law also places greater emphasis on balancing the protection of freedom of expression against protection of other human rights, such as the prohibition on racial, religious, and other forms of discrimination. The result of this framing is that treating different viewpoints differently—for example, allowing speech promoting racial equality while restricting speech advocating racial superiority—does not render a provision necessarily unlawful under human rights law. Indeed, it is not even the relevant inquiry. The framing instead assumes that judges and other government decision makers are capable of making good-faith, substantively sound decisions that distinguish intolerably harmful forms of speech.

Despite this fundamental tension in both approach and outcomes, the United States has played an important leadership role in the negotiation, drafting, and interpretation of the major human rights instruments addressing freedom of expression, including with respect to hate speech. Specifically invoking the First Amendment, the United States consistently has emphasized the importance of a "clear and present danger" of unlawful violence as the tocsin for regulation of speech, and has repeatedly warned against the risk of abuse. As a result, although greater regulation of speech is allowable under human rights law than under the First Amendment, freedom of expression is widely respected as a core human right, and US engagement has fended off ongoing efforts to allow broader restrictions on the right.

Negotiating Global Freedom of Expression

As noted, three major international treaties prohibit incitement and other forms of hateful speech: the Genocide Convention, the ICCPR, and the Race Convention. In the struggle over the drafting of these provisions from 1946 to 1966, the positions of various states regarding the appropriate scope of freedom of expression played out across a spectrum marked by, on the one side, the United States, and on the other, the Soviet Union. Both the United States and the Soviet Union participated actively in the negotiation of all three instruments, with the United States chairing much of the drafting of both the Genocide Convention and the ICCPR. Engagement by the United States and its ideological allies on the principle of freedom of expression ultimately secured stronger protection for freedom of expression and the narrowing—though not the elimination—of the incitement/hate speech clauses in all three treaties.

The Genocide Convention: Direct Incitement to Genocide

The prologue to the debates over international regulation of hate speech came with the 1948 Genocide Convention. The brain child of Raphael Lemkin and a direct response to Nazi racial and religious persecution and the Holocaust, the Convention obligates states to criminalize all acts of genocide, including "direct and public incitement to commit genocide." This incitement provision itself was not highly controversial in the negotiations. The initial draft of the treaty was prepared by US State Department career diplomat John Maktos, who also served as US representative and chair of the drafting committee, and contained a similar provision.[19] However, the Soviet Union actively promoted adding an additional "propaganda" article, which would have required punishment of all "public propaganda, tending by [its] systematic and hateful character to provoke genocide," or "to make it appear as a necessary, legitimate or excusable act." The provision was justified on the grounds that "propaganda is even more dangerous than direct incitement to commit genocide," because "genocide cannot take place unless a certain state of mind has been created."[20]

In commenting on the draft Convention in 1947, the United States urged that the propaganda article be deleted. The United States explained that under Anglo-American law, "the right to free speech is not to be interfered with unless there is a clear and present danger that the utterance might interfere with the rights of others," and that propaganda that reached the level of a "clear and present danger" would be covered by the incitement provision.[21]

The ensuing negotiations became in part a debate over the scope of US First Amendment protections. The Soviet delegate modified his proposal to prohibit "public propaganda . . . aimed at inciting racial, national or religious enmity or hatred and on provoking the commission of the crime of genocide." US representative Maktos, as Chairman, stated he still could not support the propaganda article, which was contrary to the Bill of Rights and free press protections. The Soviet delegate contended that the proposal was consistent with US constitutional jurisprudence, since Justice Holmes had acknowledged that freedom of speech did not protect falsely crying "Fire!" in a theater.[22]

But the United States was joined by other states in its resistance to prohibiting expression beyond direct incitement to genocide. Ultimately, the Soviet proposals for a separate propaganda clause were rejected. The United States voted to support the final language requiring criminalization of "direct and public incitement."

Thus, in 1948, the United States managed to hold a position regarding criminalization of hateful speech in the Genocide Convention that was limited to direct incitement to genocide. Although the US representative invoked the "clear and present danger" standard, the US negotiating position and the resulting treaty text were perhaps more protective of freedom of expression than contemporaneous Supreme Court interpretations, because direct incitement to violence would not clearly be constitutionally required until *Brandenburg*.

The Universal Declaration and the ICCPR

The preparation of the Universal Declaration of Human Rights and the ICCPR also commenced in 1946 and proceeded together for the first two years. The drafting began in a drafting committee of the UN Commission on Human Rights, with the two instruments reviewed by the Third Committee of the UN General Assembly, and ultimately adopted by the General Assembly in 1948 and 1966, respectively. Eleanor Roosevelt served as Chairperson of the Commission from 1946 to 1951, and she and her fellow US delegates asserted a powerful influence throughout the drafting of both documents.

The Universal Declaration of Human Rights and the ICCPR overtly built upon President Roosevelt's "four freedoms." Numerous states put forward proposals regarding the rights that should be internationally protected, and there was no dispute regarding the importance of freedom of expression. There was, however, some debate, particularly in drafting Articles 19 and 20 of the ICCPR, regarding the scope and possible limitations on the right. [of free speech]

ICCPR Article 19(3): Limitations on Freedom
of Expression

Like most modern international human rights, and in notable contrast to the US Bill of Rights, freedom of expression in international human rights law is framed in terms of both the right that is protected and the restrictions or "limitations" that may be imposed on that right. Thus, Article 19(2) of the ICCPR states:

> Everyone shall have the right to freedom of expression; this right shall include freedom to seek, receive and impart information and ideas of all kinds, regardless of frontiers, either orally, in writing or in print, in the form of art, or through any other media of his choice.

Article 19(3) then provides that exercise of these rights may be subject only to such restrictions "as are provided by law" and are "necessary" to advance certain legitimate government aims: "respect of the rights or reputations of others," "protection of national security," "public order (*ordre public*)," and "public health or morals."

In drafting what became Article 19(3), various proposals were put forward regarding limitations that governments could impose on exercise of freedom of expression, including limitations for "discrimination" and "hatred." Thus, repeatedly from 1949 to 1952, and again in 1961, the Soviet and Yugoslav delegates proposed that Article 19(3) state that freedom of expression would not protect war propaganda, racial discrimination, and incitement of hatred or enmity among peoples or nations. The United States and others successfully opposed these proposed amendments, on the grounds that they were too vague and might be used to justify censorship. "Propaganda, prejudice and similar evils were best overcome by giving free play to all views, thus permitting truth to prevail." Finally in 1961, the US delegate did propose allowing limitations for measures necessary "to prevent incitement to violence by fostering national, racial or religious hatred," while expressly prohibiting restrictions on criticizing government.[23] The United States thus sought to restrict any such limitation to "incitement to violence." Ultimately, however, all the proposed limitations to Article 19 regarding hatred, discrimination, and incitement failed, as the drafters decided to address the issue solely in Article 20. The US proposal for a short, generally worded set of limitations ultimately became the basis for Article 19(3).[24]

The Universal Declaration: Incitement to Discrimination

The initial drafts of the Universal Declaration of Human Rights and the ICCPR did not address incitement to racial hatred, discrimination, or violence. However, in November 1947, the Soviet delegate proposed that the article on nondiscrimination should broadly *criminalize* any advocacy of racial, religious, or national hatred or hostility. Thus, the Soviet Union proposed that

> any advocacy of national, racial and religious hostility or of national exclusiveness or hatred and contempt, as well as any action establishing a

privilege or a discrimination based on distinctions of race, nationality or religion, [shall] constitute a crime and shall be punishable under the law of the State.[25]

Amendments by the Chinese delegate and others quickly moderated the proposal by limiting advocacy to "incitement to violence" and by replacing "constitute a crime" with "be forbidden under the law of the State."[26] These changes were significant in constraining the scope of the prohibition and in clarifying that criminal penalties were not required. Civil or administrative penalties could also be imposed. Ultimately, however, as a result of opposition from the United States, United Kingdom, and others,[27] the only such language in the Universal Declaration of Human Rights appeared in Article 7 on nondiscrimination: "All are entitled to equal protection against any discrimination in violation of this Declaration and against any *incitement to such discrimination*."

ICCPR Article 20: Incitement to Discrimination, Hostility, or Violence

The Soviet Union persisted in pressing for an article to prohibit advocacy of national, racial, or religious hostility in the ICCPR, based on the amended 1947 proposal, in what ultimately became Article 20(2). In 1949, the Soviet delegate emphasized the need to proactively prohibit racist and nationalist propaganda, given the millions who had perished due to such speech at the hands of the Nazis, and the postwar resurgence of such rhetoric.[28] The US delegate responded by quoting the recent decision in *Terminiello* to the effect that "democracy was better served by allowing individuals to create disputes and dissension than by suppressing their freedom of speech," while the Soviet delegate pointed to the dissent's objection to protecting Fascist views.[29]

In the years of deliberation that followed, amendments were adopted to change "national, racial or religious hostility" in the amended 1947 Soviet proposal to "national, racial or religious hatred." "Incitement to violence" was changed to "incitement to hatred and violence," and ultimately to "incitement to discrimination, hostility or violence."[30]

During the discussions, representatives from the Soviet Union, Yugoslavia, Chile, France, and other states argued that prohibiting advocacy of racial and religious hatred or discrimination should not only be allowed under Article 19(3) but also be required. Moreover, in their view, restricting the prohibition to "incitement to violence" was too narrow, and would not address the root cause of racial and nationalist violence—for example, hostility and discrimination.[31]

Delegates from other states, including the United States, Australia, Belgium, Greece, Lebanon, Uruguay, the Netherlands, and the United

Kingdom, expressed concern about the vagueness of concepts such as "incitement," "hatred," and "national or religious hostility." They also expressed skepticism at the appropriateness and efficacy of requiring that all countries adopt legislation prohibiting incitement to racial hatred, given the different institutions and traditions in different states. They emphasized the importance of freedom of expression for democracy and the potential for abuse in suppressing speech. And they underscored that if necessary, legislation to prohibit racist or other propaganda could be adopted under Article 19(3). In an early response to the Soviet proposal to prohibit racist speech, Eleanor Roosevelt argued that the United States wanted the proposed article deleted altogether, since "any criticism of public or religious authorities might all too easily be described as incitement to hatred" and could be exploited by totalitarian states. In her view, the article was "not merely unnecessary, it was also harmful."[32] Delegates also debated the effectiveness of the "marketplace of ideas" in defending against propaganda and abuse. Some emphasized the free exchange of views as the best way to identify truth; others felt that a "marketplace" approach was easily dominated by the views of powerful voices and powerful states.

The arm-wrestling over the protection of freedom of expression, on the one hand, and prohibiting racist speech, on the other, initially played out against the ever-present backdrop of Nazi propaganda, and later moved to Cold War politics, nationalist struggles against European colonialism, and South African apartheid. UN membership increased by forty-one states between 1948, when the Genocide Convention and Universal Declaration of Human Rights were adopted, and 1960, and the growing pluralism of states contributed to the ultimate support for a clause prohibiting racist speech. Not unnoticed in the negotiations, of course, were the mixed signals coming from the United States regarding protection of free speech during the era, from the variable approaches of the Supreme Court to the actions of Senator Joseph McCarthy and the House Un-American Activities Committee. The United States' own history of racial oppression and violence contributed to skepticism regarding the US position. In 1953, for example, the Ukrainian delegate speculated that the United States' opposition to prohibiting racist propaganda could reflect US support for such views, pointing to a Mississippi law that criminalized speech promoting racial equality. The US delegate responded by invoking the recent *Beauharnais* decision as upholding legislation making it unlawful to publish any matter that exposed any group to hatred and contempt on the grounds of race or color. He observed that while such domestic laws were "highly desirable," requiring legislation against criminal libel was inappropriate in an international instrument.[33]

Nazi racial persecution was a continuous theme in the negotiations and was frequently invoked, particularly by Communist states. But Nazi propaganda had lessons for both sides of the debate. Joseph Goebbels' notorious Propaganda Ministry had aggressively advanced racist, religious, and nationalist ideologies, but had also suppressed all contrary speech. Nazi laws dictated the daily contents of newspapers and criminalized foreign media, and book burnings to purge "un-German" elements had provoked protests by hundreds of thousands in the United States. As nineteenth-century German author Heinrich Heine had ominously foretold, "where one burns books, one will soon burn people." Thus, a common refrain in US domestic and international arguments justifying protection of "ideas we hate" was that it was precisely such tolerance that distinguishes free governments from the Third Reich and other totalitarian states (which during the Cold War, of course, included the Soviet Union).

The final text of Article 20(2) was agreed to in 1961, based on a proposal by sixteen non-Western states to include advocacy that constituted incitement to "discrimination" and "hostility," as well as violence.[34] The United States abstained, and other states from the UN Western European and Others (WEOG) regional group almost uniformly either voted against the article or abstained.

Although the final version of Article 20(2) was not limited to incitement to violence, as the United States had urged, it nevertheless reflected a substantial narrowing from the original Soviet proposal. The final text does not require the prohibition of all nationalist, racist, or antireligious speech. Its application was facially limited to *advocacy* of national, racial, or religious *hatred* that *also* constitutes *incitement* to discrimination, hostility, or violence. Each of these terms constrains the scope of the speech that states are obligated to prohibit, and leaves room for potentially further narrowing (or broadening) interpretations. And unlike the original Soviet proposal, the clause does not require criminal punishment, but only that such speech "be prohibited by law," leaving states significant discretion regarding the penalties imposed.

[handwritten margin note: Much More narrow]

The Race Convention: Criminalizing Dissemination of Ideas

The Race Convention substantially expanded the international law mandate to prohibit, and criminalize, racially hateful speech. By the time the UN General Assembly called for the preparation of a treaty on racial discrimination in December 1962, decolonization was in full swing and the scourge of racial and religious hatred and discrimination—in the Palestinian-Israeli conflict, apartheid South Africa, the American South, and elsewhere—were prominent international concerns. A UN General Assembly resolution in December 1960 condemned all manifestations of racial, religious, and national hatred, and in 1962, the Czech delegate in the Third Committee proposed that a race convention should include an obligation to prevent and criminally punish incitement or manifestation of racial hatred.[35]

Like the initial efforts to address advocacy of racial hatred in the ICCPR, the first draft of what became Article 4 of the Race Convention was limited to incitement to violence or situations "likely to cause acts of violence."[36] The drafting of the Convention proceeded quite quickly, and the draft that went to the Third Committee still obligated states to criminalize only incitement to racial discrimination that "result[ed] in acts of violence," as well as all acts of violence and incitement to such acts. That draft, however, also obligated states to "prohibit by law" organizations or their activities, and organized propaganda activities, "which promote and incite racial discrimination"—a prohibition on organizations that the Soviet Union had unsuccessfully proposed for the declaration and ICCPR in 1948.[37]

As with the ICCPR, tying incitement to violence was contested by states that wanted to also prohibit dissemination of "ideas" of racial hatred and superiority. Their position in turn was opposed by the United States, the United Kingdom, and a number of Latin American states, in particular, which urged, as the Colombian delegate put it, that ideas should be fought "with ideas and reasons."[38] To respond to such concerns, Nigeria successfully proposed amending the article to provide that states should implement their obligations under the article "with due regard" to the principles in the Universal Declaration of Human Rights and the rights in Article 5 of the Race Convention (which included freedom of expression)—the latter language having been proposed by five powers, including the United States. The United States accepted this amendment, interpreting the "due regard" clause to mean that Article 4 did "not impose on a State party the obligation to take any action impairing the right to freedom of speech and freedom of association."[39]

Nevertheless, Argentina, Austria, Chile, Costa Rica, Italy, and others continued to press for a version that focused on incitement to violence and did not prohibit dissemination of ideas. A group of Latin American states even launched an unsuccessful last-ditch effort on the floor of the General Assembly to remove reference to "dissemination of ideas based on racial superiority or hatred," to make clear that mere ideas simpliciter should not be punished.[40]

The final Article 4 of the Race Convention went much further than the ICCPR in requiring states to prohibit hateful speech. The final text reads as follows:

Article 4
States Parties condemn all propaganda and all organizations which are based on ideas or theories of superiority of one race or group of persons of one colour or ethnic origin, or which attempt to justify or promote racial hatred and

discrimination in any form, and undertake to adopt immediate and positive measures designed to eradicate all incitement to, or acts of, such discrimination and, to this end, with due regard to the principles embodied in the Universal Declaration of Human Rights and the rights expressly set forth in article 5 of this Convention, inter alia:

(a) Shall declare an offence punishable by law all dissemination of ideas based on racial superiority or hatred, incitement to racial discrimination, as well as all acts of violence or incitement to such acts against any race or group of persons of another colour or ethnic origin, and also the provision of any assistance to racist activities, including the financing thereof;

(b) Shall declare illegal and prohibit organizations, and also organized and all other propaganda activities, which promote and incite racial discrimination, and shall recognize participation in such organizations or activities as an offence punishable by law;

(c) Shall not permit public authorities or public institutions, national or local, to promote or incite racial discrimination.

Article 4 provided that states should make the following an "offense punishable by law": "dissemination of ideas," "incitement to racial discrimination," and participation in organizations that "promote and incite racial discrimination." States must also "declare illegal and prohibit" any such organizations. The criminalization of such conduct as "offenses" was also a major departure from the ICCPR, which the Colombian delegation declared a "retrograde measure," adopted "without seriously pondering on the dangers involved in authorizing penalties under criminal law for ideological offenses."[41] Also, in a significant shift from Article 20 of the ICCPR only four years earlier, the article was adopted overwhelmingly, with eighty-eight votes in favor, none opposed, and five abstentions. The United States voted for the final version, pointing to the "due regard" clause as protecting First Amendment concerns.

In explaining the United States' vote supporting the final draft of the Race Convention in the Third Committee, US Ambassador to the United Nations and former Supreme Court Justice Arthur Goldberg explained that "the freedom of speech guaranteed to every American by the Bill of Rights was among the nation's most precious national rights and possessions." Accordingly,

the United States took the view that article 4 did not place a State under obligation to take action that would prohibit its citizens from freely and fully expressing their opinions on any subject, even if those opinions were obnoxious. ... A government should act only where the expression of those opinions was associated with, or threatened imminently to lead to, action against which the public had a right to be protected.

Whitney.

Quoting Justice Brandeis, Goldberg observed that "if there be time to expose through discussion the falsehood and fallacies, to avert the evil by the process of education, the remedy to be applied is more speech, not enforced silence."[42]

* * *

The United States' engagement in the drafting of the Genocide Convention, the ICCPR, and the Race Convention clearly had a moderating effect on the most ambitious efforts to provide for suppression of hateful speech at the international level. No other state so frequently or forcefully advanced its own domestic laws and judicial doctrines as a basis for informing international understandings of freedom of expression. The United States also was not alone in advocating free speech principles. Its commitment to the value of a robust, uninhibited marketplace of ideas, free from government interference, was embraced by many states, including other advanced Western democracies, as well as a number of Latin American states, Lebanon, Japan, and others. As a result, even with respect to the Race Convention, the international rules that were developed reflected a compromise between the position of the United States and that of opposing states—compromises that were significantly informed by US concerns regarding restrictions on speech.

Particularly during the negotiations over the Genocide Convention and the ICCPR, which took place in the era of *Beauharnais,* the United States' international negotiating position perhaps was more absolutist in its defense of freedom of expression from government interference than contemporary US constitutional doctrine. This may have reflected the United States' desire to clearly differentiate in the international arena its commitment to free speech and other core democratic principles from the position of Communist states. The United States may also have felt it was particularly important to ensure robust protection for freedom of expression internationally, when those principles often would be applied in states with weaker traditions of free speech and press and judicial independence.

On the other hand, the US negotiating position appeared to soften substantially during the debates over Article 4 of the Race Convention, which it interpreted as consistent with the First Amendment. In other words, the United States' international position appeared to become more accepting of language that tolerated (or required) regulation of hate speech during the 1960s, even as domestic constitutional doctrine hardened in the opposite direction. The reason for this dichotomy is unclear. It may, however, have simply reflected an effort to secure the best outcome in an increasingly pluralistic international negotiation context.

The evolution in US constitutional law disfavoring restrictions on speech—including hateful speech—also continued. As a result, by the time the United States finally ratified these conventions (the Genocide Convention in 1988, the ICCPR in 1992, and the Race Convention in 1994), it adopted reservations that precluded obligations inconsistent with the First Amendment. The United States implementing legislation for the Genocide Convention also criminalizes incitement only when the speaker "urges another to engage imminently in [genocidal] conduct in circumstances under which there is a substantial likelihood of imminently causing such conduct."[43]

The hate speech provisions also proved controversial for other states, and various states have adopted reservations or declarations to Article 20(2) and Article 4 to be consistent with freedom of expression. Japan, for example, has explained to the expert body overseeing implementation of the Race Convention (the Committee on the Elimination of Racial Discrimination [CERD]) that "Article 4 may cover an extremely wide range of acts" and subjecting them all to punitive laws could be contrary to freedom of expression.[44]

Hate Speech Applied

International Jurisprudence: The CERD and HRC

Despite broad obligations to prohibit or to criminalize certain racist and other hate speech in widely ratified international human rights treaties, international doctrine and practice relating to prohibition of hate speech remain uneven. As a general matter, advanced democratic states often have not adopted prohibitions coterminous with the treaty requirements, and enforcement has largely been limited to the most significant violations. This underimplementation and enforcement reflects, in part, ongoing concerns respecting freedom of expression. On the other hand, concerns regarding abuse by authoritarian-leaning states have proven justified. Although hate speech recently has been on the rise in many parts of the world, including the United States, so too has been abuse of such laws to suppress opposition political figures; social critics; dissidents; journalists; human rights defenders; and voices of racial, ethnic, religious, and other minority groups.[45]

The CERD repeatedly has maintained that Article 4(a) of the Race Convention requires criminalization of expression falling within its scope.[46] Over time, however, the Committee has also shown greater sensitivity in applying Article 4 in relation to freedom of expression. In 2013, for example, the Committee emphasized that criminalization of racist expression should be limited to "serious cases, . . . proven beyond reasonable doubt," and that other cases should be addressed through other means. The Committee also observed that the "due regard" implies that other human rights, including freedom of opinion and expression, "must be given appropriate weight."[47] Collectively, these and other moves appear to constrain the broadest interpretations of Article 4.

In reviewing the compliance of states with the ICCPR, the Human Rights Committee (HRC) routinely recommends that states combat hate speech and criminalize hate *crimes*. It also frequently warns against abuse of laws restricting speech.[48] In its best-known case on the subject, *Faurisson v. France*,[49] the Committee found that France's conviction of an academic Holocaust denier did not violate Article 19 of the ICCPR. Faurisson was convicted for statements such as stating that "the myth of the gas chambers is a dishonest fabrication" under the French Gayssot Act, which criminalized contesting crimes against humanity that were prosecuted at Nuremberg. France defended the prosecution on the grounds that "the denial of the genocide of the Jews during World War Two fuels debates of a profoundly anti-semitic character, since it accuses the Jews of having fabricated themselves the myth of their extermination."

The Committee found that under the specific circumstances of the case, the prosecution did not violate Article 19. Because Faurisson's statements in context "were of a nature as to raise or strengthen anti-semitic feelings," the French law protected "the [right] of the Jewish community to live free from fear of an atmosphere of anti-semitism." As to whether the measure was "necessary," the Committee noted France's submission that the act "was intended to serve the struggle against racism and anti-semitism," and that in France Holocaust denial was "the principal vehicle for anti-semitism." In the absence of any contrary argument from the author, the Committee concluded that the restriction in Faurisson's case satisfied Article 19(3).

It is not clear how generalizable that decision from 1996 is today. In 2011, the HRC took the position that "laws that penalize the expression of opinions about historical facts are incompatible with . . . respect for freedom of opinion and expression." The Committee also has since underscored that the necessity prong of Article 19(3) requires that laws limiting freedom of expression must be strictly tailored, and has expressed strong concerns about criminalizing expression. It has recommended, for example, that states decriminalize defamation and held that imprisonment is never an appropriate penalty for defamation.[50]

The Committee to date has had only one case addressing the merits of an Article 20(2) claim. *Rabbae v. The Netherlands*[51] involved a claim by three Moroccan Muslims in the Netherlands who contended that they had been personally harmed by numerous anti-Islam, anti-immigrant, and racist remarks by the right-wing Dutch politician, Geert Wilders, and that the Netherlands had not adequately prohibited the conduct. Wilders was prosecuted for anti-immigrant anti-Islam speeches calling on the Netherlands to close the borders to non-Westerners, warning of an Islamic "tsunami," and claiming that "one out of five Moroccan youngsters has a police record." Wilders was charged with "incitement to hatred and discrimination on grounds of religion or race" under the implementing legislation for Article 20 of the ICCPR and Article 4 of the Race Convention, but was ultimately acquitted on the grounds that his speech primarily constituted criticism of religious tenets of Islam and political views regarding Dutch immigration policy, both of which were legally protected. The claimants argued that the acquittal failed to fulfill the Netherlands' obligation under the ICCPR Article 26 prohibition on discrimination and the Article 20(2) obligation to prohibit incitement to discrimination, hostility, and violence.

In analyzing the claim, the Committee observed that Article 20(2) serves as a bridge between the Article 19 protection of freedom of expression and the Article 26 prohibition of discrimination under the Covenant. Accordingly, "article 20(2) secures the right . . . to be free from hatred and discrimination under article 26 by requiring States to prohibit certain conduct and expression by law." The Committee also emphasized that Article 20(2) was crafted narrowly to ensure that freedom of expression is not infringed:

> Freedom of expression embraces even expression that may be regarded as deeply offensive. Moreover, the free communication of information and ideas about public and political issues between citizens, candidates and elected representatives is essential to the promotion and protection of free expression. . . . [P]rohibitions of displays of lack of respect for a religion or other belief system, including blasphemy laws, are incompatible with the Covenant, except in the specific circumstances envisaged in article 20(2). Similarly, such prohibitions may not be used to prevent or punish criticism of religious leaders or commentary on religious doctrine and tenets of faith.

The Committee underscored that Article 20(2) does not require criminal penalties, but only that advocacy be "prohibited by law," which may also include civil and administrative penalties. The Committee also noted that the Dutch law criminalized "incitement" to hatred or discrimination restrictively, by punishing "inflammatory behaviour that incites the commission of *criminal offenses or acts of violence.*" The statute also criminalized incitement "only against persons, not religions, since criticism of even the most deeply-held convictions . . . is protected by freedom of expression." In light of the Dutch legal framework in place, the prosecution pursued, and the legal avenues afforded to the authors, the Committee concluded that the Netherlands had complied with its obligation to " 'prohibit' statements made in violation of article 20(2)." Reasoning that

Article 20(2) does not require that a defendant "will invariably be convicted by an independent and impartial court of law," the Committee found no violation of Articles 26 and 20(2) of the Covenant.

The Netherlands' approach of limiting criminal penalties under Article 20(2) to incitement of "criminal offences or acts of violence," which the Committee approved in *Rabbae*, brings Article 20 closer to the *Brandenburg* standard for incitement to imminent violence, and was appropriate for a number of reasons. It is consistent with the Committee's jurisprudence under Article 19, which urges great caution in the imposition of criminal penalties that punish speech. It is also consistent with the approach to criminal penalties for hate speech adopted by other international human rights bodies.[52]

Regional Jurisprudence: Europe

The largest body of supranational jurisprudence regarding regulation of hate speech has been developed by the European Court of Human Rights, interpreting the European Convention on Human Rights. That instrument protects freedom of expression under Article 10 and allows, but does not require, prohibition of hateful or discriminatory speech. The European system is also distinct from international human rights law in granting states a "margin of appreciation," or some domestic latitude, in interpreting European Convention on Human Rights obligations.

Most hate speech cases before the European court have involved claims of improper suppression of speech, not a state's failure to adequately prohibit speech. For example, in *Jersild v. Denmark*,[53] the court found that the conviction of a Danish journalist for airing a TV program featuring the racist attitudes of Danish "Greenjacket" youths violated the Convention, because the journalist was not advocating the racist views the show portrayed, but bringing them to public attention. The Greenjacket youths themselves had also been convicted for stating that "niggers" and "foreign workers" were "animals"—statements that might be compared to those of the Ku Klux Klan speaker that *Brandenburg* found protected. However, the court concluded that the speakers themselves were not protected under Article 10 of the European Convention on Human Rights.

In more extreme cases, the European court has found claims involving hateful speech to fall entirely outside of the Convention's protections. In *Norwood v. United Kingdom*,[54] for example, the court held that a conviction for displaying a poster with the legend "Islam out of Britain—Protect the British People" did not implicate any rights under the Convention.

The European court has also been less tolerant than the United States of speech that allegedly constitutes incitement to violence. In *Sürek v. Turkey (No.*

1),[55] the court upheld the conviction of an owner of a publishing company that had published two letters in a newsletter from readers that accused the "fascist Turkish army" of committing atrocities against Kurds in Eastern Turkey. Although the defendant was not an author, or even the editor, of the letters, and had not associated himself with their views, the court concluded that, in the context of ongoing violence with the Kurdistan Workers' Party (PKK) in the region, he had "provided their writers with an outlet for stirring up violence and hatred," which justified their suppression.

Even in a case diverging so substantially from US constitutional approaches, however, the dissent was homage to the enduring influence of the First Amendment.

Judge Bonello drew directly from Justice Holmes' *Abrams* dissent to argue that punishment would only be justifiable if the incitement created "a clear and present danger":

> I borrow what one of the mightiest constitutional jurists of all time had to say about words which tend to destabilise law and order: "We should be eternally vigilant against attempts to check the expression of opinions that we loathe and believe to be fraught with death, unless they so imminently threaten immediate interference with the lawful and pressing purposes of the law that an immediate check is required to save the country."

Conclusion

Despite the divergent approaches to regulating extremist speech, much in the approach of international human rights law to protection of freedom of expression would sound intimately familiar to an American. In interpreting Article 19 of the ICCPR, for example, the Human Rights Committee has developed extensive jurisprudence recognizing that freedom of expression is "indispensable . . . for the full development of the person" and is "the foundation stone for every free and democratic society."[56] The right thus protects even expression that may be "deeply offensive." Freedom of expression is essential to participation in public affairs, and the media must be able to "comment on public issues and to inform public opinion without censorship or restraint." States must prevent silencing of persons exercising the right to freedom of expression. Moreover,

> the value placed . . . upon uninhibited expression is particularly high in the circumstances of public debate in a democratic society concerning figures in the public and political domain. . . . [A]ll public figures,

including those exercising the highest political authority such as heads of state and government, are legitimately subject to criticism and political opposition.

With respect to the allowable restrictions on freedom of expression, the Committee has recognized that "since any restriction on freedom of expression constitutes a serious curtailment of human rights," restrictions must be strictly necessary and proportionate to a legitimate government aim set forth in Article 19(3). Restrictions must be "directly related to the specific need on which they are predicated," "must not be overbroad," but "must be the least intrusive instrument . . . which might achieve their protective function." Furthermore, a state "must demonstrate in specific and individualized fashion the precise nature of the threat" being addressed, and establish "a direct and immediate connection between the expression and the threat." To put this in US constitutional parlance, one might say that restrictions on freedom of expression must serve a compelling government interest, must not be vague or overbroad, and must be narrowly tailored to the compelling interest.

The committee accordingly expresses concern at laws punishing disrespect for authority, disrespect for flags and symbols, and defamation of heads of state, as well as laws protecting the honor of public officials. Defamation laws must be carefully crafted to not stifle freedom of expression. Restrictions relating to national security and terrorism must be imposed with "extreme care" and cannot be applied to "suppress or withhold from the public information of legitimate public interest that does not harm national security or to prosecute journalists [or others] for having disseminated such information."

Each of these standards reflects the permeation of First Amendment principles into international norms protecting free speech. The United States has been a crucial benchmark for the requirements of compelling governmental interests, narrow tailoring, and prohibitions on vagueness and overbreadth, and the international community substantially has followed that guidance. Moreover, as this review of the evolution of international and regional law and practice makes clear, since the dawn of the postwar human rights movement, the First Amendment has been invoked as a tocsin against government restrictions on speech, including racist and extremist speech.

In the context of hate speech, the United States' unique historical commitment to freedom of expression as the ultimate democratic liberty, the fact that the United States was never directly subjected to the ravages of Nazi propaganda, and perhaps the fact that the United States has never fully grappled with its own history of racial subjugation have led it on a distinct path. Nevertheless, whether as a beacon to be followed or a foil to be distinguished, the United States' protection of freedom of speech has fundamentally informed the shape of international human rights treaty protections, including in the context of hate speech. It continues to exert a constraining influence on treaty interpretation and jurisprudence, and it continues to serve as a magnetic force in countering global political and social currents that would erode protections for freedom of expression.

PART FOUR

NEW TECHNOLOGIES AND THE FIRST AMENDMENT OF THE FUTURE

The Unintentional Press

How Technology Companies Fail as Publishers

EMILY BELL

The rapid concentration of economic and cultural power among a small set of private companies is the most pressing question facing the free press in the United States and potentially the world. As the mission creep of what were once intermediary companies starts to bleed into questions of censorship and access, we are faced with challenging questions about the accidental regulation of an unintentional press.

While there are sound economic, legal, and cultural reasons that social media companies and platforms such as Facebook, Twitter, and Google have strongly resisted a description that categorizes them as publishers, their decisions and behavior are increasingly indistinguishable from those of editorial organizations. This chapter sets out to describe how platforms became the gatekeepers of free expression and why this concentration of power of private companies leaves us at a dangerous point in democracy and freedom of the press.

* * *

In October 2017, Serbian journalist Stevan Dojcinovic noticed something unusual. Stories produced by his investigative nonprofit news organization KRIK were suddenly being seen by fewer than half the number of people he would normally expect to read them. Upon further investigation, he noticed he could not find his stories on Facebook, the social media platform that directs the majority of traffic toward KRIK and other similar news publishers.

There had been no communication or notice from Facebook about why this might be happening, but in a handful of smaller nations scattered across the globe, journalists and editors were noticing the same phenomenon. In Guatemala, Slovakia, Serbia, Bolivia, Sri Lanka, and Cambodia, Facebook had

Essentially censorship changed how it showed stories from publishers and news outlets to its users. Instead of appearing in the main Facebook news feed as normal, the stories had been shifted to a separate area, kept for news. The result was that people did not see the stories as often.

KRIK's experience of seeing its traffic halved was somewhat better than others fared. In Slovakia, the number of times readers interacted with news from the top sixty news publisher sites on Facebook dropped by 66 percent. In Guatemala, it was the same. "The Facebook explore tab killed 66 percent of our traffic. Just destroyed it . . . years of really hard work were just swept away. . . . It has been catastrophic, and I am very, very worried," said Dina Fernandez,[1] a journalist and member of the editorial board at the Guatemalan news site Soy502. The Guatemalan news site had been an enthusiastic adopter of the new publishing tools being offered by Facebook, using its Facebook Live broadcasting platform to live-stream corruption trials. These too suffered from the algorithm change.[2]

Writing in the *New York Times*, Dojcinovic set out the democratic threat posed by Facebook's actions:

> Attracting viewers to a story relies, above all, on making the process as simple as possible. Even one extra click can make a world of difference. This is an existential threat, not only to my organization and others like it but also to the ability of citizens in all of the countries subject to Facebook's experimentation to discover the truth about their societies and their leaders.[3]

Facebook's sudden reorganization of press visibility in countries where the democracies were sometimes fragile or relatively new was introduced with little foresight about what it might mean for their citizens or for journalism. Unlike many public media outlets and newspapers, Facebook had no line of accountability, no editorial structure through which to explain itself. Instead, a post appeared from Adam Mosseri, Facebook's head of News Feed, on its media blog:

> The goal of this test is to understand if people prefer to have separate places for personal and public content. We will hear what people say about the experience to understand if it's an idea worth pursuing any further. There is no current plan to roll this out beyond these test countries or to charge pages on Facebook to pay for all their distribution in News Feed or Explore. Unfortunately, some have mistakenly made that interpretation—but that was not our intention.[4]

Three months later, with some refinements, Facebook announced that it would be making similar changes to its news feed algorithm in the rest of the world. The new policy was not identical to the test programs, but it was close enough to send publishers all over the world scrambling to reckon with what it might mean for their own publications. One thing was clear, however: Facebook can, with a small experiment, change the visibility and discussion of serious news across continents—even if that is not its intention.

When Google changed its search engine algorithm to try to marginalize unconventional and extremist publishers cluttering up its main news feed, it also destroyed the traffic going to smaller sites that reported on extremist content. AlterNet, one such site, saw traffic drop by 63 percent. It might be that this was just an unfortunate edge case of misclassification. But AlterNet also produced a regular flow of critical articles about Silicon Valley companies, including Google.[5] Did this contribute to the downweighting? Google denied that the change was anything but an accidental side effect of tackling a major problem. The obscurity of how the search algorithm works means that we will never know for sure.

When Nazis marched in the streets of Charlottesville, Virginia, in August 2017, the Daily Stormer, the Fascist website that helped organize the march, found itself denied a host of web services by a number of large companies. This included Cloudflare, a security company that shields around 10 percent of all internet traffic from being hacked. Having pulled Daily Stormer's access to the service, Cloudflare's chief executive published a blog that expressed anxiety about the lack of due process that large-scale technology companies are subjected to when it comes to matters of speech: "Without a clear framework as a guide for content regulation, a small number of companies will largely determine what can and cannot be online."[6]

There are urgent questions created by this convergence between the public sphere and private enterprise that center on the institutions and norms we think of as creating a healthy democracy. How have the technology companies changed the operation of the free press? Do social media platforms now get to decide what we see and discuss? And if they do, then are press freedom and the rights of citizens to receive information adequately protected? And finally, what can be done to define and safeguard these rights and freedoms in a fluid environment increasingly dominated by a small number of players?

Gatekeepers of Unprecedented Size

The number of Facebook accounts in 2017 sat at over two billion, not far behind the global headcount of Christians, ahead of the number of Muslims, and about seven hundred million more than the population of China. In terms of registered users, it is far ahead of even the other technology behemoths.

Amazon and Apple, though larger and richer as companies, have only a few hundred million registered accounts each. Even Google, which is more widely used on a daily basis than Facebook, has only a mere billion accounts using its Gmail service.

Never in history has there been an intermediary for human expression with either the scale or role of Facebook. And never in the relatively recent history of commercial media has there been such a concentration of money and human attention in a small handful of companies. The scale of large technologies has rocked the world of advertising-dependent businesses, which account for most of the world's media. Around two-thirds of all advertising expenditure globally now goes to just five companies: 50 percent goes to Google and Facebook; the ascendent technology companies in the East—Alibaba, Baidu, and Tencent—account for another 15 percent between them.

By 2017, Google was bigger than the entire global print industry, in terms of advertising, and Facebook was larger than the entire global commercial radio business. An industry that had taken two hundred years to build was replaced in a decade.

The global technology companies are reshaping our concepts of what we mean by mass media, the independent press, and the public sphere. Their collective advertising model takes all the aggregate data created by trillions of human–computer interactions a day—searching, writing, posting, liking, sharing, watching, arguing, talking—and turns it into devastatingly effective microtargeting businesses for identifying consumers who are most likely to be receptive to commercial messages.

This engineering feat of bewilderingly fast iteration has allowed little time for the evaluation of effects on the institutional press, public discourse, and the role of communications businesses in democracy. For publishing and journalism, this upheaval has proved to be singularly unmooring. So much of what enabled journalists to do their jobs was instantaneously improved and then subsequently destroyed by large-scale search and technology platforms, and their relationship has been fraught with crossed wires and confused signals.

For all social media and search companies, the business model is broadly the same. We call them "platforms," as they carry a variety of different types of content—but at heart, they are data intermediaries. They work by creating a virtuous circle of content, attention, and data collected from users. The targeting capabilities created by vast amounts of attention data are sold to advertisers through automated, real-time trading systems. The introduction of a human step into this automated data-laundering cycle creates both friction and expense. Human intervention can be necessary for tasks that computers cannot perform, but the platform companies will always try to avoid it if they can.

The companies do not see themselves as publishers, or as having a role in creating and shaping public opinion. Google's head of news, Richard Gingras, when pressed on the issue by BBC journalist Nick Robinson, said: "We are not making media, we are organizing the world's information."[7]

Mark Zuckerberg, the chief executive and founder of Facebook, consistently denied that his platform was a media business, until 2017 when he changed his language to suggest Facebook was a "new type of company." His chief operating officer, Sheryl Sandberg, insisted even after this that it was wrong to categorize Facebook as anything other than a technology company. "At our heart we're a tech company; we hire engineers. We don't hire reporters, no one's a journalist, we don't cover the news," she said.[8] Decisions about what is kept on a social platform or deleted from it are not made by editors, Sandberg noted, but by teams of policy experts who have legal backgrounds.

To outsiders, those attempts to draw a line between publishers and platforms can often seem like a distinction without a difference. In 2016, when Facebook launched a product called Facebook Live that could stream live video onto the platform from anyone's phone, it had a dedicated policy team of about twenty deciding how the material ought to be viewed. Moreover, Facebook itself paid many media outlets and individuals to create live videos. That model looks close enough to the commissioning and editing process employed by traditional publishers to make Facebook's attempts to differentiate itself seem unpersuasive.

All social platforms, including Google, Facebook, Twitter, and Snapchat, have "partnership" teams that work with creators—either journalists or individual "influencers"—who use their platforms.

Twitter, a social platform that has had journalists and news organizations as its most influential group of users since it was launched in 2007, has been less rigid in self-definition and has been punished accordingly. It has faced a series of campaigns and lawsuits from parties alternately suggesting it has been either too liberal in what it allows on its platform or too censorious.

Twitter has made a policy of banning accounts that have violated its terms of use, including technology journalist-turned Breitbart commentator Milo Yiannopoulos and alt-right troll Chuck Johnson. In 2018, Johnson launched a lawsuit claiming the "private public square" of Twitter had violated his First Amendment rights, leaning on the precedent of a previous case, *Packingham v. North Carolina*.[9] That case cast social media as the "modern public square" when North Carolina sought to ban child molesters and pedophiles from access to public media.

Legal scholars agree that Johnson's case had little merit, because Twitter is a private company, not the government, but this does not mean there isn't a case for examining the powerful reach and function of social platforms.

In general, the law has agreed with the position that platforms are not like newspapers by shielding them from the responsibility for what their users publish under the terms of Section 230 of the Communications Decency Act of 1996.[10] A growing number of critics and legal scholars have, however, suggested that a clause drawn up a decade before most social media (as we know them today) existed is in need of reform.

Definitions either in law or corporate statements melt in the furnace of public opinion. The main reason to think that platform companies have taken over the role previously played by the press lies not so much in statistical analysis or even documentary evidence, but more in how their behavior is discussed and interpreted by others.

How Platform Companies Make Editorial Decisions

The convergence of the public commons with private technology is happening in two directions. Journalism practice is being reshaped by the technologies that are available to reporters and editors, and technology platforms are being reshaped by the way communities adopt and use the platforms. The audience for news now gathers as much on social platforms as anywhere else. In the United States, the majority of citizens see some news through social media, and a growing number would list Facebook, Twitter, Google, or YouTube as a primary conduit for news, if not an actual creator of it.

Citizens use the platforms as reporting tools too, and social platforms treat the material they generate in an editorial manner. Breaking news, discussion, and opinion have moved away from the former gatekeepers of the press and broadcast media and out onto the social web. Citizen media have become the bedrock of breaking news. Crucial video for news reporting from natural disasters such as the 2004 tsunami in Asia or from terrorist attacks such as the London Tube bombings of 2005, the Boston Marathon bombing in 2013, and the shootings at the Charlie Hebdo offices in Paris in 2015 all came from eyewitnesses at the scene. The proliferation of camera phones since 2002 has made everyone into a potential video journalist.

People who do not routinely have access to mainstream media can benefit from the egalitarian nature of modern social publishing tools. In cases of police violence, such as the choking to death of Black street seller Eric Garner[11] or the shooting of Philando Castile, the official versions of law enforcement officers were challenged by video recordings that were widely disseminated or streamed on social media. In the case of Philando Castile's shooting, his partner captured and live-streamed shocking footage, which Facebook took down because it had been flagged by the platform's automatic moderation tools. Facebook later reinstated the video and the feed, saying its temporary removal had been a mistake.[12]

Eyewitness media have created new sources and methods for reporting breaking news. Newsrooms now construct often highly detailed accounts of stories entirely through the material shot or reported at the time on social media. Citizens will act as reporters or witnesses, adding their own commentary or shooting with professional accuracy during newsworthy incidents. The sheer volume of material that is captured and published makes it impossible for employees of any platform to make individual decisions on particular words and images. The content must be monitored automatically by algorithms that might be trying to remove violent content or nudity. When the automatic processes cannot distinguish between an image of cultural significance, such as an artwork or a meaningful news event, then human judgment can override those processes. Both the construction of algorithms and the human process of curation are informed not just by legality but also by value judgments from the companies employing them. The extent to which these are editorial processes is debatable, but their effects are undeniable in shaping what can and cannot be published, and what will or will not be seen.

Beyond news, personalities have built vast followings on social media, particularly YouTube. Personalities who create popular channels are cultivated and guided by partnership teams at Google-owned YouTube, specifically around how to make their material. When transgressions in taste and decency occur, or terms of use are violated, influencers are "demonetized," which means they won't receive preferential placement or advertising against their material. When YouTuber Logan Paul made an ill-judged and tasteless video about suicide in Japan and posted it to his fifteen million subscribers, it caused outrage in mainstream media and on social channels. Paul was shamed into deleting the video, and YouTube cut him from its YouTube Preferred channel.[13] He was also dropped from an original series being developed for the platform. Influencer networks test the platform companies' assertions that they are not in fact exactly like traditional media companies. It is the set of relationships where they are least like other carriage technologies. Phone companies did not cultivate film stars, and cable companies would not scout entertainment talent. YouTube, Snapchat, and Instagram might contend that they do not elevate talent—the audience does— even as they perform some of the functions of a studio system: advising, paying, and grooming performers who often have no other institutional support. On the WeChat platform in China, writers are given tip jars and other monetization tools alongside their work.[14] Fueled by recommendation algorithms and paid promotion, individuals can far outperform large corporations in their ability to reach audiences.

The Twitter silencing of trolls like Chuck Johnson and the banishing of Logan Paul from the front page of YouTube are the more high-profile examples of how platform companies exercise control over creators. Legal scholars have argued persuasively that this gatekeeping function means that a new set of norms for what constitutes acceptable speech is being arbitrated through the terms of use of platform companies.[15] To claim that this function when practiced at scale on a daily basis does not in some way "edit" our news and our discourse is a denial of the obvious.

The Tipping Point of the 2016 Election

The 2016 presidential election in the United States provides a comprehensive case study in the role of social media in our democracy. One meeting at Facebook's headquarters in May 2016 provides an example of how Facebook's resistance to being defined as a media company drove decisions that had a significant impact on American politics.

Mark Zuckerberg met a group of twenty-five right-wing commentators, publishers, and politicians at his company's plush new campus in Menlo Park, California. The purpose of the meeting was for Zuckerberg to placate those alarmed by a story claiming that Facebook curators deliberately suppressed right-leaning stories on its Trending Topics page.

The allegations came from one anonymous, disaffected content curator who had told the technology website Gizmodo about the secret practices Facebook implemented to edit a "Trending" list that featured popular stories of the day.[16] These included removing or downplaying stories that often came from highly partisan sites, so they did not appear at the top of the list. The title "Trending" and the blue line graph logo on the page gave the appearance of a computational sorting system, an algorithm that informed Facebook users which stories were currently popular among other users. And the revelation that this promotional list of stories was not in fact sorted by a computer program or algorithm, but chosen by people who might have political motives, was seized on by the aggrieved right-wing publishers and politicians as a further extension of a "liberal media conspiracy."

The meeting between Facebook and representatives of a right-wing political movement during an election cycle was illustrative of the rising power of Facebook as a purveyor of news, whose scale and influence was overtaking that of the traditional broadcast and print distribution models. Facebook had itself been actively resisting any suggestion that it was at all biased or making editorial decisions, constantly reinforcing that it was a technology company, a neutral platform to elevate all types of speech.

After the roasting by the Right, Zuckerberg posted a reaffirmation that Facebook would never suppress differing political views: "We've built Facebook to be a platform for all ideas. Our community's success depends on everyone feeling comfortable sharing anything they want. It doesn't make sense for our mission or our business to suppress political content or prevent anyone from seeing what matters most to them," wrote Zuckerberg.[17]

With hindsight, Zuckerberg's statement gave clues as to how the company's naïve philosophy toward neutrality and free speech subsequently led to a major crisis for both Facebook and US democracy. To say that "it doesn't make sense" to "suppress political content or prevent anyone from seeing what matters most to them" puts a positive spin on a corporate choice to not exercise responsibility for political content.

If "political content" was, as it turned out to be, advertising bought by Russian actors and welded into a highly sophisticated social media campaign or totally fabricated "fake news" stories, then Zuckerberg was wrong. It made sense from a civic and commercial perspective for Facebook to both be aware of it and prevent it.

When anxiety emerged over the control of the social media commons, politicians, executives, and commentators from the right saw Facebook as the central point of arbitration for their grievances. They viewed Facebook as an important actor in deciding how their work was distributed, and the opaque power that the social media company was exercising over their words was enough to force them to engage with what many of them think of as an outpost of liberal media. The insistence from Facebook that it was neutral reflected how the platform saw its role not as preventative but positive—it should give people what they wanted. The confrontation forced Facebook to make changes, though, which had an impact on what citizens saw in their news feeds. It also signaled that the company was not ready to think through or enact value-based judgments, which were easily legible to consumers.

Aside from Zuckerberg's reassurances in a Facebook post, the company sought to remedy the situation by firing all its human curators, and instead turned the sorting of articles and trending subjects over to algorithms. In reality, the implication that decision making had been surrendered to some great, impartial machine intelligence was misleading. Using algorithms to make trillions of different decisions about who should see what content is certainly a more abstract process than having human editors comb through news items and use their judgment, but the automated processes still reflect human priorities and values. Facebook decided, though, that the idea of neutrality was better performed through machines and mathematical formulae than through humans.

The decision was one of the factors that shaped the platform's role in the 2016 elections. But even the most sophisticated algorithms cannot reliably identify political propaganda or "fake news." In abandoning even the low level of human intervention it had been using, Facebook showed that its priority was to avoid negative publicity rather than to support the quality of the information on its network.

A year beyond the fateful meeting in Menlo Park, things looked very different. Donald Trump had become president despite losing the popular vote to Hillary Clinton. His victory hinged on sixty-six thousand votes in swing states, where the focus became how a campaign that lagged in the polls had pulled off such an unlikely victory. The answer seemed, at least in part, to be found in how the campaigns had addressed the public. Hillary Clinton's campaign had relied on cable television backed up with some digital campaigning. Trump had combined his skillful cable TV presence with $70 million of digital advertising spent through Facebook. Researchers and journalists revealed that voters on both sides of the political divide might have been discouraged or encouraged to vote by messages, advertising, and even made-up stories—colloquially known as "fake news"—circulating on social platforms.

Most shockingly and damagingly for Facebook, researchers and journalists found that foreign actors, including the Russian-sponsored Internet Research Agency, had used American platform technologies to create targeted material and propaganda intended to influence the American vote. Facebook had even taken advertising money, through its automated systems, from Russian trolls to target US voters. Ironically, the episode underwrote how undiscriminating the automated processes of Facebook actually were. Facebook, Google, and Twitter were called to judicial hearings on Capitol Hill in October 2017 to answer questions from lawmakers about how a mixture of advertising, propaganda, and other social interactions conducted by a foreign agency might have moved through their platforms to influence the US election.

The narrative around Facebook's responsibility for the use of its platform turned from a circular specialist debate into an issue of global political interest. The issue was no longer the rights of individuals or organizations to publish but rather the rights of citizens to hear and receive relevant and accurate information.

Journalism at Scale

The giants of Silicon Valley are not just central to the distribution of news and information; they are also reshaping every other feature of the media landscape. One of the key questions of the past decade for news organizations has been how far they should integrate themselves into the structures and processes of social media platforms. Large teams of "curators" or editors now work in the most advanced newsrooms solely to produce material for third-party platforms. Even staid institutions such as the *Wall Street Journal* might have a team of five or six dedicated to making stories for Snapchat.

That the means of production shape the journalism is nothing new. But the age of big tech has also required a different approach to newsgathering and reporting. It is impossible to report properly on the modern world without adopting the same technologies that are disrupting the news industry. An important new phenomenon resulting from large-scale digitization of information has been the "deluge leak": the release of vast caches of documents too numerous for humans to parse efficiently, easily circulated on thumb drives and CDs.

WikiLeaks is a radical transparency organization that has used the statelessness of the commercial internet and the connectivity of social media to spread leaks and other hacked material. In 2010, WikiLeaks obtained and released three major sets of documents: 77,000 that pertained to the war in Afghanistan, 390,000 related to the Iraq war, and just over 251,000 diplomatic cables that disclosed years of previously secret communication between the United States and foreign governments. In total, 750,000 documents were obtained by Chelsea Manning, who was a relatively low-ranking soldier working in surveillance in Iraq. She, in turn, handed them to WikiLeaks founder Julian Assange. WikiLeaks partnered with the *New York Times*, the *Guardian*, and other international news outlets to publish the leaks, with each news organization chosen at least in part for its digitally advanced newsroom's pioneering work with large datasets. The question for newsrooms when the diplomatic cables dropped was, how could you sort and extract sense from 251,000 different documents?

Another leap in leak scale happened in 2013, when security analyst Edward Snowden leaked a trove of material from the National Security Agency so vast that the full extent and size of the material he captured is not known. Just one folder of the Snowden leaks contained 430,000 documents, and when Snowden fled with the material first to Hong Kong and later to Russia from his home in Hawaii, he could transport all the material on a couple of laptops. Manning and Snowden, along with Daniel Ellsberg's release of the Pentagon Papers, showed to what degree the centralization and digitization of government data had expanded the amount of information stored, and how the analysis needed far more people and therefore much wider access given to civilians. It also challenged news organizations working with these new types of deluge leaks to analyze such vast troves that even the leakers themselves had little idea of the contents.[18] Commercial technologies like Google Docs, email, and even phone lines were insecure for communication about the material.

When commercially available digital systems were used to support the publication of the documents from WikiLeaks, such as to collect donations from members of the public to sustain them, services like Amazon servers, Paypal, and Mastercard all initially pulled their products from WikiLeaks until the pressure of sustained hacking and a public backlash led them to reverse their decision. The convergence of surveillance and commercial technologies places watchdog journalists within mechanisms of networked power, while simultaneously requiring them to report on it.

In 2016, a set of tax documents taken from a firm based in Panama provided a study of a new journalistic phenomenon. A story of the size of the Panama Papers could not have been reported adequately by just one news outlet. The quantity of leaked information, the range of the global material, and the territorial threats to publication presented a new set of challenges. A network of 107 media organizations scattered across the world coordinated by the International Consortium of Investigative Journalists worked secretly on the Papers for months before publication. The creation of a "virtual newsroom" supported by Online Collaborative Software (OCS) has been closely studied as a new model for journalism, called by some "a newsroom in the cloud."[19] This networked model of journalism, which evolved in response to the needs of the story, used commercial software applications, particularly Slack, a tool from a San Francisco startup that has become the default intranet for most professional newsrooms. The software enables entirely new types of journalistic collaboration to emerge, to investigate and publish stories in different ways. Deluge leaks are a new phenomenon created by modern data collection and storage, and reporting on them properly is possible only by using modern collaborative tools. Some of these tools, such as Document Cloud, have been built by journalists themselves, but the majority are commercial products from companies that would not view themselves as journalistic. In fact, on Slack's own website, it advertises that its other clients include government agencies such as the General Services Administration. Newsrooms have largely retreated from building and maintaining their own software, outside their content management systems, simply because technology companies produce far more efficient and reliable means of transmitting and sharing material and ideas. However, reliance on these types of applications is not without risk.

The trade-off for news organizations is between independent tools that can be very difficult to build and support, and systems that are commercially and journalistically efficient but subject to the decisions of the companies that control them. Slack is encouraging the multistakeholder conversations of news organizations and journalists, and promising through its commercial contracts and terms of use to keep them secure. But if the use of its platform could be proven to encourage harmful, distasteful, or even democratically damaging activities, what then? Would a set of bad actors organizing racist material be able to operate untroubled on the service?

Many of the new organizations that have sprung up in the past decade have labeled themselves as "social first." They have gone a step beyond relying on platform technologies for certain functions and have designed their entire business models around optimizing for social media. Companies such as BuzzFeed employ dozens of journalists creating content that lives only on other companies' platforms, including Facebook, Instagram, and Snapchat. "Social first" news companies were the ultimate manifestation of optimism about the benefits of integration between journalistic creativity and platform production and distribution. But what seemed like a mutually beneficial relationship concealed fundamental differences in approach and priorities. At the end of 2017, when Facebook decided it no longer wanted to prioritize news, many of those organizations found themselves suddenly forced to lay off staff. For all their efforts, their close relationships with the platforms, and the good journalism they produced, they were powerless to stop the rug from being pulled out from under their feet. They were simply collateral damage created by Facebook's reorganizing its priorities. They were dependent on social media in a way that social media was not dependent on them. The contribution that these news organizations can make to the public debate, accountability journalism, and diversity of perspectives has been muted. If we accept that Facebook and other software companies are, in reality, publishers and gatekeepers, their inconsistent relationship with journalism and the free press raises the question of what kind of custodians they are.

Audience of One

As Facebook, Twitter, and YouTube grapple with their roles with respect to news, information, and the public sphere, there is a looming possibility that the complex responsibilities are just too hard a problem for these companies to shoulder.

As worried as we might have been about the prospect of opaque private platforms meddling in the operation of the free press, a more concerning possibility must be that they will instead marginalize the important or difficult news over the bland and entertaining. Or, if that were not dystopian enough, they could make news another product of the surveillance web.

To see how unchecked or mishandled information systems can work against free press principles, consider this instructive, and worrying, example. In the same week that Facebook changed its algorithm in the United States to lower users' exposure to news, a much larger but less discussed story broke. Xinhua, China's official news agency, announced a new initiative called the Media Brain.

The project aimed to build a newsroom around "information technology and human machine collaboration."[20] The Media Brain would be executed with the partnership of the Chinese search company Alibaba. The idea was to use a whole host of technologies currently associated with surveillance, such as facial recognition, voice synthesis, and automated scripting from structured data. It is, in effect, an automated story machine hooked into the surveillance web, spitting out stories identifying people and geographies in a matter of seconds and targeting them to specific individuals. Even outside repressive regimes, tactics that include exposing personal information about people online (doxxing), mass shaming through hashtag campaigns or Twitter bots, and professional trolling can chill participation and warp our unmoderated civic discourse.

When we think about the public sphere in relation to today's platforms of data collection and aggregation, this type of application could be as much the future as Facebook's news feed algorithm. The technologies cannot be uninvented; they can only be developed and adapted, either through internal redesign or external regulation.

However they define themselves, it is important that the new gatekeepers of public discourse understand the role they play in the creation and maintenance of a networked public sphere. This means considering the rights of the audience as a group of citizens, rather than individual consumers, and in particular their rights to receive timely, high-quality, relevant information and to be protected from the effects of misinformation. The elevating of the important over the popular and ensuring equality of access are remits social platforms struggle to balance.

The largest platforms know the most and guard their data closely. When the methods of distribution and the consumption patterns of news are secret, building common understanding and norms is hard. In the absence of shared experiences or even agreed-upon facts, the ability to self-govern begins to decay. Under the current design of social platforms, there are no incentives for the creation of an inclusive public sphere; the business model of technology is segmentation and personalization. High-quality news reporting, and the mechanisms for managing news and discussion of matters of common interest, are siloed into interest groups or "filter bubbles." Refinement of web analytics, mobile data collection, and personalization technologies reinforce this segmentation. A new set of platform technologies, including voice, augmented reality, and virtual reality, are alternate worlds built to increase our immersion in media. But they also abstract the user even further from the source of information. The "fake news" revelations of 2016 were not an anomaly but a small warning shot of what is to come—a world where every piece of digitized material can be manipulated to appear real and targeted at us through black-box systems.

It has been convenient for larger technology companies to deny publishing responsibilities for a number of legal and cultural reasons. Aside from their Communications Decency Act (CDA) Section 230 protections, technology companies are as precious about their culture as news publishers. Technologists of the type that Facebook and Google recruit like to build things that will make users happy or make them use their products more. News publishing at its most vital is a contentious and dangerous activity. However, the 2016 presidential election changed many self-perceptions in Silicon Valley and began a discussion of the role and responsibilities of social media companies that reverberated far beyond the tech industry. Had Facebook known what would unfold over the political cycle of 2016 and 2017, it would have done things very differently. What is concerning now is the possibility that a powerful platform for connectivity such as Facebook retreats from all civic responsibility, and consequently makes it almost impossible for people to be reached by messages that either they or their government does not want them to hear. When Facebook changes its news feed, is it trying to create a better public sphere, or is it trying to advance its business in China and other dictatorships where platforms both cooperate with government and censor their users?

Despite the pressure on lawmakers to intervene in technology platforms after the 2016 election, the political and commercial momentum in the United States is running toward less rather than more regulation in the media environment. The 2017 rollback of net neutrality rules by the Federal Communications Commission was part of a move to implicitly increase competition for platform companies by allowing much greater consolidation between already large cable, telephone, and media companies.

Sociologist Paul Starr, in his book *The Creation of the Media*, describes how revolutions are "constitutive moments" where choices can be made about how things are built and how they work.[21] The revolution of the commercial internet and the peer-to-peer communications it enables is one such moment, but the responses so far have not been able to adequately answer concerns that new institutions have too much power. Starr suggests that these are opportunities for discussions not just about the purpose and principles of the new technologies, but about the rules and relationships around them. So far the "constitutive moment" for the internet and the public sphere has provoked very different responses that lack cohesion or agreement, largely dictated by geographical and cultural imperatives.

Territories like Europe have leaned heavily on a regulatory intervention, largely through the European Parliament and courts. A variety of interventions have sought to increase platform liability. For instance, a "right to be forgotten" ruling by the European Court of Justice in 2013 placed a requirement on Google to respond to requests for de-indexing certain search results.[22]

Countries like the United Kingdom and Germany have stepped up government intervention in speech. Rules included Germany's "NetzDG" law, which heavily fined platforms for failing to adequately respond to complaints made under existing German speech laws. The response of social platforms to the heavy-handed NetzDG provoked a strong backlash as politicians and satirical magazines found themselves kicked off social media, and the example served to highlight how hastily made reactive rules could be counterproductive in their effects.[23]

In India, a movement formed to protest the introduction of Facebook Free Basics, a low-cost mobile package that necessitated users having Facebook as part of that package. Objectors successfully lobbied the Indian government to reject a product that would have meant that the next hundred million people accessing the mobile internet in India would do so through Facebook. In Myanmar, Facebook was successful in implementing Free Basics, which helped social media and mobile penetration in the country skyrocket. Facebook does not have an office in Myanmar, however, so when stories started to circulate about the undesirability of Rohingya Muslims, including "fake news" about the threat they posed, Facebook was not on hand to respond. The Myanmar authorities are enthusiastic users of Facebook, where the official communications officers for the government often post, and as the pressure on Rohingya increased, Facebook became an unmediated weapon for repressing and harassing the minority.[24] It failed to police the platform to stop the deadly propaganda justifying the slaughtering and purging of Rohingya and complied with pressure from authorities to mark Rohingya groups as "dangerous." *Real consequences*

Facebook and other technology platforms can only achieve their enormous scale at relatively low cost by employing uniform design and policies across products in every country. Facebook's platform design is not appropriate for all global contexts, and it is positively dangerous in many. By abandoning publishing responsibility or inadequately thinking through harms that might result from its behavior in certain markets, Facebook could be seen as acting recklessly or unethically, growing its market share irrespective of consequences. Facebook is seen in many emerging democracies as a lifeline for free expression, but its influence and tools are often more easily adapted to the tactics of authoritarian dictators than to those of human rights organizations or independent journalists. In places like Myanmar or the Philippines, where social media has been co-opted expressly for the purpose of furthering authoritarianism, regimes use tech platforms to launch harassment campaigns against opposing voices, to target journalists, and to spread propaganda. If unchecked, Facebook runs the risk of accidentally replicating a kind of digital colonialism, its impact if not its actions reminiscent of American conglomerates such as the United Fruit Company, which notoriously contributed to the disruption of economic and political processes in South American countries in the twentieth century.

Conclusion

The rise of social media and the consequent extension of Silicon Valley's financial and cultural influence in the world initially inspired great optimism. The transformative technologies that allowed citizens to connect with each other, in an apparently unmediated environment, sparked great hopes for human creativity, expression, and freedom from the narrowness and perspectives of packaged media in the professional press. To many, the real-time social web represented freedom from mass commercialized media that could too often be noninclusive, trivializing, and didactic. The reality has been more complex, and more troubled. Society's views of the new technologies have been characterized by iterative rounds of euphoria and despair.

Nobody wants to return to the days of an information landscape so sparse that we have to rely on Walter Cronkite at 8 p.m. to find out what is going on in the world. However, there is a real concern that the institutions that have replaced the quasi-monopolistic channels and press structures of the past have not proved as beneficial as techno-optimism had promised.

The rapid outgrowth of social platforms has brought with it a series of problems that directly threaten aspects of democracy and public expression. Opaque distribution systems that target individuals according to personal behavior and sociodemographic categorization have undermined the notion that everyone in a society should broadly know the same information to enable them to make informed choices. Today we have personal facts, filter bubbles, and a new type of propaganda and advertising so subtle it makes the outlawed subliminal advertising of the 1970s look laughably innocuous by comparison.

The aggregation of data and attention, and therefore superior targeting methods, has also drained the financial support from whole areas of the commercial press. Local journalism in America is suffering a crisis so acute that Google announced it would cofund a Report for America initiative, philanthropically dropping journalists into local newsrooms around the country to cover local politics and teach newsrooms how to use Google's tools.[25]

In one sense there is no real threat to free expression; expression is everywhere. But that is not the whole story. Anyone can reach a million people, so long as their content is engaging or outrageous enough, and if the algorithms and platforms allow them to. As sociologist Zeynep Tufekci put it:

> Yes, mass discourse has become far easier for everyone to participate
> in—but it has simultaneously become a set of private conversations

happening behind your back. Behind everyone's backs. Not to put too fine a point on it, but all of this invalidates much of what we think about free speech—conceptually, legally, and ethically.[26]

With regard to press freedom and journalism, Paul Starr's "constitutive moment" is here, but the solutions to what institutions and interventions modern journalism needs to keep it sustainable and relevant are unclear. To restock newsrooms to a level where local and regional government can be adequately covered needs a significant transfer of wealth—from readers, owners, or advertisers—or a rethinking of public media institutions. In the United States there is little expectation that this will come from government subsidy. It now seems a remote possibility that it will come from commercial technology platforms either.

Any systemic change that allows more government control over the press is a wholly bad idea. However, a movement that might inspire a new type of public media is not. Media scholar Ethan Zuckerman has written about the necessity for new institutions of democratic power, such as the technology platforms, needing "counterdemocratic institutions" to check on their power (not to be confused with antidemocratic institutions).[27] The press has always been a powerful, counterdemocratic institution. But it needs to change in response to the disproportionately larger information ecosystem of which journalism is a small, dependent element.

A substantial amount of recent legal scholarship on the issue of platform power in the United States has centered on how to reinterpret the role of platforms,[28] how to adjust the protections of CDA Section 230,[29] and how to require greater transparency through the introduction of information fiduciaries.[30]

However legal responses develop, they are likely to only be part of an effective process if we are to forge a better civic environment for news and discourse. Economic regulation or data regulation would, at this point, seem not only necessary but also urgent. The opacity of data use practiced by big tech, and particularly the use of data for personally targeted advertising, is susceptible to being curbed by regulation such as the European Union's General Data Protection Regulation.[31]

The scale of change wrought by technology platforms is not a simple corporate problem; it is a profound cultural shift. Societies take time to readjust to cultural change, and the abandonment of long-held beliefs or norms is part of that change. In America, one aspect of cultural readjustment might be the abandonment of the idea that good journalism is necessarily sustained by a free market. Flowing from that is a renewed focus on the importance of a strong system of public media. We will need collaborations and institutional alliances aimed at reconstructing a truly public sphere, through schools, universities, libraries, philanthropic foundations, public media, and similarly aligned institutions of knowledge. But we will also need the most powerful tools of social publishing and search to be part of this solution too.

To drive progress in a direction that improves the general news environment, supports journalism, and strengthens democracy is a task that will stretch beyond the current generation of technologies, their creators, and their users. But the task will only become harder if we allow the currently fluid environment to crystallize into an opaque and ungovernable landscape.

Defining the Boundaries of Free
Speech on Social Media

MONIKA BICKERT

The increase in online consumption of news media has led many to think of social media as a primary news source. And yet in at least two important ways, social media companies stand apart from traditional media outlets. First, they generally do not create or choose the content shared on their platform; instead, they provide the virtual space for others to speak. Second, because of this intermediary role, American law provides social media companies broad protection from civil and criminal liability for the content that users post on their services.

This protection is not a constitutional rule but a legislative one, set forth in Section 230(c) of the Communications Decency Act, which makes clear that social media companies, along with other online intermediaries, are not treated as the publisher or speaker of content posted by others. One goal of Section 230 is to free online intermediaries from the need to screen every single online post, a need that would render impossible the real-time interactivity that people expect when they engage on social media. Section 230 further protects social media companies from legal liability as they work to maintain notice-and-takedown systems, whereby users flag offending material and social media companies review and remove it where appropriate.

But because the largest social media companies, like Facebook, Google, and Twitter, operate across the world, they must also learn how to operate in nations where they do not enjoy similar statutory protections. Moreover, because different nations have different rules about which speech is prohibited, these companies grapple with the challenge of addressing online speech that is legal in some communities but illegal in others.

How are these companies to decide where to draw the lines, and does that role belong to them alone?

* * *

In May 2016, the European Commission convened a special meeting in Brussels, to which it invited representatives of Facebook, Twitter, Google, and Microsoft. The purpose of the meeting was to sign and announce a code of conduct[1] committing the social media companies to taking certain steps to remove from their services speech that violates European hate speech laws. At the time of the announcement, European Commissioner for Justice, Consumers and Gender Equality Vera Jourova characterized the code of conduct as "an important step forward to ensure that the internet remains a place of free and democratic expression, where European values and laws are respected."[2]

This announcement was not the first instance of government authorities pushing for social media companies to apply specific speech laws to content on the internet. Indeed, censorship demands from governments to these companies have become so routine that the largest companies publish semiannual reports documenting the receipt and response to such demands.[3]

Nor are governments the only ones demanding removal of content. Increasingly, nongovernmental organizations devoted to issues including privacy, women's safety, LGBT rights, and freedom of expression are reaching out to social media companies to request that certain speech be removed or protected. These groups sometimes disagree on where social media companies should draw the line, but they generally agree that there should be a line. And like Commissioner Jourova, they want that line to respect the values that they hold most dear.

For social media companies based in the United States, including Facebook, Twitter, Microsoft, and Google, there are limits to how far they can be required to go in enforcing speech boundaries. Federal legislation, including Section 230(c) of the Communications Decency Act,[4] protects them from being held liable as a publisher or speaker of most content on their services.[5] Consequently, they do not need to proactively monitor their sites for content, such as child pornography, that falls outside the protections of the First Amendment. Instead, they can wait until specific content is brought to their attention before assessing any legal obligation to remove it.

Once content has been brought to the company's attention, there are some situations in which they are legally obligated to remove it. Section 230 excludes child pornography and obscene speech from its protection, and makes clear that it is not intended to have any effect on federal criminal law, federal and state communication privacy and intellectual property laws, and qualifying state laws. Section 230 also does not protect companies from liability for speech for which they have accepted money or speech that the companies have themselves created. Notwithstanding these limitations, Section 230 is fundamental to the current model of social media companies. Because of its protections, companies do not have to proactively assess the legality of content, and that means they can allow for conversations to happen as quickly online as they do offline.

Nevertheless, social media companies face many challenges in constructing speech boundaries that satisfy legal and social expectations. Many governments around the world expect social media providers to remove from their sites locally illegal speech. And even where there is no legal restriction on a piece of content, users may nevertheless find the content objectionable, and their disapproval can spur consequences just as grave as those from a court. As companies try to draw lines on which content to allow on their sites, which values should form the basis for these decisions? When values conflict, which should prevail? Is it desirable, or even possible, to create a system of standards that vary by country? And how can companies ensure that the content standards they construct can be consistently and efficiently applied in online communities so large that they generate millions of posts, photos, and minutes of video per day?

Thesis

In this chapter, I explore the role of social media companies in setting boundaries for acceptable online speech, as well as the companies' efforts to define and rank the values that should determine those boundaries. I also explore the challenges the companies face in implementing their content standards across communities that are often large and diverse, and whether those challenges justify the protection that federal legislation like Section 230 currently provides.

Should Social Media Companies Have Any Role in Setting Boundaries for Speech on Their Platforms?

Critics sometimes maintain that private companies should not be determining the boundaries for speech, arguing instead for government regulation,[6] external advisory boards,[7] or simply an elimination of company-imposed boundaries.[8]

The dissatisfaction with companies setting their own content standards is not surprising, considering the contrasting regulatory approaches and online social norms from around the world. Different cultures have very different levels of tolerance for speech. But even if sites like Facebook, Google, and Twitter operated only within the United States, there would still be some question as to whether they should be able to set their own content standards. Legislators in the United States have argued that social media companies have shown irresponsibility in setting their own standards, and therefore do not deserve the broad protections of Section 230.[9] Alternatively, one could argue that companies who want to avail themselves of Section 230 should have to pay the price of permitting all speech protected by the First Amendment.[10]

Despite those critics, technology companies necessarily play a critical role in content governance. The practicality of implementing standards in communities this large simply requires a heavy hand from the companies. Even if online speech standards were set by an outside authority, the level of attention required to implement any standard at such a large scale means that companies must play a primary role in the ultimate decision to remove or leave on site any given piece of content.

Facebook, for instance, receives more than a million daily reports of potential violations of its content standards. In evaluating these reports, Facebook relies on thousands of content reviewers and a robust automated infrastructure to assist in the review.[11] The company's policy team, which sets the content standards, updates the standards frequently in response to feedback from the team of content reviewers or automated review systems, either of which might flag new abuse trends or areas of policy ambiguity. A global team of engineers works full time on the infrastructure for receiving and reviewing user complaints, and additional engineers work on systems for more quickly detecting abuse on the site before it is ever reported.

Each component—the content reviewers, the automated systems, the policy writers, the engineers—depends on the other components for input and refinement. The content reviewers, for instance, might in the course of their daily work see that teenagers in France are using a new term to encourage self-harm. Because Facebook's content standards prohibit the encouragement of self-harm, the policy team would consider updating the self-harm implementation standards so that all reviewers are aware that the term is encouragement of self-harm. Before doing so, the policy team might run a test with other reviewers and data specialists to understand all of the ways the word is being used in French, whether the word is being used in other languages, and what benign content might also be removed if the team should begin to remove references to the new term.

Engineers might become involved in other ways, such as if the term is appearing in known viral images that automation could detect. Still other employees, such as lawyers or safety specialists, often play a role in the policy enforcement effort and might have to determine whether a certain use of the term is a threat of physical harm that should be brought to the attention of government authorities.

Considering the interdependency of all these internal teams, transferring that role of content standard management entirely to governments or external bodies is not just impractical; it is impossible to do in a way that does not require the external body to become a smaller version of the same social media company.

Social media companies must then have some role in setting and enforcing content standards in their online communities. But this does not mean they should act alone. Voices outside the company have roles to play in crafting on-line speech boundaries. In considering the appropriate scope of those roles, it is instructive to consider who in society has traditionally set speech boundaries, and how those boundaries and the resulting consequences compare to the boundaries of online speech on today's social media platforms.

Who Has Historically Determined the Boundaries of Acceptable Speech?

Roughly speaking, speech boundaries have taken several forms: government laws and regulations, formal rules of nongovernmental or private entities, and informal social norms.

Government Laws and Regulations

Throughout history, governments have set boundaries on speech in the form of laws. In Germany and France, it is a crime to deny that the Holocaust happened. In Pakistan, laws prohibit blasphemy of religious figures. Even in the United States, with its broad First Amendment protections, it is a federal crime to dis-seminate child pornographic imagery.[12] Those who run afoul of these boundaries can face severe punishments.[13]

While such laws aren't always popular, they are often the result of public input, even just the indirect influence of a democratic election. The laws are therefore likely to reflect, at least in democracies, the social values of the local population. This is true even in the United States. Although the First Amendment often limits the ability of majorities to impose their social values on the speech of others, the past few years have seen an increase in legislation criminalizing speech-based conduct such as bullying and the nonconsensual sharing of nude imagery.

Formal Rules of Private Entities

Of course, criminalization is not the only way to limit speech. Private entities of different forms, including clubs, companies, universities, and even small businesses, commonly have some discretion within the law to set speech boundaries within their space. This is particularly true in the United States, where private entities are almost completely free to set their own speech rules, but it is also true in countries with more restrictive laws governing the actions of pri-vate organizations and entities. This includes social media companies, although they are unlike most other entities in both size and diversity of membership. The smaller or more private the institution or club, the more likely the standards are to reflect the social values of its members. Although violating these boundaries will not lead to a prison sentence, the threat of exclusion for noncompliance may nevertheless be enough to change behavior. An eager food connoisseur, for instance, is likely to agree to forego swearing for a few hours in exchange for a chance to eat at his favorite Michelin-rated restaurant.[14]

Informal Social Norms

Finally, communities themselves traditionally set speech boundaries in the form of social norms. Children learn from an early age what words will land them in trouble at home. As they get older, they also may learn that telling a racist joke or making a homophobic comment may lead to social alienation.

In some settings, the consequences of social norms may be minimal—not everyone cares what his or her neighbors or coworkers think of him or her—but such norms may nevertheless create real limits on speech, particularly among young populations. Social campaigns to stop bullying often try to capitalize on this phenomenon.[15] In encouraging bystanders to become active voices against the bully, such campaigns implicitly recognize that the disapproval of peers can bring about a social consequence for the bully that may well discourage him or her from further bullying.

A recent global anti-Semitism survey conducted by the Anti-Defamation League suggests that social norms may also play a significant role in curbing unwelcome speech in adult populations.[16] The survey, which asked people in nineteen countries a series of questions to measure anti-Semitic attitudes, found a lower level of anti-Semitism in countries like the United States, the United Kingdom, and Denmark, where there are no laws against denying the Holocaust, than in Greece, Hungary, and Romania, where denying the Holocaust is a crime. Of course, there are a number of factors that influence anti-Semitic attitudes. The laws in Greece, Hungary, and Romania may well be effective in reducing anti-Semitism from what would otherwise be even higher levels. However, the lower measured rate of anti-Semitism in the countries without Holocaust-related speech restrictions suggests that social norms play a role in curbing such speech.

Who Should Determine the Boundaries for Speech on Social Media?

None of these three sources of speech restriction—governments, entities, or social norms—neatly lends itself to the creation of speech boundaries for social media platforms, or even to the determination of which social values a platform's content standards should aim to serve.

The Role of Government Laws and Regulations

Laws can play a role in determining social media content standards, but that role is limited. The borderless and dynamic nature of social media communications requires standards that are globally applied—and speech laws are ill-suited for global application.

Global Standards Are Preferable to Country-Specific Standards

Social media platforms offer a place to communicate with a larger and more diverse audience than any offline audience. On the largest platforms, the global nature of online communities is particularly visible. As of July 2017, YouTube was available in more than eighty-five countries,[17] and Facebook in more than one hundred languages. More than 79 percent of Twitter users[18] and 85 percent of Facebook users are from outside the United States, where both companies were founded. Significantly, these social media sites are not one-way content distribution mechanisms. Instead, users engage in a web of interactions: someone in Norway posts a photo of a temple she saw while on vacation in India; someone in Australia comments on the photo, asking the name of the temple; someone in India responds to the comment with the name of the temple; someone else in India writes, "There's an even more impressive temple in that city"; the Norwegian then posts another photo with the comment, "Is it this one? I didn't like it!" and a lively discussion follows. To preserve this sort of dialogue, people need to be seeing the same content, and they need to be able to engage in real time. And for that, they need one set of global content standards.

Country-specific guidelines would, at the very least, slow down policy enforcement, and would in many cases lead to users seeing only part of a conversation. The current model that companies like Facebook, YouTube, and Twitter use, where content reviewers evaluate reported content against one set of concrete, global standards, already requires the focus of thousands of people.[19] Having those reviewers evaluate the same content against a lengthy list of laws from dozens of countries would be incalculably more difficult. Laws differ from country to country, not only in their text, but also in how their enforcement is pursued by authorities and how they are applied by courts. Even within the confines of one country, and even within common law jurisdictions, courts differ in their interpretation of laws. To complicate matters, laws evolve. New laws are passed, old laws are amended, and courts invalidate some laws altogether.

Even assuming a company could employ a team of lawyers sufficient to dispense legal advice on such a massive volume of content, it would certainly slow down the speed of review to evaluate content against multiple, subjective, evolving laws. That reality would force social media companies to choose between a rock and a hard place. Leave content on the site until the legal analysis is complete, potentially risking the safety of users, or restrict the visibility of content until it can be reviewed. The latter could be accomplished by imposing a lag between the time a post is submitted to and published on a site, but such a system would significantly increase the volume of reviewed content.[20] Companies could also temporarily remove any content that has been reported and restore the content only after it has been reviewed and found acceptable, but such a system would unfairly disadvantage unpopular but acceptable speech. Either system would destroy the real-time nature of social media communications on today's platforms.

This is not to say that laws should have no place in influencing social media content standards. Indeed, social media companies must and do consider how local laws apply to their content, as discussed later in this chapter. But it would be quite different, and impractical, to rely on each nation's laws as the basis for governing social media content in individual countries.[21] Moreover, there are benefits to using global standards wherever possible, even if just for the sake of efficiency. Laws are often a valuable source of input for company-crafted global standards, but they cannot substitute for a set of standards specifically crafted for a large, global community.

Laws Are Not Suitable for Global Application

Some people have argued that one set of laws can and should form the basis for a global set of policies.[22] But even assuming one government's laws represent the social norms of its people, those laws will not represent the norms of every person on a global social media service. Danish speech laws, for example, may accurately reflect the values of most Danish people, but that does not mean they reflect the values of people in Turkey, Vietnam, or Uganda. On Facebook, Danish people are a two-million-person slice of the broader two-billion-person pie composing many different legal systems and cultural norms.[23] Even if Danes uniformly agree with laws that restrict their speech, an unlikely event in any pluralistic society,[24] those laws become somewhat arbitrary restrictions when imposed on people who have no affiliation with Denmark. And if social media companies were to simply layer the laws of different countries and globally remove speech that violates the law of any country, users from countries with legal structures more like that of the United States would find themselves unable to engage in what they would consider benign, lawful speech.

Academics and free speech advocates were quick to point out the dangers of such a model when the Canadian Supreme Court ruled in *Google Inc. v. Equustek Solutions* that the Supreme Court of British Columbia had the authority to require Google to globally remove search results for violating Canadian law. Canadian law professor Michael Geist asked, "What happens if a Chinese court orders it to remove Taiwanese sites from the index? Or if an Iranian court orders it to remove gay and lesbian sites from the index?"[25] The Electronic Frontier Foundation said in a statement, "Issuing an order that would cut off access to information for U.S. users would set a dangerous precedent for online speech," and a spokesperson for OpenMedia, a Canadian group campaigning for freedom of expression online, said, "There is great risk that governments and commercial entities will see this ruling as justifying censorship requests that could result in perfectly legal and legitimate content disappearing off the web because of a court order in the opposite corner of the globe."[26]

Laws Can Play a Role in Augmenting Global Standards

Although content standards work best when they can be applied globally, and laws are therefore not well suited to global application, laws can nevertheless play a limited role in augmenting global content standards. Major social media companies have built tools that allow them to block content in one country but leave it visible elsewhere. This means they have the technical ability to apply different content standards in different countries. And, in fact, social media companies implement this sort of "geoblocking" solution with some regularity, as shown in their transparency reports.[27] For example, when the South Korean government asked Google to remove a YouTube video of the South Korean president giving a speech, where the president's voice had been dubbed, Google restricted the YouTube video from view in South Korea only, leaving the video visible to viewers in other countries.[28] Similarly, the Indian government has on occasion asked Facebook to remove photos showing disrespect of national symbols including the Indian national flag. Consistent with Indian law, Facebook has blocked those photos in India but left them visible to the rest of the world.[29]

These types of country-specific restrictions do have costs in terms of both efficiency and the completeness of the borderless experience. In judging the role of laws in augmenting content standards, those costs need to be weighed against the value such restrictions provide to users. Country-specific restrictions based on national laws can sometimes help companies approximate user preferences at a more local level. They may also be the essential component in companies retaining operating privileges in countries with restrictive speech laws, where a blasphemous post could lead a government to fine a company, arrest its employees, or block its service altogether. The latter could significantly limit the speech and information available to individuals in the affected country. Although these benefits sometimes lead companies to geoblock content, the amount of locally illegal content that governments have asked social media companies to block has remained a very small percentage of the overall content on the site.

The Role of Informal Social Norms

In an ideal world, social media companies could neatly build into their content standards the social norms of their users. An understanding of each user's preferred speech boundaries and the strength of the user's convictions about those boundaries could help a company devise a set of standards that, if it pleases no one, at least displeases people equitably. There are, however, practical challenges to determining social norms and philosophical reasons to be cautious in proceeding down this path.

A social media company could use its site to provide users with a global survey to measure their preferences for where to draw the speech boundary. There are, however, limits to the information such a survey could accurately provide. Content standards must span a variety of topics, including hate speech, threats of violence, graphic content, bullying, harassment, terrorist recruitment, identity theft, spam, child abuse, sexual exploitation, pornography, regulated-goods sales, and defamation. For each of these topics, an assessment of a person's tolerance would require several questions. Questions around graphic content, for instance, might include the following basic questions:

1. On a scale of one to five, what is your tolerance level for images that show violence or gore?
2. What counts as gore? A stabbing where no blood is visible but the victim appears to die? An open wound with bone showing, even though the wound does not appear life-threatening? A man beating a woman with his fists? Two ten-year-old boys in a fist fight?
3. Should our standards take into account whether the image was posted for a positive social reason, such as raising awareness of a human rights violation?
4. Should our standards vary by the age of the viewer? If so, how much?
5. Should policies differentiate between videos and photos?
6. Should those depicted in the images have a right to request removal?
7. Should we measure degrees of severity? For instance, should we never allow certain types of graphic images, such as beheading videos, but allow other types of images, such as open-wound videos, when shared for medical or news purposes?
8. Should fictional images, such as movie trailers, be exempted from the policy? How should reviewers tell whether an image is real or fictional?

Of course, such questions only scratch the surface of the issues companies must decide when defining policies for graphic content. Given that social media content policies often span more than a dozen areas,[30] the number of questions in a survey could easily exceed fifty. Because survey completion rates decrease with the addition of each question to a survey,[31] however, companies would have to choose between an incomplete assessment of an individual's preferences or a low completion rate among those surveyed.

Companies would also have to contend with possible bias against groups who have historically been socially or economically disadvantaged. For instance, women in some countries are less likely than men to join social media platforms because of factors including safety concerns or lack of financial resources.[32] Survey results for such countries might perpetuate those disadvantages by disproportionately representing the views of men, who might, for example, have a higher tolerance for harassing material than the women in their community have. Arguably, such results would be fair input for a company's content boundaries, because they reflect the values of the users from a community, even if they do not reflect the values of all potential users from that community. But if social media companies want all people to feel welcome, their goal should be to measure the sentiment of all people in a community, rather than those who are already comfortable enough to join social media. Companies would also need to find a way to keep such information current. Demographics will evolve and attitudes about social media will shift, particularly in the wake of offline events like elections or terror attacks.

Of course, user sentiment surveys can add value in some cases, and social media companies have used them from time to time.[33] But surveys alone are unlikely to provide guidance to companies in a way that is granular enough to implement and that truly reflects the norms of the global population. And because companies refine their policies regularly to account for changing speech trends, such as new racial slurs or new trends in self-harm, surveys alone cannot spare companies the responsibility of making their own decisions about content boundaries.

How Should Social Media Companies Value External Sources in Creating Speech Boundaries?

Because of the limitations of law and user sentiment surveys in shaping online speech boundaries, social companies have crafted their own rules, with each company providing terms of service that define its boundaries for speech. Companies are the sole authors of these content standards, such as Facebook's Community Standards or the Twitter Rules, but that does not mean the standards were determined by the company alone. Rather, content standards often benefit significantly from external sources including laws, experts, and user sentiment measurements.

The Dual Benefit of Considering External Sources

Companies consider input from these sources not only because such input helps ensure that the standards optimally reflect the speech values of potential users around the world but also because the sources themselves—namely, governments, users, advertisers, and the media—can exert pressure on the companies' commercial success. Simply put, there are business reasons that a big social media company must pay attention to what the world thinks of its speech rules.

At the same time, there is separate risk that these external forces could push companies to adopt policies that could limit democratic discourse in a dangerous way. One such example is the recent calls on companies to remove "fake news," however vaguely defined, and become arbiters of the truth. Another example is the negative media attention companies sometimes receive when they allow criticism of public figures on their services.[34] Companies who go too far in bowing to external criticisms might well fail their communities by limiting the very discourse that they were created to foster.

As companies craft and refine these standards, then, they must determine how much weight to assign each source, and what to do when sources give conflicting guidance on what speech to allow. There is no perfect way to determine how much absolute or relative weight to give each source, and the companies learn by trying, failing (often very publicly),[35] and iterating.

A newly created social media company, for instance, may initially assign little weight to factors beyond its own speech ideology. That ideology may reflect the values of the company's founders or the values of its target audience. Either way, the content boundaries of new social media platforms tend to be permissive. Twitter, for instance, branded itself early on as a platform with permissive speech boundaries, calling itself the "free speech wing of the free speech party."[36] In defense of similarly loose boundaries, the founder of social media site Ask.fm urged people concerned about teen bullying to focus on offline efforts to reform the bullies, saying, "[bullying] is not about the site."[37]

Although laws of the company's home country provide a hard stop on some issues, such as child pornography, small companies might initially get away with content standards based primarily on their own views of acceptable speech. As companies grow, however, so does public awareness of the content on their sites and, in turn, pressure from external sources. As a result, companies will often assign more value to external inputs, not just to reflect community values but to survive financially.

As already mentioned, laws outside the company's home country are one clear example of a source that larger companies must consider. If companies want to grow, they will inevitably have to restrict speech that will expose the company to liability, fines, or blocking of the service.

For instance, in the run-up to the municipal election in Turkey in May 2014, the Turkish government blocked YouTube and Twitter for failing to remove videos the government claimed violated national security laws.[38] The blocks were costly, not only for YouTube and Twitter, but also for the Turkish people, who now had fewer available avenues to discuss the election, or anything else, online. Social media companies who seek to promote discourse around the world have to weigh this nonfinancial cost in their analysis of whether to comply with a government's request to censor content. If the company can keep its service available to the people of a country by depriving those same people of one single piece of unlawful content, the company may choose to block the single piece of content in the broader interest of speech. This is true even where the law underlying the censorship request is inconsistent with the speech values of the company's users locally or globally.

Companies can try to mitigate the effect of conflicts between laws and sentiment by putting in place procedural hurdles, including requiring governments to submit censorship requests in the form and through the appropriate authority as dictated by that country's laws. They have also built "geoblocking" tools, discussed earlier, that permit the company to block only the precise post or photo or other piece of content that is illegal, and block it in only the country where it is illegal. And by reporting in their publicly available semiannual transparency reports any government requests to remove illegal content, they may deter requests to block political speech.

In addition to considering laws as an input for their content standards, companies must also consider user and advertiser preferences. Business interests dictate that companies focus on customer satisfaction, a reality that can impact the boundaries of speech on social media platforms.

If social media companies want to stay in the good graces of governments, advertisers, and users, they must also worry about negative attention from news media and other influential public voices. One bad news story that paints a social media company as socially irresponsible can attract scrutiny from governments, who want to please their constituents, and from advertisers, who want to please their consumers.

Company Efforts to Incorporate External Sources into Content Standards

Because the largest social media platforms operate in many of the same countries, serve many of the same users and advertisers, and appear in the same news media outlets, it should come as no surprise that their content standards have converged over time as their user bases have grown. A larger user base translates into increased media, government, and advertiser scrutiny, exacerbated by a growing public awareness of and interest in social media. Over time, therefore, companies have assigned more weight to input from these sources. Even companies like Twitter, Ask.fm, and Reddit, who publicly touted their permissive speech boundaries, now publicly tout their efforts to curb bullying, harassment, and hate speech on their services.[39] As laws and speech norms continue to evolve, and as companies' users change in terms of age, geography, and gender, the policies will have to evolve as well.

Accordingly, technology companies are increasingly eager to predict regulation and discern user and advertiser preferences so they can adjust their policies to keep up with the times and thereby avoid risk to their business. Facebook, Twitter, Google, and Microsoft have hired regional public policy experts who liaise regularly with relevant government officials, with the dialogue occasionally leading to announcements like the EU Hate Speech Code of Conduct.

Companies also employ community liaisons who build relationships with knowledgeable external subject matter experts and civil society voices, and the companies use their guidance to refine content standards.

One such example is Facebook's Global Safety Network, or GSN. The GSN grew out of Facebook's Safety Advisory Board, a panel of ten external experts in online safety,[40] whom Facebook originally convened in 2011 and has since consulted on everything from potential new products to specific content policies. As Facebook became more international, the policy team sought to broaden its available sources of advice on safety issues ranging from bullying and child exploitation to adult harassment and sexual extortion. The company invited representatives from known safety organizations to regional roundtable discussions in Asia, Africa, Europe, and the Americas, and has since added 250 of those organizations to the GSN.

Facebook engages with the GSN organizations through online social media groups and provides exclusive channels through which GSN organizations can report safety risks they see on Facebook. Facebook also invites GSN organizations to summits where the GSN experts collaborate with Facebook employees. For example, in February 2017, Facebook hosted a summit where eighty organizations represented nineteen countries. The input of GSN organizations has led to refinements of Facebook's policies on rape threats, child physical abuse, and prostitution, as well as when to limit certain content so that only adults can see it.

The GSN is just one example. Facebook also talks regularly to academics who research terrorist communication trends, medical professionals who study self-harm indicators and trends, anti-hate organizations that are well placed to understand emerging racial or ethnic slurs, and international organizations like UNICEF, UNESCO, and WePROTECT. In addition to providing general guidance, these external stakeholders become well versed in Facebook content standards and sometimes provide a valuable service in alerting Facebook to violations of those standards or errors Facebook has made in enforcing them.

In recent years, social media companies have begun to engage external sources in shared venues. For instance, in April 2016, Google and Facebook hosted a two-day child safety summit in Ireland,[41] and in June 2017, Facebook, Microsoft, YouTube, and Twitter launched the Global Internet Forum to Counter Terrorism,[42] a consortium of many social media companies, civil society groups, and government officials focused on countering terrorist use of social media platforms. These joint ventures allow companies to share the expense and effort involved in convening external sources and learn from one another about the best ways to incorporate the input they receive.

How Should Social Media Companies Enforce Their Standards?

Drawing the lines for acceptable content is only the first step for social media companies in responding to government, user, and advertiser demands for speech boundaries. The second step is enforcing those lines.

Identifying Content to Review

Large social media services have an enormous volume of new content each day, including more than four hundred thousand hours of video on YouTube and more than one billion posts on Facebook.[43] Unless social media companies want to employ millions of people to proactively review all of that content (and explain to civil liberties groups why and how they are doing so consistent with privacy expectations), the companies need to find some way to sort the likely good speech from the likely bad speech before undertaking a more in-depth analysis.

Some argue that the companies can and should review all content on their service, and that technology can solve both the privacy and manpower concerns. In its current state, however, technology is simply not that advanced. Companies use automation to identify content policy violations where they can, such as using photo-matching software to determine whether a photo is a known image of child pornography. But what works for finding known child pornography will not necessarily work to identify other types of bad content. The laws of most countries consider child pornography criminal speech regardless of why the person posted it. Even where there may be small differences in the law from country to country, the general idea is the same: a prohibition on depictions of sexually explicit nude images of children. Every major social media service has adopted a similar prohibition in its content standards. Under both the law and applicable content standards, child pornography is relatively easy to define. Other speech is not so easy to categorize.

Facebook, YouTube, and Twitter each have policies prohibiting more than a dozen categories of content, including categories of hate speech, bullying, harassment, and threats, where context is critical to determining whether the speech boundary has been crossed. "I'm going to kill you" could be a threat from a violent ex-husband, but it may also be a high school student joking around with her friends after they surprised her with a singing birthday telegram. A photo of ISIS leader Abu Bakr al-Baghdadi could be part of a terrorist recruiting pitch, or it could be someone sharing a list of the worst criminals in modern society. Right now, the most reliable way to tell the difference is to have someone look at the content. And that, in turn, means that companies have much to gain from focusing human resources on reviewing only that content likely to violate the standards.

In addition to technical means for flagging certain speech for human review, companies also rely heavily on reports from users. While reporting structures for new companies can be rudimentary, such as an email address to report bad content, most large social media companies have nuanced reporting channels that ask the user to explain why the content may breach the platform's content policies.[44] Some companies also receive reports from civil society partners, such as Facebook's GSN or YouTube's "trusted flagger" community.

Companies use the information they receive from these on-site reporting options to route content for review against their standards. At Facebook, review often means review by an employee with subject matter expertise and, where text is involved, who speaks the relevant language.

Reviewing Selected Content

Once companies have identified potentially violating content for review, they need to apply their content standards consistently and quickly to meet legal requirements and the expectations of their communities. Given the sheer volume of content involved, companies are likely to make many mistakes in their review decisions, particularly where context, such as the intent of the person posting the content, is a factor in the review decision. A company that reviews a hundred thousand pieces of content per day and maintains a 99 percent accuracy rate may still have up to a thousand errors.

Companies take measures to minimize errors, and those measures often take the form of hiring specialized reviewers, auditing reviewer decisions, accepting appeals from users, and investing in technical advancements that help reviewers assess content. In each of these areas, company efforts depend on the same factors that influence the policy line, namely, serving the social values of the potential user base and business interests of the company, all informed by laws and the sentiment of users, advertisers, and the media. In the case of enforcement, companies will also want to consider laws and sentiment about privacy in addition to laws and sentiment about speech boundaries. After all, even if the vast majority of users agree that harassment should not be tolerated, they may not similarly agree that a social media company should review all users' messages in a hunt for harassing comments.

The more resources a company has to review content, the more nuanced its content standards can be. Take, for instance, the relatively simple task[45] of crafting content standards around nudity and pornography. If a company wants to allow nonsexual nudity but disallow sexual nudity, it will have to provide guidance to its content reviewers or automated systems on how to differentiate between the two. If the company wants its review to be quick, consistent across the globe, and highly accurate, its guidance will need be objective, so that reviewers from different cultural backgrounds do not reach different decisions about what is "sexual," and simple, so that reviewers do not get confused weighing factors against one another.

If a company had a small number of reviewers and no automated systems, it could nevertheless promote quick, consistent, and accurate decisions through a simple policy: remove any image that appears to depict a real person where the person's genitals are in any way visible. Of course, this policy would be far from perfect in reflecting the desired outcome of allowing nonsexual nudity but disallowing sexual nudity. Reviewers would remove nonsexual photos like that of a baby in a bathtub or a family on a nude beach, while photos showing people engaged in sex would be allowed so long as genitals are not explicitly visible, and graphic cartoons showing rape scenes would be allowed even with visible genitals.

With more resources, companies can afford to be more nuanced in the development and implementation of their policies. They can, for example, provide different standards for cartoons and photographs of real people; distinguish between babies, children, and adults; and take into consideration the apparent reason that the user shared the nude image. A drawing of a penis that demonstrates reproductive function or educates users about a disease may be allowed, while a rape cartoon would be removed; a photo of a couple engaged in sex may be removed based on the pose and lack of clothing, even if genitals are not clearly visible.

Even with more nuanced policies, however, there will still be areas where companies would not be able to accurately demarcate the line between sexual and nonsexual imagery, especially because different cultures around the world will have different ideas of what those terms mean.

Is the System Working?

Social media companies have increasingly invested in drawing speech boundaries that reflect the values and laws of their global populations and in better enforcing those boundaries. Nevertheless, policymakers and the media regularly point to areas where the companies are falling short of expectations. Sometimes the discontent is a function of the policies not matching the values of a certain segment of society, such as Twitter's hate speech policies failing to proscribe removal of speech that the European Union considers illegal.[46] Other times, the disappointment is in the companies' failure to quickly identify and remove content that violates content standards, such as YouTube's failure to remove certain terrorist propaganda[47] or Facebook's delay in removing videos of murder.[48]

Despite these shortcomings, companies are learning, as are the governments, users, advertisers, and civil society groups who so significantly shape the companies' speech boundaries. Offline and online behavior are not the same, and enforcement options are not the same. Speakers often enjoy some degree of anonymity that may reduce the effect of informal social norms in deterring bad speech, and difficulty in identifying recidivist accounts makes it hard to effectively punish offenders, who can simply sign up for new accounts and engage in the same behavior.

Governments may find it tempting to turn to legislation as a means of forcing improvement, but they should think twice before doing so. Legislation that imposes particular content standards will lead to slower and less effective enforcement as companies are forced to balkanize their standards and "geoblock" content in specific countries. Legislation that demands certain levels of accuracy in review will create a disincentive for companies to identify and review more potentially violating content. And legislation that imposes a duty to proactively monitor such massive volumes of content for legality would make it all but impossible for companies to function in those jurisdictions.

Instead, social media companies, governments, and civil society groups should commit to working together, voluntarily, to create well-informed content standards and effective enforcement mechanisms. Companies should invest in external relationships, adequate content review staffing, and technical tools to better flag and facilitate review of potentially violating content. Governments should take the time to learn the practical challenges companies face so that they can help shape speech boundaries in a way that best serves their citizens. And society at large, including civil society groups, parents, and educators, should invest in teaching people, especially those who are young or new to the social media, how to be civil and socially responsible online. For companies, good policy is not just about doing the right thing. It's good business. And where the incentives of business, governments, and the public are aligned, there is every reason to expect that the system can work.

Is the First Amendment Obsolete?

TIM WU*

The First Amendment was a dead letter for much of American history. Unfortunately, there is reason to fear it is entering a new period of political irrelevance. We live in a golden age of efforts by governments and other actors to control speech, discredit and harass the press, and manipulate public debate. Yet as these efforts mount, and as the expressive environment deteriorates, the First Amendment has been confined to a narrow and frequently irrelevant role. Hence the question: When it comes to political speech in the twenty-first century, is the First Amendment obsolete?

The most important change in the expressive environment can be boiled down to one idea: it is no longer speech itself that is scarce, but the attention of listeners. Emerging threats to public discourse take advantage of this change. As Zeynep Tufekci puts it, "censorship during the Internet era does not operate under the same logic [as] it did under the heyday of print or even broadcast television."[1] Instead of targeting speakers directly, it targets listeners or it undermines speakers indirectly. More precisely, emerging techniques of speech control depend on (1) a range of new punishments, like unleashing "troll armies" to abuse the press and other critics, and (2) "flooding" tactics (sometimes called "reverse censorship") that distort or drown out disfavored speech through the creation and dissemination of fake news, the payment of fake commentators, and the deployment of propaganda robots. As journalist Peter Pomerantsev writes, these

* This chapter is being published as part of the Knight First Amendment Institute at Columbia University's *Emerging Threats* series. These ideas were first formulated at the Knight Institute's opening event, "DISRUPTED: Speech and Democracy in the Digital Age," during a panel discussion with Zeynep Tufekci. David Pozen, the Knight Institute's inaugural visiting scholar, served as editor of this chapter. A longer version of this piece is being published in the *Michigan Law Review*. I am also grateful to Jeffrey Stein for research assistance.

techniques employ "information . . . in weaponized terms, as a tool to confuse, blackmail, demoralize, subvert and paralyze."[2]

The First Amendment first came to life in the early twentieth century, when the main threat to the nation's political speech environment was state suppression of dissidents. The jurisprudence of the First Amendment was shaped by that era. It presupposes an information-poor world, and it focuses exclusively on the protection of speakers from government, as if they were rare and delicate butterflies threatened by one terrible monster.

But today, speakers are more like moths—their supply is apparently endless. The massive decline in barriers to publishing makes information abundant, especially when speakers congregate on brightly lit matters of public controversy. The low costs of speaking have, paradoxically, made it easier to weaponize speech as a tool of speech control. The unfortunate truth is that cheap speech may be used to attack, harass, and silence as much as it is used to illuminate or debate. And the use of speech as a tool to suppress speech is, by its nature, something very challenging for the First Amendment to deal with. In the face of such challenges, First Amendment doctrine seems at best unprepared. It is a body of law that waits for a pamphleteer to be arrested before it will recognize a problem. Even worse, the doctrine may actually block efforts to deal with some of the problems described here.

It may sound odd to say that the First Amendment is growing obsolete when the Supreme Court has an active First Amendment docket and there remain plenty of First Amendment cases in litigation. So that I am not misunderstood, I hasten to add that the First Amendment's protection of the press and political speakers against government suppression is hardly useless or undesirable. With the important exception of cases related to campaign finance,[3] however, the "big" free speech decisions of the last few decades have centered not on political speech but on economic matters like the right to resell patient data[4] or the right to register offensive trademarks.[5] The safeguarding of political speech is widely understood to be the core function of the First Amendment. Many of the recent cases are not merely at the periphery of this project; they are off exploring some other continent. The apparent flurry of First Amendment activity masks the fact that the Amendment has become increasingly irrelevant in its area of historic concern: the coercive control of political speech.

What might be done in response is a question without an easy answer. One possibility is simply to concede that the First Amendment, built in another era, is not suited to today's challenges. Instead, any answer must lie in the development of better social norms, adoption of journalistic ethics by private speech platforms, or action by the political branches. Perhaps constitutional law has reached its natural limit.

On the other hand, in the 1920s Justices Oliver Wendell Holmes and Louis Brandeis and Judge Learned Hand also faced forms of speech control that did not seem to be matters of plausible constitutional concern by the standards of their time. If, following their lead, we take the bolder view that the First Amendment should be adapted to contemporary speech conditions, I suggest it may force us to confront buried doctrinal and theoretical questions, mainly related to state action, government speech, and listener interests. We might, for instance, explore "accomplice liability" under the First Amendment. That is, we might ask when the State or political leaders may be held constitutionally responsible for encouraging private parties to punish critics. I suggest here that if the president or other officials direct, encourage, fund, or covertly command attacks on their critics by private mobs or foreign powers, the First Amendment should be implicated.

Second, given that many of the new speech control techniques target listener attention, it may be worth reassessing how the First Amendment handles efforts to promote healthy speech environments and protect listener interests. Many of the problems described here might be subject to legislative or regulatory remedies that would themselves raise First Amendment questions. For example, consider a law that would bar major speech platforms and networks from accepting money from foreign governments for materials designed to influence American elections. Or consider a law that broadened criminal liability for online intimidation of members of the press. Such laws would likely be challenged under the First Amendment, which suggests that the needed evolution may lie in the jurisprudence of what the Amendment permits.

These tentative suggestions and explorations should not distract from the main point of this chapter, which is to demonstrate that a range of speech control techniques have arisen from which the First Amendment, at present, provides little or no protection. In the pages that follow, I first identify the core assumptions that proceeded from the founding era of First Amendment jurisprudence. I then argue that many of those assumptions no longer hold, and I detail a series of techniques that are used by governmental and nongovernmental actors to censor and degrade speech. I conclude with a few ideas about what might be done.

Core Assumptions of the Political First Amendment

As scholars and historians know well, but the public is sometimes surprised to learn, the First Amendment sat dormant for much of American history, despite its absolute language ("Congress shall make no law . . . ") and its placement in the Bill of Rights. It is an American "tradition" in the sense that the Super Bowl is an American tradition—one that is relatively new, even if it has come to be defining. To understand the basic paradigm by which the law provides protection, we therefore look not to the Constitution's founding era but to the First Amendment's founding era, in the early 1900s.

As the story goes, the First Amendment remained inert well into the 1920s. The trigger that gave it life was the federal government's extensive speech control program during World War I. The program was composed of two parts. First, following the passage of new Espionage and Sedition Acts,[6] men and women voicing opposition to the war, or holding other unpopular positions, were charged with crimes directly related to their speech. Eugene Debs, the former and future presidential candidate for the Socialist Party, was arrested and imprisoned for a speech that questioned the draft, in which he memorably told the crowd that they were "fit for something better than slavery and cannon fodder."[7]

Second, the federal government operated an extensive domestic propaganda campaign. The Committee on Public Information, created by Executive Order 2594, was a massive federal organization of over 150,000 employees. Its efforts were comprehensive and unrelenting. As George Creel put it: "The printed word, the spoken word, the motion picture, the telegraph, the cable, the wireless, the poster, the sign-board—all these were used in our campaign to make our own people and all other peoples understand the causes that compelled America to take arms."[8] The Committee on Public Information's "division of news" supplied the press with content "guidelines," "appropriate" materials, and pressure to run them. All told, the American propaganda effort reached a scope and level of organization that would be matched only by totalitarian states in the 1930s.[9]

The story of the judiciary's reaction to these new speech controls has by now attained the status of legend. The federal courts, including the Supreme Court, widely condoned the government's heavy-handed arrests and other censorial practices as necessary to the war effort. But as time passed, some of the most influential jurists—including Hand, followed by Brandeis and Holmes—found themselves unable to stomach what they saw, despite the fact that each was notably reluctant to use the Constitution for antimajoritarian purposes. Judge Hand was the only one of the three to act during wartime,[10] but eventually the thoughts of these great judges (mostly expressed in dissent or in concurrence) became the founding jurisprudence of the modern First Amendment.[11] To be sure, their views remained in the minority into the 1950s and '60s, but eventually the dissenting and concurring opinions would become majority holdings,[12] and by the 1970s the "core" political protections of the First Amendment had become fully active, achieving more or less the basic structure we see today.

In its time, for the conditions faced, the founding jurisprudence was as imaginative, convincing, and thoughtful as judicial writing can be. It has the unusual distinction of actually living up to the hype. Rereading the canonical opinions is an exciting and stirring experience not unlike rewatching *The Godfather* or *Gone with the Wind*. But that is also the problem. The paradigm established in the 1920s and fleshed out in the 1960s and '70s was so convincing that it is simply hard to admit that it has grown obsolete for some of the major political speech challenges of the twenty-first century.

Consider three main assumptions that the law grew up with. The first is an underlying premise of informational scarcity. For years, it was taken for granted that few people would be willing to invest in speaking publicly. Relatedly, it was assumed that with respect to any given issue—say, the war—only a limited number of important speakers could compete in the "marketplace of ideas." The second notable assumption arises from the first: listeners are assumed not to be overwhelmed with information but rather to have abundant time and interest to be influenced by publicly presented views. Finally, the government is assumed to be the main threat to the "marketplace of ideas" through its use of criminal law or other coercive instruments to target speakers (as opposed to listeners) with punishment or bans on publication. Without government intervention, this assumption goes, the marketplace of ideas operates well by itself.

Each of these assumptions has, in one way or another, become obsolete in the twenty-first century, due to the rise in importance of attention markets and changes in communications technologies. It is to those phenomena that we now turn.

Attentional Scarcity and the Economics of Filter Bubbles

As early as 1971, Herbert Simon predicted the trend that drives this chapter. As he wrote:

> In an information-rich world, the wealth of information means a dearth of something else: a scarcity of whatever it is that information consumes. What information consumes is rather obvious: it consumes the attention of its recipients. Hence a wealth of information creates a poverty of attention and a need to allocate that attention efficiently among the overabundance of information sources that might consume it.[13]

In other words, if it was once hard to speak, it is now hard to be heard. Stated differently, it is no longer speech or information that is scarce, but the attention of listeners. Unlike in the 1920s, information is abundant and speaking is easy, while listener time and attention have become highly valued commodities. It follows that one important means of controlling speech is targeting the bottleneck of listener attention, instead of speech itself.

Several major technological and economic developments over the last two decades have transformed the relative scarcity of speech and listener attention. The first is associated with the popularization of the internet: the massive decrease since the 1990s in the costs of being an online speaker, otherwise known (in Eugene Volokh's phrase) as "cheap speech," or what James Gleick calls the "information flood."[14] Using blogs, microblogs, or platforms like Twitter or Facebook, just about anyone, potentially, can disseminate speech into the digital public sphere. This has had several important implications. As Jack Balkin, Jeffrey Rosen, and I have argued, it gives the main platforms—which do not consider themselves to be part of the press—an extremely important role in the construction of public discourse.[15] Cheap speech also makes it easier for mobs to harass or abuse other speakers with whom they disagree.

The second, more long-term, development has been the rise of an "attention industry"—that is, a set of actors whose business model is the resale of human attention.[16] Traditionally, these were outfits like broadcasters or newspapers; they have been joined by the major internet platforms and publishers, all of which seek to maximize the amount of time and attention that people spend with them. The rise and centrality of advertising to their business models has the broad effect of making listener attention ever more valuable.

The third development is the rise of the "filter bubble."[17] This phrase refers to the tendency of attention merchants or brokers to maximize revenue by offering audiences a highly tailored, filtered package of information designed to match their pre-existing interests. Andrew Shapiro and Cass Sunstein were among the first legal writers to express concern about filter bubbles (which Sunstein nicknamed "the Daily Me"). Over the 2010s, filter bubbles became more important as they became linked to the attention-resale business model just described. A platform like Facebook primarily profits from the resale of its users' time and attention: hence its efforts to maximize "time on site."[18] That, in turn, leads the company to provide content that maximizes "engagement," which is information tailored to the interests of each user. While this sounds relatively innocuous (giving users what they want), it has the secondary effect of exercising strong control over what the listener is exposed to, and blocking content that is unlikely to engage.

The combined consequence of these three developments is to make listener attention scarce and highly fought for. As the commercial and political value of attention has grown, much of that time and attention has become subject to furious competition, so much so that even institutions like the family or traditional religious communities find it difficult to compete. Additionally, some form of celebrity, even "microcelebrity," has become increasingly necessary to gain any attention at all.[19] Every hour—indeed, every second—of our time has commercial actors seeking to occupy it in one way or another.

Hopefully the reader (if he or she hasn't already disappeared to check his or her Facebook page) now understands what it means to say that listener attention has become a major speech bottleneck. With so much alluring, individually tailored content being produced—and so much talent devoted to keeping people clicking away on various platforms—speakers face ever greater challenges in reaching an audience of any meaningful size or political relevance. I want to stress that these developments matter not just to the hypothetical dissident sitting in his or her basement, who fared no better in previous times, but to the press as well. Gone are the days when the CBS evening news might reach the nation automatically, or whatever made the front cover of the *New York Times* was known to all. The challenge, paradoxically, has only increased in an age when the president himself consumes so much of the media's attention.[20] The population is distracted and scattered, making it difficult even for those with substantial resources to reach an audience.

The revolutionary changes just described have hardly gone unnoticed by First Amendment or internet scholars. By the mid-1990s, Volokh, Kathleen Sullivan, and others had prophesied the coming era of cheaper speech and suggested it would transform much of what the First Amendment had taken for granted. (Sullivan memorably described the reaction to the internet's arrival as "First Amendment manna from heaven."[21]) Lawrence Lessig's brilliant "code is law" formulation suggested that much of the future of censorship and speech control would reside in the design of the network and its major applications.[22] Rosen, Jack Goldsmith, Jonathan Zittrain, Christopher Yoo, and others, including myself, wrote of the censorial potential that lay either in the network infrastructure itself (hence "net neutrality" as a counterweight) or in the main platforms (search engines, hosting sites, and later social media).[23] The use of infrastructure and platforms as a tool of censorship has been extensively documented overseas and now also in the United States, especially by Balkin.[24] Finally, the democratic implications of filter bubbles and similar technologies have become their own cottage industries.[25]

Yet despite the scholarly attention, no one quite anticipated that speech itself might become a censorial weapon, or that scarcity of attention would become such a target of flooding and similar tactics.[26] While the major changes described here have been decades in the making, we are nonetheless still in the midst of understanding their implications for classic questions of political speech control. We can now turn to the ways these changes have rendered basic assumptions about the First Amendment outmoded.

Obsolete Assumptions

Much can be understood by asking what "evil" any law is designed to combat. The founding First Amendment jurisprudence presumed that the evil of government speech control would be primarily effected by criminal punishment of publishers or speakers (or the threat thereof) and by the direct censorship of disfavored presses. These were, of course, the devices used by the Espionage and Sedition Acts in the 1790s and variations from the 1910s through the 1960s.[27] On the censor's part, the technique is intuitive: it has the effect of silencing the speaker him- or herself, while also chilling those who might fear similar treatment. Nowadays, however, it is increasingly *not* the case that the relevant means of censorship is direct punishment by the State, or that the State itself is the primary censor.

The Waning of Direct Censorship

Despite its historic effectiveness, direct and overt government punishment of speakers has fallen out of favor in the twenty-first-century media environment, even in nations without strong free speech traditions. The point comes through most clearly when observing the techniques of governments that are unconstrained by similar constitutional protections. Such observation reveals that multiple governments have increasingly turned away from high-profile suppression of speech or arrest of dissidents, in favor of techniques that target listeners or enlist government accomplices.[28]

The study of Chinese speech control provides some of the strongest evidence that a regime with full powers to directly censor nonetheless usually avoids doing so. In a fascinating ongoing study of Chinese censorship, Gary King, Jennifer Pan, and Margaret Roberts have conducted several massive investigations into the government's evolving approach to social media and other internet-based speech.[29] What they have discovered is a regime less intent on stamping out forbidden content but instead focused on distraction, cheerleading, and preventing meaningful collective action. For the most part, they conclude, the State's agents "do not censor posts criticizing the regime, its leaders, or their policies" and "do not engage on controversial issues."[30] The authors suggest that the reasons are as follows:

> Letting an argument die, or changing the subject, usually works much better than picking an argument and getting someone's back up. . . . [S]ince censorship alone seems to anger people, the [Chinese] program has the additional advantage of enabling the government to actively control opinion without having to censor as much as they might otherwise.[31]

A related reason for avoiding direct speech suppression is that under conditions of attentional scarcity, high-profile government censorship or the imprisonment of speakers runs the risk of backfiring. The government is, effectively, a kind of celebrity whose actions draw disproportionate attention. And such attention may help overcome the greatest barrier facing a disfavored speaker: that of getting heard at all. In certain instances, the attention showered on an arrested speaker may even, counterintuitively, yield financial or reputational rewards— the opposite of chill.

In internet lore, one term for this backlash potential is the "Streisand effect."[32] Named after celebrity Barbra Streisand, whose lawyer's efforts to suppress aerial photos of her beachfront resort attracted hundreds of thousands of downloads of those photos, the term stands for the proposition that "the simple act of trying to repress something . . . online is likely to make it . . . seen by many more people." To be sure, the concept's general applicability might be questioned, especially with regard to viral dissemination, which is highly unpredictable and rarer than one might imagine.[33] Even still, the possibility of creating attention for the original speaker makes direct censorship less attractive, given the proliferation of cheaper—and often more effective—alternatives.

As suggested in the introduction, those alternatives can be placed in several categories: (1) online harassment and attacks; (2) distorting and flooding, or so-called reverse censorship; and (3) control of the main speech platforms. (The third topic is included for completeness, but it has already received extensive scholarly attention.) These techniques are practiced to different degrees by different governments abroad. Yet given that they could be used by US officials as well—and that they pose a major threat to the speech environment whether or not one's own government is using them—all are worth exploring in our consideration of whether the First Amendment, in its political aspects, is obsolete.

Troll Armies

Among the newer emerging threats is the rise of abusive online mobs who seek to wear down targeted speakers and have them think twice about writing critical content, thus making political journalism less attractive. Whether directly employed by, loosely associated with, or merely aligned with the goals of the government or particular politicians, the technique relies on the low cost of speech to punish speakers.

While there have long been internet trolls, in the early 2000s the Russian government pioneered their use as a systematic speech control technique with the establishment of a "web brigade" (Веб-бригады), often called a "troll army." Its methods, discovered through leaks and the undercover work of investigative reporters,[34] range from mere encouragement of loyalists, to funding groups that pay commentators piecemeal, to employing full-time staff to engage in around-the-clock propagation of progovernment views and attacks on critics.[35]

There are three hallmarks of the Russian approach. The first is obscuring the government's influence. The hand of the Kremlin is not explicit; funding comes from "pro-Kremlin" groups or nonprofits, and those involved usually disclaim any formal association with the Russian state.[36] In addition, individuals sympathetic to the cause often join as de facto volunteers. The second is the use of vicious, swarmlike attacks over email, telephone, or social media to harass and humiliate critics of Russian policies or President Putin. While the online hate mob is certainly not a Russian invention,[37] its deployment for such political objectives seems to be a novel development. The third hallmark is its international scope. Although these techniques have mainly been used domestically in Russia, they have also been employed against political opponents elsewhere in the world, including in the Ukraine and in countries like Finland, where trolls savagely attacked journalists who favored joining the North Atlantic Treaty Organization (NATO) (or questioned Russian efforts to influence that decision).[38] Likewise, these tactics have been deployed in the United States, where paid Russian trolls targeted the 2016 presidential campaign.[39]

Journalist Peter Pomerantsev, who was among the first to document the evolving Russian approach to speech control, has presented the operative questions this way:

> What happens when a powerful actor systematically abuses freedom of information to spread disinformation? Uses freedom of speech in such a way as to subvert the very possibility of a debate? And does so not merely inside a country, as part of vicious election campaigns, but as part of a transnational military campaign? Since at least 2008, Kremlin military and intelligence thinkers have been talking about information not in the familiar terms of "persuasion," "public diplomacy" or even "propaganda," but in weaponized terms, as a tool to confuse, blackmail, demoralize, subvert and paralyze.[40]

Over the last two years, the basic elements of the Russian approach have spread to the United States. As in Russia, journalists of all stripes have been targeted by virtual mobs when they criticize the American president or his policies. While some of the attacks appear to have originated from independent actors who borrowed Russian techniques, others have come from the (paid) Russian force itself; members of the Senate Select Committee on Intelligence have said that over a thousand people on that force were assigned to influence the US election in 2016.[41] For certain journalists in particular, such harassment has become a regular occurrence, an ongoing assault. As David French of the

National Review puts it: "The formula is simple: Criticize Trump—especially his connection to the alt-right—and the backlash will come."[42]

Ironically, while sometimes the president himself attacks, insults, or abuses journalists, this behavior has not necessarily had censorial consequences in itself, as it tends to draw attention to the speech in question. In fact, the improved fortunes of media outlets like CNN might serve as a demonstration that there often is a measurable Streisand effect.[43] We are speaking here of a form of censorial punishment practiced by the government's *allies*, which is much less newsworthy but potentially just as punitive, especially over the long term.

Consider, for example, French's description of the response to his criticisms of the president:

> I saw images of my daughter's face in gas chambers, with a smiling Trump in a Nazi uniform preparing to press a button and kill her. I saw her face photo-shopped into images of slaves. She was called a "niglet" and a "dindu." The alt-right unleashed on my wife, Nancy, claiming that she had slept with black men while I was deployed to Iraq, and that I loved to watch while she had sex with "black bucks." People sent her pornographic images of black men having sex with white women, with someone photoshopped to look like me, watching.[44]

A similar story is told by Rosa Brooks, a law professor and popular commentator, who wrote a column in late January 2017 that was critical of President Trump and speculated about whether the military might decline to follow plainly irrational orders, despite the tradition of deference to the Commander in Chief. After the piece was picked up by Breitbart News, where it was described as a call for a military coup, Brooks experienced the following:

> By mid-afternoon, I was getting death threats. "I AM GOING TO CUT YOUR HEAD OFF . . . . BITCH!" screamed one email. Other correspondents threatened to hang me, shoot me, deport me, imprison me, and/or get me fired (this last one seemed a bit anti-climactic). The dean of Georgetown Law, where I teach, got nasty emails about me. The Georgetown University president's office received a voicemail from someone threatening to shoot me. New America, the think tank where I am a fellow, got a similar influx of nasty calls and messages. "You're a fucking cunt! Piece of shit whore!" read a typical missive.

The angry, censorial online mob is not merely a tool of neofascists or the political right, although the association of such mobs with the current Administration merits special attention. Without assuming any moral equivalence, it is worth noting that there seems to be a growing, parallel tendency of leftist mobs to harass and shut down disfavored speakers as well.[45]

It is of course not terribly new to suggest that private suppression of speech may matter as much as state suppression. For example, John Stuart Mill's *On Liberty* seemed to take Victorian sensibilities as a greater threat to freedom than anything the government might do.[46] But what has increased is the ability of nominally private forms of punishment—which may be directed or encouraged by government officials—to operate through the very channels meant to facilitate public speech.

Reverse Censorship, Flooding, and Propaganda Robots

Reverse censorship, which is also called "flooding," is another contemporary technique of speech control. With roots in so-called astroturfing,[47] it relies on counterprogramming with a sufficient volume of information to drown out disfavored speech, or at least distort the information environment. Politically motivated reverse censorship often involves the dissemination of fake news (or atrocity propaganda) to distract and discredit. Whatever form it takes, this technique clearly qualifies as listener-targeted speech control.

The Chinese and Russian governments have led the way in developing methods of flooding and reverse censorship.[48] China in particular stands out for its control of domestic speech. China has not, like North Korea, sought to avoid twenty-first-century communications technologies. Its embrace of the internet has been enthusiastic and thorough. Yet the Communist Party has nonetheless managed to survive—and even enhance—its control over politics, defying the predictions of many in the West who forecast that the arrival of the internet would soon lead to the government's overthrow.[49] Among the Chinese methods uncovered by researchers are the efforts of as many as two million people who are paid to post on behalf of the party. As King, Pan, and Roberts have found:

> The [Chinese] government fabricates and posts about 448 million so-cial media comments a year. In contrast to prior claims, we show that the Chinese regime's strategy is to avoid arguing with skeptics of the party and the government, and to not even discuss controversial issues. We show that the goal of this massive secretive operation is instead to distract the public and change the subject, as most of these posts involve cheerleading for China, the revolutionary history of the Communist Party, or other symbols of the regime.[50]

In an attention-scarce world, these kinds of methods are more effective than they might have been in previous decades. When listeners have highly limited bandwidth to devote to any given issue, they will rarely dig deeply, and they are less likely to hear dissenting opinions. In such an environment, flooding can be just as effective as more traditional forms of censorship.

Related to techniques of flooding is the intentional dissemination of so-called fake news and the discrediting of mainstream media sources. In modern times, this technique seems, once again, to be a key tool of political influence used by the Russian government. In addition to its attacks on regime critics, the Russian web brigade also spreads massive numbers of false stories, often alleging atrocities committed by its targets.[51] While this technique can be accomplished by humans, it is aided and amplified by the increasing use of human-impersonating robots, or "bots," which relay the messages through millions of fake accounts on social media sites like Twitter.

While the technique was pioneered overseas, it is clear that flooding has come to the United States. Here, the most important variant has been the development and mass dissemination of so-called fake news. Consider in this regard the work of Philip Howard, who runs the Computational Propaganda Project at Oxford University. As Howard points out, voters are strongly influenced by what they think their neighbors are thinking; hence, fake crowds, deployed at crucial moments, can create a false sense of solidarity and support. Howard and his collaborators studied the linking and sharing of news on Twitter in the week before the November 2016 US presidential vote. Their research produced a startling revelation: "Junk news . . . was just as, if not more, prevalent than the amount of information produced by professional news organizations."[52]

Howard's group believes that bots were used to help achieve this effect. These bots pose as humans on Facebook, Twitter, and other social media, and they transmit messages as directed. Researchers have estimated that Twitter has as many as 48 million bot users,[53] and Facebook has previously estimated that it has between 67.65 million and 137.76 million fake users.[54] Some percentage of these, according to Howard and his team, are harnessed en masse to help spread fake news before and after important events.

Robots have even been employed to attack the "open" processes of the administrative state. In the spring of 2017, the Federal Communications Commission (FCC) put its proposed revocation of net neutrality up for public comment. In previous years, such proceedings attracted vigorous argument by (human) commentators. This time, someone directed robots to impersonate—via stolen identities—over one hundred thousand people, flooding the system with fake comments, all of which were purportedly against federal net neutrality rules.[55]

What Might Be Done

What I have written suggests that the First Amendment and its jurisprudence is a bystander in an age of aggressive efforts to propagandize and control online speech. While it does wall off the most coercive technique of the government—directly punishing disfavored speakers or the press—that's just one part of the problem.

If it seems that the First Amendment's main presumptions are obsolete, what might be done? There are two basic answers to this question. The first is to admit defeat and suggest that the role of the political First Amendment will be confined to harms that fall within the original 1920s paradigm. There remains important work to be done here, as protecting the press and other speakers from explicit government censorship will continue to be essential. And perhaps this is all that might be expected from the Constitution (and the judiciary). The second—and more ambitious—answer is to imagine how First Amendment doctrine might adapt to the kinds of speech manipulation described previously. In some cases, this could mean that the First Amendment must broaden its own reach to encompass new techniques of speech control. In other cases, it could mean that the First Amendment must step slightly to the side and allow different legal tools—like the enforcement of existing or as-yet-to-be-created criminal statutes—to do the lion's share of the work needed to promote a healthy speech environment.

First Amendment Possibilities

Could First Amendment doctrine find a way to adapt to twenty-first-century speech challenges? How this might be accomplished is far from obvious, and I will freely admit that this chapter is of the variety that is intended to ask the question rather than answer it. The most basic stumbling block is well known to lawyers. The First Amendment, like other guarantees in the Bill of Rights, has been understood primarily as a negative right against coercive government action—not as a right against the conduct of *non*governmental actors, or as a right that obliges the government to ensure a pristine speech environment. Tactics such as flooding and purposeful generation of fake news are, by our current ways of thinking, either private action or, at most, the government's own protected speech.

A few possible adaptations present themselves, and they can be placed into two groups. The first concerns the "state action" doctrine. The second suggests that the project of realizing a healthier speech environment may depend more on what the First Amendment *permits* rather than on what it prevents or requires.

State Action—Accomplice Liability

The state action doctrine, once again, limits constitutional scrutiny to (as the name suggests) actions taken by the State. However, in the "troll army" model, punishment of the press and political critics is conducted by ostensibly private parties or foreign governments. Hence, at a first look, such conduct seems un-reachable by the Constitution.

Yet as many have observed, the current American president has seemingly directed online mobs to go after his critics and opponents, particularly members of the press.[56] Even members of the president's party have reportedly been nervous to speak their minds, not based on threats of ordinary political reactions but for fear of attack by online mobs.[57] And while the directed-mob technique may have been pioneered by Russia and employed by Trump, it is not hard to imagine a future in which other presidents and powerful leaders sic their loyal mobs on critics, confident that in so doing they may avoid the limits imposed by the First Amendment.

But the state action doctrine may not be as much of a hindrance as this end-run supposes. The First Amendment already has a nascent accomplice liability doctrine that makes state actors, under some circumstances, "liable for the actions of private parties."[58] In *Blum v. Yaretsky*, the Supreme Court explained that the State can be held responsible for private action "when it has exercised coercive power or has provided such significant encouragement, either overt or covert, that the choice must in law be deemed to be that of the State."[59] *Blum* itself was not a First Amendment case, and it left open the question of what might constitute "significant encouragement" in various settings.[60] However, lower courts have held, for example, that state officials who demand or encourage employees to be fired have "acted" for purposes of the First Amendment analysis.[61]

In the political "attack mob" context, an official who encourages attacks on the press or other speakers, or demands that they be fired, should be deemed to have acted for purposes of the First Amendment. If a private mob attacks critics of the State merely because they feel inspired to do so by an official's own critique, that does not present a case of state action. (If burdensome enough, however, the original attack might be a matter of First Amendment concern.) But more direct encouragement or demands may yield a First Amendment constraint. Consider, for example, the following scenarios:

- If the president or other government officials name individual speakers and suggest they should be punished, yielding a foreseeable attack
- If the president or other officials call upon companies or media organizations to fire or otherwise discipline employees for their speech
- If the government is found to be directly funding third-party efforts to attack or flood critics of the government, or organizing or coordinating with those who provide such funding
- If the president or other officials order private individuals or organizations to attack or punish critics of the government

Based on the standards enumerated in *Blum* and other cases, these scenarios should result in a finding of state action and, depending on the case, a First Amendment violation. In other words, an official who spurs private censorial mobs to attack a disfavored speaker might—in an appropriately brought lawsuit, contingent on the usual questions of standing and immunity—be subject to a court injunction or even damages, just as if he or she performed the attack herself.

This is a result that is largely consistent with accomplice or secondary liability doctrines in other areas of public and private law. In the criminal law, the Model Penal Code (and many states) hold the intentional encourager or commander of criminal acts to bear the same liability as the perpetrator, and even holds liable one who solicits a crime, even if the crime is never committed.[62] In the copyright law, which frequently faces instances of mass illegality encouraged by some third party, as the Supreme Court has put it, one is liable for "intentionally inducing or encouraging [violation of the law]."[63] The argument is not based on a theory that the mob is an "agent" of the State, but rather on a theory that the knowing encouragement or inducement creates its own liability.

Statutory or Law Enforcement Protection of Speech Environments and the Press

Many of the efforts to control speech described in this chapter may be best countered not by the judiciary using the First Amendment but rather by law enforcement using already existing or newly enacted laws. Consider several possibilities, some of which target trolling and others of which focus on flooding:

- Extensive enforcement of existing federal or state anti-cyberstalking laws to protect journalists or other speakers from individual abuse
- The introduction of antitrolling laws designed to better combat the specific problem of "troll army"–style attacks on journalists or other public figures
- New statutory or regulatory restrictions on the ability of major media and internet speech platforms to knowingly accept money from foreign governments attempting to influence American elections
- New laws or regulations requiring that major speech platforms behave as public trustees, with general duties to police fake users, remove propaganda robots, and promote a robust speech environment surrounding matters of public concern

The enactment and vigorous enforcement of these laws would yield a range of challenging constitutional questions that I cannot address in their entirety. But the important doctrinal question held in common is whether the First Amendment would give sufficient room for such measures. To handle the political speech challenges of our time, I suggest that the First Amendment must be interpreted to give wide latitude for new measures to advance listener interests, including measures that protect some speakers from others.

As a doctrinal matter, such new laws would bring renewed attention to classic doctrines that accommodate the interests of listeners—such as the doctrines of "true threats" and "captive audiences"—as well as to the latitude that courts have traditionally given efforts to protect the electoral process from manipulation. Such laws might also redirect attention to a question originally raised by the Federal Communications Commission's fairness doctrine and the *Red Lion Broadcasting Co. v. FCC* decision: how far the government may go solely to promote a better speech environment.[64]

We might begin with the prosecution of trolls, which could be addressed criminally as a form of harassment or threat. Current case law is relatively receptive to such efforts, for it allows the government to protect listeners from speech designed to intimidate them by creating a fear of violence.[65] The death threat and burning cross serve as archetypical examples. As we have seen, trolls frequently operate by describing horrific acts, and not in a manner suggesting good humor or artistic self-expression.[66] In the Supreme Court's most recent statement on the matter, it advised that "intimidation in the constitutionally proscribable sense of the word is a type of true threat, where a speaker directs a threat to a person or group of persons with the intent of placing the victim in fear of bodily harm or death."[67] The fact that threats are often not carried out is immaterial; the intent to create a fear of violence is sufficient.[68]

But what of the argument that, given that such threats are so common and so few actually are carried out, could a jury or court really find a specific intent to create a fear of violence? I would think so, in the ordinary case—for what purpose does the troll mob attack its victim if not intimidation and creating fear? If the purpose is mere public expression of views, that might be done publicly, and without the terrifying barrage of direct communication to the victim using every available medium. But it is also relevant that some courts have held that the specific intent to cause a fear of violence is not even necessary. Courts construing the federal threat statute, 18 U.S.C. 875(c), have held that objectively threatening language may suffice: "Circumstances were such that an ordinary, reasonable recipient familiar with the context of the communication would interpret it as a true threat of injury."[69] In the context of an online attack mob, this would amount to a jury question.

Given this doctrinal backdrop, there is reason to believe that the First Amendment can already accommodate increased prosecution of those who try to intimidate journalists or other critics. This belief is supported by the outcome of *United States v. Moreland*, which appears to be the first lower court decision to consider the use of the federal cyberstalking statute to protect a journalist

from an aggressive troll.[70] Jason Moreland, the defendant, directed hundreds of
aggressive emails, social media comments, and physical mailings at a journalist
living and reporting in Washington, DC. Many of his messages referenced violence and "a fight to the death." In the face of a multifaceted First Amendment
challenge, the federal district court wrote:

> His communications directly referenced violence, indicated frustration
> that CP would not respond to his hundreds of emails, reflected concern
> that CP or someone on her behalf wanted to kill Moreland, stated that it
> was time to "eliminate things" and "fight to the death," informed plain-
> tiff that he knew where her brother was, and repeatedly conveyed that
> he expected a confrontation with CP or others on her behalf. . . . [T]he
> Court concludes that the statute is not unconstitutional as applied, as
> the words are in the nature of a true threat and speech integral to crim-
> inal conduct.[71]

Cases like *Moreland* suggest that while efforts to reduce trolling might present
a serious enforcement challenge, the Constitution will not stand in the way so
long as the trolling at issue looks more like threats and not just strongly expressed
political views.

The constitutional questions raised by government efforts to fight flooding
are more difficult. Much depends on the extent to which these efforts are
seen as serving important societal interests. Consider, for instance, a ban on
political advertising—including payments to social media firms—by foreign governments or even foreigners in general. Such a ban, if challenged as
censorship, might be justified by the State's arguably compelling interest in
defending the electoral process and the "national political community," in the
same manner that the government has justified laws banning foreign campaign
contributions. As a three-judge panel of the DC District Court explained in
a recent ruling: "The United States has a compelling interest for purposes of
First Amendment analysis in limiting the participation of foreign citizens in
activities of American democratic self-government, and in thereby preventing
foreign influence over the U.S. political process."[72] It should not be any great
step to assert that the United States may also have a compelling interest in
preventing foreign interests from manipulating American elections through
propaganda campaigns conducted through social media platforms.

I have left for last the question presented by potential new laws premised
solely on an interest in improving the political speech environment. These laws
would be inspired by the indelible dictum of Alexander Meiklejohn: "What is
essential is not that everyone shall speak, but that everything worth saying shall
be said"[73]—and, to some meaningful degree, heard. Imagine, for instance, a law
that makes any social media platform with significant market power a kind of

trustee operating in the public interest, and requires that it actively take steps to promote a healthy speech environment. This could, in effect, be akin to a "fairness doctrine" for social media.

For those not familiar with it, for decades the fairness doctrine obligated broadcasters to use their power over spectrum to improve the conditions of political speech in the United States.[74] It required that broadcasters affirmatively cover matters of public concern and do so in a "fair" manner. Furthermore, it created a right for anyone to demand the opportunity to respond to opposing views using the broadcaster's facilities.[75] At the time of the doctrine's first adoption in 1949, the First Amendment remained largely inert; by the 1960s, a constitutional challenge to the regulations became inevitable. In the 1969 *Red Lion* decision, the Supreme Court upheld the doctrine and in doing so described the First Amendment's goals as follows:

> It is the right of the viewers and listeners, not the right of the broadcasters, which is paramount. It is the purpose of the First Amendment to preserve an uninhibited marketplace of ideas in which truth will ultimately prevail, rather than to countenance monopolization of that market, whether it be by the Government itself or a private licensee.[76]

While *Red Lion* has never been explicitly overruled, it has been limited by subsequent cases, and it is now usually said to be dependent on the scarcity of spectrum suitable for broadcasting.[77] The FCC withdrew the fairness doctrine in 1987, opining that it was unconstitutional,[78] and *Red Lion* has been presumed dead or overruled by a variety of government officials and scholars.[79] Nonetheless, in the law, no doctrine is ever truly dead. All things have their season, and the major changes in our media environment seem to have strengthened the constitutional case for laws explicitly intended to improve political discourse.

To make my own preferences clear, I personally would not favor the creation of a fairness doctrine for social media or other parts of the web. That kind of law, I think, would be too hard to administer, too prone to manipulation, and too apt to flatten what has made the internet interesting and innovative. But I could be overestimating those risks, and my own preferences do not bear on the question of whether Congress has the power to pass such a law. Given the problems discussed in this chapter, among others, Congress might conclude that our political discourse has been deeply damaged, threatening not just coherent governance but the survival of the republic. On that basis, I think the elected branches should be allowed, within reasonable limits, to try returning the country to the kind of media environment that prevailed in the 1950s. Stated differently, it seems implausible that the First Amendment cannot allow Congress to cultivate more bipartisanship or nonpartisanship online. The justification for such a law would turn on the trends described earlier: the increasing scarcity of human attention, the rise to dominance of a few major platforms, and the pervasive evidence of negative effects on our democratic life.

Conclusion

It is obvious that changes in communications technologies will present new challenges for the First Amendment. For nearly twenty years now, scholars have been debating how the rise of the popular internet might unsettle what the First Amendment takes for granted. Yet the future retains its capacity to surprise, for the emerging threats to our political speech environment are different from what many predicted. Few forecast that speech itself would become a weapon of censorship. In fact, some might say that celebrants of open and unfettered channels of internet expression (myself included) are being hoisted on their own petard, as those very same channels are today used as ammunition against disfavored speakers. As such, the emerging methods of speech control present a particularly difficult set of challenges for those who share the commitment to free speech articulated so powerfully in the founding—and increasingly obsolete—generation of First Amendment jurisprudence.

Epilogue

Stone: As I reflect on the evolution of First Amendment jurisprudence over the past century, I'd like to make two observations. First, the Supreme Court's protection of free speech has expanded exponentially over time. In its decisions in 1919, the Court initially held that government could punish even expressly political speech if it had even a tendency to cause harm. In practical effect, the First Amendment placed no meaningful constraint on government. Gradually, however, the Court learned from experience and began to give the First Amendment more bite. In cases like *Cantwell v. Connecticut*,[1] for example, the Court in 1940 overturned a conviction because the speech at issue did not create a clear and present danger of interfering with a substantial government interest, and in 1949, the Court held that a speaker could not constitutionally be punished for disorderly conduct because his speech had the capacity to stir people to anger.[2]

But the Court remained hesitant. In *Feiner v. New York*,[3] for example, the Court in 1951 upheld the conviction of an individual who angered his audience to the point where they might become violent, and that same year in *Dennis v. United States*,[4] the Court upheld the convictions of all of the leaders of the Communist Party under the Smith Act. Thus, although the Court had moved cautiously in a more speech-protective direction, it still refused to give truly robust protection to the freedom of speech. Moreover, at the same time that the Court began to give some meaningful protection to some forms of free speech, it declared that certain categories of expression—including defamation, threats, obscenity, and commercial advertising—were wholly outside the protection of the First Amendment.[5]

The critical shift in the Court's protection of free speech occurred with the Warren Court. In a series of decisions, exemplified by *Brandenburg v. Ohio*,[6] *New York Times v. Sullivan*,[7] and *NAACP v. Alabama*,[8] the Court now gave robust protection to free speech in situations in which the Court in prior eras would readily have found the speech unprotected. The vision of Oliver Wendell Holmes and Louis Brandeis was now, finally, coming to fruition.

For the most part, this dramatic shift in First Amendment doctrine was brought about by Justices who were generally understood to be "liberal," such as Earl Warren, Hugo Black, William Douglas, William Brennan, and Thurgood Marshall. The more conservative Justices in this era tended to be more skeptical. It was thus widely assumed that the expanded protection of speech under the First Amendment was essentially a "liberal" project and that free speech was primarily a "liberal" value. Indeed, Justices Black and Douglas went so far as to maintain that even obscenity was fully protected by the First Amendment.[9]

With the rise of the Burger, Rehnquist, and Roberts Courts, the general assumption was that the constitutional protection of free speech would hit a wall. Indeed, in the last half century, thirteen of the seventeen Justices appointed to the Court were appointed by Republican presidents, all of whom were determined, in varying degrees, to appoint "conservative" Justices. So much, one might have thought, for the First Amendment. But then a surprising thing happened, for in recent years a Court largely controlled by Republican-appointed Justices who tended generally to be "conservative" in their views of constitutional law moved the Court in a *more* speech-protective direction. Moreover, this was especially true of the *most* "conservative" of these Justices—Antonin Scalia, Clarence Thomas, John Roberts, and Samuel Alito. Although these Justices tended to take a very speech-restrictive view of sexual expression, they embraced a dramatically speech-protective approach on issues involving campaign finance, corporate speech, commercial advertising, and antiabortion speech. Moreover, in many of these cases the more "liberal" Justices took a *less* speech-protective approach and tended to be more willing than their more "conservative" counterparts to uphold restrictions of speech in these domains.[10]

Thus, the two observations I would take away from the past century of First Amendment jurisprudence are, first, that the scope of free speech protection has grown exponentially over the century, and second, that at least on some issues there has been a sharp "liberal/conservative" divide in which, perhaps surprisingly, the more "conservative" Justices have embraced a much more speech-protective approach than their more "liberal" colleagues.

Bollinger: I think there is a deep ambivalence about the status of the First Amendment, and it is reflected in our chapters here. On the one hand, as you point out, the scope of speech and press protected by the First Amendment has expanded far beyond what anyone would have guessed possible fifty or, certainly, one hundred years ago. And those protections have never been more secure. If a case such as *Schenck, Debs*, or *Dennis*[11] were to come up today, there is no doubt that it would be decided differently. There may be philosophical differences between liberal and conservative Justices and judges as to the purposes of free speech and press, but they now stand together on the outcomes of these issues.

At the same time, there is a profound and palpable unease about the First Amendment. This has many sources. First and foremost, it is related to a sharp decline in confidence we are currently witnessing, not only in America but also around the world, about the capacities of democracies to address major social and political problems. The sudden and unexpected rise of strongmen-style leaders, who exhibit alarming authoritarian tendencies, in many nations, including the United States, is evidence of this underlying anxiety (see, e.g., Ginsburg). Of course, these leaders themselves pose direct and imminent threats to free speech, which is itself a reason for concern about what the future holds.

But the deeper and more vexing issue is the paradoxical claim that a major cause of this turn of events is our particular interpretation of the First Amendment. Here too there are many variations, and we see many of them reflected in the chapters in this volume: the idea that protection of extreme views inevitably legitimates those extreme ideas, reinforces harms experienced by those targeted by such speech, and over time crowds out moderate and sensible speech and speakers (see, e.g., MacKinnon, Sachs, and Strauss on the central argument of China, Singapore, and other countries seeking to discredit the US approach to freedom of speech and press); the idea that First Amendment jurisprudence has become so encompassing of expressive activities that it has lost its core meaning for many people (see, e.g., Schauer); the idea that we have interpreted freedom of speech so rigidly that there is no longer any room for public regulation that corrects for defects in human nature or other systemic flaws (see, e.g., Abrams and Lessig); the idea that we are not accommodating reasonable societal concerns about genuine threats to the society (see, e.g., Sunstein); the idea that our free speech framework is too fixed for an era that is now dissolving right before our eyes and is being replaced by one with completely different circumstances and problems, such as the rise of the internet and the fragmentation of audiences and the corresponding rapid decline of trustworthy media (see, e.g., Bell and Wu); the idea that we have lost the sense of, and the capacity to articulate, the larger purposes of the First Amendment that animated those early, and so generative, voices, and that is absolutely necessary, given the counterintuitive nature of the principle of freedom of speech and press, to bring each new generation into the First Amendment fold (see, e.g., Blasi); and the idea that, despite our positive narrative of a century-long creation of the greatest free speech regime in history, it is a fact that there are many cases with regressive results (see, e.g., *Schenck, Frohwerk, Debs, Feiner, Beauharnais,* and *Dennis*) that have never been explicitly overruled and that, hence, reside silently in our jurisprudence awaiting the next period of national instability when they can reassert their ways of thinking.[12]

Perhaps it is always true that a strong commitment to freedom of speech and press can never rest comfortably. Nor should it resist challenge and even change, if the facts of life call for it. But the facts should be as clear and near certain as life permits.

Stone: Looking to the future, I see several major challenges to First Amendment jurisprudence. I will mention two that I see as most important. First, like Larry Lessig, I think the Court has gone off the deep end in its decisions about campaign finance, and I think those decisions pose a serious danger to the functioning of our democracy. Although the Justices are right to be concerned about the risk that legislators who enact such regulations might be more interested in benefiting their own political party or furthering their own re-election, the Justices who have voted consistently to invalidate such laws (most notably Roberts, Scalia, Kennedy, Thomas, and Alito) have seriously underestimated the risk that unregulated money in our political process can seriously corrupt and distort our electoral process and the performance of our elected representatives. Ironically, this is an instance in which a too-robust protection of free speech has undermined the very system of government that the protection of free speech was designed to protect.

Second, there was a time when the advent of social media was thought to be a boon to democracy. Suddenly, it would be possible for individuals to reach hundreds, perhaps thousands, perhaps millions of fellow citizens with their thoughts, concerns, and arguments about public policy. Social media promised that Justice Oliver Wendell Holmes' "marketplace of ideas" would finally become a reality. Alas, the current state of social media now poses a serious threat to the very functioning of our democracy.

One facet of this threat concerns the issue of "fake news." There was once a time, not all that long ago, when most Americans got their news from reasonably mainstream and generally reliable sources, such as CBS, NBC, ABC, the *New York Times*, the *Wall Street Journal*, the *Washington Post*, and the *Chicago Tribune*. Although these and similar sources of news and information were imperfect, and sometimes had their own biases, they were generally committed to providing accurate information to the American public.

Moreover, to ensure that radio and television stations served the fundamental needs of American democracy, Congress created the Federal Communications Commission (FCC) in 1934 and gave it the authority to regulate radio and television stations in "the public interest, convenience, or necessity." Under the authority of this legislation, the FCC adopted the Fairness Doctrine, which required the holders of broadcast licenses to present controversial issues of public importance in a manner that was both fair and balanced. The Supreme Court held that this regulatory scheme was consistent with the First Amendment.[13]

Unfortunately, Congress under the Reagan administration repealed the Fairness Doctrine in 1987, and with the advent of cable and then social media, our national political discourse has since deteriorated to the point where citizens increasingly obtain their news and information from wholly unreliable, dishonest, and manipulative sources. This has led not only to the polarization of American public opinion but also to the ever-growing prevalence of "fake news" designed to mislead and deceive our citizens.

This is an intolerable state of affairs in a democracy. The problem is what to do about it. One approach would be to educate American citizens to the danger and to encourage them to turn to more reliable sources for their news and information. This is certainly something that can and should be done in our educational process and in public discourse more generally. Indeed, a concerted public effort to educate our citizens about the need for skepticism in this regard is essential.

Beyond that, we look to internet sites like Facebook, Twitter, and Google to remove "fake news" from their sites. The problem here, of course, is that this would impose an extraordinary burden on those websites to screen billions of posts and tweets to identify which assertions are "false" and which are "true." As a practical matter, as Monika Bickert demonstrates, this would be an impossible burden. Moreover, by giving them the authority to determine which assertions are "true" and which are "false," such a solution would empower these entities to shape our public discourse in ways that would be extremely dangerous to our democracy. Who, after all, are *they* to exercise such power?

Another approach would be to make the intentional posting of "fake news" a criminal offense. Interestingly, under current First Amendment jurisprudence, such an approach would violate the Constitution. This is so because although intentional false statements designed to manipulate public discourse do not contribute in a positive way to the "marketplace of ideas," courts have always been extremely wary of giving government officials the power to decide which false statements to prosecute and which to ignore.

The fear, which is certainly well founded, is that government officials invested with this authority would use it to manipulate public discourse by prosecuting the speech of their critics and ignoring the speech of their supporters. Thus, the judgment has been that we are better off forbidding criminal prosecutions of intentionally false statements in public discourse and relying instead on the "marketplace of ideas" to correct the falsehoods and inform our citizens of the truth. The challenge today, though, is that however well that strategy may have worked in the past, it seems clear that the extraordinary proliferation of "fake news" on social media, combined with the polarization of our citizens, has rendered the "marketplace of ideas" ineffective as a means of addressing this problem.

These are both, I submit, profoundly important challenges for the future.

Bollinger: I share your perspective. The future vitality of the First Amendment depends on two critical characteristics: We will always need an eloquent articulation of the essential roles that the principle of freedom of speech and press plays in our efforts to reach the ideals of a democratic and civilized society and the courage to insist that we live by those ideals, especially when it becomes hard, or even seems unreasonable, to do so. And, of equal importance, we must recognize that this does not mean there is no place for the other branches of government to help in realizing this vision. As we have already noted, there are strands in the jurisprudence of the First Amendment we now inherit that can guide us in nurturing this partnership. Through the system of public funding for public broadcasting, through the vast array of engagements with public education (including such programs as the National Endowments for the Arts and Humanities), through limited regulatory interventions in broadcasting to expand the range of voices on public issues and to equalize the opportunities of political candidates to address the voters—all these and many other examples of government support of speech provide a viable foundation within both public policy and constitutional jurisprudence for developing ideas needed for grappling with similar problems in the future, especially those that so often accompany the emergence of new technologies of communication.[14]

So, we arrive at this conclusion of the first Free Speech Century with an extraordinary body of knowledge and experience to draw on, with a broad set of narratives and stories that are Shakespearean in their dramatic engagement, and with an intricate web of legal doctrine that enlists and excites our intellects while connecting our minds to the most profound human aspirations. In so many ways, it is a happy coincidence that the idea of freedom of speech and press has been formulated primarily in the context of constitutional law and the judiciary. Our thoughts about grand ideas benefit from being grounded in real-life controversies, involving actual people and institutions and posing hard choices with real consequences. Judges must struggle not only with what decisions to reach but also with writing opinions that will explain what and why the court has done what it has and why it all fits within the body of pre-existing case law. It is also notable that our most memorable and consequential decisions under the First Amendment have emerged in times of national crises, when passions are at their peak and when human behavior is on full display at its worst and at its best, in times of war and when momentous social movements are on the rise. Freedom of speech and press taps into the most essential elements of life—how we think, speak, communicate, and live within the polity. It is no wonder that we are drawn again and again into its world.

NOTES

Dialogue

1. Schenck v. United States, 249 U.S. 47 (1919); Frohwerk v. United States, 249 U.S. 204 (1919); Debs v. United States, 249 U.S. 211 (1919).
2. Abrams v. United States, 250 U.S. 616 (1919).
3. *Id.*, at 630 (Holmes, J., dissenting).
4. New York Times Co. v. Sullivan, 376 U.S. 254 (1964).
5. New York Times Co. v. United States, 403 U.S. 713 (1971).
6. Citizens United v. Fed. Election Comm'n, 558 U.S. 310 (2010).
7. Hugo Black, *The Bill of Rights*, 35 N.Y.U. L. REV. 865, 874, 879 (1960).
8. 249 U.S., at 52.
9. *See* Robert H. Bork, *Neutral Principles and Some First Amendment Problems*, 47 IND. L. REV. 1, 26–28 (1971).
10. *See* Masses Publishing Co. v. Patten, 244 F. 535 (S.D.N.Y. 1917).
11. 250 U.S., at 630 (Holmes, J., dissenting).
12. *Id.*, at 630.
13. ALEXANDER MEIKLEJOHN, FREE SPEECH AND ITS RELATION TO SELF-GOVERNMENT (New York: Harper and Brothers, 1948), 24–27.
14. *See* Vincent Blasi, *The Pathological Perspective and the First Amendment*, 85 COLUM. L. REV. 449 (1985); GEOFFREY R. STONE, PERILOUS TIMES: FREE SPEECH IN WARTIME (New York: W. W. Norton & Company, 2004), 542–550.
15. *See* LEE C. BOLLINGER, THE TOLERANT SOCIETY (New York: Oxford University Press, 1986).
16. *See* LEE C. BOLLINGER, UNINHIBITED, ROBUST, AND WIDE-OPEN: A FREE PRESS FOR A NEW CENTURY (New York: Oxford University Press, 2010), 29–43.
17. *See, e.g.,* Holder v. Humanitarian Law Project, 561 U.S. 1 (2010) (addressing the rights of US citizens to interact with foreign groups with less First Amendment protection than would be true with respect to groups within US borders).

Chapter 1

1. 198 U.S. 45, 74 (1905).
2. *See* Learned Hand, *Due Process of Law and the Eight-Hour Day*, 21 HARV. L. REV. 495 (1908).
3. *See* PHILIPPA STRUM, LOUIS D. BRANDEIS: JUSTICE FOR THE PEOPLE (Cambridge, MA: Harvard University Press, 1984), 114–131.
4. ALEXANDER MEIKLEJOHN, FREE SPEECH AND ITS RELATION TO SELF-GOVERNMENT (New York: Harper and Brothers, 1948).
5. 244 F. 535 (S.D.N.Y. 1917).

6. *See* United States v. Nearing, 252 F. 223 (S.D.N.Y. 1918); Gerald Gunther, *Learned Hand and the Origins of Modern First Amendment Doctrine: Some Fragments of History*, 27 STAN. L. REV. 719 (1975).

7. Letter from Learned Hand to Zechariah Chafee Jr., January 2, 1921, reprinted in Gunther, *supra* note 6, at 769, 770.

8. Letter from Learned Hand to Zechariah Chafee Jr., January 8, 1920, reprinted in Gunther, *supra* note 6, at 764, 765. Gunther, *supra* note 4, at 765.

9. *Id.* at 766.

10. 244 F. at 540.

11. *See* REASON AND IMAGINATION: THE SELECTED CORRESPONDENCE OF LEARNED HAND 1897–1961, ed. Constance Jordan (New York: Oxford University Press, 2013) (Letter of January 29, 1952), 311.

12. Abrams v. United States, 250 U.S. 616, 630 (1919) (Holmes, J., dissenting).

13. Oliver Wendell Holmes, *Natural Law*, 32 HARV. L. REV. 40 (1918).

14. Abrams v. United States, 250 U.S. at 630.

15. OLIVER WENDELL HOLMES JR., THE COMMON LAW (Boston: Little, Brown and Company, 1881), 1.

16. Holmes, *supra* note 12, at 40.

17. *Id.* at 43. Some students of Holmes believe that his harrowing experience as a Civil War soldier left him preoccupied with forces beyond human control. He was wounded three times, twice nearly mortally. During triage on the battlefield at Antietam, the first attending surgeon classified Holmes as among the badly wounded not worth trying to save, but a medic demurred and had him moved to a farmhouse for treatment. *See* LIVA BAKER, THE JUSTICE FROM BEACON HILL: THE LIFE AND TIMES OF OLIVER WENDELL HOLMES (New York: HarperCollins, 1991), 132–133. His less serious third wound, a heel injury suffered near Fredericksburg, probably saved his life. It required a few months' convalescence back in Boston. This prevented Captain Holmes from joining his regiment at the Battle of Gettysburg, where on the third day the Twentieth Massachusetts was stationed on Cemetery Ridge at the very apex of Pickett's Charge. That day, two-thirds of the officer corps of the Twentieth died. *See* GEORGE A. BRUCE, THE TWENTIETH REGIMENT OF MASSACHUSETTS VOLUNTEER INFANTRY 1861–1865 (New York: Houghton, Mifflin and Company, 1906), 292–298.

18. Holmes, *supra* note 12, at 42.

19. Commonwealth v. Davis, 26 L.R.A. 712 (Mass. 1895).

20. McAuliffe v. New Bedford, 155 Mass. 216 (1892).

21. Patterson v. Colorado, 205 U.S. 454 (1907).

22. Fox v. Washington, 236 U.S. 273 (1915).

23. *See* Schenck v. United States, 249 U.S. 47 (1919); Debs v. United States, 249 U.S. 211 (1919); Frohwerk v. United States, 249 U.S. 204 (1919).

24. *See* Sheldon M. Novick, *The Unrevised Holmes and Freedom of Expression*, 1991 SUP. CT. REV. 303, 343.

25. Abrams v. United States, 250 U.S. 616, 630 (1919) (Holmes, J., dissenting).

26. United States v. Schwimmer, 279 U.S. 644, 653 (1929) (Holmes, J., dissenting).

27. *See* LOUIS MENAND, THE METAPHYSICAL CLUB (New York: Farrar, Straus, Giroux, 2001).

28. Letter from Oliver Wendell Holmes, Jr. to Harold J. Laski, May 12, 1919.

29. *See* Thomas C. Grey, *Holmes, Pragmatism, and Democracy*, 71 ORE. L. REV. 521 (1992). I have developed this interpretation of Holmes' market metaphor in detail elsewhere. *See* Vincent Blasi, *Holmes and the Marketplace of Ideas*, 2004 SUP. CT. REV. 1.

30. 274 U.S. 357, 372–380 (1927) (Brandeis, J., concurring).

31. *Id.* at 375.

32. *See* PHILIPPA STRUM, *supra* note 3, at 237–238.

33. Every law clerk and extended relative of Brandeis was urged by him to read Alfred Zimmern's book, *The Greek Commonwealth*, a celebration of fifth-century Athens, the central chapter of which is about the Funeral Oration. Strum, *supra* note 27, at 242.

34. In his oral history, Learned Hand recounted how this quality of Brandeis used to unnerve him during their encounters. "I'd have this strange sense of deference to him. I'd say to myself: 'Here you are, what do you do? You sit around and talk a good deal, haven't any very definite convictions. You're not spending your life trying to leave the world better for being in

it. You drink too much. . . . I used to leave him feeling, 'You poor, self-indulgent, inadequate person!' "

35. Henry J. Friendly, *Mr. Justice Brandeis: The Quest for Reason*, 108 U. PA. L. REV. 985, 998–999 (1960).

36. *See* Strum, *supra* note 3, at 66.

37. 283 U.S. 359, 369 (1931).

38. 283 U.S. 697, 717 (1931).

39. 310 U.S. 88, 103 (1940).

40. 314 U.S. 252, 270 (1941).

41. 315 U.S. 568, 579 (1942).

42. 316 U.S. 52, 55 (1942).

43. 319 U.S. 624, 641 (1943).

44. *See, e.g.*, Glickman v. Wileman Bros. & Elliott, Inc., 521 U.S. 476, 505, n. 3 (Thomas, J., dissenting).

45. *See* Citizens United v. Fed. Election Comm'n, 558 U.S. 310, 451 (Stevens, J., dissenting).

46. *See, e.g.*, Pacific Gas & Elec. Co. v. Public Utilities Comm'n, 475 U.S. 1, 18 (1986); Riley v. Nat'l Fed'n of the Blind of N.C., 487 U.S. 781, 797 (1988); Ariz. Free Enter. Club PAC v. Bennett, 564 U.S. 721, 742 (2011).

47. 564 U.S. 721 (2011).

48. 424 U.S. 1, 54–58 (1976).

49. Fulsome recognition of discrete individual autonomy interests is not the only way that some members of the current Court accord less weight to the claims of majority rule than did Hand, Holmes, and Brandeis. A different method is to hold speech regulations that operate by taking into account the subject matter of the speech or the legal status of the speaker as equivalent, in terms of requiring extraordinary justification and precise tailoring, to regulations that are viewpoint discriminatory. This move is by no means a recent invention, but it reached its most extreme application to date in Justice Thomas' majority opinion in *Reed v. Town of Gilbert*, 135 S. Ct. 2218 (2015), disabling a municipality concerned about visual clutter from regulating event-directional signs more restrictively than political advocacy signs. The principle against viewpoint discrimination follows directly from the commitment to republican government and majority rule, as Judge Hand noted almost a century ago. It is not illogical from the standpoint of majority rule to treat subject matter and speaker sensitivity as possibly problematic in that they sometimes do indeed function as proxies for differential treatment based on viewpoint. In that regard, the restriction on majority rule embraced by the Reed majority is not free-floating. Nevertheless, the proxy phenomenon is occasional and context specific rather than chronic or predominant. As Justice Kagan explained in her concurring opinion in the case, *id.* at 2236, preventing governments from taking subject matter or speaker status into account regardless of context or other indicia of viewpoint discrimination severely limits widespread, long-standing regulatory practices.

   Citizens United v. FEC, 558 U.S. 310 (2010) treated regulation that takes into account the speaker's legal status as equivalent to viewpoint discrimination. However, in that case, the possibility that speaker-status regulation was actually functioning as a proxy for viewpoint discrimination was at least arguable. *Citizens United* evinced a troubling undervaluing of majority rule not so much by its result, but rather by its indiscriminate disfavoring of all speaker-sensitive regulations resulting in its failure to analyze in detail, despite the availability of a voluminous congressional record, whether in the context of campaign finance regulation differential treatment based on the speaker's legal status did indeed serve as a proxy for viewpoint discrimination.

50. For an elaboration of this view, *see* Sorrell v. IMS Health, Inc., 564 U.S. 552, 580 (2011) (Breyer, J., dissenting).

Chapter 2

1. 249 U.S. 47 (1919).

2. Debs v. United States, 249 U.S. 211 (1919). Debs in fact ran for president as a Socialist five times. In 1912 he received over nine hundred thousand votes, which was 6 percent of the total votes cast. He did not run in 1916, and the last of his presidential campaigns was in 1920

when, despite being in prison at the time of the election, Debs nevertheless again received in excess of nine hundred thousand votes.

3. 250 U.S. 616, 624 (1919) (Holmes, J., dissenting).

4. "The best test of truth is the power of the thought to get itself accepted in the competition of the market...," 250 U.S. at 624. The exact phrase "marketplace of ideas" did not appear in a Supreme Court opinion until Justice William Douglas employed it in his concurrence in *United States v. Rumely*, 345 U.S. 41 (1951). The phrase was widely used outside of the Supreme Court even before that in the late 1940s and early 1950s, and its first appearance in the legal literature came, ironically, in an anonymous student-written article urging measures against the "Communist menace" and stressing the importance of "keeping Communists out of vital positions in our government and economy." Note, *Control of Communist Activities*, 1 STAN. L. REV. 85 (1948).

5. 249 U.S. 204 (1919).

6. 249 U.S. at 206.

7. *See* James J. Fisher, *He Lost His Battle in WWI—Fighting for Press Freedom*, KANSAS CITY STAR (March 6, 1981), A1. *See also* THOMAS HEALY, THE GREAT DISSENT: HOW OLIVER WENDELL HOLMES CHANGED HIS MIND—AND CHANGED THE HISTORY OF FREE SPEECH IN AMERICA (New York: Metropolitan Books, Henry Holt and Company, 2013), 84–85; Mark Goodman, *The Praxis of Coercion by American Presidents in Times of Crisis*, 8 COMM. L. REV. 25 (2009).

8. Some of the articles written by Shewalter were apparently among those that were edited by Frohwerk and published in the *Missouri Staats-Zeitung*, and which provided part of the basis for the charges against Frohwerk.

9. An interesting bit of trivia is that Frohwerk served as editor of the Leavenworth prison newspaper—the *New Era*—during the period of his incarceration.

10. 198 U.S. 45 (1905).

11. 198 U.S. at 75 (Holmes, J., dissenting).

12. *See, e.g.*, Nebbia v. New York, 291 U.S. 502 (1934); West Coast Hotel Co. v. Parrish, 300 U.S. 379 (1937); Olsen v. Nebraska, 313 U.S. 236 (1941).

13. United States v. Carolene Products Co., 304 U.S. 144 (1938).

14. *See, e.g.*, Ferguson v. Skrupa, 372 U.S. 726 (1963); Williamson v. Lee Optical of Oklahoma, Inc., 348 U.S. 483 (1955).

15. The phrase "bad tendency," intended to describe a standard of review substantially less stringent than "clear and present danger," and thus permitting regulating of that which is speculative, remote, and probabilistically less likely, is attributable to Zechariah Chafee Jr., *Freedom of Speech in War Time*, 32 HARV. L. REV. 932 (1919). The highly deferential standard of review even for speech cases that is embodied in the now-discredited *Gitlow v. New York*, 268 U.S. 652 (1925), is thus frequently described as the "bad tendency" test.

16. 395 U.S. 444 (1969).

17. The Supreme Court's unsigned per curiam opinion in *Brandenburg*, which uses the word "directed," is not entirely clear about whether speech in order to be permissibly restricted must be intended to have a certain consequence, or explicit about the speaker's preferred outcome, or both.

18. For a sampling of the issues and of the various interpretations of *Brandenburg*, see Susan M. Gilles, Brandenburg v. State of Ohio: *An "Accidental," "Too Easy," and "Incomplete" Landmark Case*, 38 CAP. U. L. REV. 517 (2010); Gerald Gunther, *Learned Hand and the Origins of Modern First Amendment Doctrine: Some Fragments of History*, 27 STAN. L. REV. 719 (1975); Hans A Linde, *Clear and Present Danger Reexamined: Dissonance in the Brandenburg Concerto*, 22 STAN. L. REV. 1163 (1970); Frank Strong, *Fifty Years of "Clear and Present Danger": From Schenck to Brandenburg—and Beyond*, 1969 SUP. CT. REV. 41.

19. 376 U.S. 254 (1964).

20. *See, e.g.*, Steven Shiffrin, *Defamatory Non-Media Speech and First Amendment Methodology*, 25 UCLA L. REV. 915 (1978).

21. *See* Florida Star v. B.J.F., 491 U.S. 524 (1089); Neil M. Richards, *The Puzzle of Brandeis, Privacy, and Speech*, 63 VAND. L. REV. 1295 (2010).

22. *See* Lorillard Tobacco Co. v. Reilly, 533 U.S. 525 (2001); Cent. Hudson Gas & Elec. Co., 447 U.S. 557 (1980); Virginia State Bd. of Pharmacy v. Virginia Citizens Consumer Council, 425 U.S. 748 (1976).

23. *See*, most recently, Reed v. Town of Gilbert, Arizona, 135 S. Ct. 2218 (2015).
24. For example, and recently, Walker v. Texas Division, Sons of Confederate Veterans, Inc., 135 S. Ct. 2239 (2015).
25. *See* Gooding v. Wilson, 405 U.S. 518 (1972).
26. On the definition of the legally obscene, *see* Miller v. California, 413 U.S. 15 (1973). On the permissible forms of regulation for the sexually explicit but not legally obscene, *see* Renton v. Playtime Theatres, Inc., 475 U.S. 41 (1986).
27. New York Times Co. v. United States (Pentagon Papers Case), 403 U.S. 713 (1971).
28. Red Lion Broadcasting Co. v. FCC, 395 U.S. 367 (1969).
29. Unless, of course, some burden-raising restriction on a different constitutional right (equal protection, freedom from unreasonable searches and seizures, etc.) is implicated.
30. 241 U.S. 1 (1918).
31. 248 U.S. 37 (1918).
32. 248 U.S. 65 (1918).
33. 248 U.S. 90 (1918).
34. 249 U.S. 100 (1919).
35. 248 U.S. 139 (1918).
36. 248 U.S. 215 (1918).
37. 248 U.S. 349 (1919).
38. St. Louis Poster Advertising Co. v. City of St. Louis, 249 U.S. 269 (1919).
39. Some of the cases in the forgoing list were cases involving state and not federal regulation, and thus it might be thought that the failure even to note the First Amendment could be a product only of the fact that the Supreme Court did not explicitly recognize that the First Amendment was applicable to the states until 1925, in *Gitlow v. New York*, 268 U.S. 652 (1925). But Holmes himself had recognized the possible application of the First Amendment to the states as early as 1907, in *Patterson v. Colorado*, 205 U.S. 454 (1907), and again in 1915, in *Fox v. Washington*, 236 U.S. 273 (1915), and the issue had been recognized by Justice Field in 1892 (*O'Neil v. Vermont*, 144 U.S. 323 (1892) (Field, J., dissenting)) and by Justice Harlan in 1908 (*Turner v. New Jersey*, 211 U.S. 78 (1908) (Harlan, J., dissenting)). As a result, it is implausible to conclude that the failure even to mention the First Amendment in a number of 1918 term state cases involving language was a function of the belief that the First Amendment had nothing to do with state regulation and constrained only the federal government.
40. Although the exact coverage-protection terminology is mine, the first appearance of the idea in First Amendment context appears to have come in Laurent B. Frantz, *The First Amendment in the Balance*, 71 YALE L.J. 1424 (1962), distinguishing the "scope" of the First Amendment from its "strength," and shortly thereafter Harry Kalven contrasted the "ambit" of the First Amendment from its "level" of protection in *The Reasonable Man and the First Amendment: Hill, Butts, and Walker*, 1967 SUP. CT. REV. 267. My own earlier discussions of the issue are in FREDERICK SCHAUER, FREE SPEECH: A PHILOSOPHICAL ENQUIRY (New York: Cambridge University Press, 1982); Frederick Schauer, *The Boundaries of the First Amendment: A Preliminary Exploration of Constitutional Salience*, 117 HARV. L. REV. 1765 (2004); Frederick Schauer, *Categories and the First Amendment: A Play in Three Acts*, 34 VAND. L. REV. 265 (1981); Frederick Schauer, *Codifying the First Amendment*: New York v. Ferber, 1982 SUP. CT. REV. 285; Frederick Schauer, *Can Rights Be Abused?* 31 PHIL. Q. 225 (1981). The most recent (and best) analysis is Mark Tushnet, *The Coverage/Protection Distinction in the Law of Freedom of Speech—An Essay on Meta-Doctrine in Constitutional Law*, 25 WM. & MARY BILL OF RTS. J. 1073 (2017).
41. *See* FREDERICK SCHAUER, PLAYING BY THE RULES: A PHILOSOPHICAL EXAMINATION OF RULE-BASED DECISION-MAKING IN LAW AND IN LIFE (Oxford: Clarendon Press, 1991). As applied to the First Amendment, *see* Frederick Schauer, *The Second-Best First Amendment*, 31 WM. & MARY L. REV. 1 (1989).
42. 26 Stat. 209 (1890), 15 U.S.C. §§ 1–7.
43. *See* Am. Column & Lumber Co. v. United States, 257 U.S. 377 (1921).
44. *See*, e.g., Richard A. Samp, *Courts Are Arriving at a Consensus on Food and Drug Administration Speech Regulation*, 58 FOOD AND DRUG L. J. 313 (2003).
45. *See*, e.g., Aleta G. Estreicher, *Securities Regulation and the First Amendment*, 24 GEORGIA L. REV. 223 (1990).

46. *See* KENT GREENAWALT, SPEECH, CRIME, AND THE USES OF LANGUAGE (New York: Oxford University Press, 1989).
47. United States v. Alvarez, 567 U.S. 709 (2012).
48. Snyder v. Phelps, 562 U.S. 443 (2011).
49. United States v. Stevens, 559 U.S. 460 (2010).
50. Packingham v. North Carolina, 137 S. Ct. 368 (2017).
51. Indeed, this applies not only to the First Amendment but also to constitutional constraints generally, which are most important when they invalidate seemingly good policies in the service of deeper and longer-term principles and values. *See* Frederick Schauer, *The Annoying Constitution: Implications for the Allocation of Interpretive Authority*, 58 WM. & MARY L. REV. 1689 (2017); Frederick Schauer, *Constitutionalism and Coercion*, 54 B.C. L. REV. 1881 (2013).
52. Virginia State Board of Pharmacy v. Virginia Citizens Consumer Council, Inc., 425 U.S. 748 (1976). The current "test," far stronger than rational basis but significantly weaker than the *Brandenburg* "full protection" standard, requires that the state interest be "substantial" and the regulation of speech be such that it "directly advances" the substantial interest. Central Hudson Gas & Electric Corporation v. Public Service Commission, 447 U.S. 557 (1980); Lorillard Tobacco Co. v. Reilly, 533 U.S. 525 (2001).
53. Ohralik v. Ohio State Bar Association, 436 U.S. 447 (1978).
54. *See* Vincent Blasi, *The Pathological Perspective and the First Amendment*, 85 COLUM. L. REV. 449 (1985). For an opposing perspective, *see* John D. Inazu, *More Is More: Strengthening Free Exercise, Speech, and Association*, 99 MINN. L. REV. 485 (2014).
55. Some years ago I infelicitously speculated that First Amendment doctrine might be analogized to an oil spill, such that it thins out as it expands. Frederick Schauer, *Codifying the First Amendment, supra* note 40, at 315. *See also* Blasi, *supra* note 54. Recently, *see* Morgan N. Weiland, *Expanding the Periphery and Threatening the Core: The Ascendant Libertarian Speech Tradition*, 69 STAN. L. REV. 1389 (2017).
56. For a recent plea for such an approach, *see* Expressions Hair Design v. Schneiderman, 137 S. Ct. 1144 (2017) (Breyer, J., concurring in the judgment).
57. The Supreme Court has occasionally urged such a historical approach—*see* Brown v. Entm't Merch. Ass'n, 564 U.S. 786 (2011); United States v. Stevens, 559 U.S. 460 (2010)—but with little attention, other than occasionally using the word "coverage," to the distinction between coverage and protection, and even less to the complications surrounding the application of historical approaches to the rapidly changing world of communication. Nor has the Court considered the relationship between a historical approach and the fact that most issues of noncoverage have never reached the courts at all. *See* Frederick Schauer, *Out of Range: On Patently Uncovered Speech*, 128 HARV. L. REV. F. 346 (2015), *responding to* Genevieve Lakier, *The Invention of Low-Value Speech*, 128 HARV. L. REV. 2166 (2015).
58. And this is the regrettable but likely true conclusion in Schauer, *The Boundaries of the First Amendment, supra* note 40.
59. *See* Leslie Kendrick, *First Amendment Expansionism*, 56 WM. & MARY L. REV. 1199 (2015).
60. *See, e.g.*, Lorraine Weinreb, *Comment, in* EUROPEAN AND U.S. CONSTITUTIONALISM, ed. Georg Nolte (New York: Cambridge University Press, 2005), 70–74.

Chapter 3

1. *Report of the Committee to Oppose Judicial Recall, to Be Presented at the Meeting of the ABA, September 4–6, 1917, in* ROME G. BROWN, ADDRESSES, DISCUSSIONS, ETC. (Minneapolis: R. G. Brown, 1917) ("power").
2. Letter from Theodore Roosevelt to Herbert David Croly (Feb. 29, 1912), Theodore Roosevelt Papers, Library of Congress Manuscripts Division, http://www.theodorerooseveltcenter.org/Research/Digital-Library/Record.aspx?lOp.cit.=o224709. On judicial recall, *see* KENNETH P. MILLER, DIRECT DEMOCRACY AND THE COURTS (New York: Cambridge University Press, 2009), 191–199; WILLIAM G. ROSS, A MUTED FURY: POPULISTS, PROGRESSIVES, AND LABOR UNIONS CONFRONT THE COURTS, 1890–1937 (Princeton, NJ: Princeton University Press, 1994), ch. 5.
3. Zechariah Chafee, *Freedom of Speech in War Time*, 32 HARV. L. REV. 932–973 (1919).

4. Whitney v. California, 274 U.S. 357, 373 (1927); Editorial, *The Conduct of the Scopes Trial*, NEW REPUBLIC (Aug. 19, 1925), 332–333.
5. Walter Nelles, *Suggestions for Reorganization of the National Civil Liberties Bureau* (undated), American Civil Liberties Union Records, The Roger Baldwin Years, 1917–1950, Seeley G. Mudd Manuscript Library, Public Policy Papers, Princeton University, NJ (ACLU Papers), reel 16, vol. 120.
6. *American Conditions and Historical Review*, NEW YORK LEGISLATIVE DOCUMENTS, vol. 18 (Albany, 1921), 1979–1980 (name change); Proposed Reorganization of the Work for Civil Liberty, undated, ACLUR, reel 5, vol. 43 ("situation").
7. ACLU, THE FIGHT FOR FREE SPEECH: A BRIEF STATEMENT OF PRESENT CONDITIONS IN THE UNITED STATES AND OF THE WORK OF THE AMERICAN CIVIL LIBERTIES UNION AGAINST FORCES OF SUPPRESSION (New York: American Civil Liberties Union, 1921), 4; Walter Nelles, *Suggestions for Reorganization of the National Civil Liberties Bureau*, undated, ACLUR, reel 16, vol. 120.
8. THE INDIVIDUAL AND THE STATE: THE PROBLEM AS PRESENTED BY THE SENTENCING OF ROGER N. BALDWIN (1918), 9–10 ("impatien[ce]"); ACLU, THE FIGHT FOR FREE SPEECH: A BRIEF STATEMENT OF PRESENT CONDITIONS IN THE UNITED STATES AND OF THE WORK OF THE AMERICAN CIVIL LIBERTIES UNION AGAINST FORCES OF SUPPRESSION (New York: American Civil Liberties Union, 1921), 4 ("property interests").
9. NCLB, THE MEANING OF "INDUSTRIAL ACTION" (New York, 1918).
10. Albert DeSilver and Roger Baldwin, on behalf of the ACLU, to ACLU members, September 1921, ACLU Papers, reel 7, vol. 69 ("power"); "Proposed Reorganization of the Work for Civil Liberty," ACLU Papers, reel 5, vol. 43 ("ceaseless").
11. *Danger Ahead*, NATION (Feb. 8, 1919).
12. *See, e.g.*, Executive Committee Minutes, 21 June 1920, *in* ACLU, *Minutes* (amending the ACLU's statement of principles to "stat[e] the social value of the principle of civil liberty at all times, not only when a class is struggling for expression").
13. ACLU friends of civil liberty, 17 February 1920, ACLUS, box 1; Walter Nelles to Roger Baldwin, 23 January 1926, ACLUR, reel 22, vol. 159A ("propaganda"); Walter Nelles, *Objections to Labor Injunctions, in* CIVIL LIBERTY, ed. Edith M. Phelps (New York: H. W. Wilson Co., 1927), 156 ("Judges"); Editorial, *The Conduct of the Scopes Trial*, NEW REPUBLIC (Aug. 19, 1925), 332.
14. Letter from Felix Frankfurter to Walter Nelles (25 January 1926), ACLUR, reel 22, vol. 159A; letter from Roger Baldwin to Robert Whitaker (6 April 1934), ACLUR, reel 105, vol. 678; letter from Roger Baldwin (undated), ACLUR, reel 38, vol. 274.
15. ACLU, LIBERTY UNDER THE NEW DEAL: THE RECORD FOR 1933–34 (New York: American Civil Liberties Union, 1934), 3; letter from Alexander Meiklejohn to Roger Baldwin (20 May 1935), ACLUR, reel 116, vol. 780; John Dewey, *Liberalism and Civil Liberties*, 2 SOC. FRONTIER 137–138, 138 (February 1936).
16. ACLU executive committee minutes, 26 October 1925, ACLUR, reel 40, vol. 281 ("affirmative").
17. *In the Courts*, CIV. LIBERTIES Q., June 1931, 2 ("no hope").
18. IJA, *Curbing the Courts*, 1937, WGRP, box 19, folder 7.
19. Preliminary Report of the American Civil Liberties Union Temporary Committee concerning the Supreme Court (undated), ACLUR, reel 143, vol. 978 ("widening").
20. Letter from Victor S. Gettner to Lucille Milner (30 March 1937), ACLUR, reel 142, vol. 969 ("dangerous"); National Lawyers Guild, *Resolutions Adopted at the First Annual Convention*, Washington, DC, 20–22 February 1937, GCP, box 80, folder 121 ("unwarranted").
21. National Lawyers Guild, *A Call to American Lawyers*, ATVP, box 130, folder "National Lawyers Guild" ("concern"); William J. Donovan, *An Independent Supreme Court and the Protection of Minority Rights*, 23 ABA J. 254–260, 295–296, 254 (1937) ("independent").
22. *Criticism of the Judiciary*, 8 LAW NOTES 307 (July 1904) (describing "liberty is not license" as a "hackneyed phrase"); *Current Events*, 6 ABA J. 131–132 (1920) ("extreme"); PAUL L. MURPHY, The MEANING OF FREEDOM OF SPEECH: FIRST AMENDMENT FREEDOMS FROM WILSON TO FDR (Westport, CT: Greenwood Publishing Company, 1972), 42 (quoting Benjamin W. Oppenheim).

23. *Report of the Committee to Oppose the Judicial Recall*, ABA ANN. REP. 37 (1912); Cordenio A. Severance, *The Constitution and Individualism*, 8 ABA J. 535–542, 542 (1922) ("our constitution"); John Dewey, *Liberty and Social Control*, 2 SOC. FRONTIER 41–42 (1935) ("almost").

24. Meyer v. Nebraska, 262 U.S. 390, 401 (1923); Nicholas Murray Butler, *The Changing Foundations of Government*, 8 ABA J. 7, 10 (1922).

25. Roger Baldwin, *Civil Liberties under the New Deal*, 24 October 1934, ACLUR, reel 109, vol. 717.

26. John Dewey, *Liberty and Social Control*, 2 SOC. FRONTIER 41–42 (1935).

27. Roger Baldwin, *Civil Liberties under the New Deal*, 24 October 1934, ACLUR, reel 109, vol. 717 ("right to exploit"); John Dewey, *Liberty and Social Control*, 2 SOC. FRONTIER 41–42 (1935): ("politically dominant"); Panel Discussion, 31, *Liberty of Expression in the Press, Radio, and Motion Pictures*, Institute of Public Affairs, University of Virginia, 17 July 1936, GCP, series VIII, box 83, folder 53 ("freedom of the press"); *Urges Citizens to Guard Rights from Congress*, CHICAGO TRIBUNE (April 16, 1936) ("one of").

28. Letter from Arthur Vanderbilt to Frank Grinnell (18 March 1937), ATVP, box 113, folder "Correspondence 1937" ("best idea"); George Wharton Pepper, *Plain Speaking: The President's Case against the Supreme Court*, 23 ABA J. 247–251, 250 (1937) ("best friend").

29. NLRB v. Jones and Laughlin Steel, 301 U.S. 1, 33 (1937).

30. Frank J. Hogan, *Important Shifts in Constitutional Doctrines*, 25 ABA J. 629–638, 630 (1939) ("devastating"); Brief on Behalf of Petitioner the Associated Press at 101, Associated Press v. NLRB, 301 U.S. 103 (1937) (No. 365); Associated Press v. NLRB, 301 U.S. at 135 (Sutherland, J. dissenting).

31. *Through the Editor's Specs*, NATION'S BUSINESS, March 1937, 7 ("What passes"); Walter J. Kohler, *Address at Annual Meeting*, Chamber of Commerce of the United States, 27–29 April 1937, CCUSR, box 31; H. W. Prentis, past President, NAM, "Safeguarding American Freedom," February 1945, NAMP, box 2, folder 100 ("vital"); Public Relations Advisory Group, October 23 (no year), NAMP, box 112, folder "Committee – Public Relations Advisory Committee 1939" ("link").

32. Arthur Vanderbilt to Grenville Clark, 27 June 1938, GCP, box 235, folder 15 ("more conservative"); Grenville Clark, *Conservatism and Civil Liberty*, 24 ABA J. 640–644 (1938); Arthur Vanderbilt to Grenville Clark, 27 June 1938, GCP, box 235, folder 15; Frank J. Hogan, *Justice, Sure and Speedy, for All*, Address to the Annual Meeting of the ABA, 29 July 1938, GCP, box 83, folder 45 ("well worn").

33. Zechariah Chafee to Grenville Clark, 28 September 1938, GCP, box 78, folder 11 ("depriv[ing]"); Frank Hogan to the board of governors, 8 June 1939, ATVP, box 123, folder "Correspondence September 1938–June 1939" ("remarkably"). On Lusky's service to the ABA committee and its relationship to his earlier role in drafting Carolene Products footnote four, *see* LAURA WEINRIB, The TAMING OF FREE SPEECH (Cambridge, MA: Harvard University Press, 2016), ch. 7.

34. R. S. C. to George Alger, 11 March 1938, ACLUR, reel 156, vol. 1080 ("outwardly").

35. ACLU, *Presenting the American Civil Liberties Union, Inc., November 1941* 3 (1941) ("battleground").

36. Charles O. Gregory, *Peaceful Picketing and Freedom of Speech*, 26 ABA J. 709–715, 714–715 (1940).

37. Teamsters Union v. Vogt, 354 U.S. 284 (1957).

38. ACLU, IN DEFENSE OF OUR LIBERTIES: A REPORT OF THE AMERICAN CIVIL LIBERTIES UNION IN THE THIRD YEAR OF THE WAR (New York: American Civil Liberties Union, 1944), 23.

39. Whitney v. California, 274 U.S. at 373 (Brandeis, J., concurring).

40. Edwin Borchard to Osmond Fraenkel, 4 February 1937, ACLU Papers, reel 143, vol. 978.

41. IJA, *Civil Liberties and the NLRB*, reprinted from speech by Nathan Greene, 8 March 1940, MSC, folder 54:17, 5 (emphasis in original).

42. Radio Address by Hon. Robert M. La Follette Jr., 13 February 1937, ACLUR, reel 143, vol. 978.

Chapter 4

1. Kentucky and Virginia's responses to the Alien and Sedition Acts are prominent examples, as is the storied role juries played early in our history.

2. Heather Gerken, *Federalism as the New Nationalism: An Overview*, 123 YALE L.J. 1889 (2014).

3. *See, e.g.*, FRANK R. BAUMGARTNER AND BRYAN D. JONES, AGENDAS AND INSTABILITY IN AMERICAN POLITICS, 2nd ed. (Chicago: University of Chicago Press, 2009); ROGER

W. COBB AND CHARLES D. ELDER, PARTICIPATION IN AMERICAN POLITICS: THE DYNAMICS OF AGENDA-BUILDING, 2nd ed. (Baltimore: John Hopkins University Press, 1983); JOHN W. KINGDON, AGENDAS, ALTERNATIVES, AND PUBLIC POLICIES, 2nd ed. (Boston: Longman, 2010); WILLIAM H. RIKER, LIBERALISM AGAINST POPULISM: A CONFRONTATION BETWEEN THE THEORY OF DEMOCRACY AND THE THEORY OF SOCIAL CHOICE, repr. ed. (Prospect Heights, IL: Waveland Press, 1988).

4. See, e.g., Garcetti v. Ceballos, 547 U.S. 410 (2006).

5. For a more in-depth exploration of these ideas, see Gerken, Dissenting by Deciding, 57 STAN. L. REV. 1745 (2005).

6. See, e.g., PAUL HORWITZ, FIRST AMENDMENT INSTITUTIONS (Cambridge, MA: Harvard University Press, 2013); Frederick Schauer, Towards an Institutional First Amendment, 89 MINN L. REV. 1256 (2005).

7. See, e.g., Thomas P. Crocker, Displacing Dissent: The Role of "Place" in First Amendment Jurisprudence, 75 FORDHAM L. REV. 2587 (2007).

8. See, e.g., Owen M. Fiss, Why the State?, 100 HARV. L. REV. 781 (1987); Larry W. Yackle, Confessions of a Horizontalist: A Dialogue on the First Amendment, 27 U. KAN. L. REV. 541 (1979).

9. One might be especially worried given that search engines function to push people to already popular sites. As one academic observed, "obscurity hurts." Frank Pasquale, Internet Nondiscrimination Principles: Commercial Ethics for Carriers and Search Engines, 2008 U. CHI. LEGAL F. 263, 264–265.

10. Luisita Lopez Torregrosa, After Filibuster, a Star Rises in Texas, N.Y. TIMES (July 23, 2013), http://www.nytimes.com/2013/07/24/us/24iht-letter24.html.

11. For a full description, see Heather Gerken, Foreword: Federalism All the Way Down, 124 HARV. L. REV. 4 (2010). For ease of exposition, then, I will use several terms interchangeably in describing these institutional arrangements: federalism-all-the-way-down, federalism and localism, decentralization, and "Our Federalism."

12. Gerken, Dissenting by Deciding, supra, note 5.

13. Here I mean to describe when the ground shifted in favor of same-sex marriage. Hawaii, of course, really jumpstarted the debate when its Supreme Court threatened to make same-sex marriage a reality there. See Baehr v. Lewin, 852 P.2d 44 (1993). That decision, of course, ignited the debate that led Congress to pass DOMA in the first place. For an overview, see MICHAEL J. KLARMAN, FROM THE CLOSET TO THE ALTAR: COURTS, BACKLASH, AND THE STRUGGLE FOR SAME-SEX MARRIAGE (New York: Oxford University Press, 2013), 57–60.

14. Cf. Ernest A. Young and Erin C. Blondel, Federalism, Liberty, and Equality in United States v. Windsor, 2012–2013 CATO SUP. CT. REV. 117, 119 (2012) ("Federalism has structured our national conversation about same-sex marriage.").

15. Note, for instance, that the Compassionate Conservative in Chief—George W. Bush—endorsed civil unions in the year after same-sex marriages took place in San Francisco and Massachusetts. Elizabeth Bumiller, Bush Says His Party Is Wrong to Oppose Gay Civil Unions, N.Y. TIMES (Oct. 25, 2004), at A21.

16. Agenda setting may be the most powerful tool minorities wield in a majoritarian system. See Adrian Vermeule, Submajority Rules: Forcing Accountability upon Majorities, 13 J. POL. PHIL. 74, 80–83 (2005).

17. https://fivethirtyeight.blogs.nytimes.com/2013/03/01/poll-finds-record-support-for-same-sex-marriage-in-california/?_r=0.

18. For a fuller account, see Gerken, Dissenting by Deciding, supra, note 5, at 1763–1765.

19. Id. at 1764–1765.

20. Edward Epstein, Governor Fears Unrest Unless Same-Sex Marriages Are Halted, S. F. CHRON. (Feb. 23, 2004), http://www.sfgate.com/politics/article/Governor-fears-unrest-unless-same-sex-marriages-2819189.php, archived at http://perma.cc/JN5R-4BM8.

21. Maura Dolan and Lee Romney, S.F. Wedding Planners Are Pursuing a Legal Strategy, L.A. TIMES (Feb. 22, 2004), at A1, http://articles.latimes.com/2004/feb/22/local/me-marry22/3, archived at http://perma.cc/Y5ZM-PYT2.

22. Some of the best work on this subject has been done by Cristina Rodríguez. See Cristina M. Rodríguez, The Significance of the Local in Immigration Regulation, 106 MICH. L. REV. 567 (2008); Cristina M. Rodríguez, Negotiating Conflict through

Federalism: Institutional and Popular Perspectives, 123 YALE L.J. 2094 (2013); Cristina Rodríguez, *Federalism and National Consensus* (working paper) (on file with the Boston University Law Review).

23. This idea may even undergird *Romer v. Evans*, 517 U.S. 620 (1996), the first gay-rights victory at the Supreme Court. *See*, e.g., Nicholas S. Zeppos, *The Dynamics of Democracy: Travel, Premature Predation, and the Components of Political Identity*, 50 VAND. L. REV. 445, 452–455 (1997).

24. For a description of these networks, *see* Jessica Bulman-Pozen, *Partisan Federalism*, 127 HARV. L. REV. 1077, 1124–1130 (2013); Judith Resnik, *Law's Migration: American Exceptionalism, Silent Dialogues, and Federalism's Multiple Ports of Entry*, 115 YALE L.J. 1564 (2006); Heather K. Gerken and Charles Tyler, *The Myth of the Laboratories of Democracy* (2013) (unpublished manuscript) (on file with author).

25. For an exploration of these ideas, *see* Jessica Bulman-Pozen and Heather K. Gerken, *Uncooperative Federalism*, 118 YALE L.J. 1256, 1285–1287 (2009); *and* Heather K. Gerken, *The Federalis(m) Society*, 36 HARV. J.L. & PUB. POL'Y 941, 944–947 (2013).

26. Bulman-Pozen and Gerken, *supra*, note 25.

27. Nestor M. Davidson, *Cooperative Localism: Federal-Local Collaboration in an Era of State Sovereignty*, 93 VA. L. REV. 959 (2007).

28. *See*, e.g., Jerry L. Mashaw, *Accountability and Institutional Design: Some Thoughts on the Grammar of Governance, in* PUBLIC ACCOUNTABILITY: DESIGNS, DILEMMAS AND EXPERIENCES, ed. Michael W. Dowdle (New York: Cambridge University Press, 2006), 115, 142–144; John T. Scholz et al., *Street-Level Political Controls over Federal Bureaucracy*, 85 AM. POL. SCI. REV. 829 (1991). *See generally* MICHAEL LIPSKY, STREET-LEVEL BUREAUCRACY: DILEMMAS OF THE INDIVIDUAL IN PUBLIC SERVICE (New York: Russell Sage Foundation, 1980).

29. Some have argued that the shift in federal policy has, in turn, fueled still more change at the state level. Doug NeJaime, for instance, notes that states banning same-sex marriage keep "those couples from significant federal rights and benefits." H. Douglas NeJaime, *Windor's Right to Marry*, 123 YALE L.J. ONLINE 219, 243 (2013), a fact that some believe has influenced the outcome of at least one of the lawsuits being brought. *See* Marc. R. Poirier, *"Whiffs of Federalism" in* United States v. Windsor: *Power, Localism, and Kulturkampf*, 85 COLO. L. REV. 935, 988–990 (2014) (discussing *Garden State Equal. v. Dow*, 82 A.3d 336 (N.J. Super. Ct. Law Div. 2013)).

30. Robert A. Mikos, *On the Limits of Supremacy: Medical Marijuana and the States' Overlooked Power to Legalize Federal Crime*, 62 VAND. L. REV. 1421, 1425 (2009).

31. *Id.* For other examples of state defiance, *see* Bulman-Pozen and Gerken, *supra*, note 25 (discussing Patriot Act and environmental regulation).

32. Heather K. Gerken, *The Loyal Opposition*, 123 YALE L.J. 1626 (2014).

33. Martin Luther King, *Remaining Awake through a Great Revolution, Address at the National Cathedral*, Washington DC (March 31, 1968), *in* 114 CONG. REC. 9397 (1968).

34. As I have detailed elsewhere, "Congress has a readymade workaround to bypass the anti-commandeering doctrine, it can usually write in a jurisdictional element to satisfy *Lopez*, it can borrow a page from Justice O'Connor's 'drafting guide' to fit its regulations within the ambit of *Raich*, it can turn to its taxing power when the Commerce Clause won't do, and it will presumably have no trouble evading the dictates of *Sebelius* (unless the Court lends some oomph to its Spending Clause ruling)." Heather K. Gerken, *Slipping the Bonds of Federalism*, 128 HARV. L. REV. 85 (2014).

35. Shelby County v. Holder, 133 S.Ct. 2612 (2013).

36. There are any number of constitutionally viable solutions to revive Section 5 of the Voting Rights Act. *See*, e.g., Heather K. Gerken, *A Third Way for the Voting Rights Act: Section 5 and an Opt-In Approach*, 106 COLUM. L. REV. 708 (2006). Here again, what's stopping us isn't law, but politics.

Chapter 5

1. *See* Snyder v. Phelps, 562 U.S. 443 (2011); United States v. Stevens, 559 U.S. 460 (2010); United States v. Alvarez, 567 U.S. 709 (2012).

2. Machinists v. Street, 367 U.S. 740, 788 (1961) (Black, J., dissenting).

3. Thomas v. Collins, 323 U.S. 516, 545 (1945).

4. Eu v. S.F. Cty. Democratic Cent. Comm., 489 U.S. 214, 223 (1989) (citation omitted).

5. Ronald Dworkin, *The "Devastating" Decision*, N.Y. REV. OF BOOKS (Feb. 25, 2010), http://www.nybooks.com/articles/2010/02/25/the-devastating-decision/.

6. Richard L. Hasen, *Money Grubbers*, SLATE (Jan. 21, 2010), http://www.slate.com/articles/news_and_politics/jurisprudence/2010/01/money_grubbers.html.

7. Jamie Raskin, 'Citizens United' *and the Corporate Court*, NATION (Sept. 13, 2012), https://www.thenation.com/article/citizens-united-and-corporate-court/.

8. Daniel I. Weiner, Citizens United *Five Years Later*, BRENNAN CTR. FOR JUST. 2 (2015), https://www.brennancenter.org/sites/default/files/analysis/Citizens_United_%205_%20Years_%20Later.pdf.

9. Austin v. Mich. Chamber of Commerce, 494 U.S. 652, 659 (1990) (citation omitted).

10. *Id.* at 660.

11. Citizens United v. Fed. Election Comm'n, 558 U.S. 310, 455 (2010) (Stevens, J., dissenting).

12. Supplemental Brief for the Appellee at 17, Citizens United v. Fed. Election Comm'n, 558 U.S. 310 (2010) (No. 08-205).

13. *Id.*

14. Supplemental Brief of *Amici Curiae* Senator John McCain, Senator Russell Feingold, Former Representative Christopher Shays, and Former Representative Martin Meehan in Support of Appellee at 2, Citizens United v. Fed. Election Comm'n, 558 U.S. 310 (2010) (No. 08-205).

15. *Id.* at 2–3.

16. Supplemental Brief of *Amici Curiae* Representatives Chris Van Hollen, David Price, Michael Castle, and John Lewis in Support of Appellee at 2, 4, Citizens United v. Fed. Election Comm'n, 558 U.S. 310 (2010) (No. 08-205).

17. Brief of the Democratic National Committee as *Amicus Curiae* in Support of Appellee at 7–8, Citizens United v. Fed. Election Comm'n, 558 U.S. 310 (2010) (No. 08-205).

18. Editorial, *The Court's Blow to Democracy*, N.Y. TIMES (Jan. 21, 2010), http://www.nytimes.com/2010/01/22/opinion/22fri1.html.

19. Editorial, *The Supreme Court Removes Important Limits on Campaign Finance*, WASH. POST (Jan. 22, 2010), http://www.washingtonpost.com/wp-dyn/content/article/2010/01/21/AR2010012104482.html.

20. *Money Talks, High Court Rules*, S.F. CHRON. (Jan. 22, 2010), http://www.sfgate.com/opinion/editorials/article/Money-talks-high-court-rules-3202187.php.

21. Bob Kerrey, *The Senator from Exxon-Mobil?*, HUFFINGTON POST (March 23, 2010), http://www.huffingtonpost.com/bob-kerrey/the-senator-from-exxon-mo_b_431245.html.

22. JEFFREY D. CLEMENTS, CORPORATIONS ARE NOT PEOPLE: WHY THEY HAVE MORE RIGHTS THAN YOU DO AND WHAT YOU CAN DO ABOUT IT (San Francisco: Berrett-Koehler Publishers, 2012), xi.

23. *Id.*

24. *See* SpeechNOW.org v. Fed. Election Comm'n, 599 F.3d 686 (D.D.C. 2010).

25. EXXON MOBIL CORPORATION POLITICAL ACTION COMMITTEE (EXXONMOBIL PAC) *PAC Disbursements*, FED. ELECTION COMM'N, https://www.fec.gov/data/committee/C00121368/?cycle=2016&tab=disbursements (last visited June 9, 2017).

26. *500*, FORTUNE, http://beta.fortune.com/fortune500/list (last visited Sept. 1, 2017); *Global 500*, FORTUNE, http://beta.fortune.com/global500/list (last visited Sept. 1, 2017).

27. Unless otherwise noted, all data and figures are sourced from the Center for Responsive Politics. *See* https://www.opensecrets.org.

28. *Table 2 PAC Contributions 2007–2008 through December 31, 2008*, FED. ELECTION COMM'N, http://classic.fec.gov/press/press2009/20090415PAC/documents/2contrib2008.pdf (last visited Sept. 26, 2017).

29. *PAC Table 2 PAC Contributions to Candidates January 1, 2011–December 31, 2012*, FED. ELECTION COMM'N, http://classic.fec.gov/press/summaries/2012/tables/pac/PAC2_2012_24m.pdf (last visited Sept. 26, 2017).

30. *PAC Table 2 PAC Contributions to Candidates January 1, 2015 through December 31, 2016*, FED. ELECTION COMM'N (May 4, 2017), http://classic.fec.gov/press/summaries/2016/tables/pac/PAC2_2016_24m.pdf.

31. Ezra Klein, *We Got Way Too Excited over Money in the 2012 Elections*, WASH. POST (May 6, 2013), https://www.washingtonpost.com/news/wonk/wp/2013/05/06/we-got-way-too-excited-over-money-in-the-2012-elections/?utm_term=.4c013917093b.

32. Editorial, *Republicans Audition for Big Money*, N.Y. TIMES (July 31, 2015), https://www.nytimes.com/2015/08/01/opinion/republicans-audition-for-big-money.html?mcubz=0&_r=0.

33. Jack Shafer, *Three Cheers for Citizens United!*, POLITICO (Aug. 25, 2015), http://www.politico.com/magazine/story/2015/08/citizens-united-2016121739_full.html?print#.Walt8mXeOOo.

34. *Id.*

35. Joel M. Gora, *In the Business of Free Speech: The Roberts Court and* Citizens United, *in* BUSINESS AND THE ROBERT COURT, ed. Jonathan H. Adler (New York: Oxford University Press, 2016), 254.

36. Doug Weber, *The Power of One*, OPENSECRETS.ORG (May 8, 2017), https://www.opensecrets.org/news/2017/05/environment-power-of-1/.

37. *Id.*

38. Emily Dalgo and Ashley Balcerzak, *Seven Years Later: Blurred Boundaries, More Money*, OPENSECRETS.ORG (Jan. 19, 2017), https://www.opensecrets.org/news/2017/01/citizens-united-7-years-later/.

39. Joel M. Gora, *The Legacy of* Buckley v. Valeo, 2 ELECTION L.J. 55, 58 (2003).

40. Scott Turow, *The High Court's 20-Year-Old Mistake*, N.Y. TIMES (Oct. 12, 1997), Section 4, p. 15.

41. Buckley v. Valeo, 424 U.S. 1, 19 (1976).

42. *Id.* at 57.

43. *Id.* at 48–49 (citation omitted).

44. Note 15, *supra.*

45. *Dark Money Basics*, OPENSECRETS.ORG, https://www.opensecrets.org/dark-money/basics (last visited June 13, 2017).

46. *Id.*

47. David Ignatius, *A Manifesto to Mend Our Politics*, WASH. POST (April 21, 2016), https://www.washingtonpost.com/opinions/a-manifesto-to-mend-american-politics/2016/04/21/77c519cc-07de-11e6-a12f-ea5aed7958dc_story.html?utm_term=.5503494ebd89.

48. Note 12, *supra*, at 371.

49. *Campaign Finance Disclosure: The Devil Is in the Details*, CTR. FOR COMPETITIVE POL., http://www.campaignfreedom.org/wp-content/uploads/2013/12/2014-08-19_Policy-Primer_Disclosure.pdf (last visited June 15, 2017).

50. *Statement of Justice John Paul Stevens (Ret.)*, SENATE RULES AND ADMIN. COMMITTEE HEARING ON CAMPAIGN FIN. L. (April 30, 2014), https://www.supremecourt.gov/publicinfo/speeches/JPSSpeech(DC)04-30-2014.pdf.

Chapter 6

1. Citizens United v. Fed. Election Comm'n, 558 U.S. 310, 339 (2010).

2. Austin v. Michigan, 494 U.S. 652 (1990).

3. *Id.* at 658.

4. Brief for Appellants at 18–19, Austin v. Michigan, 494 U.S. 652 (1990) (No. 88-1569).

5. *Id.* at 31–33.

6. 494 U.S. at 658–659.

7. Brief for Appellants at 31, Austin v. Michigan, 494 U.S. 652 (1990) (No. 88-1569).

8. 494 U.S. at 668–669.

9. *See*, e.g., ALEXANDER MEIKLEJOHN, FREE SPEECH AND ITS RELATION TO SELF-GOVERNMENT (New York: Harper and Brothers, 1948).

10. 558 U.S. 310.

11. *Id.* at 365, 340 ("the Government may not suppress political speech on the basis of the speaker's corporate identity"); *id.* at 359–350 ("laws that burden political speech are 'subject to strict scrutiny'").

12. *Id.* at 341, 350.

13. *Id.* at 345, 361.
14. *Id.*
15. *Id.*
16. *Id.*
17. 424 U.S. 1.
18. *Id.* at 14–15.
19. 599 F. 3d 686.
20. *Id.* at 694–696.
21. *Id.*
22. 558 U.S. at 356–358.
23. Transcript, *The Whole Truth Pilot*, Public Broadcasting Service, 11/29/11 (on file with author).
24. *Citizens United*, 558 U.S. at 345, 356–361.
25. *Id.*
26. Wikipedia keeps a list. *See Category: American Politicians Convicted of Bribery*, https:// en.wikipedia.org/wiki/Category:American_politicians_convicted_of_bribery (last visited Oct. 24, 2017).
27. *See* Randall Kennedy, *Reconstruction and the Politics of Scholarship*, 98 YALE L.J. 521, n. 51 (1989) (*citing* JOHN T. NOONAN, JR., BRIBES (Berkeley: University of California Press 1987) 455–459); Rebecca E. Zietlow, James Ashley, *The Great Strategist of the Thirteenth Amendment*, 15 GEO. J. L. & PUB. POL'Y 265, 299 (2017).
28. 424 U.S. at 26–27.
29. 424 U.S. at 27.
30. 134 S.Ct. 1434, 1468–1471.
31. U.S. CONST. art. 1, § 3, cl. 1, cl. 2 (*amended by* U.S. CONST. amend. XVII).
32. U.S. CONST. art. 1, § 2.
33. THE FEDERALIST NO. 52 (James Madison).
34. THE FEDERALIST NO. 57 (James Madison).
35. THE FEDERALIST NO. 52 (James Madison).
36. *Id.* ("the people *alone*") (emphasis added).
37. *See generally*, MODEL RULES OF PROF'L CONDUCT Preamble, r. 1.6 (Am. Bar Ass'n 1983).
38. *Id.*
39. *Id.* r. 1.7, 1.8.
40. *See* LAWRENCE LESSIG, REPUBLIC, LOST: HOW MONEY CORRUPTS CONGRESS—AND A PLAN TO STOP IT. rev. ed. (New York: Twelve, 2015), 240–241, n. 33–34 (citing references).
41. *See* Baker v. Carr, 369 U.S. 186, 301 (1962) (*citing* FREDERIC AUSTIN OGG, ENGLISH GOVERNMENT AND POLITICS, 2nd ed. (New York: The Macmillan Company, 1936), 257–259); *see also* LESSIG, REPUBLIC, LOST, *supra* note 40, at 18.
42. *See supra*, note 23.
43. *See* LESSIG, REPUBLIC, LOST, *supra*, note 40, at 269.
44. *See generally*, LESSIG, REPUBLIC, LOST, *supra*, note 40, at 138, n. 43 (citing references).
45. *See Donor Demographics*, OpenSecrets.org, https://www.opensecrets.org/overview/ donordemographics.php (last visited Oct. 24, 2017).
46. *See supra*, note 23.
47. *Id.*
48. *Id.*
49. *Id.*
50. *Id.*
51. 424 U.S. 1, 45 (1976).
52. *See also* Floyd Abrams, Citizens United: *Predictions and Reality, supra*, 81–94. *See* Matt Bai, *How Much Has Citizens United Changed the Political Game*, N.Y. TIMES MAG. (July 17, 2012), http://www.nytimes.com/2012/07/22/magazine/how-much-has-citizens-united-changed-the-political-game.html, *citing* Brief Amicus Curiae of Senator Mitch McConnell in Support of Petitioners at *7, American Tradition Partnership, Inc. v. Bullock, 2012 WL 1513830 (2012) (stating that not a single Fortune 100 company contributed to a candidate's super PAC during 2012's Republican primaries).

53. *Buckley*, 424 U.S. at 102.
54. *See Citizens United,* 558 U.S. at 356 ("When Government seeks to . . . command where a person may get his or her information or what distrusted source he or she may not hear, it uses censorship to control thought. This is unlawful. The First Amendment confirms the freedom to think for ourselves.").
55. *Citizens United,* 558 U.S. at 360.
56. *Id.* at 345, 361.
57. *See generally* Derigan Silver and Dan V. Kozlowski, *The First Amendment Originalism of Justice Brennan, Scalia and Thomas,* 17 COMM. LAW AND POL'Y 385, 390 (2012).
58. *See generally Citizens United,* 558 U.S. at 356–361.
59. *See,* e.g., Silver, *supra* note 57, at 386–387.
60. *See* Speech by Attorney General Edwin Meese, III, before The Federalist Society Lawyers Division on November 15, 1985, https://fed-soc.org/commentery/publications/the-great-debate-attorney-general-ed-meese-iii-november-15-1985, *citing* Brief for the United States as Amicus Curiae in Support of Appellants, Thornburgh v. Am. Coll. of Obstetricians and Gynecologists, 1985 WL 669620 at 24 (1985) (Nos. 84-495 and 84-1379).
61. *See* Brief of Amicus Curiae of Professor Lawrence Lessig in Support of Appellee at *9-10 and Appendix at 23a, McCutcheon v. Fed. Election Comm'n, 2013 WL 3874388 (No. 12-536) 2013.
62. *See* http://csac.history.wisc.edu/nc_marcus2.pdf. *See also* Commentaries on the Constitution, Volume XVI: Commentaries on the Constitution, No. 4, http://rotunda.upress.virginia.edu/founders/default.xqy?keys=RNCN-print-03-16-02&mode=TOC. Marcus 2 was likely by James Iredell. *See* http://csac.history.wisc.edu/nc_the_marcus_essays.pdf.
63. *See* Brief of Amicus Curiae of Professor Lawrence Lessig in Support of Appellee at *9 and Appendix at 23a, McCutcheon v. Fed. Election Comm'n, 2013 WL 3874388 (No. 12-536) 2013.
64. *Id.*
65. *Id.* at *10.
66. *Id.*
67. *See supra,* 102 and note 57.
68. *See supra,* 96–97 and note 19.
69. *See supra,* 96–97, 102 and 11, note 19 and note 57.
70. THE FEDERALIST NO. 52 (James Madison).
71. U.S. CONST. amend. XVII ("The Senate of the United States shall be composed of two Senators from each State, elected by the people thereof . . .").
72. *Id.*

Chapter 7

1. Patterson v. Colorado, 205 U.S. 454, 462 (1907) (Holmes, J.). Even as late as 1915, Harlan Fiske Stone, the future author of footnote four of *Carolene Products,* could summarize "the more important" aspects of the Bill of Rights as including "freedom of religious worship, the right peaceably to assemble, the right to bear arms, the right to be free from unreasonable searches and seizures, the right to a speedy trial by jury, the right not to be compelled to testify against oneself in a criminal trial, the right not to be deprived of life, liberty, or property without due process of law, and the like." HARLAN F. STONE, LAW AND ITS ADMINISTRATION (New York: Columbia University Press, 1915), 140. It is remarkable that in this long list Stone does not even mention freedom of expression.
2. ROBERT C. POST, CITIZENS DIVIDED: CAMPAIGN FINANCE REFORM AND THE CONSTITUTION (Cambridge, MA: Harvard University Press, 2014).
3. CHARLES HORTON COOLEY, SOCIAL ORGANIZATION: A STUDY OF THE LARGER MIND (New York: Scribners, 1956), 118.
4. Letter from Learned Hand to Zechariah Chafee, Jr., January 8, 1920 (on file in the Chafee Papers, box 4, folder 20, Harvard Law Library, Treasure Room), *as reprinted in* Gerald Gunther, *Learned Hand and the Origins of Modern First Amendment Doctrine: Some Fragments of History,* 27 STAN. L. REV. 719, 764–766 (1975).

5. Stromberg v. California, 283 U.S. 359, 369 (1931).
6. Thornhill v. Alabama, 310 U.S. 88, 95 (1940).
7. Masses Publishing Co. v. Patten, 244 F. 535 (S.D.N.Y.), *rev'd*, 246 F. 24 (2d Cir. 1917). Hence *Thornhill*:

> The freedom of speech and of the press guaranteed by the Constitution embraces at the least the liberty to discuss publicly and truthfully all matters of public concern without previous restraint or fear of subsequent punishment. The exigencies of the colonial period and the efforts to secure freedom from oppressive administration developed a broadened conception of these liberties as adequate to supply the public need for information and education with respect to the significant issues of the times. . . . Freedom of discussion, if it would fulfill its historic function in this nation, must embrace all issues about which information is needed or appropriate to enable the members of society to cope with the exigencies of their period.

   Id. at 101–102.
8. Valentine v. Chrestensen, 316 U.S. 52, 54 (1942).
9. Rosenberger v. Rectors and Visitors of the University of Virginia, 515 U.S. 819, 828–829 (1995). *See* Reed v. Town of Gilbert, 135 S.Ct. 2218, 2226 (2015) (The state "'has no power to restrict expression because of its message, its ideas, its subject matter, or its content.' Content-based laws—those that target speech based on its communicative content—are presumptively unconstitutional and may be justified only if the government proves that they are narrowly tailored to serve compelling state interests.").
10. Hustler Magazine, Inc. v. Falwell, 485 U.S. 46, 51 (1988). *See* Bose Corp. v. Consumers Union of U.S., Inc., 466 U.S. 485, 504 (1984); Old Dominion Branch No. 496 v. Austin, 418 U.S. 264, 284 (1974).
11. Agency for Int'l Dev. v. Alliance for Open Soc'y Int'l, 570 U.S. 205, 213 (2013) (quoting Rumsfeld v. F. for Acad. and Institutional Rts., 547 U.S. 47, 61 (2006) *and* Turner Broadcasting Sys. v. Fed. Comm. Commission, 512 U.S. 622, 641 (1994)).
12. Harper & Row Publishers, Inc. v. Nation Enters., 471 U.S. 539, 559 (1985) (quoting Estate of Hemingway v. Random House, Inc., 244 N.E.2d 250, 255 (1968)). "There is certainly some difference between compelled speech and compelled silence, but in the context of protected speech, the difference is without constitutional significance, for the First Amendment guarantees 'freedom of speech,' a term necessarily comprising the decision of both what to say and what *not* to say." Riley v. Nat'l Fed'n of the Blind of N.C., Inc., 487 U.S. 781, 796–797 (1988). "Just as the First Amendment may prevent the government from prohibiting speech, the Amendment may prevent the government from compelling individuals to express certain views." United States v. United Foods, 533 U.S. 405, 410 (2001). *See* Wooley v. Maynard, 430 U.S. 705, 714 (1977); West Virginia Bd. of Educ. v. Barnette, 319 U.S. 624 (1943).
13. Brown v. Hartlage, 456 U.S. 45, 60 (1982).
14. POST, *supra* note 2.
15. *See* ROBERT C. POST, DEMOCRACY, EXPERTISE & ACADEMIC FREEDOM: A FIRST AMENDMENT JURISPRUDENCE FOR THE MODERN STATE (New Haven, CT: Yale University Press, 2012).
16. *See* John Rawls, *Reply to Habermas*, 92 J. PHIL. 132, 140–141 (1995).
17. Hence the Court's ruling that within public discourse even deliberate falsehoods can receive First Amendment protection. United States v. Alvarez, 132 S.Ct. 2537 (2012).
18. ALEXANDER MEIKLEJOHN, POLITICAL FREEDOM: THE CONSTITUTIONAL POWERS OF THE PEOPLE (New York: Harper and Brothers, 1948), 12.
19. Glickman v. Wileman Bros. and Elliott, Inc., 521 U.S. 457, 478 (1997) (Souter, J., dissenting).
20. Va. State Bd. of Pharmacy v. Va. Citizens Consumer Council, Inc., 425 U.S. 748 (1976).
21. Robert C. Post, *Compelled Commercial Speech,* 117 W. VA. L. REV. 867 (2015).
22. Zauderer v. Office of Disciplinary Counsel, 471 U.S. 626 (1985).
23. Cent. Hudson Gas & Elec. Corp. v. Pub. Serv. Comm'n, 447 U.S. 557, 566 (1980).
24. Illinois ex rel. Lisa Madigan v. Telemarketing Assocs., Inc., 538 U.S. 600 (2003).
25. King v. Governor of New Jersey, 767 F.3d 216, 229 (3d Cir. 2014); *see* Wollschlaeger v. Florida, 848 F.3d 1293, 1307 (11th Cir. 2017) (en banc).

26. *See,* e.g., Sorrell v. IMS Health Inc., 131 S.Ct. 2653 (2011); United States v. United Foods, Inc., 533 U.S. 405 (2001).

27. *See,* e.g., Amanda Shanor, *The New Lochner,* 2016 WISC. L. REV. 133.

28. *See* Robert C. Post and Amanda Shanor, *Adam Smith's First Amendment,* 128 HARV. L. F. 165 (2015).

29. Scott Jaschik, *DeVos vs. the Faculty,* INSIDE HIGHER EDUC. (Feb. 24, 2017), https://www.insidehighered.com/news/2017/02/24/education-secretary-criticizes-professors-telling-students-what-think?utm_source=Inside+Higher+Ed&utm_campaign=00ea4196f1-DNU20170224&utm_medium=email&utm_term=0_1fcbc04421-00ea4196f1-197462733&mc_cid=00ea4196f1&mc_eid=e7d1eb30be. *See* Graham W. Bishai, *With Provocative Speakers, New Group Aims to 'Test' Free Speech Values,* HARV. CRIMSON (April 6, 2017), https://www.thecrimson.com/article/2017/4/7/free-speech-club/#.WOdkwlvMeVM.email.

30. Lisa Marie Segarra, *Colleges Are an 'Echo Chamber of Political Correctness.' Read Jeff Sessions' Speech on Campus Free Speech,* TIME (Sept. 26, 2017), http://time.com/4957604/jeff-sessions-georgetown-law-speech-transcript/.

31. *Id.*

32. *Id.*

33. JONATHAN ZIMMERMAN, CAMPUS POLITICS: WHAT EVERYONE NEEDS TO KNOW (New York: Oxford University Press, 2016), 5. *See* Jacqueline Pfeffer Merrill, *YES: Students Must Consider All Ideas,* CHRONICLE (WILLIMANTIC, CONNECTICUT) (Nov. 3, 2016), at 5 (referring to "rising campus ambivalence about free expression").

34. Jennifer Schuessler, *Can Cries of 'Free Speech' Be a Weapon? Students Say Yes,* N.Y. TIMES (Oct. 16, 2016), http://www.nytimes.com/2016/10/17/arts/pen-warns-that-college-students-often-see-free-speech-as-a-cudgel.html?_r=0.

35. Cindi Andrews, *Academic Fascism Begins with Curbing Free Speech,* CINCINNATI ENQUIRER (Aug. 16, 2015), at 5 ("Once leftists gain control, as they have at many universities, free speech becomes a liability and must be suppressed.").

36. Editorial, *Standing for Campus Free Speech,* TAMPA BAY TIMES (Oct. 8, 2016), at 10. *See* Amanda Hoover Staff, *Can a Halloween Costume Be Hate Speech?: A Costume Depicting Donald Trump Hanging Hillary Clinton and President Obama from a Noose Sparked Outrage at a University of Wisconsin Football Game. Are There Controversial Costumes That Don't Fall under Free Speech Protections?,* CHRISTIAN SCI. MONITOR (Oct. 31, 2016).

37. Sally Jenkins, *Free Speech? Columbia Wrestlers Can Pay the Price,* WASH. POST (Nov. 16, 2016), at D08.

38. Susan Svrluga, *Writer's Speech at U-Md Canceled,* WASH. POST (Oct. 26, 2016), at B01.

39. Campus Free Speech Protection Act, 2017 Bill Text TN S.B. 723, http://www.capitol.tn.gov/Bills/110/Amend/SA0333.pdf. *See* Peter Schmidt, *Tennessee Law Is Hailed as Offering Unprecedented Protection of Campus Speech,* CHRON. OF HIGHER EDUC. (May 10, 2017), http://www.chronicle.com/blogs/ticker/tennessee-law-is-hailed-as-offering-unprecedented-protection-of-campus-speech/118311; Peter Schmidt, *A State's Effort to Head Off Campus Speech-Fights Gets Mixed Reviews,* CHRON. OF HIGHER EDUC. (May 16, 2017), http://www.chronicle.com/article/A-State-s-Effort-to-Head-Off/240088?cid=trend_au&elqTrackId=6d39ab8080af4fd1b466de696acbbef2&elq=e9311457c81c451a8a07cd2e11ec27d9&elqaid=13978&elqat=1&elqCampaignId=5833. The Tennessee statute is evidently the leading edge of a coming wave of state legislative protections for free speech on campus. *See* Chris Quintana and Andy Thomason, *The States Where Campus Free-Speech Bills Are Being Born: A Rundown,* CHRON. OF HIGHER EDUC. (May 15, 2017), http://www.chronicle.com/article/The-States-Where-Campus/240073?cid=at&utm_source=at&utm_medium=en&elqTrackId=ddc8c04f9ace45d1b98525b7161c83bc&elq=bb12c0f09bee4686a72e62ba086a8ab7&elqaid=13919&elqat=1&elqCampaignId=5804.

40. Janet Napolitano, *It's Time to Free Speech on Campus Again,* BOS. GLOBE (Oct. 2, 2016), at K3.

41. Jerry Shenk, *How Political Correctness Will Kill Higher Ed.,* LEBANON DAILY NEWS (Oct. 8, 2016), at A5.

42. Website of FIRE, https://www.thefire.org/.

43. Available at https://www.thefire.org/about-us/mission/.

44. On distinguishing respect for students from respect for their ideas, *see* MATTHEW W. FINKIN AND ROBERT C. POST, FOR THE COMMON GOOD: PRINCIPLES OF AMERICAN ACADEMIC FREEDOM (New Haven, CT: Yale University Press, 2009), 105.

45. *See* Robert C. Post, *Community and the First Amendment*, 29 ARIZ. ST. L.J. 473, 479–480 (1997). Abusive, degrading, offensive, and outrageous speech is protected in public discourse for reasons that derive from the value of self-governance. *See* Robert C. Post, *The Constitutional Concept of Public Discourse: Outrageous Opinion, Democratic Deliberation, and* Hustler Magazine v. Falwell, 103 HARV. L. REV. 601 (1990).

46. "Students are entitled to an atmosphere conducive to learning . . . ," AAUP, *A Statement of the Association's Council: Freedom and Responsibility*, available at https://www.aaup.org/report/freedom-and-responsibility.

47. FINKIN AND POST, *supra* note 44, at 79–111.

48. JOHN HENRY CARDINAL NEWMAN, THE IDEA OF A UNIVERSITY DEFINED AND ILLUSTRATED (London: Longmans, Green, 1888), xvi (*Preface*).

49. American Association of University Professors, *Declaration of Principles on Academic Freedom and Tenure* (1915), *reproduced in* FINKIN AND POST, *supra* note 44, at 174.

50. *Id.*

51. RICHARD RORTY, PHILOSOPHY AND SOCIAL HOPE (New York: Penguin Books, 1999), 123, 125.

52. *Declaration, supra* note 49, at 167–168.

53. AAUP, *Statement on Professional Ethics*, available at https://www.aaup.org/report/statement-professional-ethics.

54. *Id.*

55. *See* Robert C. Post, *Debating Disciplinarity*, 35 CRITICAL INQUIRY 749 (2009).

56. ALLAN GIBBARD, THINKING HOW TO LIVE (Cambridge, MA: Harvard University Press, 2003), 226–227.

57. Thomas L. Haskell, *Justifying the Rights of Academic Freedom in the Era of "Power/Knowledge,"* *in* THE FUTURE OF ACADEMIC FREEDOM, ed. Louis Menand (Chicago: University of Chicago Press, 1996), 45–46.

58. Haskell, *supra* note 57, at 47.

59. Arthur O. Lovejoy, *Academic Freedom, in* ENCYCLOPEDIA OF THE SOCIAL SCIENCES, eds. Edwin R. A. Seligman and Alvin Johnson (London: Macmillan, 1930), 384–385.

60. Red Lion Broad. v. FCC, 395 U.S. 367, 390 (1969).

61. Gloria Franke, *The Right of Publicity vs. The First Amendment: Will One Test Ever Capture the Starring Role*, 79 CALIF. L. REV. 945, 958 (2006).

62. MICHAEL WALZER, SPHERES OF JUSTICE: A DEFENSE OF PLURALISM AND EQUALITY (New York: Basic Books, 1983), 310.

63. FINKIN AND POST, *supra* note 44, at 53–77.

64. *Declaration, supra* note 49, at 163.

65. *Id.* at 173. On the relationship between academic freedom and a theory of knowledge, *see* John R. Searle, *Two Concepts of Academic Freedom, in* THE CONCEPT OF ACADEMIC FREEDOM, ed. Edmund L. Pincoffs (Austin: University of Texas Press, 1975), 88–89, 92.

66. *Declaration, supra* note 49, at 179–180. Hence the conclusion of Thomas Haskell: "Historically speaking, the heart and soul of academic freedom lie not in free speech but in professional autonomy and collegial self-governance. Academic freedom came into being as a defense of the disciplinary community (or, more exactly, the university conceived as an ensemble of such communities)." Haskell, *supra* note 57, at 54.

67. In this chapter I do not consider situations where speakers come to campus based exclusively on private resources and without explicit university sanction, because in such circumstances the connection between speakers and universities becomes particularly difficult to define. I consider instead situations in which universities are asked to expend their resources to sustain speakers.

68. Under ordinary principles of academic freedom, students have little standing to challenge the professional judgments of faculty about the value of an outside speaker with respect to the attainment of either educational or research goals. Universities therefore have little tolerance for student efforts to shut down faculty-invited outside speakers.

69. *See supra*, note 67.
70. The Supreme Court has approved a law school policy authorizing student programs to encourage "tolerance, cooperation, and learning among students." Christian Legal Soc'y v. Martinez, 561 U.S. 661, 689 (2010). The Court held that the school could limit expressive association to serve these goals. The school policy supporting student organizations was theorized as a limited purpose public forum.
71. *See, e.g.,* Manny Fernandez and Richard Pérez-Peña, *As Two Oklahoma Students Are Expelled for Racist Chants, Sigma Alpha Epsilon Vows Wider Inquiry,* N.Y. TIMES (March 10, 2015), http://www.nytimes.com/2015/03/11/us/university-of-oklahoma-sigma-alpha-epsilon-racist-fraternity-video.html?_r=0.
72. *See, e.g.,* Pickering v. Bd. of Educ., 391 U.S. 563 (1968).
73. In the 1960s, the freedom-of-speech movement sought precisely to oppose this concept of education. *See* Robert C. Post, *Constitutionally Interpreting the FSM Controversy, in* THE FREE SPEECH MOVEMENT: REFLECTIONS ON BERKELEY IN THE 1960S, eds. Robert Cohen and Reginald E. Zelnik (Berkeley: University of California Press, 2002), 401.
74. *See, e.g.,* Eliza Gray, *Civil Libertarians Say Expelling Oklahoma Frat Students May Be Illegal,* TIME (March 10, 2015), http://time.com/3739268/sigma-alpha-epsilon-university-of-oklahoma-expel-free-speech/.
75. *See* Robert C. Post, *Between Governance and Management: The History and Theory of the Public Forum,* 34 UCLA L. REV. 1713 (1987). Another way to put this point is that the First Amendment does not require the state to protect speech within courtrooms, bureaucracies, and prisons as though the values of self-government were at stake.
76. Widmar v. Vincent, 454 U.S. 263, 268 n.5 (1981).
77. *Id.* at 277 (citing Healy v. James, 408 U.S. 169, 189 (1972)).
78. *See* Post, *supra*, note 75.
79. *See* Tyler Kingkade, *Texas Tech Frat Loses Charter Following "No Means Yes, Yes Means Anal" Display,* HUFFINGTON POST (Oct. 9, 2014), http://www.huffingtonpost.com/2014/10/08/texas-tech-frat-no-means-yes_n_5953302.html.
80. *See supra*, note 45.
81. The famous Woodward Report issued by Yale University on December 23, 1974, effectively obscures these questions when it simultaneously asserts *both* that "the primary function of a university is to discover and disseminate knowledge by means of research and teaching," *and* that a university "is not primarily a fellowship, a club, a circle of friends. . . . Without sacrificing its central purpose it cannot make its primary and dominant value the fostering of friendship, solidarity, harmony, civility, or mutual respect." The Woodward Report, http://yalecollege.yale.edu/deans-office/policies-reports/report-committee-freedom-expression-yale. These two propositions are in serious tension; in extreme situations, they cannot be reconciled except through a theory of education that runs contrary to the experience of virtually all university teachers and administrators. It is no wonder, therefore, that the report is almost always read to subordinate the goal of teaching and to elevate "free speech over every other university goal or purpose." JONATHAN ZIMMERMAN, CAMPUS POLITICS: WHAT EVERYONE NEEDS TO KNOW (New York: Oxford University Press, 2016), 113. But a university that abandons the goal of teaching can no longer remain true to its raison d'être.
82. Note that under the recently enacted "Campus Individual Rights Act" of Utah, available at https://le.utah.gov/~2017/bills/static/HB0054.html#53b-27-101, the direct imposition of First Amendment "public forum" principles onto public campuses would prevent a university from regulating this demonstration on the grounds of content or viewpoint. *See* Reed v. Town of Gilbert, 135 S.Ct. 2218 (2015).
83. Glickman v. Wileman Bros. and Elliott, Inc., 521 U.S. 457, 478 (1997) (Souter, J., dissenting).

Chapter 8

1. For accounts of these events, *see* GEOFFREY R. STONE, PERILOUS TIMES: FREE SPEECH IN WARTIME FROM THE SEDITION ACT OF 1978 TO THE WAR ON TERRORISM (New York: W. W. Norton, 2004), 500–502; DAVID RUDENSTINE, THE DAY THE PRESSES STOPPED: A HISTORY OF THE PENTAGON PAPERS CASE (Berkeley: University of California Press, 1996), 27–42; SANFORD UNGAR, THE PAPERS AND THE PAPERS: AN ACCOUNT OF THE

LEGAL AND POLITICAL BATTLE OVER THE PENTAGON PAPERS (New York: Dutton, 1972), 22–27.

2. New York Times Co. v. United States, 403 U.S. 713 (1971).

3. *Id.* at 730 (Stewart, J., concurring). Only Justice White joined Justice Stewart's opinion, but at least three other justices—Justices Black, Douglas, and Brennan—would have adopted an even more restrictive standard. Justice Stewart's standard was therefore the narrowest ground on which a majority of the Court agreed.

4. The Court's holding concerned only whether a court could enjoin the publication, not whether the *Times* and *Post*, or their editors, might have committed a crime by publishing the Papers. On the significance of this distinction, *see infra*, 133–134.

5. *See* Snepp v. United States, 444 U.S. 507 (1980).

6. *See, e.g.,* Michael B. Kelley, *NSA: Snowden 1.7 Million Classified Documents*, http://www.businessinsider.com/how-many-docs-did-snowden-take-2013-12.

7. *See* GLENN GREENWALD, NO PLACE TO HIDE: EDWARD SNOWDEN, THE NSA, AND THE U.S. SURVEILLANCE STATE (New York: Metropolitan Books, Henry Holt and Company, 2014), 48.

8. For an important discussion of how the emergence of WikiLeaks and other recent developments threaten the Pentagon Papers equilibrium, *see* Patricia L. Bellia, *WikiLeaks and the Institutional Framework for National Security Disclosures*, 121 YALE L.J. 1448 (2012). Specifically on WikiLeaks and its role in the Snowden disclosures, *see id.* at 1473–1477.

9. *See id.* at 1477. The United States refused to answer.

10. *See id.* at 1479.

11. On this point, and many other relevant issues, see the comprehensive discussion in David E. Pozen, *The Leaky Leviathan: Why the Government Condemns and Condones Unlawful Disclosures of Information*, 127 HARV. L. REV. 512, 534–536 and nn. 113, 114, 121 (2013).

12. 18 U.S.C. § 793.

13. 18 U.S.C. § 793(d).

14. 18 U.S.C. § 798 makes it a crime to "transmit, or otherwise make available to an unauthorized person, or publish, or use in any manner prejudicial to the safety or interest of the United States" such classified information.

15. Intelligence Identities Protection Act, 50 U.S.C. § 421. The statute that generally forbids stealing from the United States, 18 U.S.C. § 641, is also sometimes used in connection with leaks; that statute makes it a crime to "convey or dispose of any record, voucher, money, or thing of value of the United States or of any department or agency thereof." Someone who took physical records could be prosecuted under this statute; the courts disagree about whether information not embodied in physical property belonging to the government is covered by the statute. For a list of statutes that are potentially applicable to leaks, *see* Pozen, *supra* note 11, 127 HARV. L. REV. at 523–524.

16. *See* United States v. Morison, 844 F.2d. 1047 (4th Cir. 1988). Morison, a US Navy analyst, disclosed classified information about Soviet military capabilities to a British trade journal.

17. *See* 403 U.S. at 737 ("I would have no difficulty in sustaining convictions [under the Espionage Act] on facts that would not justify the intervention of equity and the imposition of a prior restraint."). *See also* the discussion in Bellia, *supra* note 8, 121 YALE L.J. at 1470.

18. The specific history of the Espionage Act, in particular, would also arguably have precluded such a prosecution. *See* the discussion in Stone, *supra* note 1, at 507–508.

19. Haig v. Agee, 423 U.S. 280 (1981). That case concerned not a criminal prosecution but the government's decision to revoke the passport of an individual accused of violating the statute. But the opinion did not leave much doubt that the First Amendment would permit a prosecution as well.

20. *See, e.g.,* Ungar, *supra* note 1, 83–84.

21. *See, e.g.,* the discussion in Pozen, *supra* note 11, 127 HARV. L. REV. at 527 and nn. 63–64.

22. *See, e.g.,* Dun & Bradstreet, Inc. v. Greenmoss Builders, Inc., 472 U.S. 749, 784 (Brennan, J., joined by Marshall, Blackmun, and Stevens, dissenting); *id.* at 773 (White, J., concurring in the judgment), cited in Citizens United v. Fed. Election Comm'n, 558 U.S. 310, 352 (2010).

23. *See, e.g.,* AMY GAJDA, THE FIRST AMENDMENT BUBBLE: HOW PRIVACY AND PAPARAZZI THREATEN A FREE PRESS (Cambridge, MA: Harvard University Press, 2015).

Chapter 9

1. For discussion, *see*, e.g., Catharine A. MacKinnon, *Substantive Equality: A Perspective*, 96 MINN. L. REV. 1–27 (2011).
2. Abrams v. United States, 250 U.S. 616, 624 (1919); Gitlow v. New York, 268 U.S. 652, 672 (1925); Whitney v. California, 274 U.S. 357, 372 (1927).
3. Dennis v. United States, 341 U.S. 494, 579 (1951); *id.* at 581.
4. *Abrams*, 250 U.S. at 628 (Holmes, J., dissenting).
5. *Dennis*, 341 U.S. at 589 (Douglas, J., dissenting).
6. *Id.* at 588.
7. *Id.*
8. Brown v. Socialist Workers '74 Campaign Committee (Ohio), 459 U.S. 87, 88 (1982).
9. Beauharnais v. Illinois, 343 U.S. 250, 251 (1952).
10. *Id.* at 253.
11. *Id.* at 251.
12. Excellent scholarship on this point can be found in KIMBERLÉ WILLIAMS CRENSHAW, RICHARD DELGADO, CHARLES R. LAWRENCE III, AND MARI J. MATSUDA, WORDS THAT WOUND: CRITICAL RACE THEORY, ASSAULTIVE SPEECH, AND THE FIRST AMENDMENT (Boulder: Westview Press, 1993).
13. 343 U.S. at 272.
14. Chaplinsky v. New Hampshire, 315 U.S. 568, 573 (1942).
15. 376 U.S. 254 (1964).
16. Herbert Wechsler, *Toward Neutral Principles of Constitutional Law*, 73 HARV. L. REV. 1–35 (1959).
17. 347 U.S. 483 (1954).
18. Wechsler, *Toward Neutral Principles* at 33.
19. *Brandenburg*, 395 U.S. at 444.
20. *Id.*
21. *Id.*
22. *Id.* at 446.
23. *Id.*
24. On Klan violence during the Reconstruction era, *see*, e.g., ALLEN W. TRELEASE, WHITE TERROR: THE KU KLUX KLAN CONSPIRACY AND SOUTHERN RECONSTRUCTION (New York: Harper and Row, 1971); Lisa Cardyn, *Sexualized Racism/Gendered Violence: Outraging the Body Politic in the Reconstruction South*, 100 MICH. L. REV. 675–867 (2002).
25. *Brandenburg*, 395 U.S. at 447.
26. *Id.*
27. Collin v. Smith, 578 F.2d 1197 (7th Cir. 1978), *cert. denied*, 439 U.S. 916 (1978).
28. *Id.* at 1200.
29. *Id.* at 1201.
30. *Id.* at 1202.
31. *Id.* at 1203 (*quoting* Gertz v. Robert Welch, Inc., 418 U.S. 323, 339 (1974)).
32. *Id.* at 1199.
33. *Smith*, 439 U.S. at 919 (Blackmun & White, JJ., dissenting).
34. Schacht v. United States, 398 U.S. 58, 63 (1970).
35. Geoffrey R. Stone, *Kenneth Karst's Equality as a Central Principle in the First Amendment*, 75 U. CHI. L. REV. 37, 39 (2008).
36. Barbier v. Connolly, 113 U.S. 27, 32 (1885).
37. 408 U.S. 92 (1972).
38. *Id.* at 96.
39. *Id.*
40. The classic articulation of this principle was Kenneth Karst, *Equality as a Central Principle in the First Amendment*, 43 U. CHI. L. REV. 20 (1975).
41. *Id.* at 35.
42. *Mosley*, 408 U.S. at 96.
43. Karst, *supra* note 42, at 39.

44. United States v. O'Brien, 391 U.S. 367 (1968).

45. *See, e.g.,* Catharine A. MacKinnon, *The Road Not Taken: Sex Equality in* Lawrence v. Texas, 65 OHIO ST. L. J. 1081–1096 (2004).

46. 530 U.S. 640 (2000).

47. *Id.* at 653.

48. 530 U.S. at 653.

49. *See, e.g.,* Lawrence v. Texas, 539 U.S. 558 (2003) and the gay marriage cases.

50. 413 U.S. 376 (1973).

51. Karst, *supra* note 42, at 33.

52. 468 U.S. 609 (1984).

53. *Id.* at 610.

54. *Id.* at 609.

55. *Id.* at 628.

56. Keyishian v. Board of Regents of the University of the State of New York, 385 U.S. 589, 603 (1967).

57. For a fuller discussion, *see* Catharine A. MacKinnon, *On Academic Freedom: From Powerlessness to Power, in* BUTTERFLY POLITICS (Cambridge, MA: Harvard University Press, 2017), 242–262.

58. 505 U.S. 377 (1992).

59. *Id.* at 380.

60. *Id.* at 381.

61. *Id.* at 391.

62. *Id.*

63. *Id.* at 392.

64. *Id.* at 391.

65. *Id.* at 380.

66. Virginia v. Black, 538 U.S. 343 (2003).

67. *Id.* at 362.

68. *Id.* at 352–357.

69. *Id.* at 357.

70. 561 U.S. 1 (2010).

71. *See* EDWARD DE GRAZIA, GIRLS LEAN BACK EVERYWHERE: THE LAW OF OBSCENITY AND THE ASSAULT ON GENIUS (New York: Random House, 1992).

72. United States v. Williams, 553 U.S. 285, 310 (2008) (Souter & Ginsburg, JJ., dissenting).

73. *See* Corita R. Grudzen et al., *Comparison of the Mental Health of Female Adult Film Performers and Other Young Women in California,* 62 PSYCHIATRIC SERVICES, 641–642 (2011). The preconditions and characteristics of abuse, inequality, and poverty found there are similar to those of persons exploited in prostitution. *See, e.g.,* Catharine A. MacKinnon, *Trafficking, Prostitution, and Inequality,* 46 HARV. CIV. RTS.-CIV. LIBERTIES L. REV. 276–280 (2011) (referring to multiple studies).

74. *See, e.g.,* NATALIE J. PURCELL, VIOLENCE AND THE PORNOGRAPHIC IMAGINARY: THE POLITICS OF SEX, GENDER, AND AGGRESSION IN HARDCORE PORNOGRAPHY (New York: Routledge, 2012), 179–181.

75. Melissa Farley, *"Renting an Organ for Ten Minutes": What Tricks Tell Us about Prostitution, Pornography, and Trafficking, in* PORNOGRAPHY: DRIVING THE DEMAND IN INTERNATIONAL SEX TRAFFICKING, eds. David E. Guinn and Julie DiCaro (Los Angeles: Captive Daughters Media, Captive Daughters Media, 2007), 146.

76. *See, e.g.,* Paul J. Wright et al., *A Meta-Analysis of Pornography Consumption and Actual Acts of Sexual Aggression in General Population Studies,* 66 J. OF COMM'N 201 (2016) (finding "little doubt" that more pornography consumption "on average" predicts more "actual acts of sexual aggression" than less consumption does); Mike Allen et al., *Exposure to Pornography and Acceptance of Rape Myths,* 45 J. OF COMM'N 18–19 (1995); Mike Allen et al., *A Meta-Analysis Summarizing the Effects of Pornography II: Aggression After Exposure,* 22 HUM. COMM'N RES. 267, 271, 274 (1995). Studies have also rejected the hypothesis that these correlations can be explained by aggressive persons consuming pornography conforming to their predispositions. *See id.* at 199; *see also* Gert Martin Hald et al., *Pornography and*

Attitudes Supporting Violence against Women: Revisiting the Relationship in Nonexperimental Studies, 36 AGGRESSIVE BEHAV. 14, 18 (2010) (finding, in meta-analysis, that pornography consumption significantly predicts stronger attitudes supporting violence against women). *See also* Max Waltman, *The Politics of Legal Challenges to Pornography: Canada, Sweden, and the United States,* STOCKHOLM STUD. IN POL. 90-140, 160 (PhD dissertation, Stockholm University, 2014), https://ssrn.com/abstract=2539998.

77. 354 U.S. 476 (1957).
78. *Id.* at 491.
79. *Id.* at 484, 487.
80. Redrup v. New York, 386 U.S. 767 (1967).
81. Miller v. California, 413 U.S. 15, 24 (1973).
82. 413 U.S. 15.
83. A few successful prosecutions do exist. *See,* e.g., United States v. Ira Isaacs, 359 Fed. Appx. 875 (9th Cir. 2014); United States v. Little, 365 Fed. Appx 159 (11th Cir. 2010).
84. A self-administered anonymous computer survey conducted in the United States in 2014 estimated that 46 percent of the men and 16 percent of the women used pornography during any given week. *See* Mark Regnerus et al., *Documenting Pornography Use in America: A Comparative Analysis of Methodological Approaches,* 53 J. OF SEX RES. 875-876, 878, table 4 (2016).
85. *See* EMILIE BUCHWALD, PAMELA FLETCHER, AND MARTH ROTH, eds., TRANSFORMING A RAPE CULTURE, rev. ed. (Minneapolis: Milkweed Editions, 2005).
86. MacKinnon, *Sex Equality, supra* note 48, at 1688-1689 (listing sources). Recent research shows that "the global pornography industry is expected to reach US$100 billion in the near future." Melinda Tankard Reist and Abigail Bray, *Introduction, in* BIG PORN INC: EXPOSING THE HARMS OF THE GLOBAL PORNOGRAPHY INDUSTRY, EDS. MELINDA TANKARD REIST AND ABIGAUL BRAY (North Melborne: Spinifex Press, 2011), xiv.
87. Brown v. Entertainment Merchants Ass'n, 564 U.S. 786, 793 (2011).
88. Ginsberg v. New York, 390 U.S. 629, 632 (1968).
89. *See* Ashcroft v. Free Speech Coalition, 535 U.S. 234, 256, 258 (2002).
90. City of Los Angeles v. Alameda Books, Inc., 535 U.S. 425, 457 (2002) (Souter, Stevens, & Ginsburg, JJJ., dissenting).
91. Osborne v. Ohio, 495 U.S. 103, 125-126 (1990).
92. 535 U.S. at 256, 258.
93. *Id.* at 267 (Rehnquist, C.J., dissenting).
94. 771 F.2d at 324.
95. *Id.* at 328.
96. *Id.*
97. *Id.* at 328, 328, 329.
98. *Id.* at 329, 331.
99. *Id.* at 332, 332.
100. 475 U.S. 1001. Chief Justice Burger, Justice Rehnquist, and Justice O'Connor dissented.
101. Empirical details in this hypothetical are provided by my own research.
102. 413 U.S. at 24.
103. *See* Catharine A. MacKinnon, *Not a Moral Issue,* 2 YALE L. AND POL'Y REV. 321-345 (1984).
104. Brandenburg, 395 U.S. at 449.
105. Chaplinsky, 315 U.S. at 573.
106. R.A.V., 505 U.S. at 393.
107. Hudnut, 771 F.2d at 324.
108. 771 F.2d at 328-329.
109. Mishkin v. New York, 383 U.S. 502, 505 (1966).
110. Per the USA Patriot Act definition, as "material support to terrorism," upheld by *Holder v. Humanitarian Law Project,* 561 U.S. 1 (2010).
111. *Id. See* 28 C.F.R. § 0.85(l) (2017).
112. 336 U.S. 490 (1949). For one mapping of the considerable and expanding contemporary vitality of this doctrine, *see* Eugene Volokh, *The 'Speech Integral to Criminal Conduct' Exception,* 101 CORNELL L. REV. 981 (2016).
113. *Id.* at 498.

114. 18 U.S.C. § 1117 (2017).
115. Ashcroft, 535 U.S. at 250.
116. *Id.*
117. *See* People v. Fixler, 56 Cal.App.3d 321 (1976); People v. Freeman, 758 P.2d 1128 (1988).
118. Abrams, 250 U.S. at 627 (Holmes, J., dissenting).
119. United States v. Stevens, 559 U.S. 460, 475, 476 (2010).
120. *Id.* at 491.
121. Osborne, 495 U.S. 103.
122. Stevens, 559 U.S. at 492–493.
123. *Id.* at 493.
124. Most women in prostitution, of which pornography is an arm, are pimped, further crimes. A synthesis averaging the estimates from eighteen sources estimated that 84 percent of prostituted women were under the control of third parties or subjected to pimping or human trafficking. *See* Melissa Farley et al., *Online Prostitution and Trafficking,* 77 ALB. L. REV. 1041–1042, n. 14 (2014).
125. *See Attorney General's Commission on Pornography,* ATTORNEY GENERAL'S COMMISSION ON PORNOGRAPHY: FINAL REPORT, 2 vols. 1: 291–297; 2: 1037–1238 (Washington, DC: US Department of Justice, 1986).
126. 535 U.S. 747 (1982).
127. Stevens, 559 U.S. at 494 (Alito, J., dissenting) (quoting Ferber 535 U.S. at 250).
128. Brown v. Entertainment Merchants Ass'n, 564 U.S. at 841 (Breyer, J., dissenting).
129. *Id.* at 790. Justice Breyer disagreed. *See id.* at 849, 851, 852.
130. *Id.* at 789 (quoting Cal. Civ. Code Ann. § 1746 (d)(1).
131. *Id.* at 799 (quoting United States v. Playboy Entertainment Group, 529 U.S. 803, 822–823 (2000)).
132. *Id.* at 799.
133. Andrea Dworkin, *Pornography Happens to Women, in* THE PRICE WE PAY: THE CASE AGAINST RACIST SPEECH, HATE PROPAGANDA, AND PORNOGRAPHY, eds. Laura J. Lederer and Richard Delgado (New York: Hill and Wang, 1995), 128–129.
134. Catharine A. MacKinnon, *Pornography as Trafficking,* 26 MICH. J. OF INT'L L. 1–15 (2005).
135. Letter from Steve Johnson to John M. Harrington, June 5, 1986, 1, 2.
136. R.A.V., 505 U.S. at 390.
137. 249 U.S. at 52.
138. 395 U.S. at 449.
139. 564 U.S. at 791.
140. 561 U.S. 1. (And *Stevens* did not so hold.)
141. 564 at 792.
142. 561 U.S. at 39.
143. City of Los Angeles v. Alameda Books, 535 U.S. 425 (2002).
144. 535 U.S. at 256–258.
145. Brief for American Booksellers Ass'n, Inc. et al. as Amicus Curiae Supporting Respondent, New York v. Ferber, 458 U.S. 747 (1982) (No. 81-55), 1982 WL 608539.
146. *See* Andrews v. Law Society of British Columbia, 1 S.C.R. 143 (Can. 1985); R. v. Kapp, 2 S.C.R. 483 (Can. 2008).
147. R. v. Keegstra, 3 S.C.R. 697 (Can. 1990).
148. Offenses Tending to Corrupt Morals, R.S.C., c C-46 § 163(8) (Can. 1985).
149. *See* Butler v. R., 1 S.C.R. 452 (Can. 1992).
150. JOHN STUART MILL, ON LIBERTY (London: John W. Parker and Son, 1859), 53.

Chapter 10

1. *See* INTERAGENCY WORKING GRP. ON SOC. COST OF CARBON, U.S. GOV'T, TECHNICAL SUPPORT DOCUMENT: TECHNICAL UPDATE OF THE SOCIAL COST OF CARBON FOR REGULATORY IMPACT ANALYSIS UNDER EXECUTIVE ORDER 12866 (2013), 2–3, https://www.whitehouse. gov/sites/default/files/omb/inforeg/social_cost_of_carbon_for_ria_2013_update.pdf.
2. *See* CASS R. SUNSTEIN, THE COST-BENEFIT STATE: THE FUTURE OF REGULATORY PROTECTION (Chicago: Section of Administrative Law and Regulatory Practice, American

Bar Association, 2002). On the philosophical issues, *see* MATTHEW D. ADLER, WELL-BEING AND FAIR DISTRIBUTION: BEYOND COST-BENEFIT ANALYSIS (New York: Oxford University Press, 2011).

3. *See* Exec. Order No. 13,563, 76 Fed. Reg. 3,821 (Jan. 18, 2011), *supra* note 2. Distributive impacts, equity, and human dignity may all be taken into account. *Id.*

4. *See, e.g.,* Whitman v. American Trucking, 531 U.S. 457 (2001).

5. *See* CASS R. SUNSTEIN, VALUING LIFE: HUMANIZING THE REGULATORY STATE (Chicago: University of Chicago Press, 2014).

6. For a vivid account, see FRANK ACKERMAN AND LISA HEINZERLING, PRICELESS: ON KNOWING THE PRICE OF EVERYTHING AND THE VALUE OF NOTHING (New York: New Press, 2004).

7. *Id.; see also* JALE TOSUN, RISK REGULATION IN EUROPE: ASSESSING THE APPLICATION OF THE PRECAUTIONARY PRINCIPLE (New York: Springer, 2012).

8. *Id.*

9. *See* DANIEL STEEL, PHILOSOPHY AND THE PRECAUTIONARY PRINCIPLE: SCIENCE, EVIDENCE, AND ENVIRONMENTAL POLICY (Cambridge: Cambridge University Press, 2014), 25; Cass R. Sunstein, *Irreversible and Catastrophic*, 91 CORNELL L. REV. 841 (2006); *see also* JON ELSTER, EXPLAINING TECHNICAL CHANGE: A CASE STUDY IN THE PHILOSOPHY OF SCIENCE (New York: Cambridge University Press, 1983), 185.

10. *See* INDUR M. GOKLANY, THE PRECAUTIONARY PRINCIPLE: A CRITICAL APPRAISAL OF ENVIRONMENTAL RISK ASSESSMENT (Washington, DC: CATO, 2001).

11. *See* Nassim Nicholas Taleb et al., *The Precautionary Principle (with Application to the Genetic Modification of Organisms)* (NYU School Engineering Working Paper Series, 2014), 2, https://arxiv.org/pdf/1410.5787.pdf.

12. On the underlying issues, *see* FREDERICK F. SCHAUER, FREE SPEECH: A PHILOSOPHICAL ENQUIRY (New York: Cambridge University Press, 1982).

13. *See* AMARTYA SEN, POVERTY AND FAMINES: AN ESSAY ON ENTITLEMENT AND DEPRIVATION (New York: Oxford University Press, 1983).

14. *See* Amartya Sen, *Utilitarianism and Welfarism*, 76 J. PHIL. 463 (1979).

15. *See* MARC SAGEMAN, MISUNDERSTANDING TERRORISM (Philadelphia: University of Pennsylvania Press, 2017).

16. 341 U.S. 494 (1951).

17. *Id.*

18. *Id.* at 510.

19. *Id.*

20. United States v. Carroll Towing Co., 159 F.2d 169 (2d. Cir. 1947).

21. Whitney v. California, 274 U.S. 357 (1927) (Brandeis, J., concurring).

22. *Id.*

23. *Id.*

24. *See* Masses Pub. Co. v. Patten, 244 F. 535, 541 (S.D.N.Y.), rev'd, 246 F. 24 (2d Cir. 1917).

25. Gerald Gunther, *Learned Hand and the Origins of Modern First Amendment Doctrine. Some Fragments of History*, 27 STAN. L. REV. 719, 770 (1975).

26. *Id.* at 725.

27. *See* JOHN STUART MILL, 'ON LIBERTY' AND OTHER WRITINGS, ed. Stefan Collini (New York: Cambridge University Press, 1989 [1859]).

28. If people are risk seeking or risk averse, of course, expected value might not be enough.

29. *See* THOMAS HEALY, THE GREAT DISSENT: HOW OLIVER WENDELL HOLMES CHANGED HIS MIND—AND CHANGE THE HISTORY OF FREE SPEECH IN AMERICA (New York: Metropolitan Books, Henry Holt and Company, 2013).

30. 395 U.S. 444 (1969).

31. *See* Memorandum from Carlos Monje, Assistant Sec'y for Pol'y, Dep't of Transp. & Kathryn Thomson, Gen. Counsel, Dep't of Transp., to Secretarial Officers and Modal Administrators (June 17, 2015), https://www.transportation.gov/sites/dot.gov/files/docs/VSL2015_0.pdf.

32. *See* AMARTYA SEN, DEVELOPMENT AS FREEDOM (New York: Knopf, 1999).

33. *See* GEOFFREY R. STONE, PERILOUS TIMES: FREE SPEECH IN WARTIME FROM THE SEDITION ACT OF 1798 TO THE WAR ON TERRORISM (New York: W. W. Norton, 2004).

34. *See* CASS R. SUNSTEIN, SIMPLER: THE FUTURE OF GOVERNMENT (New York: Simon and Schuster, 2013).

35. *See* Michael Greenstone, *Toward a Culture of Persistent Regulatory Experimentation and Evaluation, in* NEW PERSPECTIVES ON REGULATION, eds. David Moss and John Cisternino (Cambridge: Tobin Project, 2009), 111.

Chapter 11

1. *The Appointment of the Judges*, Const. Ct. S. Afr., http://www.constitutionalcourt.org.za/site/thecourt/history.htm#judges (last visited Oct. 8, 2017).

2. *See, e.g.,* W. Va. State Bd. of Educ. v. Barnette, 319 U.S. 624, 642 ("If there is any fixed star in our constitutional constellation, it is that no official, high or petty, can prescribe what shall be orthodox in politics, nationalism, religion, or other matters of opinion or force citizens to confess by word or act their faith therein.").

3. The First Amendment's centrality to the American ethos has also been explored by prominent American constitutional scholars. *See, e.g.,* Akhil Reed Amar, *The First Amendment's Firstness*, 47 U.C. DAVIS L. REV. 1015, 1029 (2014) (noting that the Amendment "truly is first in our text and first in our hearts"); Edmond Cahn, *The Firstness of the First Amendment*, 65 YALE L.J. 464, 474 (1956) ("In insisting on the firstness of the First Amendment, modern thinkers . . . are continuing and advancing the American vision of a good society.").

4. This statutory regime of censorship included the Riotous Assemblies Act of 1956, the Unlawful Organizations Act of 1960, the Sabotage Act of 1967, and the Internal Securities Act of 1976. *See generally* CHRISTOPHER MERRETT, A CULTURE OF CENSORSHIP: SECRECY AND INTELLECTUAL REPRESSION IN SOUTH AFRICA (Macon, GA: Mercer University Press, 1995).

5. For a comprehensive list of South Africans who were subject to such orders, *see Banned*, S. Afr. Hist. Online, http://www.sahistory.org.za/article/banned (last visited Oct. 8, 2017).

6. *See* Suppression of Communism Act 44 of 1950 § 9 (S. Afr.).

7. *See* ALBIE SACHS, JUSTICE IN SOUTH AFRICA (Berkeley: University of California Press, 1973).

8. *See* Albie Sachs, *A Freedom Charter for South African Artists*, 9, no. 4 STAFFRIDER, 45, 48 (1991).

9. As authorized by the Publications and Entertainment Act 26 of 1963 (S. Afr.).

10. *See, e.g.,* ROBERT ROSS, A CONCISE HISTORY OF SOUTH AFRICA (Cape Town: Cambridge University Press, 2008), 114 (noting that the Publications Control Board reflexively banned the children's book simply "on the basis of its name").

11. NELSON MANDELA, *Freedom in Our Lifetime, in* MANDELA, TAMBO, AND THE AFRICAN NATIONAL CONGRESS: THE STRUGGLE AGAINST APARTHEID, 1948–1990, eds. Sheridan Jones and R. Hunt Davis Jr. (Oxford: Oxford University Press, 1991), 48–49.

12. For an original perspective on the religious freedom philosophies that animated the First Amendment's drafting, *see* JAMES MADISON, A MEMORIAL AND REMONSTRANCE AGAINST RELIGIOUS ASSESSMENTS (1785).

13. *See, e.g., Religion and the Founding of the American Republic: America as a Religious Refuge*, Libr. Cong., https://www.loc.gov/exhibits/religion/rel01.html (last visited Oct. 8, 2017).

14. *See generally* Evarts B. Greene, *The Anglican Outlook on the American Colonies in the Early Eighteenth Century*, 20 AM. HIST. REV. 64 (1914).

15. *By the King, a Proclamation, for Suppressing Rebellion and Sedition*, Nat'l Archives, http://www.archives.gov/historical-docs/todays-doc/?dod-date=823 (last visited Oct. 8, 2017) (displaying King George III's 1775 proclamation that "transformed loyal subjects into traitorous rebels").

16. Notwithstanding Thomas Jefferson's famous claim that the principle of equality is "self-evident." THE DECLARATION OF INDEPENDENCE para. 2 (U.S. 1776).

17. *See* STEPHEN E. AMBROSE, TO AMERICA: PERSONAL REFLECTIONS OF AN HISTORIAN (New York: Simon and Schuster, 2002), 2 (describing Jefferson as "a racist, incapable of rising above the thought of his time and place, and willing to profit from slave labor").

18. S. AFR. CONST. pmbl., 1996 ("We, the people of South Africa, [r]ecognise the injustices of our past").

19. *Id.* at ch. 1, § 1(a)–(d).
20. *Id.* at ch. 2.
21. *Id.* at ch. 3–5 (providing for cooperative government, parliament, and the president and national executive, respectively).
22. *Id.* at ch. 2, § 7(1).
23. *Id.* at ch. 2, § 9–16.
24. *Id.* at ch. 2, § 16(1)(a)–(d).
25. *Id.* at ch. 2, § 16(2)(a)–(c).
26. *Id.* at ch. 2, § 36(1) (setting out the limitation of rights).
27. *See* Criminal Procedure Act 51 of 1977 § 154(3) (S. Afr.).
28. *See, e.g.,* Mtyhopo v. South African Municipal Workers Union National Provident Fund 2015 (11) BCLR 1393 (CC) (S. Afr.) (holding that a "prior restraint of speech is among the most serious infringements of freedom of expression" and that an interdict could not be constitutionally granted against a disgruntled union member).
29. N.Y. Times v. United States, 403 U.S. 713 (1971).
30. N.Y. Times v. Sullivan, 376 U.S. 254 (1964).
31. SIMON S. C. TAY, *The Future of Civil Society: What Next?,* in SINGAPORE IN THE NEW MILLENNIUM: CHALLENGES FACING THE CITY-STATE, ed. Derek da Cunhua (Singapore: Institute of Southeast Asian Studies, 2002), 88.
32. Kenya's High Court only just struck down the country's criminal defamation law as unconstitutional in February 2017. *See* Nani Jansen Reventlow and Catherine Anite, *Kenyan Court Knocks Down Criminal Defamation, Safeguards Freedom of Expression,* BERKMAN KLEIN CTR. FOR INTERNET & SOC'Y (Feb. 8, 2017), http://clinic.cyber.harvard.edu/2017/02/08/kenyan-court-knocks-down-criminal-defamation-safeguards-freedom-of-expression/.
33. Malaysia's Court of Appeal also recently abandoned the country's decades-long defamation law regime, holding that "public officials must be open to public criticism and hence should be precluded from suing the media for defamation in their official capacity." Bernama, *Court of Appeal Says Public Officials Should Be Open to Criticism,* NEW STRAIT TIMES (June 9, 2016), http://www.nst.com.my/news/2016/06/150787/court-appeal-says-public-officials-should-be-open-criticism.
34. N.Y. *Times,* 403 U.S. at 723–724 (Douglas, J., concurring) (noting that "[the] dominant purpose of the First Amendment was to prohibit the widespread practice of governmental suppression of embarrassing information").
35. *See, e.g.,* Observer & Guardian v. United Kingdom, 216 Eur. Ct. H.R. (ser. A) (1991) (holding that injunctions restraining the publication of reporting on *Spycatcher,* an ex-MI5 officer's candid biography, interfered with the right of freedom of expression under the European Convention on Human Rights).
36. Most famously noting "that debate on public issues should be uninhibited, robust, and wide-open." *Sullivan,* 376 U.S. at 270.
37. *Id.* at 300 (Goldberg, J., concurring).
38. Collin v. Smith, 578 F.2d 1197 (7th Cir. 1978), *cert. denied,* 439 U.S. 916 (1978).
39. Strafgesetzbuch [StGB] [Criminal Code], § 130, *translation at* http://www.gesetze-im-internet.de/englisch_stgb/englisch_stgb.html#p1246 (Ger.).
40. *See* Carole Cadwalladr, *Antisemite, Holocaust Denier . . . Yet David Irving Claims Fresh Support,* GUARDIAN (Jan. 14, 2017), http://www.theguardian.com/uk-news/2017/jan/15/david-irving-youtube-inspiring-holocaust-deniers.
41. *See* R.A.V. v. City of St. Paul, Minn., 505 U.S. 377, 391 (1992) (holding that an ordinance that had been narrowly construed by the Minnesota Supreme Court to only apply to "symbols or displays that amount to 'fighting words'" was still facially unconstitutional because its prohibitions were content based). *But see* Virginia v. Black, 538 U.S. 343, 362 (2003) (holding that a Virginia statute that bans cross burning *with intent to discriminate* is constitutional because it "does not single out for opprobrium" speech about "specified disfavored topics") (emphasis added).
42. *Cf.* Antonin Scalia, *Originalism: The Lesser Evil,* 57 U. CIN. L. REV. 849 (1989).
43. Print Media South Africa and Another v. Minister of Home Affairs and Another 2012 (6) SA 443 (CC) (S. Afr.).
44. Case and Another v. Minister of Safety and Security and Others, Curtis v. Minister of Safety and Security and Others 1996 (3) SA 617 (CC) (S. Afr.).

45. South African National Defence Union v. Minister of Defence 1999 (4) SA 469 (CC) (S. Afr.).
46. De Reuck v. Director of Public Prosecutions (Witwatersrand Local Division) and Others 2004 (1) SA 406 (CC) (S. Afr.).
47. In accordance with Section 36(1) of the Constitution of South Africa. See supra note 26 and accompanying text.
48. Sullivan, 376 U.S. at 280.
49. See Gertz v. Robert Welch, Inc., 418 U.S. 323, 342 (1974).
50. Khumalo and Others v. Holomisa 2002 (5) SA 401 (CC) at para. 18 (S. Afr.).
51. Id. at para. 44–47.
52. Id. at para. 43.
53. S. AFR. CONST., ch. 2, § 39(2), 1996.
54. Id. at ch. 2, § 39(1)(a)–(c).
55. Khumalo and Others v. Holomisa 2002 (5) SA 401 (CC) at para. 43 (S. Afr.) (holding that "the defence of reasonable publication avoids therefore a winner-takes-all result and establishes a proper balance between freedom of expression and the value of human dignity").
56. Id. (noting that "the defence of reasonable publication will encourage editors and journalists to act with due care and respect for the individual interest in human dignity prior to publishing defamatory material, without precluding them from publishing such material when it is reasonable to do so").
57. See 2017 World Press Index, Reporters without Borders, http://rsf.org/en/ranking (last visited Oct. 8, 2017) (ranking South Africa 27th out of 180 countries, above both the United States and the United Kingdom).
58. Complaints, Press Council, http://presscouncil.org.za/Complaints?prev=http%3A%2F%2Fpresscouncil.org.za%2F (last visited Oct. 8, 2017) (setting out available sanctions for press transgressions ranging from "wrongly spelled names" to "inaccurate or unfair reporting" and "allowing commercial, political, personal or other non-professional considerations to influence or slant reporting").
59. Media, Diversity, and Ownership, Afr. Nat'l Cong., http://www.anc.org.za/docs/discus/2010/mediad.pdf (last visited Oct. 8, 2017) (republishing a 2010 ANC Discussion Document that proposed a media appeals tribunal). This proposal prompted significant backlash in the media and has not been adopted. See Zach Zagger, South Africa Journalists "Appalled" by Proposed Media Regulation, JURIST (Aug. 8, 2010), http://www.jurist.org/paperchase/2010/08/south-africa-journalists-appalled-by-proposed-media-regulation.php.
60. See David Smith, Jacob Zuma Goes to Court over Painting Depicting His Genitals, GUARDIAN (May 21, 2012), http://www.theguardian.com/world/2012/may/21/jacob-zuma-court-painting-genitals.
61. Campbell v. Acuff-Rose Music, Inc., 510 U.S. 569 (1994).
62. See, e.g., Laugh It Off Promotions CC v. South African Breweries International (Finance) BV t/a Sabmark International and Another 2006 (1) SA 144 (CC) at para. 77 (S. Afr.) (exploring the "paradox of parody").
63. ERIC SCHLOSSER, REEFER MADNESS: SEX, DRUGS, AND CHEAP LABOR IN THE AMERICAN BLACK MARKET (Boston: Houghton Mifflin, 2003), 113–114.
64. See generally CATHERINE A. MACKINNON, ONLY WORDS (Cambridge, MA: Harvard University Press, 1993).
65. Phillips and Another v. Director of Public Prosecutions and Others 2003 (3) SA 345 (CC) (S. Afr.).
66. Id. at para. 30.
67. Islamic Unity Convention v. Independent Broadcasting Authority 2002 (4) SA 294 (CC) (S. Afr.).
68. Id. at para. 2.
69. Id. at para. 21.
70. Id. at para. 24 (quoting S v. Mamabolo 2001 (3) SA 409 (CC) at para. 37 (S. Afr.)).
71. See supra notes 22–25 and accompanying text.
72. See supra note 67, at para. 27.
73. Id.
74. Id. at para. 28.
75. Id. (quoting S v. Mamabolo 2001 (3) SA 409 (CC) at para. 41 (S. Afr.)).

76. *Id.* at para 43.
77. *Id.*
78. *Id.*
79. *Id.* at para 49.
80. *Equality Courts*, Dep't Just. and Const. Dev., http://www.justice.gov.za/EQCact/eqc_faq. html (last visited Oct. 8, 2017).
81. ANC v. Sparrow 2016 ZAEQC 1 (S. Afr.).
82. *See*, e.g., *South African Fined $10,000 over "Monkey" Facebook Post*, ASSOCIATED PRESS (June 10, 2016), http://www.sandiegouniontribune.com/sdut-south-african-fined-10000-over-monkey-facebook-2016jun10-story.html.
83. *See supra* note 25 and accompanying text.
84. *See supra* note 26 and accompanying text.
85. Cape Party-Kaapse Party v. Iziko-S. Afr. Nat'l Gallery EC02/2017 (EQC) (S. Afr.).
86. The magistrate judge went on to note: "The fear of losing the debate in the battle of ideas, is not enough reason to take the battle to the legal trenches and hope to have the canons of judgments from the courtrooms to shoot down and repress, curb or kill the opposing views." *Id.* at para. 29.
87. President of the Republic of South Africa and Another v. Hugo 1997 (4) SA 1 (CC) at para. 41 (S. Afr.) ("The prohibition on unfair discrimination in the interim Constitution seeks not only to avoid discrimination against people who are members of disadvantaged groups. It seeks more than that. At the heart of the prohibition of unfair discrimination lies a recognition that the purpose of our new constitutional and democratic order is the establishment of a society in which all human beings will be accorded equal dignity and respect regardless of their membership of particular groups.").
88. City Council of Pretoria v. Walker 1998 (2) SA 363 (CC) (S. Afr.).
89. *Id.* at para. 102.
90. *Id.* at para. 132.
91. South African Human Rights Commission v. Qwelane; Qwelane v. Minister for Justice and Correctional Services [2017] ZAGPJHC 218 (S. Afr.).
92. *Id.*
93. In 2016, the Department of Justice and Constitutional Development invited comment on new hate speech legislation, which criminalizes the intentional communication of hate speech, including communications that "stir up violence against, or bring into contempt or ridicule, any person or group of persons, based on race, gender, sex." Invitation to Comment on the Prevention and Combatting of Hate Crimes and Hate Speech Bill, GN 698 of GG 40367 (24 Oct. 2016).
94. The debate surrounding the bill has included vigorous critiques and defenses. *See*, e.g., Phephelaphi Dube, *Rescuing the "Hate Speech Bill,"* NEWS24 (March 7, 2017), http:// www.news24.com/Columnists/GuestColumn/rescuing-the-hate-speech-bill-20170307 (arguing that the bill "will not pass constitutional muster"); Wendy Isaack, *South African Move on Hate Speech a Step Too Far*, HUMAN RIGHTS WATCH (Feb. 21, 2017), https:// www.hrw.org/news/2017/02/21/south-african-move-hate-speech-step-too-far (arguing that "the draft includes an over-broad and vague provision criminalizing hate speech that threatens freedom of expression, a fundamental human right"); Kyle Bowles, *The Hate Crimes Bill: Not All Doom and Gloom*, LEXOLOGY (April 26, 2017), https://www.lexology. com/library/detail.aspx?g=92f0c277-afad-40da-9803-dd60ac79b994 (stating that "while the Hate Crimes Bill may be flawed in various respects, its potential positive impact, especially in the context of the LGBTI community, must not be ignored").
95. Virginia v. Black, 538 U.S. 343, 362 (2003); *see also supra* note 41 and accompanying text.
96. *See generally Ku Klux Klan: A History of Racism*, Southern Poverty L. Ctr., http://www. splcenter.org/20110301/ku-klux-klan-history-racism (last visited Oct. 8, 2017).
97. LEONARD J. MOORE, CITIZEN KLANSMAN: THE KU KLUX KLAN IN INDIANA, 1921–1928 (Chapel Hill: University of North Carolina Press, 1991), 13.
98. *Lynching Mob in Ohio: Militia Called Out in Springfield – Negroes Taken to Dayton*, N.Y. TIMES (Feb. 28, 1906), at 1 (on file with author).
99. Steven Cuevas, *New Photo Exhibit Examines California's History of Lynching and Frontier Justice*, SOUTHERN CAL. PUB. RADIO (April 12, 2012), http://www.scpr.org/news/2012/ 04/12/32004/photo-exhibit-examines-californias-history-lynchin/.
100. Citizens United v. Fed. Election Comm'n, 558 U.S. 310 (2010).

Chapter 12

1. THE SOCIALIST CONST. OF THE DEMOCRATIC PEOPLE'S REPUBLIC OF KOREA, art. 67 ("Citizens are guaranteed freedom of speech, of the press, of assembly, demonstration and association.").
2. Schenck v. United States, 249 U.S. 47 (1919).
3. ELIZABETH POWERS, ED., FREEDOM OF SPEECH: HISTORY OF AN IDEA (Lewisburg, PA: Bucknell University Press, 2011).
4. GEORGE ATHAN BILLIAS, AMERICAN CONSTITUTIONALISM HEARD ROUND THE WORLD, 1776–1989 (New York: New York University Press, 2011).
5. Indeed, for constitutions written in the current wave, since the end of the Cold War, it is as essential as saying something about the military, and comparable to mentioning an entire branch of government. Only a handful of countries have a constitution in force that does not include freedom of expression. These include dictatorships like Brunei, Qatar, and Iran, but also, notably, Australia, which does not have a bill of rights at all. Iran's constitution includes a mention of freedom of expression in media, subject to Islamic criteria and public policy.
6. LOUIS HENKIN, THE AGE OF RIGHTS (New York: Columbia University Press, 1990). Professors Law and Versteeg call it "rights creep." David S. Law and Mila Versteeg, *The Evolution and Ideology of Global Constitutionalism*, 99, no. 5 CAL. L. REV. 1170 (Oct. 2011). Our own data show that the first modern constitutions, those written before 1825, contained only about a dozen rights from our survey, on average. This number had increased to about two dozen by the start of the twentieth century (1890–1910) and to just under three dozen in constitutions written just after World War II (1945–1955). This pattern broke around 1960. Since then, we have observed an explosion in the number of rights in constitutions, so that those written in recent years (2005–2015) entrench, on average, more than five dozen distinct rights.
7. G.A. Res. 217 (III) A, Universal Declaration of Human Rights (Dec. 10, 1948); G.A. Res. 2200A (XXI), International Covenant on Civil and Political Rights (Dec. 16, 1966); G.A. Res. 2200A (XXI), International Covenant on Economic, Social and Cultural Rights (Dec. 16 1966).
8. Zachary Elkins, Tom Ginsburg, and Beth Simmons, *Getting to Rights: Treaty Ratification, Constitutional Convergence, and Human Rights Practice*, 51, no. 4 HARV. J. OF INT'L L. 201–234 (2013).
9. IAN CRAM, CONTESTED WORDS: LEGAL RESTRICTIONS ON FREEDOM OF SPEECH IN LIBERAL DEMOCRACIES (Bodmin: MPG Books Ltd., 2006); ERIC BARENDT, FREEDOM OF SPEECH, 2nd ed., (New York: Oxford University Press, 2007); RONALD J. KROTOSYNSKI, THE FIRST AMENDMENT IN CROSS-CULTURAL PERSPECTIVE: A COMPARATIVE LEGAL ANALYSIS (New York: New York University Press, 2006); PÉTER MOLNÁR, ED., FREE SPEECH AND CENSORSHIP AROUND THE GLOBE (Budapest: Central European University Press, 2014).
10. Eduardo Andres Bertoni, *The Inter-American Court of Human Rights and the European Court of Human Rights: A Dialogue on Freedom of Expression Standards*, 3 EUR. HUM. L. REV. 332–352 (2009).
11. VICKI JACKSON, CONSTITUTIONAL ENGAGEMENT IN A TRANSNATIONAL ERA (New York: Oxford University Press, 2012); Melissa A. Waters, *The Role of Transnational Judicial Dialogue in Shaping Transnational Speech: International Jurisdictional Conflicts in Hate Speech and Defamation Law, in* PROGRESS IN INTERNATIONAL LAW, eds. Russell Miller and Rebecca Bratspies (Leiden: Martinu Nijhoff, 2008), 473–490.
12. Case of Marcel Claude Reyes et al. v. Chile, Inter-Am. Ct. H. R. (ser. C) para. 90–91 (Sept. 19, 2006). In the European case, it comes from the right to freedom of expression itself in Article 10 of the European Convention on Human Rights.
13. 395 U.S. 444 (1969).
14. Moshe Cohen-Eliya and Iddo Porat, *American Balancing and German Proportionality: The Historical Origins*, 8, no. 2 INT'L J. OF CONST. L. 263–286 (2010).
15. *National Security Act* art. 7(1).
16. CONST. OF THE REPUBLIC OF KOREA, art. 21(1) (speech); art. 22(1) (academic study); art. 19 (conscience).
17. Kuk Cho, *Tension between the National Security Law and Constitutionalism in South Korea: Security for What?*, 15 B.U. INT'L L.J. 125, 169 (1997).

18. His phrasing subsequently influenced a Supreme Court National Security Agency (NSA) case, on May 31, 1992, where the minority argued that the threat must be a "concrete and possible danger" for prosecution, under Korea's "liberal democratic basic order."

19. Cho, *Tension between the National Security Law and Constitutionalism in South Korea: Security for What?, supra* note 18, at 161.

20. Stephen Haggard and Jong-Sung You, *Freedom of Expression in South Korea*, 45, no. 1 J. OF CONTEMP. ASIA 167–179 (2015).

21. HCJ 73/53 Kol Ha'am v. Minister of Interior, 7 PD 1140 (1953).

22. 250 U.S. 616 (1919).

23. 274 U.S. 357 (1927).

24. *See generally*, Suzie Navot, *Israel: Creating a Constitution—The Use of Foreign Precedents by the Supreme Court (1994–2010), in* THE USE OF FOREIGN PRECEDENTS BY CONSTITUTIONAL JUDGES, eds. Tania Groppi and Marie-Claire Ponthoreau (Oxford: Hart Publishing, 2013).

25. HCJ 7052/03 Adalah v. The Minister of Interior, 61(2) PD 202 (2006). *See also* Aharon Barak, *Freedom of Speech in Israel: The Impact of the American Constitution*, 8 TEL AVIV UNIV. STUDIES IN L. 241 (1988); DANIEL FRIEDMAN, THE PURSE AND THE SWORD: THE TRIALS OF ISRAEL'S LEGAL REVOLUTION (New York: Oxford University Press, 2016).

26. AHARON BARAK, PROPORTIONALITY: CONSTITUTIONAL RIGHTS AND THEIR LIMITATIONS (Cambridge: Cambridge University Press, 2012).

27. Pnina Lahav, *American Influence on Israel's Jurisprudence of Free Speech*, 9 HASTINGS CONST. L. Q. 21 (1981), citing the example of Ha'aretz v. Electric Company, 32(iii) PD 337 (1977).

28. *See* HCJ 316/03 Bakri v Film Censorship Board, 58(1) IsrSC 249 (2003).

29. Akiko Ejima, *A Gap between the Apparent and Hidden Attitudes of the Supreme Court of Japans towards Foreign Precedents, in* THE USE OF FOREIGN PRECEDENTS BY CONSTITUTIONAL JUDGES, eds. Tania Groppi and Marie-Claire Ponthoreau (Oxford: Hart Publishing, 2013), 273–297.

30. Hakata Station Case [Sup. Ct.] November 26, 1969, Keishu 23(11), 1490.

31. Sarufutsu Case [Sup. Ct.] November 6, 1974, Keishu 28(9), 393.

32. The *Lady Chatterly's Lover* Case [Sup. Ct.], March 13, 1957, Keishu 11(3), 997.

33. Shigenori Matsui, *Freedom of Expression in Japan*, 38 OSAKA UNIV. L. REV. 13–43, 23 (1991).

34. [Sup. Ct.] September 28, 1990, Keishu 44(6).

35. Kim Lane Scheppele, *Democracy by Judiciary (or, Why Courts Can Sometimes Be More Democratic Than Parliaments), in* RETHINKING THE RULE OF LAW AFTER COMMUNISM, eds. Wojciech Sadurski, Martin Krygier, and Adam Czarnota (Budapest: Central European University Press, 2003).

36. Zoltán Szente, *Hungary: Unsystematic and Incoherent Borrowing of Law. The Use of Foreign Judicial Precedents in the Jurisprudence of the Constitutional Court, 1999–2010, in* THE USE OF FOREIGN PRECEDENTS BY CONSTITUTIONAL JUDGES, eds. Tania Groppi and Marie-Claire Ponthoreau (Oxford: Hart Publishing, 2013).

37. Decision 30/1992 (V.26) AB határozat (Constitutional Court of Hungary). *See* Peter Molnar, *Towards Improved Law and Policy on "Hate Speech"—The "Clear and Present Danger" Test in Hungary, in* EXTREME SPEECH AND DEMOCRACY, eds. Ivan Hare and James Weinstein (Oxford: Oxford University Press, 2009).

38. Michel Rosenfeld and András Sajó, *Spreading Liberal Constitutionalism: An Inquiry into the Fate of Free Speech in New Democracies, in* THE MIGRATION OF CONSTITUTIONAL IDEAS, ed. Sujit Choudhry (Cambridge: Cambridge University Press, 2006), 158 ("In many regards, the HCC adopted an absolutist theory of speech going beyond the US Supreme Court's position, i.e., it claimed that all speech is protected.").

39. *Id.* at 163. *See also* András Koltay, *The Appearance of The Clear and Present Danger Doctrine in Hungarian Hate Speech Laws and the Jurisprudence of the European Court of Human Rights*, SSRN (June 23, 2014), https://papers.ssrn.com/sol3/papers.cfm?abstract_id=2457903.

40. Arrowsmith v. United Kingdom, App. No. 7050/75, para. 95, 3 Eur. H.R. Rep. 218, 233 (1978).

41. Zana v. Turkey, App. No. 18954/91, 27 Eur. H.R. Rep. 667 (1997).

42. *Id.* at 691, para. 60.

43. Surek v. Turkey (No. 1), App. No. 26682/95; Surek v. Turkey (No. 3), App. No. 24735/95.

44. *Id.* (Bonello, J., partly dissenting).

45. David G. Barnum, *The Clear and Present Danger Test in Anglo-American and European Law*, 7 SAN DIEGO INT'L L. J. 263–292 (2006); Stefan Sottiaux, *The "Clear and Present Danger" Test in the Case Law of the European Court of Human Rights*, 63 ZEITSCHRIFT FÜR AUSLÄNDISCHES ÖFFENTLICHES RECHT UND VÖLKERRECHT 633–679 (2003).

46. Kim Lane Scheppele, *supra* note 36.

47. Fratanoló v. Hungary, Eur. Ct. H.R. App no. 29459/10 (2011) para. 25.

48. Human Rights Council, Rep. of the Special Rapporteur on the promotion and protection of the right to freedom of opinion and expression on his mission to Japan, U.N. Doc. A/HRC/ 35/22/Add.1.

49. Defined further as "social order" (社会秩序). The Liberal Democratic Party explanation points out that individuals who assert human rights should not cause nuisances to others. Lawrence Repeta, *Japan at Risk—The LDP's Ten Most Dangerous Proposals for Constitutional Change*, 11, issue 28, no. 3 JAPAN FOCUS (July 14, 2013), http://apjjf.org/2013/11/28/ Lawrence-Repeta/3969/article.html. As Repeta explains, "Although the public order limitation would apply to all constitutional rights, we can expect that it would have an especially powerful chilling effect on speech rights and other forms of protest. Every public march or other political demonstration slows traffic and causes 'nuisances' to others."

50. *See supra*, note 49.

51. U.N. Special Rapporteur on the right to privacy, Letter dated May 18, 2017, from the Special Rapporteur on the right to privacy to Prime Minister Shinzo Abe of Japan, U.N. Doc. OL JPN 3/2017 (May 18, 2017), http://www.ohchr.org/Documents/Issues/Privacy/OL_JPN.pdf.

52. *Defunded for Politics, Israeli Arab Theater Reaches Deal With State*, HAARETZ (March 29, 2016), http://www.haaretz.com/israel-news/.premium-1.711620; *The New Culture War in Israel*, ATLANTIC (Oct. 4, 2016), https://www.theatlantic.com/international/archive/2016/10/ israel-culture-regev-netanyahu-palestine/501245/.

53. *Attack on Free Speech or Reality Check? Israel Debates Code*, BLOOMBERG (June 26, 2017), https://www.bloomberg.com/news/articles/2017-06-25/attack-on-free-speech-or-reality-check-israel-code-fuels-debate; *U.S. Professors Who Fight Boycott of Israel Slam Plans to Gag Political Speech in Academia*, HAARETZ, June 28, 2017, http://www.haaretz.com/us-news/ .premium-1.798242; *Ethics Code Section Shushing Campus Political Speech Scrapped— Report*, TIMES OF ISRAEL (July 6, 2017), http://www.timesofisrael.com/liveblog_entry/ ethics-code-section-shushing-campus-political-speech-scrapped-report.

54. Peter Beaumont, *Israel Passes Law to Force NGOs to Reveal Foreign Funding*, GUARDIAN (July 12, 2016), https://www.theguardian.com/world/2016/jul/12/israel-passes-law-to-force-ngos-to-reveal-foreign-funding; Jonathan Lis et al., *Israel's Nationalist "Loyalty in Culture" Bill Passes Legal Test*, HAARETZ (Feb. 26, 2016), http://www.haaretz.com/israel-news/.premium-1.705312; Seymour D. Reich, *Israel's Assault on Democracy: Time to Speak Out*, JEWISH WEEK, April 26, 2016, http://jewishweek.timesofisrael.com/israels-assault-on-democracy-time-to-speak-out/; *The Economist Intelligence Unit's Democracy Index*, https://infographics.economist.com/2017/DemocracyIndex/.

55. Abrams v. United States, 250 U.S. 616 (1919); Gitlow v. New York, 268 U.S. 652 (1925); Dennis v, United States, 341 U.S. 494 (1951); Brandenburg v. Ohio, 395 U.S. 444 (1969).

Chapter 13

1. Franklin D. Roosevelt, Annual Message to Congress on the State of the Union, January 6, 1941. (The four freedoms were freedom of speech and belief and freedom from fear and want.)

2. G.A. Res. 217 (III) A, Universal Declaration of Human Rights (Dec. 10, 1948).

3. *See* Council of Europe, European Convention for the Protection of Human Rights and Fundamental Freedoms, November 4, 1950, 213 U.N.T.S. 221, E.T.S. 5, art. 10; Organization of American States, American Convention on Human Rights, November 22, 1969, O.A.S.T.S. No. 36, 1144 U.N.T.S. 123, art. 13; Organization of African Unity (OAU), African Charter on Human and Peoples' Rights ("Banjul Charter"), June 27, 1981, CAB/LEG/67/3 rev. 5, 21 I.L.M. 58 (1982), art. 9. The United States has signed, but not ratified, the American Convention.

4. UN General Assembly, Convention on the Prevention and Punishment of the Crime of Genocide, December 9, 1948, United Nations, Treaty Series, vol. 78, p. 277, art. III(c).

5. UN General Assembly, International Convention on the Elimination of All Forms of Racial Discrimination, December 21, 1965, United Nations, Treaty Series, vol. 660, p. 195 ("Race Convention"), art. 4.

6. 250 U.S. 616, 630 (1919).

7. Whitney v. California, 274 U.S. 357 (1927).

8. 310 U.S. 296 (1940).

9. 341 U.S. 494 (1951).

10. 315 U.S. 568 (1942).

11. 337 U.S. 1 (1949).

12. 343 U.S. 250 (1952).

13. 376 U.S. 254, 270 (1964).

14. 395 U.S. 444 (1969).

15. Collin v. Smith, 578 F.2d 1197 (7th Cir.), *cert. denied*, 439 U.S. 915 (1978).

16. LEE C. BOLLINGER, THE TOLERANT SOCIETY (New York: Oxford University Press, 1986), 31–33 and n. 47.

17. 505 U.S. 377 (1992).

18. 538 U.S. 343 (2003).

19. HIRAD ABTAHI AND PHILLIPA WEBB, THE GENOCIDE CONVENTION: THE TRAVAUX PRÉPARATOIRES (Leiden: Martinus Nijhoff Publishers, 2008), 237.

20. *Id.* at 239.

21. *Id.* at 376.

22. *Id.* at 903, 904, 906.

23. MARC J. BOSSUYT, GUIDE TO THE "TRAVAUX PRÉPARATOIRES" OF THE INTERNATIONAL COVENANT ON CIVIL AND POLITICAL RIGHTS (Dordrecht: Martinus Nijhoff Publishers, 1986), 392, 394–395.

24. UN General Assembly, International Covenant on Civil and Political Rights, December 16, 1966, United Nations, Treaty Series, vol. 999, p. 171, U.N. Doc. E/CN.4/433/Rev.2 (1950).

25. Document on Prevention of Discrimination and Protection of Minorities, proposal made by Mr. Borisov to the Sub-Commission, U.N. Doc. E/CN.4/Sub.2/21 (1947).

26. *Id.*; Memorandum [Received by the Secretariat from the Inter-Parliamentary Union Transmitting Extracts from Resolutions That May Be of Interest of the Commission on Human Rights]: 25/11/1947, U.N. Doc. E/CN.4/SR.35 (1947), at 11–12. The revised text stated: "Any advocacy of national, racial or religious hostility that constitutes an incitement to violence shall be prohibited by the law of the State."

27. Commission on Human Rights, Sub-Commission on the Prevention of Discrimination and the Protection of Minorities, U.N. Doc. E/CN.4/52, December 6, 1947, at 6.

28. As an example of such resurgence, the Soviet delegate pointed to Winston Churchill's "Iron Curtain" speech.

29. Commission on Human Rights, Summary Record of the One Hundred and Twenty-Third Meeting, U.N. Doc. E/CN.4/SR.123, June 10, 1949, at 4–5.

30. BOSSUYT, *supra* note 23, at 409.

31. *Id.* at 407.

32. Commission on Human Rights, Summary Record of the Hundred and Seventy-Fourth Meeting, U.N. Doc. E/CN.4/SR.174, May 8, 1950, at 6.

33. Commission on Human Rights, Summary Record of the Three Hundred and Twenty-First Meeting, U.N. Doc. E/CN.4/SR.321, June 3, 1952, at 4, 7.

34. U.N. Gen. Assembly, Third Comm., 16th Sess., U.N. Doc. A/C.3/SR.1083 (Oct. 25, 1961), paras. 57, 58 (fifty votes in favor, eighteen against, and fifteen abstentions).

35. GA Res. 1510 (XV) (Dec. 12, 1960); U.N. Gen. Assembly, Third Comm., Summary, U.N. Doc. A/C.3/SR.1165 (Oct. 29, 1962), para. 49.

36. PATRICK THORNBERRY, THE INTERNATIONAL CONVENTION ON THE ELIMINATION OF ALL FORMS OF RACIAL DISCRIMINATION: A COMMENTARY (Oxford: Oxford University Press, 2016), 43.

37. In 1948, the Soviet Union proposed that, inter alia, "organizations having a Nazi, fascist or anti-democratic character" should be forbidden by law. United Nations Economic and Social Council, Commission on Human Rights, Summary Record of the Ninety-Fifth Meeting, U.N. Doc. E/CN.4/95 (May 20, 1948), at 9, 30.

38. U.N. Gen. Assembly, Third Comm., Eighteenth Sess., Summary, U.N. Doc. A/C.3/L.1245 (five power proposal); UN Gen. Assembly, International Convention on the Elimination of All Forms of Racial Discrimination, December 21, 1965, United Nations, Treaty Series, vol. 660, p. 195, U.N. Doc. A/PV.1406 (Dec. 21, 1965), para. 70.

39. U.N. Gen. Assembly, Third Comm., Twentieth Sess., Summary, U.N. Doc. A/C.3/SR.1318, para. 59.

40. U.N. Doc. A/L.480.

41. THORNBERRY, supra note 36, at 275–278.

42. U.N. Gen. Assembly, Third Comm., Twentieth Sess., Summary, U.N. Doc. A/C.3/SR.1373 (Dec. 14, 1965), paras. 41–42.

43. 18 U.S.C. §§ 1091(c), 1093(3).

44. THORNBERRY, supra note 36, at 278–279, and n. 86.

45. Joint Declaration by the UN Special Rapporteur on Freedom of Opinion and Expression, the Organisation for Security and Cooperation in Europe Representative on Freedom of the Media, and the Organisation of American States Special Rapporteur on Freedom of Expression (2006), https://www.article19.org/data/files/pdfs/standards/four-mandates-dec-2006.pdf.

46. Opinion of the Committee on the Elimination of Racial Discrimination under Art. 14 of the International Convention on the Elimination of All Forms of Racial Discrimination (Eighty Second Session), TBB-Turkish Union in Berlin/Brandenburg v. Germany, U.N. Doc. CERD/C/82/D/48/2010 (2013); Opinion of the Committee on the Elimination of Racial Discrimination, Jewish Community of Oslo v. Norway, U.N. Doc. CERD/C/67/D/30/2003 (2005).

47. UN Committee on the Elimination of Racial Discrimination (CERD), General Recommendation No. 35: Combating Racist Hate Speech, September 26, 2013, U.N. Doc. CERD/C/GC/35 (Sept. 26, 2013), paras. 12, 15, 16, 25.

48. See e.g., UN Human Rights Committee, Concluding Observations on the Third Periodic Report of Kuwait, para. 40, U.N. Doc. CCPR/C/KWT/CO/3 (Aug. 11, 2016); UN Human Rights Committee, Concluding Observations on the Sixth Periodic Report of Ecuador, paras. 28–29, U.N. Doc. CCPR/C/ECU/CO/6 (Aug. 11, 2016); UN Human Rights Committee, Concluding Observations on the Seventh Periodic Report of the Russian Federation, paras. 10, 18–20, U.N. Doc. CCPR/C/RUS/CO/7 (April 28, 2015).

49. Opinion of the Human Rights Committee, Robert Faurisson v. France, Comm. No. 550/1993, U.N. Doc. CCPR/C/58/D/550/1993 (Views adopted November 1996).

50. UN Human Rights Committee, General Comment No. 34, U.N. Doc. CCPR/C/GC/34 (Sept. 12, 2011), paras. 47, 49; CERD Committee, General Recommendation No. 35, supra note 47.

51. Opinion of the Human Rights Committee, Comm. No. 2124/2011, U.N. Doc. CCPR/C/117/D/2124/2011 (Views adopted July 2016).

52. Individual opinion (concurring) of Committee Members Sarah Cleveland and Mauro Politi, Rabbae v. The Netherlands, Comm. No. 2124/2011, U.N. Doc. CCPR/C/117/D/2124/2011 (Views adopted July 2016).

53. App. No. 15890/89, 298 Eur. Ct. H.R. (ser. A) (1994).

54. App. No. 23131/03, 2004–XI Eur. Ct. H.R. (admissibility decision) (2004).

55. App. No. 26682/95, 1999–IV Eur. Ct. H.R. (Grand Chamber) (1999).

56. HRC, General Comment No. 34, supra note 50.

Chapter 14

1. Alex Hern, "Downright Orwellian": Journalists Decry Facebook Experiment's Impact on Democracy, GUARDIAN (Oct. 25, 2017), https://www.theguardian.com/technology/2017/oct/25/facebook-orwellian-journalists-democracy-guatemala-slovakia.

2. *Id.*

3. Stevan Dojcinovic, *Hey, Mark Zuckerberg: My Democracy Isn't Your Laboratory*, N.Y. TIMES (Nov. 15, 2017), https://www.nytimes.com/2017/11/15/opinion/serbia-facebook-explore-feed.html.

4. Adam Mosseri, *Clarifying Recent Tests*, FACEBOOK MEDIA (Oct. 23, 2017), https://media.fb.com/2017/10/23/clarifying-recent-tests/.

5. Adam Hudson, *How Google and the Big Tech Companies Are Helping Maintain America's Empire*, ALTERNET (Aug. 19, 2014), https://www.alternet.org/news-amp-politics/how-google-and-big-tech-companies-are-helping-maintain-americas-empire.

6. Matthew Prince, *Why We Terminated Daily Stormer*, CLOUDFLARE (Aug. 16, 2017), https://blog.cloudflare.com/why-we-terminated-daily-stormer/.

7. *Google News Boss: We're Not a Media Company*, BBC NEWS (Sept. 13, 2017), http://www.bbc.com/news/av/technology-41251243/donald-trump-is-symptom-of-click-bait-says-twitter-co-founder-evan-williams.

8. Erin Griffith, *Memo to Facebook: How to Tell If You're a Media Company*, WIRED (Oct. 12, 2017), https://www.wired.com/story/memo-to-facebook-how-to-tell-if-youre-a-media-company/.

9. Issie Lapowsky, *Chuck Johnson's Twitter Free Speech Suit Is Probably DOA*, WIRED (Jan. 11, 2018), https://www.wired.com/story/chuck-johnson-twitter-free-speech-lawsuit/.

10. Communications Decency Act of 1996, 47 U.S.C. § 230 (1996).

11. Ken Murray et al., *Staten Island Man Dies after NYPD Cop Puts Him in Chokehold—See the Video*, DAILY NEWS (Dec. 3, 2014), http://www.nydailynews.com/new-york/staten-island-man-dies-puts-choke-hold-article-1.1871486.

12. Andrea Peterson, *Why the Philando Castile Police-Shooting Video Disappeared from Facebook—Then Came Back*, WASH. POST (July 7, 2016), https://www.washingtonpost.com/news/the-switch/wp/2016/07/07/why-facebook-took-down-the-philando-castile-shooting-video-then-put-it-back-up/?utm_term=.8b836adc9685.

13. Erik Pedersen and Greg Evans, *Logan Paul: YouTube Deletes Business Ties with Social Star over Suicide Video*, DEADLINE (Jan. 10, 2018), http://deadline.com/2018/01/logan-paul-youtube-channel-axed-suicide-video-foursome-1202240266/.

14. Mia Shuang Li, *How WeChat Became the Primary News Source in China*, COLUM. JOURNALISM REV. (Jan. 10, 2018), https://www.cjr.org/tow_center/how-wechat-became-primary-news-source-china.php.

15. Kate Klonick, *The New Governors: The People, Rules, and Processes Governing Online Speech*, 131 HARV. L. REV. (forthcoming 2018), https://papers.ssrn.com/sol3/papers.cfm?abstract_id=2937985.

16. Michael Nunez, *Former Facebook Workers: We Routinely Suppressed Conservative News*, GIZMODO (May 9, 2016), https://gizmodo.com/former-facebook-workers-we-routinely-suppressed-conser-1775461006.

17. Mark Zuckerberg, FACEBOOK (May 18, 2016), https://www.facebook.com/zuck/posts/10102840575550621.

18. Margaret B. Kwoka, *Leaking and Legitimacy*, 48 U.C. DAVIS L. REV. 1387 (2015).

19. Mel Bunce et al., *"Our Newsroom in the Cloud": Slack, Virtual Newsrooms, and Journalistic Practice*, 00(0) NEW MEDIA & SOC'Y 1 (2017) http://journals.sagepub.com/doi/pdf/10.1177/1461444817748955.

20. Christine Schmidt, *Chinese Newsrooms Push Forward into AI Technology*, INT'L JOURNALISTS' NETWORK (Jan. 12, 2018), https://ijnet.org/en/blog/chinese-newsrooms-push-forward-ai-technology.

21. PAUL STARR, THE CREATION OF THE MEDIA (New York: Basic Books, 2004).

22. Jeffrey Toobin, *The Solace of Oblivion*, NEW YORKER (Sept. 29, 2014), https://www.newyorker.com/magazine/2014/09/29/solace-oblivion.

23. David Martin, *German Satire Magazine Titanic Back on Twitter Following "Hate Speech" Ban*, DEUTSCHE WELLE (Jan. 6, 2018), http://www.dw.com/en/german-satire-magazine-titanic-back-on-twitter-following-hate-speech-ban/a-42046485.

24. Megan Specia and Paul Mozur, *A War of Words Puts Facebook at the Center of Myanmar's Rohingya Crisis*, N.Y. TIMES (Oct. 27, 2017), https://www.nytimes.com/2017/10/27/world/asia/myanmar-government-facebook-rohingya.html.

25. REPORT FOR AMERICA, https://www.reportforamerica.org/ (last visited Jan. 27, 2018).

26. Zeynep Tufecki, *It's the (Democracy-Poisoning) Golden Age of Free Speech*, WIRED (Jan. 16, 2018), https://www.wired.com/story/free-speech-issue-tech-turmoil-new-censorship/.

27. Ethan Zuckerman, *Mistrust, Efficacy and the New Civics—A Whitepaper for the Knight Foundation*, ETHANZUCKERMAN.COM (Aug. 17, 2017), http://www.ethanzuckerman.com/blog/2017/08/17/mistrust-efficacy-and-the-new-civics-a-whitepaper-for-the-knight-foundation/.

28. Oliver Sylvain, *Intermediary Design Duties*, 50 CONN. L. REV. 1 (2017).

29. Danielle Keats Citron and Benjamin Wittes, *The Internet Will Not Break: Denying Bad Samaritans Section 230 Immunity*, 87 FORDHAM L. REV. (forthcoming 2018), https://papers.ssrn.com/sol3/papers.cfm?abstract_id=3007720.

30. Jack M. Balkin, *Information Fiduciaries and the First Amendment*, 49 U.C. DAVIS L. REV. 1183 (2016).

31. EU GENERAL DATA PROTECTION REGULATION, https://www.eugdpr.org/ (last visited Jan. 27, 2018).

Chapter 15

1. European Commission Press Release IP/17/1471, Code of Conduct on Countering Illegal Hate Speech Online (June 1, 2016), http://ec.europa.eu/justice/fundamental-rights/files/hate_speech_code_of_conduct_en.pdf.

2. European Commission Press Release IP/16/1937, European Commission and IT Companies Announce Code of Conduct on Illegal Online Hate Speech (May 31, 2016), http://europa.eu/rapid/press-release_IP-16-1937_en.htm.

3. *Removal Requests*, TWITTER (June 30, 2017), https://transparency.twitter.com/en/removal-requests.html; *Government Requests to Remove Content*, GOOGLE (Jan. 1, 2017), https://www.google.com/transparencyreport/removals/government/; *Content Removal Requests Report*, MICROSOFT (June 30, 2017), https://www.microsoft.com/about/csr/transparencyhub/crrr/; *Facebook Transparency Report*, FACEBOOK, https://govtrequests.facebook.com (last visited Jan. 9, 2018).

4. Communications Decency Act of 1996, 47 U.S.C. § 230 (2012).

5. Specifically, the Communications Decency Act provides that no provider or user of an interactive computer service shall be treated as the publisher or speaker of any information provided by another information content provider. Other important intermediary liability legislation includes the Digital Millennium Copyright Act, 17 U.S.C. § 512, which provides limited protection to internet service providers from civil liability for copyrighted material sent or posted through their service. To qualify for protection, the service providers must meet certain requirements, including providing a "notice and takedown" procedure through which rights holders can notify them of infringing content.

6. *See, e.g.,* Charles Riley, *Theresa May: Internet Must Be Regulated to Prevent Terrorism*, CNN (June 4, 2017), http://money.cnn.com/2017/06/04/technology/social-media-terrorism-extremism-london/index.html; Edward W. Felton, *Not an Easy Call*, N.Y. TIMES: ROOM FOR DEBATE (May 25, 2010), https://roomfordebate.blogs.nytimes.com/2010/05/25/should-government-take-on-facebook/ (the director of the Center for Information Technology Policy at Princeton University argues that "the strongest argument for regulation is that the notice-and-consent model" does not provide meaningful protection but instead is a scenario in which "users pretend to read privacy notices and sites pretend that users have made informed decisions to accept the notices' terms"); William McGeveran, *Save Facebook from Itself*, N.Y. TIMES: ROOM FOR DEBATE (May 25, 2010), https://roomfordebate.blogs.nytimes.com/2010/05/25/should-government-take-on-facebook/ (Professor William McGeveran, at the University of Minnesota Law School, argues that the Federal Trade Commission should establish some broad guidelines for social media. For example, he proposes that the rules might "require that users give explicit consent to make information accessible.").

7. *See, e.g.,* Leighton Andrews, *We Need European Regulation of Facebook and Google*, OPEN DEMOCRACY UK (Dec. 12, 2016), https://www.opendemocracy.net/uk/leighton-andrews/we-need-european-regulation-of-facebook-and-google ("What is needed is the necessary a

strategic alliance between other media companies, civil society organisations and academic specialists to drive an agenda forward to address the powers of internet intermediaries, in terms of content rules, competition issues and their dominance of the advertising markets which as we have seen has had the effect of undermining the newspaper industry in particular."); *Countering Islamic State Exploitation of the Internet*, COUNCIL ON FOREIGN REL. (June 18, 2015), https://www.cfr.org/report/countering-islamic-state-exploitation-internet (Council of Foreign Relations suggests that social media companies should "establish independent, periodic reviews of their implementation of content-based countermeasures" against violent extremism. "To achieve consistency across companies, this process could be centralized in an academic institution, such as Stanford University or the University of California, Berkeley.").

8. *See*, e.g., Kalev Leetaru, *Is the Internet Evolving Away from Freedom of Speech?*, FORBES (Jan. 15, 2016), https://www.forbes.com/sites/kalevleetaru/2016/01/15/is-the-internet-evolving-away-from-freedom-of-speech/#39b81dc66c37 ("[Social media companies'] shift towards moderation and censorship comes at great potential cost. Most importantly, the world we know today is a rich and vibrant quilt work of differing values, beliefs, and rules. The more the Internet takes on the role of enforcing a specific set of standards of online conduct, the more it finds itself mediating amongst these differing standards."); Kalev Leetaru, *Has Social Media Killed Free Speech?*, FORBES (Oct. 31, 2016), https://www.forbes.com/sites/kalevleetaru/2016/10/31/has-social-media-killed-free-speech/#115e147b46b1.

9. *See*, e.g., STAFF OF PERMANENT SUBCOMM. ON INVESTIGATIONS, 114TH CONG., REPORT ON BACKPAGE.COM'S KNOWING FACILITATION OF ONLINE SEX TRAFFICKING (Comm. Print 2017).

10. Increasingly at issue in such debates is the role of companies in determining the relative visibility of content on their site. Depending on the structure of the site, not all posts are treated equally in terms of visibility. For instance, users may encounter highlighted content in the form of "trending" videos selected based on popularity with other users, or recommended content selected for its relationship to content that a user has chosen to view. This chapter focuses on the binary choice companies make to display or remove content, but it is worth mentioning that nonbinary choices like algorithmic ranking will play an important role in the global conversation about companies' authority to make content-based decisions.

11. *See* Ingrid Lunden, *Facebook to Add 3,000 to Team Reviewing Posts with Hate Speech, Crimes, and Other Harming Posts*, TECHCRUNCH (May 3, 2017), https://techcrunch.com/2017/05/03/facebook-to-hire-3000-to-review-posts-with-hate-speech-crimes-and-other-harming-posts/ (utilizing thousands more people on its operations team to screen for harmful videos and other posts to respond to them more quickly in the future, using human curation in addition to algorithms); Megan Rose Dickey, *Facebook Addresses Revenge Porn with Tech to Prevent People from Re-sharing Intimate Images*, TECHCRUNCH (April 5, 2017), https://techcrunch.com/2017/04/05/facebook-addresses-revenge-porn-with-tech-to-prevent-people-from-re-sharing-intimate-images/ (Facebook has implemented a new photo-matching technology to ensure people can't reshare images previously reported and tagged as revenge porn—intimate photos of people shared without their consent).

12. *See* 18 U.S.C. §§ 2251, 2252. A first-time offender convicted of producing child pornography under Section 2251 faces fines and a statutory minimum of fifteen years to thirty years maximum in prison. A first-time offender convicted of transporting child pornography in interstate or foreign commerce under Section 2252 faces fines and a statutory minimum of five years to twenty years maximum in prison.

13. In a recent high-profile case, the British historian David Irving spent thirteen months in jail in Austria for challenging the Holocaust. Dan Bilefsky, *EU Adopts Measure Outlawing Holocaust Denial*, N.Y. TIMES (April 19, 2007), http://www.nytimes.com/2007/04/19/world/europe/19iht-eu.4.5359640.html. In Pakistan, Section 295B of the penal code proscribes life imprisonment for defiling the Quran. Section 295C proscribes a mandatory death sentence for use of derogatory remarks against Muhammad.

14. This dynamic also plays out on social media platforms, where dedicated users will comply with the platform's content standards rather than risk account termination.

15. *See,* e.g., Barbara Coloroso, *Bully, Bullied, Bystander. . . and Beyond,* TEACHING TOLERANCE MAGAZINE, Spring 2011, at 50; STOMP OUT BULLYING, http://www.stompoutbullying.org/ (last visited Jan. 10, 2018) ("When you're a bystander it's important to know that by doing nothing you are sending a message to the bully that their behavior is acceptable."); *Stop Bullying: Speak Up,* CARTOON NETWORK, http://www.cartoonnetwork.com/tv_shows/promotion_landing_page/stopbullying/index.html (last visited Jan. 10, 2018).

16. *ADL Global 100: An Index of Anti-Semitism,* ANTI-DEFAMATION LEAGUE 3 (2015), http://global100.adl.org/public/ADL-Global-100-Executive-Summary2015.pdf.

17. *See YouTube Goes (Even More) Global!,* YOUTUBE: OFFICIAL BLOG (Oct. 12, 2015), https://youtube.googleblog.com/2015/10/youtube-goes-even-more-global.html.

18. https://about.twitter.com/company (79 percent of accounts from outside the United States as of June 30, 2016).

19. *See* Lunden, *supra* note 11.

20. Facebook, Twitter, YouTube, and Microsoft do not review all content for violations. Instead, they rely heavily on systems of user reports.

21. There are other reasons society might not be well served by a system that simply uses national laws as online content standards. One could argue, for instance, that such a system would facilitate violations of Article 19 of the International Covenant on Civil and Political Rights, which states, in relevant part, that "everyone shall have the right to freedom of expression; this right shall include freedom to seek, receive and impart information and ideas of all kinds, regardless of frontiers, either orally, in writing or in print, in the form of art, or through any other media of his choice."

22. *See,* e.g., Mathew Ingram, *Here's Why We Need a First Amendment for Social Platforms,* FORTUNE (June 3, 2016), http://fortune.com/2016/06/03/social-platforms-free-speech/; Trevor Puetz, Note, *Facebook: The New Town Square,* 44 SW. L. REV. 385 (2014); Micha Nandaraj Gallo, *Facebook, Censorship, and the First Amendment,* COLUM. SCI. TECH. L. REV.: BLOG (Nov. 16, 2016), http://stlr.org/2016/11/21/4253/#_ftn8.

23. *Facebook Reports Second Quarter 2017 Results,* FACEBOOK (July 26, 2017), https://investor.fb.com/investor-news/press-release-details/2017/Facebook-Reports-Second-Quarter-2017-Results/default.aspx (Facebook now has more than two billion monthly active users).

24. Laws governing speech in Denmark have been the subject of robust debate. *See* Jacob Mchangama, *Something's Rotten: How Denmark Is Criminalizing Blasphemy through Hate Speech Law,* COLUM. GLOBAL FREEDOM OF EXPRESSION (Feb. 29, 2016), https://globalfreedomofexpression.columbia.edu/updates/2016/02/somethings-rotten-denmark-criminalizing-blasphemy-hate-speech-law/.

25. Michael Geist, *Global Internet Takedown Orders Come to Canada: Supreme Court Upholds International Removal of Google Search Results,* MICHAEL GEIST: NEWS (June 28, 2017), http://www.michaelgeist.ca/2017/06/global-internet-takedown-orders-come-canada-supreme-court-upholds-international-removal-google-search-results/.

26. David Christopher, *Disappointing Supreme Court Ruling Has Worrying Implications for Online Free Expression and Access to Information in Canada and across the Globe,* OpenMedia (June 28, 2017), https://openmedia.org/en/disappointing-supreme-court-ruling-has-worrying-implications-online-free-expression-and-access.

27. *See supra* note 3.

28. *Government Requests to Remove Content,* GOOGLE (Jan. 1, 2017), https://www.google.com/transparencyreport/removals/government/.

29. *India Transparency Report: January 2017–June 2017,* FACEBOOK, https://govtrequests.facebook.com/country/India/2016-H2/ (last visited Jan. 10, 2018).

30. *See,* e.g., *Community Standards,* FACEBOOK, http://facebook.com/communitystandards (last visited Jan. 10, 2018); *The Twitter Rules,* TWITTER, https://support.twitter.com/articles/18311 (last visited Jan. 10, 2018); *Policies and Safety,* YOUTUBE, https://www.youtube.com/yt/policyandsafety/communityguidelines.html (last visited Jan. 10, 2018).

31. *See* Brent Chudoba, *Does Adding One More Question Impact Survey Completion Rate?,* SURVEYMONKEY (Dec. 8, 2010), https://www.surveymonkey.com/blog/2010/12/08/survey_questions_and_completion_rates/.

32. *See, e.g., Bridging the Gender Gap: Mobile Access and Usage in Low and Middle-Income Countries,* GSMA 40 (2015), https://www.gsma.com/mobilefordevelopment/wp-content/uploads/2016/02/Connected-Women-Gender-Gap.pdf.

33. *See* David Cohen, *Facebook Surveys Users on Their Experiences with Pages,* ADWEEK (Apr. 1, 2015), http://www.adweek.com/digital/survey-users-pages/; Dave Lee, *Facebook to Use Surveys to Boost "Trustworthy" News,* BBC NEWS (Jan. 19, 2018), http://www.bbc.com/news/technology-42755832.

34. *See, e.g.,* Ashley Feinberg, *Another Celebrity Is Leaving Twitter—Can You Blame Her?,* GIZMODO (Feb. 19, 2015), https://gizmodo.com/how-twitter-could-beat-the-trolls-and-why-it-won-t-1623167517/1686776633; Emma Ockerman, *Daisy Ridley Quits Instagram After Harassment,* TIME (Aug. 4, 2016), http://time.com/4438463/daisy-ridley-quits-instagram/.

35. *See, e.g.,* Meredith Bennett-Smith, *Facebook Vows to Crack Down on Rape Joke Pages after Successful Protest, Boycott,* HUFFPOST (May 29, 2013), https://www.huffingtonpost.com/2013/05/29/facebook-rape-jokes-protest_n_3349319.html; Robinson Meyer, *Twitter's Famous Racist Problem,* ATLANTIC (Jul. 21, 2016), https://www.theatlantic.com/technology/archive/2016/07/twitter-swings-the-mighty-ban-hammer/492209/.

36. Josh Halliday, *Twitter's Tony Wang: "We Are the Free Speech Wing of the Free Speech Party,"* GUARDIAN (Mar. 22, 2012), https://www.theguardian.com/media/2012/mar/22/twitter-tony-wang-free-speech.

37. *Ask.fm Founder on Bullying: "It Is Not about the Site,"* THEJOURNAL.IE (Nov. 2, 2012), http://www.thejournal.ie/ask-fm-online-bullying-response-658613-Nov2012/.

38. Constance Letsch and Dominic Rushe, *Turkey Blocks YouTube amid "National Security" Concerns,* GUARDIAN (March 28, 2014), https://www.theguardian.com/world/2014/mar/27/google-youtube-ban-turkey-erdogan.

39. *See, e.g.,* Ed Ho, *An Update on Safety,* TWITTER (Feb. 7, 2017), https://blog.twitter.com/en_us/topics/product/2017/an-update-on-safety.html ("We stand for freedom of expression and people being able to see all sides of any topic. That's put in jeopardy when abuse and harassment stifle and silence those voices. We won't tolerate it and we're launching new efforts to stop it."); Josh Constine, *Reddit Cracks Down on Abuse as CEO Apologizes for Trolling the Trolls,* TECHCRUNCH (Nov. 30, 2016), https://techcrunch.com/2016/11/30/when-your-ceo-is-a-troll-too/; Amar Toor, *Ask.fm Responds to Cyberbullying Controversy with New Safety Measures,* VERGE (Aug. 19, 2013), https://www.theverge.com/2013/8/19/4635784/ask-fm-unveils-new-safety-measures-amid-cyberbullying-suicides.

40. Online safety in this context includes issues such as prevention of self-harm, child exploitation, adult sexual exploitation, bullying, harassment, and exposure to graphic content.

41. *See* Carl O'Brien, *Facebook Introduces New Tool to Tackle Harassment Online,* IRISH TIMES (April 13, 2016), http://www.irishtimes.com/news/education/facebook-introduces-new-tool-to-tackle-harassment-online-1.2609652.

42. *See* John Mannes, *Facebook, Microsoft, YouTube and Twitter form Global Internet Forum to Counter Terrorism,* TECHCRUNCH (Jun. 26, 2017), https://techcrunch.com/2017/06/26/facebook-microsoft-youtube-and-twitter-form-global-internet-forum-to-counter-terrorism/.

43. *See* Saba Hamedy, *People Now Spend 1 Billion Hours Watching YouTube Every Day,* MASHABLE (Feb. 27, 2017), http://mashable.com/2017/02/27/youtube-one-billion-hours-of-video-daily/#3AXtKo4q0Squ.

44. *See, e.g., Reporting Abusive Behavior,* TWITTER, https://support.twitter.com/articles/20169998 (last visited Jan. 10, 2018); *Safety and Abuse Reporting,* YOUTUBE, https://www.youtube.com/reportabuse (last visited Jan. 10, 2018); *Report Something,* FACEBOOK, https://www.facebook.com/help/263149623790594/ (last visited Jan. 10, 2018).

45. These standards are likely to be simpler than standards for content like harassment or threats, where the critical context for determining the user's intent may be offline and therefore unavailable. A content reviewer at Facebook will not know whether the user, who appears to threaten another person in a post, is actually referencing an offline joke between the two of them.

46. Mark Scott, *Twitter Fails E.U. Standard on Removing Hate Speech Online,* N.Y. TIMES (May 31, 2017), https://www.nytimes.com/2017/05/31/technology/twitter-facebook-google-europe-hate-speech.html.

47. *Companies Pull Ads from Google, YouTube over Racist, Terrorist Content,* NBC NEWS (March 20, 2017), http://www.nbcnews.com/card/companies-pull-ads-google-youtube-over-racist-terrorist-content-n735971.

48. *Facebook, Slammed for Videos of Murders, Will Hire 3,000 More People to Review Posts,* ASSOCIATED PRESS (May 3, 2017), http://www.latimes.com/business/technology/la-fi-tn-facebook-hires-20170503-htmlstory.html.

Chapter 16

1. ZEYNEP TUFEKCI, TWITTER AND TEAR GAS: THE POWER AND FRAGILITY OF NETWORKED PROTEST (New Haven, CT: Yale University Press, 2017), 226.

2. Peter Pomerantsev, *The Menace of Unreality: How the Kremlin Weaponizes Information, Culture and Money,* INTERPRETER (Nov. 22, 2014).

3. *See, e.g.,* Citizens United v. Fed. Election Comm'n, 558 U.S. 310 (2010).

4. Sorrell v. IMS Health Inc., 564 U.S. 552 (2011).

5. Matal v. Tam, 137 S.Ct. 1744 (2017).

6. Sedition Act of 1918, Pub. L. No. 65-150 (1918); Espionage Act of 1917, Pub. L. No. 65–24 (1917).

7. Debs v. United States, 249 U.S. 211, 214 (1919).

8. GEORGE CREEL, HOW WE ADVERTISED AMERICA: THE FIRST TELLING OF THE AMAZING STORY OF THE COMMITTEE ON PUBLIC INFORMATION THAT CARRIED THE GOSPEL OF AMERICANISM TO EVERY CORNER OF THE GLOBE (New York: Harper and Brothers, 1920), 5.

9. As described in TIM WU, THE ATTENTION MERCHANTS (New York: Knopf, 2016), and sources cited therein.

10. *See* Masses Pub. Co. v. Patten, 244 F. 535, 543 (S.D.N.Y.), rev'd, 246 F. 24 (2d Cir. 1917); *see also* Vincent Blasi, *Learned Hand and the Self-Government Theory of the First Amendment: Masses Publishing Co. v. Patten,* 61 U. COLO. L. REV. 1 (1990).

11. *See, e.g.,* Whitney v. California, 274 U.S. 357, 372 (1927) (Brandies, J., concurring); Abrams v. United States, 250 U.S. 616, 624 (1919) (Holmes, J., dissenting).

12. In cases like *Dennis v. United States,* 341 U.S. 494 (1951), and *Brandenburg v. Ohio,* 395 U.S. 444 (1969).

13. Herbert A. Simon, *Designing Organizations for an Information-Rich World,* in COMPUTERS, COMMUNICATIONS, AND THE PUBLIC INTEREST, ed. Martin Greenberger (Baltimore: John Hopkins University Press, 1971), 37, 40–41.

14. *See, e.g.,* JAMES GLEICK, THE INFORMATION: A HISTORY, A THEORY, A FLOOD (New York: Pantheon Books, 2011); Eugene Volokh, *Cheap Speech and What It Will Do,* 104 YALE L.J. 1805 (1995).

15. *See, e.g.,* Jack M. Balkin, *Old-School/New-School Speech Regulation,* 127 HARV. L. REV. 2296 (2014); Jeffrey Rosen, *The Deciders: The Future of Privacy and Free Speech in the Age of Facebook and Google,* 80 FORDHAM L. REV. 1525 (2012); Tim Wu, *Is Filtering Censorship? The Second Free Speech Tradition,* Brookings Institution (Dec. 27, 2010).

16. *See generally* Wu, *supra* note 9.

17. *See* ELI PARISER, THE FILTER BUBBLE: WHAT THE INTERNET IS HIDING FROM YOU (New York: Penguin Press, 2011). Scholarly consideration of filtering came earlier. *See, e.g.,* CASS SUNSTEIN, REPUBLIC.COM (Princeton: Princeton University Press, 2001).

18. *See* Lauren Drell, *Why "Time Spent" Is One of Marketing's Favorite Metrics,* MASHABLE (Dec. 13, 2013).

19. *See* Wu, *supra* note 9, at 303.

20. *See* Tim Wu, *How Donald Trump Wins by Losing,* N.Y. TIMES (March 3, 2017).

21. Kathleen M. Sullivan, *First Amendment Intermediaries in the Age of Cyberspace,* 45 UCLA L. REV. 1653, 1669 (1998).

22. Lawrence Lessig, *What Things Regulate Speech: CDA 2.0 vs. Filtering,* Berkman Klein Center for Internet and Society at Harvard University (May 12, 1998); *see also* LAWRENCE LESSIG, CODE AND OTHER LAWS OF CYBERSPACE (New York: Basic Books, 1999).

23. *See* Jonathan Zittrain, *Internet Points of Control,* 44 B.C. L. REV. 653 (2003); Christopher S. Yoo, *Free Speech and the Myth of the Internet as an Unintermediated Experience,* 78 GEO. WASH.

L. REV. 697 (2010); Jeffrey Rosen, *Google's Gatekeepers,* N.Y. TIMES (Nov. 28, 2008); JACK GOLDSMITH AND TIM WU, WHO CONTROLS THE INTERNET? ILLUSIONS OF A BORDERLESS WORLD (New York: Oxford University Press, 2006).

24. *See generally* Jack M. Balkin, *Old-School/New-School Speech Regulation,* 127 HARV. L. REV. 2296 (2014) (describing "new school" speech control).

25. *See, e.g.,* R. Kelly Garrett, *Echo Chambers Online?: Politically Motivated Selective Exposure among Internet News Users,* 14 J. COMPUTER-MEDIATED COMM. 265 (2009); W. Lance Bennett and Shanto Iyengar, *A New Era of Minimal Effects? The Changing Foundations of Political Communication,* 58 J. COMM. 707 (2008); Sofia Grafanaki, *Autonomy Challenges in the Age of Big Data,* 27 FORDHAM INTELL. PROP. MEDIA & ENT. L.J. 803 (2017).

26. For a notable partial exception, *see* Danielle Keats Citron, *Cyber Civil Rights,* 89 B.U. L. REV. 61 (2009).

27. For a full account of the speech-restrictive measures taken by the US government during wartime, *see* GEOFFREY STONE, PERILOUS TIMES: FREE SPEECH IN WARTIME, FROM THE SEDITION ACT OF 1798 TO THE WAR ON TERRORISM (New York: W. W. Norton, 2004).

28. *See generally* Tufekci, *supra* note 1.

29. Gary King, Jennifer Pan, and Margaret E. Roberts, *How Censorship in China Allows Government Criticism but Silences Collective Expression,* 107 AM. POL. SCI. REV. 326 (2013); Gary King, Jennifer Pan, and Margaret E. Roberts, *How the Chinese Government Fabricates Social Media Posts for Strategic Distraction, Not Engaged Argument,* 111 AM. POL. SCI. REV. 484 (2017) [hereinafter King et al., 2017 APSR].

30. King et al., 2017 APSR, *supra* note 29, at 496 (emphasis omitted).

31. *Id.* at 497.

32. The term was coined in an article about a cease-and-desist letter sent by Marco Beach Ocean Resort to Urinal.net threatening legal action unless the website stopped mentioning the resort's name alongside photos from its bathroom. The cease-and-desist letter prompted more attention than the original posts on Urinal.net. Mike Masnick, *Since When Is It Illegal to Just Mention a Trademark Online?,* TECHDIRT (Jan. 5, 2005).

33. *See* Sharad Goel et al., *The Structural Virality of Online Diffusion,* 62 MGMT. SCI. 180 (2016).

34. Max Seddon, *Documents Show How Russia's Troll Army Hit America,* BUZZFEED NEWS (June 2, 2014); Pomerantsev, *supra* note 2; *Russia Update: Questions about Putin's Health after Canceled Meetings & Vague Answers,* INTERPRETER (March 12, 2015).

35. Peter Pomerantsev, *Inside the Kremlin's Hall of Mirrors,* GUARDIAN (April 9, 2015).

36. Pomerantsev, *supra* note 2.

37. *Cf.* Citron, *supra* note 26.

38. Andrew Higgins, *Effort to Expose Russia's "Troll Army" Draws Vicious Retaliation,* N.Y. TIMES (May 30, 2016).

39. *See* Rachel Roberts, *Russia Hired 1,000 People to Create Anti-Clinton "Fake News" in Key US States During Election, Trump-Russia Hearings Leader Reveals,* INDEPENDENT (March 30, 2017).

40. Pomerantsev, *supra* note 2; *see also* Pomerantsev, *supra* note 35.

41. *See* Roberts, *supra* note 39.

42. David French, *The Price I've Paid for Opposing Donald Trump,* NATIONAL REVIEW (Oct. 21, 2016).

43. Stephen Battaglio, *Trump's Attacks on CNN Aren't Hurting It One Bit,* L.A. TIMES (Feb. 16, 2017).

44. French, *supra* note 42.

45. *See, e.g.,* Katharine Q. Seelye, *Protesters Disrupt Speech by "Bell Curve" Author at Vermont College,* N.Y. TIMES (March 3, 2017).

46. J.S. MILL, ON LIBERTY AND OTHER WRITINGS, ed. Stefan Collini (Cambridge: Cambridge University Press, 1989), 69.

47. *See generally* Adam Bienkov, *Astroturfing: What Is It and Why Does It Matter?,* GUARDIAN (Feb. 8, 2012).

48. *See* Goldsmith and Wu, *supra* note 23 (including an earlier investigation into Chinese censorship innovations).

49. Predictions of the Communist Party's downfall at the hands of the internet are surveyed in chapter 6 of Goldsmith and Wu, *supra* note 23.

50. King et al., 2017 APSR, *supra* note 29, at 484.

51. *See* Pomerantsev, *supra* note 35.

52. Philip N. Howard, et al., *Junk News and Bots during the U.S. Election: What Were Michigan Voters Sharing over Twitter?*, COMPUTATIONAL PROPAGANDA PROJECT (March 26, 2017).

53. *See* Onur Varol et al., *Online Human-Bot Interactions: Detection, Estimation, and Characterization*, INT'L AAAI CONF. WEB & SOCIAL MEDIA (March 27, 2017) (estimating that 9 to 15 percent of active Twitter users are bots).

54. Rebecca Grant, *Facebook Has No Idea How Many Fake Accounts It Has—But It Could Be Nearly 140M*, VENTUREBEAT (Feb. 3, 2014).

55. Patrick Kulp, *Bots Are the Latest Weapon in the Net Neutrality Battle*, MASHABLE (May 10, 2017).

56. *See, e.g.,* Martin Pengelly and Joanna Walters, *Trump Accused of Encouraging Attacks on Journalists with CNN Body-Slam Tweet*, GUARDIAN (July 2, 2017).

57. *See* French, *supra* note 42.

58. Blum v. Yaretsky, 457 U.S. 991, 1003 (1982).

59. *Id.* at 1004.

60. In *Blum* itself, the Supreme Court stated that the medical decisions made by the nursing home were insufficiently directed by the state to be deemed state action. 457 U.S. at 1012.

61. For example, the Sixth Circuit has held state officials liable for encouraging or demanding that private employers fire employees for speaking critically. *See* Paige v. Coyner, 614 F.3d 273 (6th Cir. 2010); Wells ex rel. Bankr. Estate of Arnone-Doran v. City of Grosse Pointe Farms, 581 F. App'x 469 (6th Cir. 2014).

62. *See, e.g.,* N.Y. Penal Law § 20.00 (McKinney); Model Penal Code §§ 2.06, 5.02 (Am. Law Inst. 2016).

63. Metro-Goldwyn-Mayer Studios Inc. v. Grokster, Ltd., 545 U.S. 913 (2005).

64. 395 U.S. 367 (1969).

65. *See, e.g.,* Virginia v. Black, 538 U.S. 343 (2003).

66. *See* Watts v. United States, 394 U.S. 705 (1969); Elonis v. United States, 135 S. Ct. 2001 (2015).

67. *Black*, 538 U.S. at 360.

68. *Id.*

69. United States v. Francis, 164 F.3d 120, 123 (2d Cir. 1999).

70. 207 F. Supp. 3d 1222 (N.D. Okla. 2016).

71. *Id.* at 1230–1231.

72. Bluman v. FEC, 800 F. Supp. 2d 281, 288 (D.D.C. 2011), aff'd, 565 U.S. 1104 (2012). A related interest—protecting elections—has been called on to justify "campaign-free zones" near polling stations. *See* Burson v. Freeman, 504 U.S. 191, 211 (1992).

73. ALEXANDER MEIKLEJOHN, FREE SPEECH AND ITS RELATION TO SELF-GOVERNMENT (New York: Harper and Brothers, 1948), 25.

74. *See Report on Editorializing by Broadcast Licensees*, 13 F.C.C. 1246 (1949).

75. Applicability of the Fairness Doctrine in the Handling of Controversial Issues of Public Importance, 29 Fed. Reg. 10426 (July 25, 1964).

76. Red Lion Broad. Co. v. FCC, 395 U.S. 367, 390 (1969).

77. *See, e.g.,* Miami Herald Pub. Co. v. Tornillo, 418 U.S. 241 (1974).

78. Syracuse Peace Council, 2 F.C.C. Rcd. 5043, 5047 (1987).

79. *See, e.g.,* Thomas W. Hazlett et al., *The Overly Active Corpse of Red Lion*, 9 Nw. J. TECH. & INTELL. PROP. 51 (2010).

Epilogue

1. 310 U.S. 296 (1940).

2. Terminiello v. Chicago, 337 U.S. 1 (1949).

3. 340 U.S. 315 (1951).

4. 341 U.S. 494 (1951).

5. *See* Chaplinsky v. New Hampshire, 315 U.S. 568 (1942); Valentine v. Chrestensen, 316 U.S. 52 (1942).

6. 395 U.S. 444 (1969).

7. 376 U.S. 254 (1964).

8. 357 U.S. 449 (1958).

9. *See* Roth v. United States, 354 U.S. 476 (1957).

10. *See,* e.g., Arizona Free Enterprise Club's Freedom Club PAC v. Bennett, 131 S. Ct. 2806 (2011) (campaign finance); Citizens United v. Fed. Election Comm'n, 558 U.S. 310 (2010) (corporate speech); Sorrell v. IMS Health, Inc., 131 S. Ct. 2653 (2011) (commercial advertising); McCullen v. Coakley, 134 S. Ct. 2518 (2014) (antiabortion speech).

11. Schenck v. United States, 249 U.S. 47 (1919); Debs v. United States, 249 U.S. 211 (1919); *Dennis* 341 U.S. 494.

12. *Schenck,* 249 U.S. 47; Frohwerk v. United States, 249 U.S. 204 (1919); *Debs,* 249 U.S. 211; *Feiner,* 340 U.S. 315; Beauharnais v. Illinois, 343 U.S. 250 (1952); *Dennis,* 341 U.S. 494.

13. *See* Red Lion Broadcasting Co. v. FCC, 395 U.S. 367 (1969).

14. *See generally,* LEE C. BOLLINGER, IMAGES OF A FREE PRESS (Chicago: University of Chicago Press, 1991); LEE C. BOLLINGER, UNINHIBITED, ROBUST, AND WIDE-OPEN: A FREE PRESS FOR A NEW CENTURY (New York: Oxford University Press, 2010).

INDEX